T0342139

Living Documentation

Part 2 Documentation

Living Documentation

Continuous Knowledge Sharing by Design

Cyrille Martraire

✦Addison-Wesley

Boston • Columbus • New York • San Francisco • Amsterdam • Cape Town
Dubai • London • Madrid • Milan • Munich • Paris • Montreal • Toronto • Delhi
Mexico City • São Paulo • Sydney • Hong Kong • Seoul • Singapore • Taipei • Tokyo

For information about buying this title in bulk quantities, or for special sales opportunities (which may include electronic versions; custom cover designs; and content particular to your business, training goals, marketing focus, or branding interests), please contact our corporate sales department at corpsales@pearsoned.com or (800) 382-3419.

For government sales inquiries, please contact governmentsales@pearsoned.com.

For questions about sales outside the U.S., please contact intlcs@pearson.com.

Visit us on the Web: informit.com/aw

Library of Congress Control Number: 2019936806

ISBN-13: 978-0-13-468932-6
ISBN-10: 0-13-468932-1

6 2024

Publisher
Mark L. Taub

Development Editor
Chris Zahn

Managing Editor
Sandra Schroeder

Senior Project Editor
Tonya Simpson

Copy Editor
Kitty Wilson

Indexer
Erika Millen

Proofreader
Linda Morris

Technical Reviewers
Rebecca Wirfs-Brock
Woody Zuill
Steve Hayes

Editorial Assistant
Cindy Teeters

Cover Designer
Chuti Prasertsith

Compositor
codeMantra

Graphics
Yunshan Xia

For my wife, Yunshan, and our children,
Norbert and Gustave.

Contents

Acknowledgments

First, I'd like to give special thanks my official reviewers, Rebecca Wirfs-Brock, Steve Hayes, and Woody Zuill, for the insightful review of the manuscript in a very short period of time, which really helped improve and organize the material better.

Many thanks to the Pearson team, starting with Chris Zahn, the developmental editor I've been lucky to work with regularly, Mark Taub, publisher, who led the whole publishing process, Kitty Wilson for the meticulous copy editing, and Tonya Simpson, it was a pleasure working with you throughout the project. I also want to thank Chris Guzikowski, executive editor, for signing the book at Pearson back in 2016.

The ideas in this book originate from people I respect a lot. Dan North, Chris Matts, and Liz Keogh derived the practice called behavioral driven development (BDD), which is one of the best examples of living documentation at work. Eric Evans, in his book *Domain-Driven Design*, proposed many ideas that, in turn, inspired BDD. Gojko Adzic proposed the term *living documentation* in his book *Specification by Example*. In this book, I elaborate on these ideas and generalizes them to other areas of a software project. DDD has emphasized how the thinking evolves during the life of a project, and its proponents have proposed unifying the domain model and code. Similarly, this book suggests unifying project artifacts and documentation.

The patterns movement and its authors, starting with Ward Cunningham and Kent Beck, have made it increasingly obvious that it is possible to do better documentation by referring to patterns, those already published or presented at Pattern Languages of Programs (PLoP) conferences.

Pragmatic Programmers, Martin Fowler, Ade Oshyneye, Andreas Rüping, Simon Brown, and many other authors have distilled nuggets of wisdom on how to do better documentation, in a better way. Rinat Abdulin first wrote on living diagrams and, indeed, coined the term. Thanks to you all of you!

Eric Evans, thanks for all the discussions, usually not on this book, and for your advice.

I would also like to thank Brian Marick for sharing his own work on visible workings with me. As encouragement matters, discussions with Vaughn Vernon and Sandro Mancuso on writing a book did help me, so thanks, guys!

Some discussions are more important than others; especially important are those that generate new ideas, lead to better understanding, or are just exciting. Thanks to George Dinwiddie, Paul Rayner, Jeremie Chassaing, Arnauld Loyer, and Romeu Moura for all the exciting discussions and for sharing your own stories and experiments.

Through the writing of this book, I looked for ideas and feedback as much as I could, particularly during open-space sessions at software development conferences. Maxime Sanglan gave me the first encouraging feedback, along with Franziska Sauerwein. Thanks, Franzi and Max! I want to thank all the participants of the sessions I have run on living documentation at these conferences and unconferences, such as in Agile France, Socrates Germany, Socrates France, Codefreeze Finland, and the Meetup Software Craftsmanship Paris round tables and several Jams of Code at Arolla in the evening.

I had been giving talks at conferences for some time but always concerning practices that are already widely accepted in our industry. With more novel content like living documentation, I also had to test acceptance from various audiences, and I thank the first conferences that took the risk of select the topic: NCrafts in Paris, Domain-Driven Design eXchange in London, Bdx.io in Bordeaux, and ITAKE Bucharest. Thanks for hosting the first versions of the talk or workshop. It was very helpful to have great feedback to inspire more effort to create the book.

I am very lucky at Arolla to have a community of passionate colleagues; thank you all for your contributions and for being my very first audience, in particular Fabien Maury, Romeu Moura, Arnauld Loyer, Yvan Vu, and Somkiane Vongnoukoun. Somkiane suggested adding stories to make the text "less boring," and it was one of the best ideas to improve the book. Thanks to the coaches of the Craftsmanship center at SGCIB for all the lunch discussions and ideas and their enthusiasm to get better at how we do software. In particular, I want to thank Gilles Philippart, who is mentioned several times in this book for his ideas, and Bruno Boucard and Thomas Pierrain.

I must also acknowledge Clémo Charnay and Alexandre Pavillon for providing early support for some of the ideas as experiments in the SGCIB commodity trading department information system and Bruno Dupuis and James Kouthon for their help making it a reality. Many of the ideas in this book have been tried in previous companies I've worked with: the Commodity department at SGCIB, the Asset Arena teams at Sungard Asset Management, all the folks at Swapstream, our colleagues at CME, and others.

Thanks to Café Loustic and all the great baristas there. It was the perfect place to work as an author, and I wrote many chapters there, usually powered by an Ethiopian single origin coffee from Caffenation. Merci papa et maman, for encouraging our free spirit. Finally, I want to thank my wife Yunshan, who's always been supportive and encouraging throughout the writing of the book. Very importantly, you also made the book a more pleasant experience, thanks to your cute pictures! Chérie, your support was key, and I want to support your own projects the same way you have this book.

About the Author

Cyrille Martraire (@cyriux on Twitter) is CTO, co-founder, and partner at Arolla (@ArollaFr on Twitter), the founder of the Paris Software Crafters community, and a regular speaker at international conferences. Cyrille refers to himself as a developer, since he has designed software since 1999 for startups, software vendors, and corporations as an employee and as a consultant.

He has worked and led multiple significant projects, mostly in capital finance, including the complete rewriting of a multilateral trading facility of interest rate swaps. In most cases he has to start from large and miserable legacy systems.

He's passionate about software design in every aspect: test-driven development, behavior-driven development, and, in particular, domain-driven design.

Cyrille lives in Paris with his wife, Yunshan, and children, Norbert and Gustave.

Introduction

I never planned to write a book on living documentation. I didn't even have in mind that this topic was worth a book.

Long ago, I had a grandiose dream of creating tools that could understand the design decisions we make when coding. I spent a lot of free time over several years trying to come up with a framework for that, only to find out it's very hard to make such a framework suitable for everyone. However, I tried the idea whenever it was helpful in the projects I was working on.

In 2013 I was speaking at Øredev on refactoring specifications. At the end of the talk I mentioned some of the ideas I'd been trying over time, and I was surprised at the enthusiastic feedback I received about the living documentation ideas. That is when I recognized the need for better ways to do documentation. I've done this talk other times since then, and the feedback has continued to be about the documentation thing and how to improve it, how to make it real-time and automated, without manual effort.

The term *living documentation* was introduced in the book *Specification by Example* by Gojko Adzic, as one of the many benefits of specification by example. But living documentation is a good name for an idea that is not limited to specifications.

I had many ideas to share about living documentation. I wrote down a list of all these things I had tried, as well as other stuff I had learned about the topic. More ideas came from other people—people I actually know and people I know only from Twitter. As all that was growing, I decided to make it into a book. Instead of offering a framework ready for use, I believe a book will be more useful to help you create quick and custom solutions to make your own living documentation.

What This Book Is About

The book *Specification by Example* introduced the idea of living documentation, where an example of behavior used for documentation is promoted into automated test. Whenever the test fails, you know the documentation is no longer in sync with the code, and you can just fix it quickly. This idea has shown that it is possible to have useful documentation that doesn't suffer the fate of becoming obsolete as soon as it is written. But we can go much further.

This book expands on Gojko's idea of living documentation, embracing a kind of documentation that evolves at the same pace as the code for many aspects of a project, from the business goals to the business domain knowledge, architecture and design, processes, and deployment.

This book combines some theory and practice, with illustrations and concrete examples. You will learn how to start investing in documentation that is always up to date and has minimal extra cost, thanks to well-crafted artifacts and a reasonable amount of automation.

You will see that you don't necessarily have to choose between working software and extensive documentation!

Who This Book Is For

This book is primarily for software developers or anyone who is not afraid of code in a source control system. It is code-centric and meant for developers, coding architects, and those in senior roles who understand code. It also addresses some needs from other stakeholders, from business analysts to managers, but through the lens of software developers who change the source code and commit files into the source control system.

This book is *not* about producing user documentation. Specific skills such as technical writing are required to do user documentation well, and that is absolutely not the topic of this book.

How to Read This Book

This book is on the topic of living documentation, and it is presented as a network of related patterns. Each pattern stands on its own and can be read independently. However, to fully understand and situate each pattern in context, it's often desirable to also look at related patterns. On the book's website, you can find pattern diagrams, which illustrate some of the relationships between the patterns.

The content of this book is organized as a progression from the problem of managing knowledge, to the inspiration from BDD, to some preliminary theory, to the different paces of knowledge changes and the corresponding documentation techniques. It then expands beyond that, focusing on the application for architecture and legacy systems, and on how to introduce living documentation in your environment.

I suggest starting with Chapter 1 and making sure you grasp the key ideas of Chapters 3 and 4 before taking a look at Chapters 5 through 9, which cover general practical techniques. Then you should take a look at the Chapter 10 for the shift of perspective. Chapters 11 through 15 cover more specific topics and provide additional examples.

Some readers have enjoyed reading this book cover to cover; however, feel free to skim, dig into a particular area, and read the text in any other order.

What This Book Covers

Chapter 1, "Rethinking Documentation," takes a fresh look at documentation from first principles, providing a foundation for the rest of the book.

Chapter 2, "Behavior-Driven Development as an Example of Living Specifications," describes how BDD is a key inspiration behind living documentation, although BDD itself is not the central topic of this book.

Chapter 3, "Knowledge Exploitation," and Chapter 4, "Knowledge Augmentation," lay a foundation on which other practices build. In particular, they discuss extracting knowledge that is there and augmenting it with what's missing.

Chapter 5, "Living Curation: Identifying Authoritative Knowledge," shows how to start turning knowledge into something useful through curation, while embracing that this knowledge is continuously changing.

Chapter 6, "Automating Documentation," expands on turning the knowledge into documentation and diagrams that live at the pace of the knowledge, mirroring each change in the knowledge.

Chapter 7, "Runtime Documentation," is an extension of the previous chapter, discussing how to use knowledge that is accessible only at runtime.

Chapter 8, "Refactorable Documentation," is more code-centric and focuses on using development tools to help keep documentation up-to-date.

In contrast to the previous chapters, Chapter 9, "Stable Documentation," explores the idea that you don't need living techniques for knowledge that doesn't change and discusses better methods of documenting such knowledge.

Chapter 10, "Avoiding Traditional Documentation," takes a more rebellious perspective, with a focus on alternative means of documentation.

After all the chapters on how to improve documentation by design, Chapter 11, "Beyond Documentation: Living Design," takes a different view: how a focus on documentation could help you improve the design itself.

Chapter 12, "Living Architecture Documentation," applies the living documentation ideas to software architecture and discusses some specific techniques.

Chapter 13, "Introducing Living Documentation to a New Environment," offers guidance on how to introduce living documentation in your environment, mostly as a social challenge.

Because we are surrounded by legacy systems, Chapter 14, "Documenting Legacy Applications," closes the book with a set of specific patterns for dealing with these tough legacy challenges.

Chapter 15, "Extra: Conspicuous Documentation," is a bonus chapter on practical advice to make all your living documentation initiatives more effective by making them more noticeable.

Register Your Book

Register your copy of *Living Documentation* at informit.com for convenient access to downloads, updates, and corrections as they become available. To start the registration process, go to informit.com/register and log in or create an account. Enter the product ISBN 9780134689326 and click Submit. Once the process is complete, you will find any available bonus content under "Registered Products."

Figure Credits

Cover image: Yunshan Xia

Globally, LOL note image: Yunshan Xia

Figures 1.1 through 1.6, 1.10 and 1.11: Yunshan Xia

Figure 1.9: Yunshan Xia

Figure 2.1: Yunshan Xia

Figure 2.4: Screenshot of Pickles © Jeffrey Cameron 2011-2012

Figures 3.3, 3.5, 3.8 through 3.11: Yunshan Xia

Figures 4.3 and 4.4: Yunshan Xia

Figure 4.5: Screenshot of Github © 2019 GitHub, Inc.

Figures 5.1 and 5.4: Yunshan Xia

Figure 5.2: Screenshot of Eclipse © Eclipse Foundation, Inc.

Figure 6.2: Screenshot of Java © Oracle

Figure 6.7: Yunshan Xia

Figure 6.10: Alistair Cockburn

Figure 6.15: Screenshot of Java © Oracle

Figure 7.1: Screenshot of Zipkin © Zipkin 2019

Figure 8.5: Screenshot of Eclipse © Eclipse Foundation, Inc.

Figure 8.6: Cyrille Martraire

Figure 10.1, 10.5, and 10.9: Yunshan Xia

Figure 10.2: Alistair Cockburn

Figure 10.3: Cyrille Martraire

Figure 10.6: Screenshot of Bug Magnet © 2015-2017 Gojko Adzic

Figure 10.8: John Arundel, http://bitfieldconsulting.com/puppet-dependency-graphs

Figures 11.1, 11.2, 11.4, and 11.7: Yunshan Xia

Figure 11.5 and 11.6: Screenshot of Word Cloud © Zygomatic

Figures 12.3, 12.4, and 12.5: Yunshan Xia

Figures 15.1, 15.4, and 15.5: Cyrille Martraire

Figures 15.2 and 15.3: Yunshan Xia

Chapter 1

Rethinking Documentation

Forget about documentation. Instead, focus on the speed of working on software. You want to deliver software faster. It isn't just about going fast right now but about going sustainably fast in the long run. It is not just about you going fast but about the whole team or company going fast.

Working on software faster involves more productive programming languages and frameworks, better tools, and higher level of skills. But the more the industry makes progress on all these aspects, the more we have to look at the other bottlenecks.

Beyond making use of technology, writing software is a lot about making decisions based on knowledge. When you don't have enough knowledge, you have to make learning experiments and collaborate with other people to discover new knowledge. This takes time, which also means this knowledge is expensive and has value. Going fast is all about learning faster when you need new knowledge or about quickly recovering any prior valuable knowledge whenever there was some. Let us illustrate that point with a little story.

A Tale from the Land of Living Documentation

We begin with a story. Imagine a software project to develop a new application as part of a bigger information system in your company. And imagine that you are a developer on this project. Your task is to add a new kind of discount for recent loyal customers.

Why This Feature?

You meet Franck, from the marketing team, and Lisa, a professional tester, and the three of you start talking about the new feature, asking questions, and looking for concrete examples. Lisa asks, "Why this feature?" Franck explains that the rationale is to reward recent loyal customers in order to increase customer retention, in a gamification approach, and suggests a link on Wikipedia about that topic. Lisa takes some notes about the main points and main scenarios.

All this goes quickly because everyone is around the table, and communication is easy. Also, the concrete examples make it easier to understand and clarify anything that starts out unclear. Once it's all clear, everyone gets back to their desk. It's Lisa's turn to write down the most important scenarios and send them to everyone. (Last time it was Franck's turn.) Now you can start coding from that.

In your previous work experience, the process did not work like this. Teams talked to each other through hard-to-read documents full of ambiguities. You smile. You quickly turn the first scenario into an automated acceptance test, watch it fail, and start writing code to make it pass to green.

You have the nice feeling that you'll be able to spend your valuable time on what matters and nothing else.

Tomorrow You Won't Need This Sketch Anymore

That afternoon, a pair of colleagues, Georges and Esther, ask the team about a design decision that needs to be made. You meet around the whiteboard and quickly evaluate each option while sketching. You don't need much UML[1] at this point, just some custom boxes and arrows. You just want to make sure everybody understands it right now. A few minutes later a solution is chosen. The plan is to use two different topics in the messaging system; the rationale for this decision is the need for full isolation between the incoming orders and the shipment requests.

Esther takes a picture of the whiteboard with her phone, just in case someone erases the whiteboard during the day. But she knows that in half a day, it will be implemented, and she can then safely delete the picture stored in her phone. One hour later, when she commits the creation of the new messaging topic, she takes care to add the rationale "isolation between incoming orders and shipment requests" in the commit comment.

The next day, Dragos, who was away yesterday, notices the new code and wonders why it's like that. He runs `git blame` on the line and immediately gets the answer.

---

1. Unified Modeling Language: http://www.uml.org/

Sorry, We Don't Have Marketing Documents!

A week later, a new marketing manager, Michelle, replaces Franck. Michelle is more into customer retention than Franck. She wants to know what's already implemented in the application in the area of customer retention, so she asks for the corresponding marketing document, and she is surprised to learn there is none.

"You can't be serious!" she first says. But you quickly show her the website with all the acceptance tests produced during each build. There's a search area on top so she can enter "customer retention" and search on it. She clicks submit and discovers the results:

```
1  In order to increase customer retention
2  As  a  marketing person
3  I want to offer a discount to recent loyal customers
4
5    Scenario: 10$ off on next purchase for recent loyal
customer
6    ...
7
8    Scenario: Recent loyal customers have bought 3 times in the
last week
9    ...
```

The result list displays many scenarios about the special discount for recent loyal customers. Michelle smiles. She didn't even have to browse a marketing document to find the knowledge she was looking for. And the level of precision of these scenarios well exceeds what she was expected.

"Could we do the same discount for purchases in euro?" Michelle asks. You reply, "I'm not sure the code manages currencies well, but let's just try." In your IDE[2], you change the currency in the acceptance test, and you run the tests again. They fail, so you know some work will need to be done to support that. Michelle has her answer within minutes. She begins to think that your team has something special compared to her former work environments.

You Keep Using This Word, but This Is Not What It Means

The next day Michelle has another question: What is the difference between a *purchase* and an *order*?

---

2. integrated development environment (IDE).

Usually she would just ask the developers to look in the code and explain the difference. However, this team has anticipated the question, and the project's website includes a glossary. "Is this glossary up-to-date?" she asks. "Yes," you reply. "It's updated during every build—automatically from the code." She's surprised. Why doesn't everybody do that? "You need to have your code closely in line with the business domain for that," you say simply, though you're tempted to elaborate on the ubiquitous language from Eric Evans's book *Domain-Driven Design*[3] you're so enthusiastic about.

Looking at the glossary, Michelle discovers a confusion that nobody has spotted before in the naming, and she suggests fixing the glossary with the correct name. But this is not the way it works here. You want to fix the name first and foremost in the code. You rename the class and run the build again, and—voilà—the glossary is now fixed as well. Everybody is happy, and you just learned something new about the business of e-commerce.

Show Me the Big Picture, and You'll See What's Wrong There

Now you'd like to remove a toxic dependency between two modules, but you're not very familiar with the full codebase, so you ask Esther for a dependency diagram, since she has the most knowledge of that. But even she does not remember every dependency. "I'll generate a diagram of the dependencies from the code. It's something I've long wanted to do. This will take me a few hours, but then it'll be done forever," she says.

Esther already knows about a few open-source libraries she can use to easily extract the dependencies from a class or a package, and she quickly wires one to Graphviz, the magical diagram generator that does the layout automatically. A few hours later, her little tool generates the diagram of dependencies. You get what you wanted, and you're happy. She then spends an extra half hour integrating this tool into the build.

But the funny thing is that when Esther first looks at the generated diagram, she notices something intriguing: a dependency between the two modules that should not be there. By comparing her mental view of the system with the generated view of the actual system, it was easy to spot the design weakness.

In the next project iteration, the design weakness is fixed, and in the next build, the dependency diagram is automatically updated. It becomes a much cleaner diagram.

---

3. Evans, Eric. *Domain-Driven Design: Tackling Complexity in the Heart of Software*. Hoboken: Addison-Wesley Professional, 2003.

The Future of Living Documentation Is Now

This tale is not about the future. It is already here, right now, and it has been here for years already. To quote fiction writer William Gibson, this "future has arrived, it's just not evenly distributed yet."

The tools are here. The techniques are here. People have been doing all this for ages, but it's not yet mainstream. That's a pity because these are powerful ideas for software development teams.

In the following chapters, we'll go through all these approaches and many others, and you'll learn how to implement them in your projects.

The Problem with Traditional Documentation

> Documentation is the castor oil of programming—managers think it is good for programmers, and programmers hate it!
> —*Gerald Weinberg*, Psychology of Computer Programming

Documentation is a boring topic. I don't know about you, but in my work experience so far, documentation has mostly been a great source of frustration.

When I'm trying to consume documentation, the information I need is always missing. When it's there, it is often obsolete and misleading, so I can't even trust it.

Creating documentation for other people is a boring task, and I'd prefer to be coding instead. *But it does not have to be this way.*

There have been a number of times when I've seen, used, or heard about better ways to deal with documentation. I've tried a lot of them. I've collected a number of stories, and you'll find many of them in this book.

There's a better way, but it requires adopting a new mindset about documentation. With this mindset and the techniques that go with it, it is possible for documentation to be as much fun as coding.

Documentation Is Not Cool, Usually

What comes to mind when you hear the word *documentation*? Here are a few of the answers you might give:

- It's boring.

- It involves writing lots of text.

- It means trying to use Microsoft Word without losing your sanity with picture placement.

- As a developer, I love dynamic, executable stuff that exhibits motion and behavior. To me, documentation is like a dead plant that's static and dry.
- It's supposed to be helpful, but it's often misleading.
- Creating documentation is a boring chore. I'd prefer to be writing code instead of doing documentation (see Figure 1.1)!

Figure 1.1 *Oh no...I'd better be coding!*

Documentation takes a lot of time to write and to maintain, it becomes obsolete quickly, it is typically incomplete at best, and it is just not fun. Documentation is a fantastic source of frustration. And I'm sorry to bring you on this journey on such a dull topic.

The Flaws of Documentation

> Like cheap wine, paper documentation ages rapidly and leaves you with a bad headache.
> —*@gojkoadzic on Twitter*

Traditional documentation suffers from many flaws and several common anti-patterns. An *anti-pattern* describes a common response to a recurring problem that is considered not a good idea and that should avoided.

Some of the most frequent flaws and anti-patterns of documentation are described in the following sections. Do you recognize some of them in your own projects?

Separate Activities

Even in software development projects that claim to be agile, deciding what to build and doing the coding, testing, and preparing documentation are too often separate activities, as illustrated in Figure 1.2.

Separate activities induce a lot of waste and lost opportunities. Basically, the *same* knowledge is manipulated during each activity, but in different forms and in different artifacts—and probably with some amount of duplication. In addition, this "same" knowledge can evolve during the process itself, which may cause inconsistencies.

| Specs | Code | Test | Doc |

Figure 1.2 *Separate activities in software development projects*

Manual Transcription

When the time comes to do documentation, members of the team select some elements of knowledge of what has been done and perform a manual transcription into a format suitable for the expected audience. Basically, it means writing another document about what has just been done in the code—like copyists before Gutenberg (see Figure 1.3).

Figure 1.3 *Manual transcription*

Redundant Knowledge

The transcription just described leads to redundant knowledge: You end up with the original source of truth (usually the code) and a bunch of copies that duplicate this knowledge in various forms. Unfortunately, when one artifact changes—for example, the code—it is hard to remember to update the other documents. As a result, the documentation quickly becomes obsolete, and you end up with incomplete documentation that you cannot trust. How useful is that documentation?

Boring Time Sink

Managers want documentation for the users and also to cope with the turnover in the team. However, developers hate writing documentation. It is not fun compared to writing code or compared to automating a task. Dead text that gets obsolete quickly and that does not execute is not particularly exciting to write for a developer. When developers are working on documentation, they'd prefer to be working on the real working software instead. Paradoxically, when they want to reuse third-party software, they often wish it had more documentation available.

Technical writers like to do documentation and are paid for that. However, to get access to the technical knowledge required, they usually need developers, and often they're still doing manual transcription of knowledge. This is all frustrating and consumes a lot of precious time (see Figure 1.4).

Figure 1.4 *Documentation is often a time sink*

Brain Dump

Because writing documentation is not fun and is done because it simply has to be done, it is often done arbitrarily, without much thinking. The result is a random brain dump of what the writer had in mind at the time of writing (see Figure 1.5). The problem is that such a random brain dump is not helpful to anyone.

Figure 1.5 *A brain dump is not necessarily useful as documentation*

Polished Diagrams

This anti-pattern is common with people who like to use CASE tools. These tools are not meant for sketching. Instead they encourage the creation of polished and large diagrams, with various layouts and validation against a modeling referential. All this takes a lot of time. Even with all the auto-magical layout features of these tools, it still takes too much time to create even a simple diagram.

Notation Obsession

It is now increasingly obvious that the UML notation is not fashionable anymore, but in the decade following its adoption as a standard in 1997, it was the *universal* notation for everything software, despite not being suited for all situations. No other notation has been popularized since that time, and teams around the world still use some UML to document stuff, even when it is not well suited for that. When all you know is UML, everything looks like one of its collection of standard diagrams.

No Notation

In fact, the opposite of notation obsession has been rather popular. Many people have simply ignored UML, drawing diagrams with custom notations that nobody understands the same way and mixing together random concerns like build dependencies, data flow, and deployment concerns in a happy mess.

Information Graveyard

Enterprise knowledge management solutions are the places where knowledge goes to die. Consider these:

- Enterprise wikis
- SharePoint
- Large Microsoft Office documents
- Shared folders
- Ticketing systems and wikis with poor search capabilities

These approaches to documentations often fail either because they make it too hard to find the right information or because it's too much work to keep the information up-to-date or both. They promote a form of *write-only documentation*, or *write-once documentation*.

On a recent Twitter exchange, the famous software developer Tim Ottinger (@tottinge) asked:

> Product category: "Document Graveyard" - are all document management & wiki & SharePoint & team spaces doomed?

James R. Holmes (@James_R_Holmes) replied:

> Our standard joke is that "It's on the intranet" leads to the response, "Did you just tell me to go ____ myself?"
> *(Note: Edited because of the original rough language; you get the idea.)*

Misleading Help

Whenever documentation is not strictly kept up-to-date, it becomes misleading, as pictured in Figure 1.6. Although it pretends to help, it is incorrect. As a result, such documentation may be interesting to read, but there's an additional cognitive load involved in trying to find out what's still correct versus what's become incorrect.

There's Always Something More Important Right Now

Writing good documentation requires a lot of time, and maintaining it takes even more time. Those who are under time pressure often skip documentation tasks or do them quickly and badly.

Figure 1.6 *Documentation can be toxic when misleading*

The Agile Manifesto and Documentation

The Agile Manifesto was written by a group of software practitioners in 2001. In it, they list what they have come to value, including the following:

- Individuals and interactions over processes and tools

- Working software over comprehensive documentation

- Customer collaboration over contract negotiation

- Responding to change over following a plan

The second preference, "Working software over comprehensive documentation," is frequently misunderstood. Many people believe that it disregards documentation completely. In fact, the Agile Manifesto does not say "don't do documentation." It's only a matter of preference. In the words of the authors of the manifesto, "We embrace documentation, but not to waste reams of paper in never-maintained and rarely-used tomes."[4] Still, with agile approaches becoming mainstream in larger corporations, the misunderstanding is still there, and many people neglect documentation.

However, I've noticed recently that the lack of documentation is a big source of frustration for my customers and colleagues, and this frustration is getting bigger. I was surprised to see some great appetite for the topic of documentation after I first mentioned living documentation at the Öredev conference in Sweden in 2013.

It's Time for Documentation 2.0

Traditional documentation is flawed, but now we know better. Since the end of the 1990s, practices like clean code, test-driven development (TDD), behavior-driven development (BDD), domain-driven design (DDD), and continuous delivery have

---

4. Martin Fowler and Jim Highsmith, http://agilemanifesto.org/history.html

become increasingly popular. All these practices have changed the way we think about delivering software.

With TDD, the tests are first considered as specifications. With DDD, we identify the code and the modeling of the business domain, breaking with the tradition of models kept separately from the code. One consequence is that we expect the code to tell the whole story about the domain. BDD borrowed the idea of the business language and made it more literal, with tool support. Finally, continuous delivery is showing that an idea that looked ridiculous a few years ago (delivering several times a day in a non-event fashion) is actually possible and even desirable if we decide to follow the recommended practices.

Another interesting thing that is happening is due to the effect of time: Even though old ideas like literate programing or HyperCard did not become mainstream, they remained slowly and quietly influential, especially in more recent programming languages communities such as F# and Clojure, which bring some of the old ideas to the foreground.

Now at last we can expect an approach to documentation that is useful, always up-to-date, low cost, and fun to create. We acknowledge all the problems of the traditional approach to documentation, and we also see that there is a need to be fulfilled. This book explores and offers guidance on other approaches to meet the needs in more efficient ways. But first, let's explore what documentation really is.

Documentation Is About Knowledge

Software development is all about knowledge and decision-making based on that knowledge, which in turn creates additional knowledge. The given problem, the decision that was made, the reason it was made that way, the facts that led to that decision, and the considered alternatives are all knowledge.

You may not have ever thought about it this way, but each instruction typed in a programming language is a decision. There are big and small decisions, but no matter the size, they are all decisions. In software development, there is no expensive construction phase following a design phase: The construction (running the compiler) is so cheap that there's only an expensive—and sometimes everlasting—design phase.

Software design can last a long time. It can last long enough to forget about previous decisions made, as well as their contexts. It can last long enough for people to leave, taking with them their knowledge, and for new people to join, lacking knowledge. Knowledge is central to a design activity like software development.

Most of the time this design activity is, for many good reasons, a team effort involving more than one person. Working together means making decisions together or making decisions based on someone else's knowledge.

Something unique with software development is that the design involves not only people but also machines. Computers are part of the picture, and many of the decisions made are simply given to the computer to execute. This is usually done through documents called *source code*. Using a formal language like a programming language, we pass knowledge and decisions to a computer in a form it can understand.

Having a computer understand source code is not the hard part, though. Even inexperienced developers usually manage to succeed at that. The hardest part is for other people to understand what has been done so that they can then do better and faster work.

The greater the ambition, the more documentation becomes necessary to enable a cumulative process of knowledge management that scales beyond what fits in our heads. When our brains and memories are not enough, we need assistance from technologies such as writing, printing, and software to help remember and organize larger sets of knowledge.

The Origination of Knowledge

Where does knowledge come from? Knowledge primarily comes from *conversations*. We develop a lot of knowledge through conversations with other people. This happen during collective work such as pair programming, or during meetings, or at the coffee machine, on the phone, or via a company chat or emails. Examples of conversations include BDD specification workshops and the three amigos in agile.

However, as software developers, we have conversations with machines, too, and we call these *experiments*. We tell something to a machine by using code in some programming language, and the machine runs it and tells us something in return: The test fails or goes green, the UI reacts as expected, or the result is not what we wanted, in which case we learn something new. Examples of experiments include TDD, emerging design, and Lean Startup experiments.

Knowledge also comes from *observation* of the context. In a company, you learn a lot by just being there, paying attention to other people's conversations, behavior, and emotions. Examples of observation include domain immersion, obsession walls, information radiators, and Lean Startup "Get out of the building" observation.

Knowledge comes from conversations with people and experiments with machines in an observable context.

How Does Knowledge Evolve?

Some knowledge can be stable for years, whereas other knowledge changes frequently over months or even hours.

Any form of documentation has to consider the cost of maintenance and make it as close to zero as possible. For stable knowledge, traditional methods of documentation work. But with frequently changing knowledge, writing text and updating it after every change is just not an option.

The effect of acceleration in the software industry is that we want to be in a position to evolve the software very quickly. The speed is such that it's impossible to spend time writing pages and pages of documentation, and yet we want all the benefits of documentation.

Why Knowledge Is Necessary

When creating software, we go through a lot of questions, decisions, and adjustments as we learn:

- What problem are we trying to solve? Everyone should know it from now on.

- What problem are we *really* trying to solve? (We try to answer this when we realize we got it wrong initially.)

- We've been confusing *trade* and *deal*, but we eventually realized that they are not synonyms. We should not confuse them again.

- We tried this new DB, and it doesn't match our needs—for three reasons. No need to try again later as long as our needs remain the same.

- We decided to decouple the shopping cart module and the payment module because we noticed that the changes to one had nothing to do with changes to the other. We should not couple them again.

- We found out by chance that this feature is useless, so we plan to delete the code next month. But we are likely to forget our rationale, and if the code remains, it will be a mystery forever.

With existing software, when we miss the knowledge developed before, we end up redoing what's already done because we don't know it's there already. We also end up putting a feature in an unrelated component because we don't know where it should be, and this makes the software bloated. Or the code about the feature becomes fragmented across various components.

If only we had the knowledge available to answer everyday questions like the following:

- Where can I fix that issue safely?

- Where should I add this enhancement?

- Where would the original authors add this enhancement?
- Is it safe to delete this line of code that looks useless?
- I'd like to change a method signature, but what impacts will result if I do?
- Do I really have to reverse engineer the code just to understand how it works?
- Do I really have to spend time reading the source code each time the business analysts need to know about the current business rules?
- When a customer asks for a feature, how do we know if it's already supported if it needs to be developed?
- We have the feeling that the way we evolve the code is the best possible, but what if we lack a complete understanding of how it works?
- How do we easily find the part of the code that deals with a particular feature?

Lack of knowledge manifests as two costs:

- **Wasted time:** That time could have been better invested in improving something else.
- **Suboptimal decisions:** Other decisions could have been more relevant, or cheaper in the long term.

These two expenses compound over time: The time spent finding missing knowledge is time *not* spent on making better decisions. In turn, suboptimal decisions compound to make our life progressively more miserable, until we have no choice but to decide that the software is no longer maintainable and start again.

It sounds like a good idea to be able to access the knowledge that is useful to perform the development tasks.

Software Programming as Theory Building and Passing

In 1985, Peter Naur's famous paper "Programming as Theory Building" perfectly revealed the truth about programming as a collective endeavor: He said that it's not so much about telling the computer what to do as it is about sharing with other developers the theory of the world (think "mental model") that has been patiently elaborated by learning, experiment, conversations, and deep reflections. In his own words:

Programming properly should be regarded as an activity by which the programmers form or achieve a certain kind of insight, a theory, of the matters at hand. This suggestion is in contrast to what appears to be a more common notion, that programming should be regarded as a production of a program and certain other texts.[5]

The problem is that most of the theory is tacit. The code only represents the tip of the iceberg. It's more a consequence of the theory in the mind of the developers than a representation of the theory itself. In Peter Naur's view, this theory encompasses three main areas of knowledge:

- The mapping between code and the world it represents: The programmer who has the theory of the program can explain how the solution relates to the affairs of the world that it helps to handle.

- The rationale of the program: The programmer who has the theory of the program can explain why each part of the program is what it is; in other words, the programmer is able to support the actual program text with a justification of some sort.

- The potential of extension or evolution of the program: The programmer who has the theory of the program is able to respond constructively to any demand for modification of the program in order to support the affairs of the world in a new manner.

Over time, we've learned a number of techniques that enable people to pass theories among themselves. Clean code and Eric Evans's domain-driven design encourage programmers to find ways of expressing the theory in their heads more literally into the code. For example, DDD's ubiquitous language bridges the gap between the language of the world and the language of the code, helping solve the mapping problem. I hope future programming languages will recognize the need to represent not only the behavior of the code but also the bigger mental model of the programmers, of which the code is a consequence.

Patterns and pattern languages also come to mind, as literal attempts to package nuggets of theories. The more patterns we know, the more we can encode the tacit theory, making it explicit and transferable to a wider extent. Patterns embody in the description of their forces the key elements of the rationale in choosing them, and they sometimes hint at how extension should happen. They might hint at the potential of the program; for example, a strategy pattern is meant to be extended by adding new strategies.

---

5. Peter Naur, "Programming as Theory Building," Microprocessing and Microprogramming, Volume 15, Issue 5, 1985, pp. 253–261.

But as we progress in the codification of our understanding, we also tackle more ambitious challenges, so our frustration remains the same. I believe Naur's sentence from 1985 will still hold in the next decades:

For a new programmer to come to possess an existing theory of a program it is insufficient that he or she has the opportunity to become familiar with the program text and other documentation.[6]

We'll never completely solve that knowledge transfer problem, but we can accept it as a fact and learn to live with it. The theory as a mental model in programmers' heads can never be fully shared with those who weren't part of the thought process that led to building it.

The conclusion seems inescapable: At least in certain kinds of large programs, the continued adaption, modification, and correction of errors is dependent on a certain kind of knowledge possessed by a group of programmers who are closely and continuously connected to each other.

It's worth noting that permanent teams that regularly work collectively don't suffer too much from this issue of theory passing.

Documentation Is About Transferring Knowledge

The word *documentation* often brings a lot of connotations to mind: written documents, Microsoft Word or PowerPoint documents, documents based on company templates, printed documents, big, heavy and boring text on a website or on a wiki, and so on. However, all these connotations anchor us to practices of the past, and they exclude a lot of newer and more efficient practices.

For the purposes of this book, we'll adopt a much broader definition of documentation:

> The process of transferring valuable knowledge to other people now and also to people in the future.

There's a logistic aspect to documentation. It's about transferring knowledge in space between people and also about transferring it over time, which technical people call *persistence* or *storage*. Overall, our definition of documentation looks like shipment and warehousing of goods, where the goods are knowledge.

---

6. Peter Naur, "Programming as Theory Building," Microprocessing and Microprogramming, Volume 15, Issue 5, 1985, pp. 253–261.

Transferring knowledge between people is actually transferring knowledge between brains (see Figure 1.7). From one brain to other brains, it's a matter of *transmission*, or diffusion (for example, to reach a larger audience). From brains now to brains later, it's about persisting the knowledge, and it's a matter of memory.

Transfer knowledge to other people.

Store knowledge for the future.

Figure 1.7 *Documentation is about transferring and storing knowledge*

> **Did you know?**
>
> The development tenure half-life is 3.1 years, whereas the code half-life is 13 years.[7] Documentation has to help with this mismatch.

Transferring knowledge from the brain of a technical person to the brains of nontechnical people is a matter of *making the knowledge accessible*. Another case of making knowledge accessible is to make it efficiently *searchable*.

And there are other situations, such as needing to put knowledge into a specific document format for compliance reasons—because you just have to.

Focusing on What Matters

As a means of transferring valuable knowledge, documentation can take many forms: written documents, face-to-face conversations, code, activity on social tools, or nothing at all when it's not necessary.

---

7. Rob Smallshire, Sixty North blog, http://sixty-north.com/blog/predictive-models-of-development-teams-and-the-systems-they-build

With this definition of documentation, we can express some important principles:

- Knowledge that is of interest for a *long period of time* deserves to be documented.

- Knowledge that is of interest to a *large number of people* deserves to be documented.

- Knowledge that is *valuable* or *critical* may also need to be documented.

On the other hand, you don't need to care about documentation of knowledge that isn't in any of these cases. Spending time or effort on it would be a waste.

The *value* of the considered knowledge matters. There's no need to make the effort to transfer knowledge that's not valuable enough for enough people over a long enough period of time. If a piece of knowledge is already well known or is useful for only one person, or if it's only of interest until the end of the day, then there's no need to transfer or store it.

The Default Is Don't

There is no point in making any specific effort at documenting knowledge unless there's a compelling reason to do it; otherwise, it's a waste. Don't feel bad about not documenting something that doesn't need to be documented.

Having reconsidered what documentation really is, in terms of knowledge transmission and preservation, and some early consequences in how it should be managed, it is now time to introduce the central idea of living documentation and its core principles.

Core Principles of Living Documentation

The term *living documentation* first became popular in the book *Specification by Example* by Gojko Adzic. Adzic described a key benefit of teams doing BDD: Their scenarios created for specifications and testing were also very useful as documentation of the business behaviors. Thanks to the test automation, this documentation was always up-to-date, as long as the tests were all passing.

It is possible to get the same benefits of living documentation for all aspects of a software development project: business behaviors, of course, but also business domains, project vision and business drivers, design and architecture, legacy strategies, coding guidelines, deployment, and infrastructure.

Living documentation involves a set of four principles (see Figure 1.8):

- **Reliable:** Living documentation is accurate and in sync with the software being delivered, at any point in time.
- **Low effort:** Living documentation minimizes the amount of work to be done on documentation, even in case of changes, deletions, or additions. It requires only minimal additional effort—and only once.
- **Collaborative:** Living documentation promotes conversations and knowledge sharing between everyone involved.
- **Insightful:** By drawing attention to each aspect of the work, living documentation offers opportunities for feedback and encourages deeper thinking. It helps reflect on the ongoing work and helps in making better decisions.

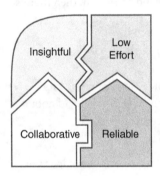

Figure 1.8 *Principles of living documentation*

Living documentation also brings the fun back for developers and other team members. They can focus on doing a better job, and at the same time they get the living documentation out of this work.

The following sections briefly describe the four core principles of living documentation that together will act as a guidance to unlock the most benefits from the approach. These important ideas are then elaborated on in the rest of the chapter and in the next three chapters.

Reliable

To be useful, documentation must be trustworthy; in other words, it must be 100% reliable. Since humans are never that reliable, we need discipline and tools to help with reliability.

To achieve reliable documentation, we rely on the following ideas:

- **Exploiting available knowledge:** Most of the knowledge is already present in the artifacts of the project, it just needs to be exploited, augmented, and curated for documentation purposes.

- **Accuracy mechanism:** An accuracy mechanism is needed to ensure that the knowledge is always kept in sync.

Low Effort

A living documentation must be low effort to be feasible and sustainable on ever-changing environments; you can achieve that thanks to the following ideas:

- **Simplicity:** Documentation is best if there is nothing to declare, but it's just obvious.

- **Standard over custom solutions:** Standards are supposed to be known, and if that's not the case, it is enough to just refer to a standard in an external reference (for example, your favorite books, authors, or Wikipedia).

- **Evergreen content:** There is always stuff that does not change or that changes very infrequently, and this material does not cost much to maintain.

- **Refactoring-proof knowledge:** Some things don't require human effort when there is a change. This can be because of refactoring tools that automatically propagate linked changes, or because knowledge intrinsic to something is collocated with the thing itself, and it changes and moves with that thing.

- **Internal documentation:** Additional knowledge about a thing is best located on the thing itself, or as close as possible.

Collaborative

A living documentation must be collaborative through the following preferences:

- **Favor conversations over formal documentation:** Nothing beats interactive, face-to-face conversations for exchanging knowledge efficiently. Don't feel bad about not keeping a record of every discussion. Even though I usually favor conversations, there is knowledge that keeps on being useful repeatedly over a long period of time or for many people. It is important to pay attention to the process of *ideas sedimentation* over time to decide what knowledge is worth the effort of recording in a persistent form.

- **Accessible knowledge:** In a living documentation approach, knowledge is often declared within technical artifacts in a source control system. This makes it difficult for nontechnical people to access it. Therefore, you should provide tools to make this knowledge accessible to all audiences without any manual effort.

- **Collective ownership:** It's not because all the knowledge is in the source control system that developers own it. Developers don't own the documentation; they just own the technical responsibility to deal with it.

Insightful

The above-mentioned principles are useful, but to realize the full potential of a living documentation, it must be insightful:

- **Deliberate decision making:** If you don't know clearly what you're doing, it shows immediately when you're about to do living documentation. This kind of feedback encourages you to clarify your decisions so that what you do becomes easy to explain. By encouraging more deliberate decision-making, this will often raise the quality of the work.

- **Embedded learning:** You want to write code and other technical artifacts that are so good that your workmates can learn the design, the business domain, and everything else just by working with the system, learning through their interactions.

- **Reality check:** Living documentation helps reveal the actual state of the system (for example, "I did not expect the implementation to be that messy," as in "I thought I was shaved correctly, but the mirror tells otherwise."). This, again, can foster improvements by accepting reality for what it is, as opposed to what you'd like it to be.

The following sections describe these principles more in details, while the next chapters expand into the related patterns and practices to implement a successful living documentation approach. But before that, an important inspiration for living documentation can be found, surprisingly, in the way ants and other social insects collaborate and exchange knowledge.

How Ants Exchange Knowledge: Stigmergy

Michael Feather (@mfeathers) recently shared a link to a fantastic article online by Ted Lewis, who introduces the concept of stigmergy in relation to our work in software as a team:

> The French entomologist Pierre-Paul Grassé described a mechanism of insect coordination he called "stigmergy"—work performed by an actor stimulates subsequent work by the same or other actors. That is, the state of a building, code base, highway, or other physical construction determines what needs to be done next without central planning or autocratic rule. The actors—insects or programmers—know what to do next, based on what has already been done. This intuitive urge to extend the work of others becomes the organizing principle of modern software development.
>
> Ants use a special type of chemical marker—pheromones—to highlight the results of their activity.[8]

Similarly, programmers manufacture their own markers through emails, GitHub issues, and all kinds of documentation that augments code. As Lewis concludes:

> The essence of modern software development is stigmergic intellect and markers embedded within the code base. Markers make stigmergy more efficient, by more reliably focusing a programmer's attention on the most relevant aspects of the work that needs to be done.[9]

Stigmergy is already the prominent way we exchange knowledge between the people and the machines involved when doing software. One key idea of living documentation is to acknowledge that this stigmergic effect is there, and to find ways to push it to the max. This starts by getting most of the knowledge out of the system you're in, like ants do.

Most Knowledge Is Already There

There is no need to record a piece of knowledge when it is already recorded in the system itself.

Every interesting project is a learning journey that produces specific knowledge. We usually expect documentation to give us the specific knowledge we need, but the

---

8. Ted Lewis, Ubiquity blog, http://ubiquity.acm.org/blog/why-cant-programmers-be-more-like-ants-or-a-lesson-in-stigmergy

9. Ted Lewis, Ubiquity blog, http://ubiquity.acm.org/blog/why-cant-programmers-be-more-like-ants-or-a-lesson-in-stigmergy

funny thing is that all this knowledge is already there: in the source code, in the configuration files, in the tests, in the behavior of the application at runtime, in memory of the various tools involved, and, of course, in the brains of all the people working on it.

In a software project, most of the knowledge is present in some form somewhere in the artifacts. It is similar to ants learning how to evolve their nest mostly from the nest itself.

Therefore: Acknowledge that most of the knowledge is already in the system itself. When needed, identify where it is located and exploit it from there.

Even if the knowledge is there somewhere, this does not mean that there is nothing to do about it. There are a number of problems with the knowledge that's already there:

- **Inaccessible:** The knowledge stored in the source code and other artifacts is not accessible to nontechnical people. For example, source code is not readable by nondevelopers.

- **Too abundant:** Huge amounts of knowledge are stored in the project artifacts, which makes it impossible to use the knowledge efficiently. For example, each logical line of code encodes knowledge, but for a given question, only one or two lines may be relevant to the answer.

- **Fragmented:** There is knowledge that we think of as one single piece but that is in fact spread over multiple places in the project's artifacts. For example, a class hierarchy in Java is usually spread over multiple files, one for each subclass, even though we tend to think about the class hierarchy as a whole.

- **Implicit:** A lot of knowledge is present *implicitly* in the existing artifacts. It may be, for example, 99% there but missing the 1% to make it explicit. For example, when you use a design pattern like a composite, the pattern is visible in the code only if you're familiar with the pattern.

- **Unrecoverable:** It may be that the knowledge is there but that there is no way to recover it because it's excessively obfuscated. For example, business logic is expressed in code, but the code is so bad that nobody can understand it.

- **Unwritten:** In the worst case, the knowledge is only in people's brains, and only its consequences are there in the system. For example, there may a general business rule, but it may have been programmed as a series of special cases, so the general rule is not expressed anywhere.

Internal Documentation

The best place to store documentation is on the documented thing itself.

You've probably seen pictures of the Google datacenters and of the Centre Pompidou in Paris (see Figure 1.9). They have in common a lot of color-coded pipes, with additional labels printed or riveted on the pipes themselves. On the Pompidou Center, air pipes are blue and water pipes are green. This logic of color-coding expands beyond the pipes: Electricity transport is yellow, and everything about moving people is red, including the elevators and stairways.

Figure 1.9 *The Centre Pompidou building is color coded*

This logic is also ubiquitous in datacenters, and even more documentation is printed directly on the pipes. There are labels to identify the pipes, and there are arrows to show the direction of the water flow in them. In the real world, such color-coding and ad hoc marking are often mandatory for fire prevention and firefighting: Water pipes for firefighters have very visible labels riveted on them, indicating where they come from. Emergency exits in buildings are made very visible above the doors. In airplanes, bright signs on the central corridors document where to go. In a situation of crisis, you don't have time to look for a manual; you need the answer in the most obvious place: right where you are, on the thing itself.

Internal Versus External Documentation

Persistent documentation comes in two flavors: external and internal.

With external documentation, knowledge is expressed in a form that has nothing to do with the chosen implementation technologies of the project. This is the case of the traditional forms of documentation, with separate Microsoft Office documents on shared folders or wikis with their own databases.

An advantage of external documentation is that it can take whatever format and tool is most convenient for the audience and for the writers. The drawback is that it's extremely hard, if not impossible, to ensure that external documentation is up-to-date with respect to the latest version of the product. External documentation can also simply be lost.

In contrast, internal documentation directly represents knowledge by using the existing implementation technology. Using Java annotations or naming conventions on the language identifiers to declare and explain design decisions is a good example of internal documentation.

The advantage of internal documentation is that it's always up-to-date with any version of the product, as it's part of its source code. Internal documentation cannot be lost because it's embedded within the source code itself. It's also readily available and comes to the attention of any developers working on the code just because it's under their eyes.

Internal documentation also enables you to benefit from all the tools and all the goodness of your fantastic IDE, such as autocomplete, instant search, and seamless navigation within and between elements. The drawback is that your expression of the knowledge is limited to the possible extension mechanisms built in to the language. For example, there's little you can do to extend the Maven XML with additional knowledge about each dependency. Another big drawback is that knowledge expressed as internal documentation is not readily accessible to nondevelopers. However, it is possible to work around that limitation with automated mechanisms that extract the knowledge and turn it into documents that are accessible to the right audience.

If you're familiar with the book *Domain-Specific Languages* by Martin Fowler and Rebecca Parsons, you'll recognize the similar concept of internal versus external domain-specific languages (DSLs). An external DSL is independent from the chosen implementation technology. For example, the syntax of regular expressions has nothing to do with the programming language chosen for the project. In contrast, an internal DSL uses the regular chosen technology, such as the Java programming language, in a way that makes it look like another language in disguise. This style is often called a *fluent* style and is common in mocking libraries.

Examples of Internal and External Documentation

It's not always easy to tell whether documentation is internal or external, as it's sometime relative to your perspective. Javadoc is a standard part of the Java programming language, so it's internal. But from the Java implementors' perspective, it's another syntax embedded within the Java syntax, so it would be external. Regular code comments are in a gray middle area. They're formally part of the language but do not provide anything more than free text. You're on your own to write them with your writing talent, and the compiler will not help check for typos beside the default spell-checking based on the English dictionary.

From the perspective of the developer, every standard technology used to build a software product can be considered a host for internal documentation, including the following:

- Feature files used for business-readable specifications and testing tools
- Markdown files and images next to the code with a naming convention or linked to from the code or feature files
- Tools manifests, including the dependency management manifest, automated deployment manifest, infrastructure description manifest, and so on

Whenever we add documentation within these artifacts, we benefit from being able to use our standard toolset and have the advantage of being in the source control, close to the corresponding implementation so that it can evolve together with it. Examples of potential media for internal documentation include the following:

- Self-documenting code and use of clean code practices, including class and method naming, using composed methods and types
- Annotations that add knowledge to elements of the programming language
- Javadoc comments on public interfaces, classes, and main methods
- Folder organization and decomposition and naming of modules and submodules

In contrast, examples of external documentation include the following:

- README and similar text files
- Any HTML or Microsoft Office document about the project

Preferring Internal Documentation

Remember what I said earlier: The best place to put documentation about a thing is on the thing itself.

As you'll see throughout this book, I'm definitely in favor of internal documentation, coupled with just enough automation for cases where it's necessary to publish more traditional documents. I suggest choosing internal documentation by default, at least for all knowledge that's at risk of changing regularly.

Even for stable knowledge, I recommend internal documentation first, and I would choose to do external documentation only when there's clearly value added, such as with a documentation that must be maximally attractive (perhaps for marketing reasons). In that case, I suggest hand-crafted slides, diagrams with careful manual layout, and appealing pictures. The point of using external documentation would be to be able to add a human feel to the final document, so I'd use Apple Keynote or Microsoft PowerPoint, select or create beautiful quality pictures, and beta test the effectiveness of the documentation on a panel of colleagues to make sure it's well received.

Note that appeal and humor can be hard to automate or to encode into formal documentation, but it's not impossible either.

In Situ Documentation

Internal documentation, also an in-situ documentation, means documentation that is "in the natural or original position or place."[10]

This implies that the documentation is not only using the same implementation technology, but is also directly mixed into the source code, within the artifact that built the product. *In situ* means bringing the additional knowledge about a thing where the thing is located, for example within the source code rather than in a remote location.

This type of documentation is convenient for developers. As in designing user interfaces, where the term *in situ* means that a particular user action can be performed without going to another window, consuming and editing the documentation can be performed without going to another file or to another tool.

---

10. By Permission. From Merriam-Webster.com © 2019 by Merriam-Webster, Inc. https://www.merriam-webster.com/dictionary/in situ.

Machine-Readable Documentation

Good documentation focuses on high-level knowledge like the design decisions on top of the code and the rationale behind these decisions. We usually consider this kind of knowledge to be of interest only to people, but even tools can take advantage of it. Because internal documentation is expressed using implementation technologies, it can usually be parsed by tools. This opens new opportunities for tools to assist developers in their daily tasks. In particular, it enables automated processing of knowledge for curation, consolidation, format conversion, automated publishing, or reconciliation.

Specific Versus Generic Knowledge

There is knowledge that is specific to your company, your particular system, or your business domain, and there is knowledge that is generic and shared with many other people in many other companies in the industry.

Knowledge about programming languages, developers' tools, software patterns, and practices belongs to the generic knowledge category. Examples include DDD, patterns, continuous integration using Puppet and Git tutorials.

Knowledge about mature business industry sectors is also generic knowledge. Even in very competitive areas like pricing in finance or supply chain optimization in e-commerce, most of the knowledge is public and available in industry-standard books, and only a small part of the business knowledge is specific and confidential—and only for a while at that.

For example, each business domain has its own essential reading list, and it might have a book that is often referred to as "The Bible" of that field (for example, *Options, Futures, and Other Derivatives* by John C Hull, *Logistics and Supply Chain Management* by Martin Christopher).

The good news is that generic knowledge is already documented in the industry literature. There are books, blog posts, and conference talks that describe it quite well. There are standard vocabularies to talk about it. There are trainings available to learn it faster from knowledgeable people.

Learning Generic Knowledge

You also learn generic knowledge by doing your job, as well as by reading books and attending trainings and conferences. This only takes a few hours, and you know beforehand what you're going to learn, how long it will take, and how much it will cost. It's as easy to learn generic knowledge as it is to go to the store to buy food.

Generic knowledge is a solved problem. This knowledge is ready-made, ready to be reused by everyone. When you use it, you just have to link to an authoritative source, and you're done documenting. This is as simple as noting an Internet link or a bibliographic reference.

Focusing on Specific Knowledge

Use documentation for specific knowledge and learn the generic knowledge from trainings.

Specific knowledge is the knowledge your company or team has that is not (yet) shared with other peers in the same industry. This knowledge is more expensive to learn than generic knowledge; it takes time practicing and making mistakes. This is the kind of knowledge that deserves most attention.

Specific knowledge is valuable and cannot be found ready-made, so it's the kind of knowledge you have to take care of. Specific knowledge deserves the biggest efforts from you and your colleagues. As a professional, you should know enough of the generic, industry standard knowledge to be able to focus on growing the knowledge that's specific to your particular ambitions.

Therefore: Make sure everyone is trained on the generic knowledge in your industry. Then focus any documentation effort on specific knowledge.

Ensuring Documentation Accuracy

You can trust documentation only if there is a mechanism to guarantee its accuracy.

When it comes to documentation, the main problem is often that it's not accurate, usually because of obsolescence. Documentation that is not 100% accurate all the time cannot be trusted. As soon as you know documentation can be misleading from time to time, it loses its credibility. It might still be a bit useful, but it will take more time to find out what's right and what's wrong in it. And when it comes to creating documentation, it's hard to dedicate time to it when you know it won't be accurate for long; its lifespan is a big motivation killer.

But updating documentation is one of the most unappreciated tasks ever. It is not interesting and doesn't seem rewarding. However, you can have nice documentation if you take it seriously and decide to tackle it with a well-chosen mechanism to enforce accuracy at all times.

Therefore: You need to think about how you address the accuracy of your documentation.

Accuracy Mechanism for Reliable Documentation

As mentioned earlier, authoritative knowledge that can be trusted already exists somewhere, usually in the form of source code. Therefore, duplicated knowledge is problematic because it multiplies the cost of keeping it updated to keep pace with changes. This applies to source code, of course, and this applies to every other artifact, too. We usually call "design" the discipline of making sure that changes remain cheap at any point in time. We need design for the code, of course, and we need the same design skills for everything about documentation.

A good approach for documentation is a matter of design. It takes design skills to design documentation that is always accurate, without slowing down the software development work.

With knowledge that can change at any time, there are a number of approaches to keeping documentation accurate. They are described in the following sections, ordered from the most desirable to the least desirable, and Chapter 3, "Knowledge Exploitation," expands on them.

Consider a piece of knowledge kept in a single source that is authoritative. This knowledge is accessible only to the people who can read the files. For example, source code is a natural documentation of itself for developers, and with good code, there's no need for anything else. For example, a manifest to configure the list of all dependencies for a dependency management tool like Maven or NuGet is natural authoritative documentation for the list of dependencies. As long as this knowledge is only of interest for developers, it's just fine as it is; there's no need for a publishing mechanism to make the knowledge accessible to other audiences.

Single Sourcing with a Publishing Mechanism

Single sourcing is the approach to favor whenever possible. With single sourcing, knowledge is kept in a single source that is authoritative. It's made available in various forms as published and versioned documents, thanks to an automated publishing mechanism. Any time there's a change, it's updated there and only there.

As an example, source code and configuration files are often the natural authoritative homes for a lot of knowledge. When necessary, the knowledge from such a single source of truth is extracted and published in another form, but it remains clear that there is only one place that is authoritative. The publishing mechanism should also be automated to be run frequently; automation prevents the introduction of errors that is common with manual documentation.

Even without the additional comments, Javadoc is a good example of this approach: The reference documentation is the source code itself, as parsed by the Javadoc Doclet, and it's published automatically as a website for everyone to browse the structure of interfaces, classes, and methods, including the class hierarchies, in a convenient and always accurate manner.

Redundant Sources with a Propagation Mechanism

Knowledge may be duplicated in various places, but reliable tools can automatically propagate any change in one place to every other place. Automated refactorings in your IDE are the best examples of this approach. The class names, interface names, and method names are repeated everywhere in the code, but it's easy to rename them because the IDE knows how to reliably chase every reference and update it correctly. This is far superior to and safer than using *Find* and *Replace*, where you run the risk of replacing random strings by mistake.

Similarly, documentation tools such as AsciiDoc offer built-in mechanisms to declare attributes that you can then embed everywhere in the text. Thanks to the built-in include and substitution features, you can rename and make changes in one place and propagate the change to many places at no cost.

Redundant Sources with a Reconciliation Mechanism

If knowledge is declared in two sources, one source may change without the other changing—and that's a problem. There's a need for a mechanism to detect whenever the two sources don't match. Such a reconciliation mechanism should be automated and run frequently to ensure permanent consistency.

BDD with automation tools such as Cucumber is an example of this approach. In this case, the code and the scenarios are the two sources of knowledge, and they both describe the same business behavior. Whenever a test running the scenarios fails, it's a signal that the scenarios and the code are no longer in sync.

An Anti-Pattern: Human Dedication

Human dedication is an anti-pattern. If knowledge is duplicated in various places, sometimes it's left to people on the team to make sure everything remains consistent at all times through a lot of dedication and hard grunt work. In practice, this does not work, and it is not a recommended approach.

When Documentation Does Not Need an Accuracy Mechanism

In some cases, such as in the following sections, you don't need an accuracy mechanism for your documentation.

Single-Use Knowledge

Sometimes accuracy is just not a concern because the knowledge recorded will be disposed of within hours or a few days after use. This kind of transient knowledge does not age and does not evolve, and hence there's no concern about its consistency—as long as it's used for only a short period of time and actually disposed of immediately after use. For example, conversations between the pair in pair programming and the code written during baby steps in TDD don't matter once the task at hand is done.

Accounts from the Past

An account of past events, such as a blog post, is not subject to issues of accuracy because it is clear for the reader that there is no promise of the text being accurate forever. The point of the post may be, for example, to describe a situation as it happened, including the thinking at the time and the related emotions.

Such knowledge that is accurate at a point in time and that's recorded in the context of that point in time is not considered obsolete documentation. The knowledge in the blog post does get outdated over time, but this is not a problem as it's clearly in the context of a blog post with a date and a story that's clearly in the past. This is a smart way to archive episodes of work and the big idea behind a story in a persistent fashion, without pretending it is evergreen. A blog post won't mislead anyone to think that it's new information as it's clear that it's an account of a past reflection. As a story anchored in the past, it's always an accurate story, even if you can't trust the particular code or examples that may be quoted. It's like reading a book on history, and there are a lot of precious lessons to be learned, regardless of the context in which they happened.

The worst that can happen to an account from the past is that it might become irrelevant, when the concerns of that time are no longer concerns.

Big Questions to Challenge Your Documentation

> Every minute crafting documents is a minute lost to other things. Is this adding value? Is this most important?
>
> —*@dynamoben on Twitter*

Imagine that your boss or a customer asks for "more documentation." A number of important questions need to be asked and answered to decide what to do next. The goal behind these questions is to make sure you're going to use your time as efficiently as possible in the long run.

The order in which you ask the important questions listed in the following sections depends on the situation, and you may skip or rearrange the questions at will. The following sections explain the thought process involved in determining how to do documentation, and once you understand it, you can make the process your own.

Questioning the Need for Documentation at All

Documentation is not an end in itself; it's a mean for a purpose that must be identified. You won't be able to make something useful unless you understand the goal. So the first question is:

> Why do we need this documentation?

If no answer comes easily, then you're definitely not ready to start investing effort in additional documentation. You should put the topic on hold until you know better. You don't want to waste time on ill-defined objectives.

Then the next question immediately follows:

> Who's the intended audience?

If the answer is unclear or sounds like "everyone," then you're not ready to start doing anything. Efficient documentation must target an identified audience. Even documentation about things "that everyone should know" has to target an audience, such as "nontechnical people with only a superficial knowledge of the business domain."

Now, still determined to avoid wasting time, you're ready for the first question of documentation.

The First Question of Documentation

Do we really need this documentation?

Someone might be tempted to create documentation on a topic that is only of interest for himself or herself or that is relevant only for the time he or she is working on it. Perhaps it does not make much sense to even add a paragraph to the wiki. But there's another, and worse, reason for asking for documentation.

Need for Documentation Because of Lack of Trust

The answer to the first question of documentation may sound something like "I need documentation because I'm afraid you don't work as much as I'd like, so I need to see deliverables to make sure you work hard enough." In this case, the main issue is not a matter of documentation.

As the duo Matt Wynne (@mattwynne) and Seb Rose (@sebrose) said at the BDD eXchange conference in 2013: "Need for detail might indicate lack of trust." In such a case, lack of documentation is just a symptom, and the root issue is lack of trust. This is a serious enough issue that you should stop reading this book and try to find ways to improve the situation. No amount of documentation alone can fix lack of trust in the first place. However, since delivering value often is a good way to build trust, sensible documentation has a side role in a remediation. For example, making the work more visible may help build trust and is a form of documentation.

Just-in-Time Documentation, or a Cheap Option on Future Knowledge

If you need documentation, you might not actually need it right away. Hence, there is another first question of documentation.

> ### The Other First Question of Documentation
> Do we really need this documentation **now**?

Creating documentation has a cost, and the benefit in the future is an uncertain benefit. The benefit is uncertain when you cannot be sure someone will have the need for the information in the future.

One thing I've learned over the years in software development is that people are notoriously bad at anticipating the future. Usually people can just bet, and their bets are often wrong. As a consequence, it is important to use a number of strategies to determine when it's important to do documentation:

- **Just-in-time:** Add documentation only when really needed.
- **Cheap upfront:** Add a little documentation now, at a very low cost.
- **Expensive upfront:** Add documentation now, even if it takes time to create it.

Just-in-Time

You may decide that the cost of documenting now is not worth it, given the uncertainty that it will be useful in the future. In such a case, you might put off doing documentation until it becomes really necessary. Typically, it is a good idea to wait for someone to initiate a documentation effort. On a big project with lots of stakeholders, you might even decide to wait for a second or third request before deciding it's worth investing time and effort in creating documentation.

Note that this assumes that you will still have the knowledge available somewhere in the team when the time comes to share it. It also assumes that the effort of documenting in the future will not be too great compared to what it would be right now.

Cheap Upfront

You might decide that the cost of documenting right now is so low that it's not worth deferring it for later, even if it's never actually used. This is especially relevant when the knowledge is fresh in mind and you run the risk that it will be much harder later to remember all the stakes and important details. And, of course, creating documentation upfront makes sense if you have cheap ways to do it, as you'll see later.

Expensive Upfront

You might decide that it's worth it to bet on the future need for this knowledge and choose to create documentation right now, even if doing so is not cheap. There's the risk it might be a waste, but you might be happy to take this risk—hopefully for some substantiated reason (for example, guidelines or compliance requirement, high confidence from more than one person that it's necessary).

It's important to keep in mind that any effort around documentation right now also has an impact on the quality of the work because it put the focus on how it's done and why and acts like a review. This means that even if it's never used in the future, it can be useful at least once, right now, for the sake of thinking clearly about the decisions and the rationale behind them.

Questioning the Need for Traditional Documentation

Assuming that there's a genuine need for additional documentation, for an identified purpose, and for an identified audience, you're now ready for the second question of documentation.

> **The Second Question of Documentation**
>
> Could we just share knowledge through conversations or working together?

Traditional documentation should never be the default choice, as it's too wasteful unless absolutely necessary. When there is a need for knowledge transfer from some people to other people, this is best done by simply talking—by asking and answering questions instead of exchanging written documents.

Working collectively, with frequent conversations, is a particularly effective form of documentation. Techniques such as pair programming, cross-programming, the three amigos in agile, and mob-programming totally change the game with respect to documentation, as knowledge transfer between people is done continuously and at the same time the knowledge is created or applied on a task.

Conversations and working collectively are the preferred forms of documentation, although sometimes they are not enough. Sometime there's a genuine need to have the knowledge formalized.

> ### Challenging the Need for Formalized Documentation
>
> Does it have to be persistent? Does it have to be shared to a large audience? Is it critical knowledge?
>
> If the answer to each of these questions is "no," conversations and working collectively should be enough, and there is no need for more formal documentation.
>
> Of course, if you ask a manager these questions, you're likely to be answered "yes" just because it's a safe choice. You can't be wrong by doing more, right? It's a bit like setting the priority on tasks; many people put a high priority flag on everything, which then makes high priority meaningless. With documentation, what seems to be the safe choice carries a higher cost, which can in turn endanger the project. The safe choice is really to consider these three questions in a balanced way rather than automatically answering "yes" or "no."

Even for the knowledge that must be shared to a large audience, that must be kept persistent for the long term or that is critical, there are several documentation options:

- Plenary meeting with the full audience attending, or a lecture-style conference talk with the audience hopefully taking notes
- Podcast or video, like a recorded conference talk or a recorded interview
- Artifacts that are self-documented or that are augmented in an internal documentation approach
- Manually written document

The point is that, even with particularly important knowledge, manually written documentation does not have to be the default choice.

Minimizing Extra Work Now

Say that you have a legitimate need to keep some knowledge in a formal form. Because, as you've learned, most knowledge already exists somewhere, in some form, you need to answer another question.

The Knowledge Location Question

Where's the knowledge right now?

If knowledge is only in the heads of the people, then it needs to be encoded somewhere—as text, code, metadata, or something else. If the knowledge is already represented somewhere, the idea is to use it (*knowledge exploitation*) or reuse it (*knowledge augmentation*) as much as possible.

You might be able to use the knowledge that's in the source code, in the configuration files, in the tests, in the behavior of the application at runtime, and perhaps in the memory of the various tools involved. This process, which is described in detail in the following chapters, involves asking the following questions:

- Is the knowledge exploitable, or obfuscated, or unrecoverable?
- Is the knowledge too abundant?
- Is the knowledge accessible for the intended audience?
- Is the knowledge in one single place or fragmented?
- What is missing that would make the knowledge 100% explicit?

When the knowledge is not fully there or is too implicit to be used, then the game becomes finding a way to add the knowledge directly into the source of the product. That is the focus of Chapter 4, "Knowledge Augmentation."

Minimizing Extra Work Later

It's not enough to create documentation once; you must consider how to keep it accurate over time. Therefore, an important question remains.

The Knowledge Stability Question

How stable is this knowledge?

Stable knowledge is easy because you can ignore the question of its maintenance. On the other end of the spectrum, living knowledge is challenging. It can change often or at any time, and you don't want to update multiple artifacts and documents over and over.

The rate of change is the crucial criterion (see Figure 1.10). Knowledge that is stable over years can be taken care of with any traditional form, such as writing text manually and printing it on paper. Knowledge that is stable over years can even survive some amount of duplication because it will not need to be updated.

Figure 1.10 *The rate of change of the knowledge is the key criterion*

In contrast, knowledge that changes every hour or more often just cannot afford traditional forms of documentation. The key concerns to keep in mind are the cost of evolution and the cost of maintaining the documentation. Changing the source code and then having to update other documents manually is not an option.

This process, which is described in the next chapters, involves the following questions:

- If it changes, what changes at the same time?
- If there's redundant knowledge, how do we keep the redundant sources in sync?

Making an Activity Fun

To make an activity sustainable, make it fun.

Fun is important for sustainable practices. If something is not fun, you'll not want to do it very often, and the practice will progressively disappear. For practices to last, they need to be fun. This is particularly important with a boring topic such as documentation.

Therefore: Choose living documentation practices that are as fun as possible. If something is fun, do more of it, and if it's totally not fun, look for alternatives, such as solving the problem in another way or through automation.

This preference for fun activities obviously assumes that working with people is on the fun side, because there's no good way around that. For example, if coding is fun for you, you'll try to document as much as possible in code. That's the idea behind many suggestions in this book. If copying information from one place to another is a chore, then it's a candidate for automation or for finding a way to avoid having to move data at all. Fixing a process and automating a part of a process tend to be fun, so these are also things you might feel like doing (see Figure 1.11)—and that's lucky.

Figure 1.11 *Fun starts with automating the chores*

Mixing Fun and Professionalism

There's nothing wrong with having fun at work, as long as you're professional in your work. This means doing your best to solve the problems that matter, delivering value, and reducing risk. With that in mind, you're free to choose the practices and tools that make your life more fun. After 18 years in programming, I'm now confident it's always possible to do professional work while having fun. The idea that work should be boring and unpleasant because it's work or because you're paid for it to compensate for this very unpleasantness is just stupid. You're paid some money to deliver value that is worth even more money. Delivering value is fun, and behaving professionally is pleasant, too. And fun is essential for working efficiently as a team in a pleasant atmosphere.

Documentation Reboot

This book could be titled *Documentation 2.0: Living Documentation*, *Continuous Documentation*, or *No Documentation*. Even with the shorter title *Living Documentation*, the key driver of this book is to reconsider the way we do documentation, starting from the purpose. From there, the universe of applicable solutions is nearly infinite. This book explores the universe of practices and techniques in various categories, organized into almost 100 patterns. Table 1.1 provides a summary of this language of patterns.

Table 1-1 *Patterns Summary*

Pattern	Brief Description
Rethinking Documentation	
Most knowledge is already there	There is no need to record a piece of knowledge that is already recorded in the system itself.
Prefer internal documentation	The best place to store documentation is on the documented thing itself.
Focus on specific knowledge	Use documentation for the specific knowledge and learn the generic knowledge from trainings.
Accuracy mechanism	You can trust documentation only if there is a mechanism to guarantee its accuracy.
Fun activity	To make an activity sustainable, make it fun.
Knowledge Exploitation	
Single-source publishing	Keep the knowledge in one single source of truth and publish from there when needed.
Reconciliation mechanism	If knowledge is repeated in more than one place, set up a reconciliation mechanism to detect inconsistencies immediately.
Consolidation of dispersed facts	Diverse facts put together become useful knowledge.
Tools history	Your tools record knowledge about your system.
Ready-made documentation	Most of what you do is already documented in the literature.

Pattern	Brief Description
Knowledge Augmentation	
Augmented code	When the code doesn't tell the full story, add the missing knowledge to make it complete.
Documentation by annotation	Extend your programming language by using annotations for documentation purposes.
Documentation by convention	Rely on code conventions to document knowledge.
Module-wide knowledge augmentation	Knowledge that spans a number of artifacts that have something in common is best factored out in one place.
Intrinsic knowledge augmentation	Only annotate elements with knowledge that is intrinsic to them.
Embedded learning	Putting more knowledge into the code helps its maintainers learn while working on it.
Sidecar files	When putting annotations within the code is not possible, put them into a file next to the code.
Metadata database	When putting annotations within the code is not possible, keep them in an outside database.
Machine-accessible documentation	Documentation that is machine accessible opens new opportunities for tools to help at the design level.
Record your rationale	The rationale behind a decision is one of the most important things to augment the code with.
Acknowledge your influences	The major influences of a team are the keys for understanding the system they've built.
Commit messages as comprehensive documentation	Carefully written commit messages make each line of code well documented.
Knowledge Curation	
Dynamic curation	Even if all the works of art are already there in the collection, there is still work to be done to make an exhibition out of it.
Highlighted core[11]	Some elements of the domain are more important than others.
Inspiring exemplars	The best documentation on how to write code is often just the best code that is already there.

---

11. Evans, Eric. *Domain-Driven Design: Tackling Complexity in the Heart of Software.* Hoboken: Addison-Wesley Professional, 2003.

Pattern	Brief Description
Guided tour, sightseeing map[12]	It is easier to quickly discover the best of a new place with a guided tour or a sightseeing map.
Automating Documentation	
Living document	A document that evolves at the same pace as the system it describes.
Living glossary	A glossary that evolves at the same pace as the system it describes, reflecting the domain language used in the code.
Living diagram	A diagram that can be generated again on any change so that it's always up-to-date.
One diagram/one story	One diagram should tell only one specific message.
Runtime Documentation	
Visible test	Tests can produce visual output for human review in domain-specific notation.
Visible workings[13]	Working software can be its own documentation at runtime.
Introspectable workings	Your code in memory can be a source of knowledge.
Refactorable Documentation	
Code as documentation	Most of the time, the code is its own documentation.
Integrated documentation	Your IDE already fulfills many documentation needs.
Plain-text diagrams	Diagrams that cannot be genuine living diagrams should be created from plain-text documents to make their maintenance easier.
Stable Documentation	
Evergreen content	Evergreen content is content that remains useful without change for a long time.
Perennial naming	Favor naming schemes that last longer than others.
Linked knowledge	Knowledge is more valuable when it is connected, provided that the connections are stable.
Link registry	An indirection can be changed to fix broken links in a single place.

---

12. Brown, Simon. Software *Architecture for Developers, Vol 2: Visualize, document, and explore your software architecture*. https://leanpub.com/visualising-software-architecture
13. Brian Marick, "Visible Workings": https://web.archive.org/web/20110202132102/http://visibleworkings.com/

Pattern	Brief Description
Bookmarked search	A search made into a link is more stable than a direct link.
Broken link checker	Detecting broken links as soon as possible helps keep the documentation trusted.
Invest in stable knowledge	Stable knowledge is an investment that pays back over a longer period of time.

How to Avoid Traditional Documentation

Pattern	Brief Description
Working collectively as continuous knowledge sharing	Working collectively is an opportunity for continuous knowledge sharing.
Coffee machine communication	Not all exchange of knowledge has to be planned and managed. Spontaneous discussions in a relaxed environment often work better and must be encouraged.
Ideas sedimentation	It takes some time to find out whether a piece of knowledge was important or not.
Throwaway documentation	Some documentation is useful for only a limited period of time before it can be deleted.
On-demand documentation	Document what you've seen is necessary to be documented.
Astonishment report	Newcomers' superpower is bringing a fresh perspective.
Interactive documentation	Documentation can try to emulate the interactivity of a conversation.
Declarative automation	Every time you automate a software task, you should take the opportunity to make it a form of documentation as well.
Enforced guidelines	The best documentation does not even have to be read if it can alert you at the right time with the right piece of knowledge.
Constrained behavior	Influence or constrain the behavior instead of documenting.
Replaceability first	Designing for replaceability reduces the need to know how things work.
Consistency first	Being consistent reduces the need for documentation.

Pattern	Brief Description
Beyond Documentation: Living Design	
Listen to the documentation	Documentation can be a signal to spot opportunities for improvements.
Shameful documentation	The presence of a free comment is often a signal of a shameful behavior in the code.
Deliberate decision making	The path to better design and better documentation starts by making more decisions deliberately.
Hygienic transparency	Transparency leads to greater hygiene because the dirt cannot hide.
Word cloud	A word cloud of the identifiers in the code should reveal what the code is about.
Signature survey[14]	Looking at the code at some level of detail can reveal its shape.
Documentation driven	Start by explaining your goal or end result, such as how the system will be used.
Abusing living documentation (anti-pattern)	Don't be dogmatic about living documentation but focus on delivering value for your users.
Living documentation procrastination	Have fun in your living documentation tools to avoid having too much fun in your production code.
Biodegradable documentation	The goal of documentation should be to make itself redundant.
Design skills everywhere	Learn and practice good design; it's equally good for your code and for your documentation.
Living Architecture	
Document the problem	It's almost useless to document a solution without explaining the problem it attempts to solve.
Stake-driven architecture	Is your biggest challenge on the domain understanding a quality attribute or socio-technical aspects?
Explicit quality attributes	Friends don't let friends guess the quality attributes for which a system was designed.

---

14. Ward Cunningham, "Signature Survey: A Method for Browsing Unfamiliar Code": https://c2.com/doc/SignatureSurvey/

Pattern	Brief Description
Architecture landscape	Organize multiple documentation mechanisms into a consistent whole for easier navigation.
Decision log	Keep the major decisions in a decision log.
Fractal architecture documentation	Your system is made of smaller systems; organize your documentation accordingly.
Architecture codex	Documenting the way you make decisions enables decentralized decision making.
Transparent architecture	Architecture is for everyone, as long as they have access to the information.
Architectural reality check	Making sure the implementation of the architecture matches its intent.
Test-driven architecture	The ultimate living architecture is test driven.
Small-scale simulation as documentation	Document a large system with a smaller version of itself.
System metaphor[15]	A concrete analogy shared by everyone—customers, programmers, and managers—can help you understand how the system works.

Introducing Living Documentation

Undercover experiments	Start with safe-to-fail experiments without much publicity.
Marginal documentation	New practices can usually only be applied to new work.
Compliance in spirit	A living documentation approach can comply with even the most demanding compliance requirements by aiming for the spirit instead of for the letter.

Documenting Legacy Applications

Fossilized knowledge	Legacy systems should not be considered blindly as reliable documentation.
Bubble context[16]	Create an isolated space where you can work without the constraint of the legacy system.
Superimposed structure	Relate the desirable structure to the existing, less desirable one.

15. Evans, Eric. *Domain-Driven Design: Tackling Complexity in the Heart of Software*. Hoboken: Addison-Wesley Professional, 2003.
   also
   Beck, Kent. *Extreme Programming Explained*. Hoboken: Addison-Wesley Professional, 2000.
16. Eric Evans, "Getting Started with DDD when Surrounded by Legacy Systems": http://domainlanguage.com/wp-content/uploads/2016/04/GettingStartedWithDDDWhenSurroundedByLegacySystemsV1.pdf

Pattern	Brief Description
Highlighted structure	Make a superimposed structure visible in relation to the existing source code.
External annotations	Sometimes you don't want to touch a fragile system just to add some knowledge to it.
Biodegradable transformation	Documentation of a temporary process should disappear when that process is done.
Agree on maxims[17]	Big changes to legacy systems are made by a number of people who share common objectives; use maxims to share the vision.
Enforced legacy rule	Legacy transformations can last longer than the people doing them; automate the enforcement of the big decisions to protect them.

Living Documentation: The Very Short Version

If you only want to spend a minute on what living documentation is all about, please remember the following big ideas:

- Favor conversations and working together over every kind of document. Most knowledge is already there and just needs to break free.

- Most of the knowledge is there already. You just need to augment it with the missing context, intent, and rationale.

- Pay attention to the frequency of change.

- Thinking about documentation is a way to draw attention to the quality or lack thereof in a system.

If this list is clear enough, you've understood the key message of this chapter.

Approaches to Better Documentation

There are many ways to consider the topic of documentation. These approaches cover a full spectrum that can be seen as a cycle that follows a progression from *avoiding documentation* to *documentation to the max* and then beyond, to

---

17. Demeyer, Serge, Stéphane Ducasse, Oscar Nierstrasz. *Object Oriented Reengineering Patterns*. San Francisco: Morgan Kaufmann Publishers, Inc., 2002.

questioning the need for documentation again and looping the cycle to less documentation again. You could also see this cycle as going from lightweight approaches to more heavyweight ones.

This cycle involves the rate of change (volatility) of the knowledge in question, from stable knowledge to knowledge that changes continuously.

The following describes the following categories of approaches to documentation, which are discussed throughout this book:

- **Avoiding documentation:** The best documentation is often no documentation because the knowledge is not worth any particular effort beyond doing the work. Collaboration with conversation or collective work is key here. Sometimes you can do even better and improve the underlying situation rather than work around it with documentation. Examples include automation and fixing the root issues.

- **Stable documentation:** Not all knowledge changes all the time. When it's stable enough, documentation becomes much simpler and much more useful at the same time. Sometimes it just takes one step to go from changing a piece of knowledge to a more stable one—and this is the type of opportunity you want to exploit.

- **Refactorable documentation:** Code, tests, plain text, and so on present particular opportunities to evolve continuously in sync, thanks to the refactoring capabilities of modern IDEs and tools. Refactorable documentation makes possible accurate documentation for little to no cost.

- **Automating documentation:** Automating documentation is the geekiest area, involving using specific tools to produce documentation automatically in a living fashion, following the changes in the software construction. A particular flavor of automating documentation involves every approach that operates at runtime, when the software is running; this is in contrast to other approaches that work at build time.

- **Beyond documentation:** Finally, we reach the beyond documentation area, where we have the opportunity to question everything and recognize that the topic of documentation can have benefits well beyond just transferring and storing knowledge. This is where we reach enlightenment and reconsider every other approach and technique in a more critical way. This aspect of living documentation is more abstract, but important. Through living documentation practices that stimulate your attention to your work, the quality of the work can be improved as a side effect.

These categories structure the main chapters of this book—but in reverse order to follow a progression from more technical and rather easy-to-grasp to more abstract and people-oriented considerations. This ordering means the chapters progress from the less important to the more important.

Across these categories of approaches, this book discusses some core principles that guide you in how to do documentation efficiently.

A Gateway to DDD

You can get closer to domain-driven design by investing in living documentation.

Living documentation can help guide a team or a set of teams in their adoptions of DDD practices. It helps make these practices more concrete and focuses some attention on the resulting artifacts. Of course, the way you work with the DDD mindset is much more important than the resulting artifacts. Still, the artifacts can at least help visualize what DDD is about, and they can help make visible any problematic practice and provide guidance on how well it's done (or not).

Domain-Driven Design in a Nutshell

Domain-driven design is an approach to tackling complexity in the heart of software development. It primarily advocates a sharp focus on the particular business domain being considered. It promotes writing code that expresses the domain knowledge literally, with no translation between the domain analysis and the executable code. As such, it calls for *modeling directly in code written in a programming language*, in contrast with a lot of literature on modeling. This is possible only if there is the possibility of frequent and close conversations with domain experts, with everyone using the same ubiquitous language—the language of the business domain.

Domain-driven design calls for focusing the efforts on the core domain, the one business area with the potential to make a difference against the competition. As such, DDD encourages developers not just to deliver code but to contribute as partners with the business in a constructive two-way relationship where the developers grow a deep understanding of the business and gain insights into the important stakes.

Domain-driven design is deeply rooted in Kent Beck's *Extreme Programming Explained: Embrace Change*. It is also built on top of the pattern literature, most notably Martin Fowler's *Analysis Patterns: Reusable Object Models* and Rebecca Wirfs-Brock's *Object Design: Roles, Responsibilities, and Collaborations*, the book that began the practice of "xDD" naming.

Eric Evans's *Domain-Driven Design: Tackling Complexity in the Heart of Software* also includes numerous patterns for applying DDD successfully. One of the most important concepts is the notion of bounded context. A *bounded context* defines an area of a system where the language can be kept precise and without ambiguity. Bounded contexts are a major contribution to system design; they simplify and partition large, complicated systems into several smaller and simpler subsystems—without much downside. Splitting systems and work between teams efficiently is quite hard, and the notion of bounded contexts is a powerful design tool to help with this.

Because Evans's *Domain-Driven Design* book was published in 2003, most of its examples were proposed for application in object-oriented programming languages, but it has become clear since then that DDD applies just as well with functional programming languages. I often make the claim that DDD advocates a functional programming style of code even in object-oriented programming languages.

Living Documentation and Domain-Driven Design

This book focuses on several aspects of DDD:

- It promotes the use of DDD in a project, in particular through the chosen examples.

- It shows how documentation can support the adoption of DDD and how it can act as a feedback mechanism to improve your practice.

- It is in itself an application of DDD on the subject of documentation and knowledge management, in the way this topic is approached.

- In particular, many of the practices of living documentation are actually directly DDD patterns from Eric Evans's book.

- The point of writing this book is to actually draw attention to design, or lack of thereof, through documentation practices that make it visible when the team is doing a poor job of design.

Do these factors make this book a book on DDD? I think so. As a fan of DDD, I would definitely love this to be the case.

Living documentation is all about making each decision explicit, with not only the consequences in code but also the rationale, the context, and the associated business stakes expressed (or perhaps *modeled*) using all the expressiveness of the code as a documentation medium.

A project is interesting if it addresses a problem for which there is no standard solution. The project must discover how to solve the problem through continuous learning and a lot of knowledge crunching while exploring the domain. As a consequence, the resulting code will change all the time, from small changes to major breakthroughs.

"Try, Try Again" requires change-friendly documentation. However, at all times it is important to keep the precious knowledge that took so much effort to learn. Once the knowledge is there, you can turn it into valuable and deliverable software by writing and refactoring source code and other technical artifacts. But you need to find ways to keep the knowledge through this process.

DDD advocates "modeling with code" as the fundamental solution. The idea is that code itself is a representation of the knowledge. Only when the code is not enough do you need something else. Tactical patterns leverage the idea that code is the primary medium, and they guide developers in how to use it as such in practice, with their ordinary programming language.

Therefore: Your investment in learning living documentation is also an investment in learning some aspects of domain-driven design. Learn one, and you learn half of the other for free!

When Living Documentation Is an Application of DDD

Living documentation not only supports DDD but is also in itself an example of applying the DDD approach on the domain of managing knowledge throughout its lifecycle. And in many cases, living documentation is a directly applied case of DDD under a slightly different name.

A Story of Mutual Roots Between BDD, DDD, XP, and Living Documentation

The term *living documentation* was introduced by Gojko Adzic in *Specification by Example*, which is a book on behavior-driven development (BDD). BDD is an approach involving collaboration between everyone involved in software development that was proposed by Dan North, who introduced the idea by combining test-driven development (TDD) with the ubiquitous language of domain-driven design. As a consequence, even the term *living documentation* already has roots in domain-driven design!

Consider that living documentation strongly adheres to the following tenets of DDD:

- **Code as the model:** Code is the model (and vice versa), so you want to have as much knowledge of the model in the code as possible—and this is, by definition, the documentation.

- **Tactical techniques to make the code express all the knowledge:** You want to exploit programming languages to the maximum of what they can express, to express even knowledge that is not executed at runtime.

- **Evolving the knowledge all the time with the DDD whirlpool:** Knowledge crunching is primarily a matter of collaboration between business domain experts and the development team. Through this process, some of the most important knowledge becomes embodied into the code—and perhaps into some other artifacts. Because all the knowledge evolves or may evolve at any time, any documented knowledge must embrace change without impediments such as maintenance costs.

- **Making clear what's important and what's not:** In other words, there needs to be a focus on curation. "Focus on the core domain" and "highlight the core concepts" are from Evans's DDD book, but there's much more you can do with curation to help keep the knowledge under control despite the limited human memory and cognition capabilities.

- **Attention to detail:** Many DDD patterns emphasize that attention to detail is important. Decisions should be deliberate and not arbitrary, and they should be guided by concrete feedback. The living documentation approach has to encourage attention to detail by making it easier to document what's deliberate and by giving insightful feedback throughout the process.

- **Strategic design and large-scale structures:** DDD offers techniques to deal with evolving knowledge at the strategic level and on a large scale, providing opportunities for smarter documentation, too.

It is difficult to mention all the correspondences between the ideas of living documentation and domain-driven design without rewriting parts of other books. But some examples are necessary to make the point (see Table 1.2).

Table 1.2 *Correspondence Between Living Documentation and DDD*

Living Documentation Pattern	DDD Pattern (from Evans's book or from later contributions)	Notes
Ready-made knowledge; acknowledge bibliography	Draw on established formalisms, when you can; read the book; apply analysis patterns	Clearly declare all the ready-made knowledge used with references to the sources.
Evergreen document	Domain vision statement	Higher-level knowledge is a great example of stable knowledge that can be written in an evergreen document.

Living Documentation Pattern	DDD Pattern (from Evans's book or from later contributions)	Notes
Code as documentation	Model-driven design; intention-revealing interfaces; declarative design; the building blocks of a model-driven design (to enable expressive code)	DDD is about modeling in plain code, with the purpose of having all the domain knowledge embodied in the code and its test.
Living glossary	Ubiquitous language	When the code literally follows the ubiquitous language, it becomes the single reference for the glossary of the domain.
Listen to the documentation	Hands-on modelers	Modeling in code with living documentation extracted from it gives fast feedback on the quality of the design, in a hands-on fashion.
Change-friendly documentation	Refactoring toward deeper insight; try, try again	"Embracing change" is a constant theme with XP, DDD, and living documentation
Curation	Highlighted core; flagged core; segregated core; abstract core	Segregating what is particularly important from the rest is a key driver in DDD; the goal is to best allocate effort and cognitive attention.

Living documentation goes beyond traditional documentation and its limitations. It elaborates on the DDD techniques and advice for knowledge about the business domain and also for knowledge about the design, as well as the infrastructure and delivery process, which are technical domains, too, with respect to the project stakeholders. The ideas from domain-driven design are essential to guiding developers in how to invest in knowledge in a tactical and strategic way, dealing with change in the short term and in the long term as well. Therefore, as you are going the living documentation route, you are learning domain-driven design, too.

Summary

Throughout this chapter, you have seen that documentation often suffers because of unchallenged traditional habits. This is good news, in a way, because it means there are many opportunities to deconstruct the topic in order to reconstruct it again from first principles, in the light of the fast-paced and change-friendly projects we deal with today.

Living documentation is all about paying attention to the knowledge involved in software making. Some knowledge is more important than other knowledge, and the most important knowledge is almost surely already somewhere in a project's artifacts. The goal, and the fun, of living documentation is to recognize the valuable knowledge, where it already is, and determine what may be missing and how often it changes in order to best benefit from it with minimal expense. In other words, it is about designing a system of knowledge within your code base itself, and it requires design skills, just like coding!

Chapter 2

Behavior-Driven Development as an Example of Living Specifications

What about documenting the business behavior? (Because as you know, business people never change their mind.)

Behavior-driven development (BDD) was the first example of living documentation. In the book *Specification by Example*, Gojko Adzic explains that many teams doing BDD say that one of the biggest benefits is that they benefit from a living documentation that explains what the application is doing, and that can be trusted because it is always up-to-date.

The following sections quickly look at what BDD is and what it is not, in relation with living documentation.

BDD Is All About Conversations

If you think BDD is about testing, forget what you think you know about it. BDD is about sharing knowledge efficiently. This means that you can do BDD without any tools. Before anything else, BDD promotes deep conversations between the three (or more) amigos shown in Figure 2.1. BDD also relies on the use of concrete scenarios—which must use the language of the business domain—to detect misunderstandings and ambiguities early.

Figure 2.1 *The three amigos*

BDD with Automation Is All About Living Documentation

BDD with just conversations provides a lot of value. However, going to the additional effort of setting up automation brings even more benefits. When using a tool like Cucumber, BDD still involves the use of a domain language between every stakeholder involved and, in particular, between the three amigos, a focus on the higher-level purpose, and frequent use of concrete examples, also known as scenarios. These scenarios then become tests in the tool, and they become living documentation at the same time.

Redundancy and Reconciliation

BDD scenarios describe the behavior of an application, but the source code of the application also describes this behavior: The scenarios and source code are redundant with each other, as shown in Figure 2.2.

On one hand, this redundancy is good news: Scenarios expressed in pure domain language, if done properly, are accessible to nontechnical audiences such as business people who could never read code. However, this redundancy is also a problem: If some scenarios or parts of the code evolve independently, then you have two problems: You must determine whether to trust the scenarios or the code, and (a bigger problem), you must in some way know that the scenarios and the code are not in sync.

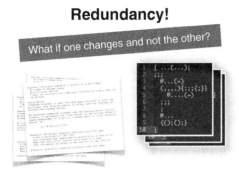

Figure 2.2 *Scenarios and code both describe the same behavior*

This is where a reconciliation mechanism is needed. In the case of BDD, you can use tests and tools like Cucumber or SpecFlow. These tools act like a Roberval balance between both redundant pieces of knowledge, as pictured in Figure 2.3.

These tools parse the scenarios in plain text and use some glue code provided by the developers to drive the actual code. The amounts, dates, and other values in the "Given" and "When" sections of the scenarios are extracted and passed as parameters when calling the actual code. The values extracted from the "Then" sections of the scenarios, on the other hand, are used for the assertions, to check what's expected in the scenario, based on the result from the code matches.

Figure 2.3 *Tools check regularly that the scenarios and the code describe the same behavior*

The tools turn scenarios into automated tests. The nice thing is that these tests also provide a way to detect when the scenarios and the code are no longer in sync. This is an example of a reconciliation mechanism, a means to ensure that redundant sets of information always match.

The Anatomy of Scenarios in a File

When using a tool like Cucumber or SpecFlow to automate scenarios into tests, you create files called *feature files*. These files are plain-text files that are stored in the source control, just like code. Usually they are stored near the tests or as Maven test resources. This means they are versioned like the code, and they are easy to diff.

Let's take a closer look at a feature file.

The Intent of a Feature File

A feature file must start with a narrative that describes the intent of all the scenarios in the file. It usually follows the pattern "In order to.... As a.... I want...." Starting with "In order to" helps you focus on the most important thing: the value you're looking for.

Here's an example of a narrative for an application about detection of potential frauds in the context of fleet management for parcel delivery:

```
1   Feature: Fuel Card Transactions anomalies
2   In order to detect potential fuel card abnormal behavior by
drivers
3   As a fleet manager
4   I want to automatically detect anomalies in all fuel card
transactions
```

Note that the tools just consider the narrative as text; they don't do anything with it except include it in the reports because they acknowledge that it's important.

Feature File Scenarios

The rest of the feature file usually lists all the scenarios that are relevant for the corresponding feature. Each scenario has a title, and scenarios almost always follow the "Given.... When.... Then..." pattern.

Here's an example of one of the many concrete scenarios for an application on detection of potential frauds, in the context of fleet management for parcel delivery:

```
1  Scenario: Fuel transaction with more fuel than the vehicle
tank can hold
2  Given that the tank size of the vehicle 23 is 48L
3  When a transaction is reported for 52L on the fuel card
4  associated with vehicle 23
5  Then an anomaly "The fuel transaction of 52L exceeds the tank
size of 48L" is reported
```

Within one feature file there are typically between 3 and 15 scenarios, describing the happy path, its variants, and the most important situations.

There are a number of other ways to describe scenarios, such as by using the outline format, and there are also ways to factor out common assumptions between scenarios with background scenarios. (For more information on outline format and background scenarios, see for example https://docs.cucumber.io/gherkin/reference/.)

Specification Details

There are many cases in which scenarios alone are enough to describe the expected behavior, but in some rich business domains, such as accounting or finance, scenarios are definitely not enough. In such cases, you also need abstract rules and formulas.

Rather than putting all this additional knowledge in a Word document or in a wiki, you can directly embed it within the related feature file, between the intent and the list of scenarios. Here's an example, from the same feature file as before:

```
1  Feature: Fuel Card Transactions anomalies
2  In order to detect potential fuel card abnormal behavior by
drivers
3  As a fleet manager
4  I want to automatically detect anomalies in all fuel card
transactions
5
6  Description:
7  The monitoring detects the following anomalies:
8  * Fuel leakage: whenever capacity > 1 + tolerance,
9  where capacity = transaction fuel quantity / vehicle tank size
```

```
10 * Transaction too far from the vehicle: whenever distance to
vehicle > threshold,
11 where distance to vehicle = geo-distance (vehicle
coordinates, gas
12 station coordinates),
13 and where the vehicle coordinates are provided by the GPS
14 Tracking by (vehicle, timestamp),
15 and where the gas station coordinates are provided by
16 geocoding its post address.
17
18 Scenario: Fuel transaction with no anomaly
19 When a transaction is reported on the fuel card
20 .../// more scenarios here
```

These specification details are just comments as free text though; the tools completely ignore it. However, the point of putting it there is to have co-located with the corresponding scenarios. Whenever you change the scenarios or the details, you are more likely to update the specification details because they are so close. As we say, "out of sight, out of mind." But there is no guarantee to do so.

Tags in Feature Files

The last significant ingredient in feature files is the ability to add tags. Each scenario can have tags, like the following:

```
1 @acceptance-criteria  @specs  @wip  @fixedincome @interests
2 Scenario: Bi-annual compound interests over one year
3   Given a principal of USD 1000
4   ...//
```

Tags are documentation. Some tags describe project management knowledge, such as @wip, which stands for *work in progress* and signals that this scenario is currently being developed. Other similar tags may even name who's involved in the development (for example, @bob, @team-red) or mention the sprint (for example, @sprint-23) or its goal (for example, @learn-about-reporting-needs). These tags are temporary and are deleted when the tasks are all done.

Some tags describe how important the scenario is. For example, @acceptance-criteria indicates that this scenario is part of the few user acceptance criteria. Other similar tags may help with curation of scenarios, such as @happy-path, @nominal, @variant, @negative, @exception, and @core.

Finally, some tags describe categories and concepts from the business domain. For example, in the example just shown, the tags @fixedincome and @interests describe that this scenario is relevant to the fixed income and interest financial areas.

Tags should be documented, too. For example, a collocated text file can list all the valid tags, along with a text description for each. And to make sure that every tag used in the feature files is documented there, my colleague Arnauld Loyer likes to add a separate unit test as yet another reconciliation mechanism.

Organizing Feature Files

When the number of feature files grows, it's necessary to organize them into folders. The organization you use is also a way to convey knowledge; the folders can tell a story.

When the business domain is the most important thing, I recommend organizing the folders by functional areas to show the overall business picture. For example, you might have the following folders:

- Accounting
- Reporting Rules
- Discounts
- Special Offers

If you have any additional content as text and pictures, you can also include it in the same folders, so that it stays as close as possible to the corresponding scenarios.

In the book *Specification by Example*, Gojko Adzic lists three ways to organize stories into folders:

- By functional areas
- Along UI navigation routes (when documenting user interfaces)
- Along business processes (when end-to-end use case traceability is required)

With this approach, the folders literally represent the chapters of your business documentation (as you can see in the example later in this chapter).

Scenarios as Interactive Living Documentation

The scenarios form the basis for living documentation. Even better, this documentation is typically interactive, as a generated interactive website. For example, if you use Pickles for SpecFlow, a specific one-page website is generated during each build (see Figure 2.4). The website shows a navigation pane that is organized by chapter, provided that your folders represent functional chapters. It displays all scenarios, together with the test results and their statistics. This is quite powerful—much more so than any paper documentation you've ever seen.

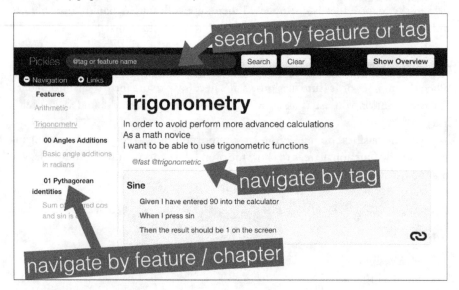

Figure 2.4 *Generated interactive documentation website, with Pickles*

A built-in search engine in Pickles allows instant access to any scenario by keyword or by tag. This is the second powerful effect of tags: They make searching more efficient and accurate.

Scenarios in Boring Paper Documents

An interactive website like the one shown in the preceding section is convenient for a team, providing fast access to the business behavior knowledge. However, in some cases, such as when there are mandatory compliance requirements, you must provide a boring paper document (a "BPD," as some call it).

There are tools for creating these documents. One of them, which was developed by my Arolla colleague Arnauld Loyer (@aloyer), is called Tzatziki[1], because it's a Cucumber sauce. It exports a beautiful PDF document out of the feature files. It goes a bit further, also including Markdown files and images that are stored alongside the feature files into the document. It therefore helps create nice explanations at the beginning of each functional area chapter.

---

1. Tzatziki, https://github.com/Arnauld/tzatziki

> **Note**
>
> If the tool you need in your context is missing, you should create it on top of or as a derivation of existing tools. The sky's the limit. Custom tools or extensions of tools can be created as fun projects, on hackathon days, or during slack time; they needn't be made by vendors or other people.

BDD is a great example of living documentation: It's not additional work to be done but is part of doing work properly. It's always in sync, thanks to the tools that act as reconciliation mechanisms. And if the feature files in the source code are not enough, the generated website illustrates how documentation can be useful, interactive, searchable, and well organized.

A Feature File Example

This section provides a full example of a fictitious yet realistic feature file in the business domain of finance. To keep it short, this example contains only one outline scenario, along with a corresponding data table. It illustrates another style of using Cucumber, SpecFlow, and equivalent tools. The scenario is evaluated for each line of the table. Here is the complete feature file example:

```
1  Feature: Calculate compound interests on a principal
2  In order to manage the company money
3  As a finance officer
4  I want to calculate the compound interests on a principal on
my account
5
6  Description:
7  Compound interest is when the bank pays interest on both the
   principal (the original amount of money) and the interest an
   account has already earned.
8
9  To calculate compound interest use the formula below.
10
11 In the formula, A represents the final amount in the account
   after t years compounded 'n' times at interest rate 'r' with
   starting amount 'p'.
12
13
```

```
14
15   A = P*(1+(r/n))^n*t
16
17
18 Scenario: Bi-annual compound interests over one year
19 Given a principal of USD 1000
20 And interests are compounded bi-annually at a rate of 5%
21 When the calculation period lasts exactly 1 year
22 Then the amount of money in the account is USD 1053.63
23
24 Scenario: Quarterly compound interests over one year
25 //... outline scenario
26
27 Examples:
28
29 | convention | rate | time | amount     | remarks          |
30 |-------------------------------------------------------|
31 | LINEAR     | 0.05 | 2    | 0.100000   | (1+rt)-1         |
32 | COMPOUND   | 0.05 | 2    | 0.102500   | (1+r)^t-1        |
33 | DISCOUNT   | 0.05 | 2    | -0.100000  | (1 - rt)-1       |
34 | CONTINUOUS | 0.05 | 2    | 0.105171   | (e^rt)-1 (rare)  |
35 | NONE       | 0.05 | 2    | 0          | 0                |
36 |-------------------------------------------------------|
```

With the support of tools, all business scenarios become automated tests and living documentation at the same time. The scenarios are just plain text in the feature files. To bridge the gap between the text in the scenarios and the actual production code, you create a little set of steps. Each step is triggered on a particular text sentence, matched by regular expressions, and calls the production code. The text sentence may have parameters that are parsed and used to call the production code in many different ways. Here is an example:

```
1   For example:
2   Given the VAT rate is 9.90%
3   When I but a book at an ex-VAT price of EUR 25
4   Then I have to pay an inc-VAT price of EUR 2.49
```

To automate this scenario, you need to define what is called a *step* for each line used within scenarios. For example, you can define that any sentence like this:

```
1   "When I but a book at an ex-VAT price of EUR <exVATPrice>"
```

Would trigger the following glue code:

```
1  Book(number exVATPrice)
2  Service  = LookupOrderService();
3  Service.sendOrder(exVATPrice);
```

In this code snippet, the tool (Cucumber or SpecFlow) passes the variable *exVAT-Price* to the glue code; the value of this variable is automatically extracted from the sentence in a scenario. For example, in the preceding scenario, the value of exVAT-Price would be 25.

Using this mechanism, the scenarios become automated tests that are driven by the scenarios and the values they declare. If you change the rounding mode of the price in the scenario without changing the code, the test will fail. If you change the rounding mode of the price in the code without changing the scenario, the test will fail, too. This is a reconciliation mechanism to signal inconsistencies between the sides of the redundancy.

A Canonical Case of Living Documentation in Every Aspect

BDD has shown that it is possible to have accurate documentation that is always in sync with the code by doing the specification work more carefully. BDD is a canonical case of living documentation, and all the core principles of living documentation are already present in BDD:

- **Collaborative:** The primary tool of BDD is talking among people, making sure that each role out of the three amigos (or more) is present.

- **Low-effort:** The conversations around concrete examples are useful for agreeing on what to build, and with some additional work they become automated tests and a living documentation: one activity, multiple benefits.

- **Reliable, thanks to a reconciliation mechanism:** Because the business behaviors are described both in text scenarios and in implementation code, tools like Cucumber and SpecFlow ensure that the scenarios and code remain always in sync (or at least show when they go out of sync). This is necessary whenever there is duplication of knowledge.

- **Insightful:** The conversations provide feedback, as do writing and automating the scenarios. For example, if a scenario is too long or awkward, it may suggest looking for the missing implicit concepts that would make the scenario shorter and simpler.

It also illustrates other ideas described later in this book:

- **Targeted audience:** All this work is targeted for an audience that includes business people, hence the focus on clear, nontechnical language when discussing business requirements.
- **Idea sedimentation:** Conversations are often enough, and not everything needs to be written down. Only the most important scenarios, the *key scenarios*, need to be written for archiving or automation.
- **Plain-text documents:** Plain text is very convenient for managing stuff that changes and for living alongside the source code in source control.
- **Accessible published snapshot:** Not everyone has or wants access to the source control in order to read the scenarios. Tools like Pickles and Tzatziki offer a solution, exporting a snapshot of all the scenarios at a current point in time as an interactive website or as a PDF document that can be printed.

Now that you've seen BDD as the canonical case of living documentation, you're ready to move on to other contexts where you can apply living documentation. Living documentation is not restricted to the description of business behaviors, as is BDD; it can help you in many other aspects of software development projects—and perhaps even outside software development.

Going Further: Getting the Best of Your Living Documentation

Feature files describing business scenarios are a great place to gather rich domain knowledge in an efficient way.

Most tools that support teams in doing BDD understand the Gherkin syntax. They expect feature files to follow a fixed format, as shown here:

```
1  Feature: Name of the feature
2
3  In order to... As a... I want...
4
```

```
5 Scenario: name of the first scenario
6 Given...
7 When...
8 Then...
9
10 Scenario: name of the second scenario
11 ...
```

Over time, teams in rich domains like finance or insurance realized that they needed more documentation than just the intent at the top and the concrete scenarios at the bottom. As a result, they started putting additional description of their business case in the middle area, and this is ignored by the tools. Tools like Pickles that generate living documentation out of the feature files adapted to this use and started to support Markdown formatting for what became called "the description area":

```
1  Feature: Investment Present Value
2
3  In order to calculate the breakeven point of the investment
opportunity
4  As an investment manager
5  I want to calculate the present value of future cash amounts
6
7
8  Description
9  ===========
10
11  We need to find the present value *PV* of the given future
cash \
12 amount *FV*. The formula for that can be expressed as:
13
14 - Using the negative exponent notation:
15
16       PV = FV * (1 + i)^(-n)
17
18 - Or in the equivalent form:
19
20       PV = FV * (1 / (1 + i)^n)
21
22 Example
23 -------
24
25    For example, n = 2, i = 8%
```

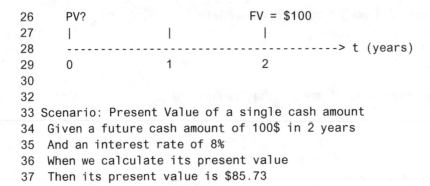

```
26    PV?                              FV = $100
27    |                  |            |
28    --------------------------------------------> t (years)
29    0                  1            2
30
32
33 Scenario: Present Value of a single cash amount
34  Given a future cash amount of 100$ in 2 years
35  And an interest rate of 8%
36  When we calculate its present value
37  Then its present value is $85.73
```

This documentation will be rendered in the living documentation website as a pretty document called "Feature: Investment Present Value."

This example illustrates how feature files provide the opportunity to gather a lot of documentation in the same place, directly within the source control. Note that this descriptive area with text, formulas, and ASCII diagrams in the middle of the file is not really living; it's is just co-located with the scenarios; if we change the scenarios, you're likely to also need to update the description nearby, but there is no guarantee.

The best strategy would be to put knowledge that does not change very often in the description section and to keep the volatile parts within the concrete scenarios. One way to do this is to clarify that the description uses sample numbers, not the numbers that are necessarily used for the configuration of the business process at any point in time.

Tools like Pickle,[2] Relish,[3] and Tzatzikinow understand Markdown descriptions and even plain Markdown files located next to the feature files. This makes it easy to have an integrated and consistent approach for the domain documentation. And Tzatziki can export a PDF from all this knowledge, as expected by the regulators in finance.

Property-Based Testing and BDD

Requirements often come naturally as properties (for example, "The sum of all amounts paid and received must be zero at all times" or "Nobody can ever be a lawyer and a judge at once"). When doing BDD or TDD, you must clarify these general properties into specific concrete examples, which will help with finding issues and building code incrementally.

---

2. Pickle, http://www.picklesdoc.com

3. Relish, http://www.relishapp.com

It's a good idea to keep track of the general properties for their documentation value. You usually do that as plain text comments in the feature file, as described earlier in this chapter. But it happens that the technique of property-based testing is precisely about exercising these properties against randomly generated samples. This is performed with a property-based testing framework that runs the same test over and over, with inputs generated from generators of samples. The canonical framework is QuickCheck in Haskell, and there are now similar tools in most other programming languages.

Integrating property-based testing into your feature files eventually makes the general properties executable, too. In practice, it's a matter of adding special scenarios describing the general property and invoking the property-based testing framework underneath, as shown here:

```
1  Scenario: The sum of all cash amounts exchanged must be zero
for derivatives
2
3  Given any derivative financial instrument
4  And a random date during its lifetime
5  When we generate the related cash flows on this date for the
payer and\
6  the receiver
7  Then the sum of the cash flows of the payer and the receiver
is\
8  exactly zero
```

Such scenarios typically use sentences like "given ANY shopping cart...." This wording is a code smell for regular scenarios, but it's okay for property-oriented scenarios on top of property-based testing tools supplementing the regular concrete scenarios.

Creating a Glossary

An ideal glossary is a living one, extracted directly from your code. However, in many cases it is not possible to create a living glossary, and you must manually create one.

It's possible to create a glossary manually as a Markdown file and to co-locate it with the other feature files. This way, it will be included in the living documentation website, too. You could even do it as dummy empty feature file.

Linking to Nonfunctional Knowledge

Not all the knowledge should be described in the same place. You don't want to mix domain knowledge with UI-specific or legacy-specific knowledge, which is important and should be stored elsewhere. And when that language is related to the domain language, you should use links to represent the relationship and make it easy to find it.

As described elsewhere in this book, you can use different approaches to linking. You may link directly to a URL, as shown here, although you risk of having a broken link whenever it changes:

```
1  https://en.wikipedia.org/wiki/Present_value
```

You may go through a link registry that you maintain to manage links and to replace broken links with working ones, as shown here:

```
1  go/search?q=present+value
```

You may also use bookmarked searches to link to places that include the related content, as shown here:

```
1  https://en.wikipedia.org/w/index.php?search=present+value
```

Linking to nonfunctional knowledge gives you a resilient way to link to related content, at the expense of letting the reader select the most relevant results each time.

Summary

BDD is the canonical example of living documentation. It primarily relies on frequent conversations between team members before anything else. It is a direct part of the necessary work to build software, and yet it preserves the knowledge collected during a project in a form that is accessible to both business people and developers. And even though it leads to redundant knowledge in the code and the scenarios, the accompanying tools make sure it all remains in sync. But BDD only deals with the business behaviors of the software. In subsequent chapters, we explore how to extrapolate these ideas for other activities related to software development.

Chapter 3

Knowledge Exploitation

For a given project or system, a lot of knowledge already exists, and it's everywhere: in the source code of the software, in the various configuration files, in the source code of the tests, in the behavior of the application at runtime, in various random files and as data within the various tools around, and in the brains of all the people involved.

Traditional documentation attempts to gather knowledge into convenient documents, in paper form or online. These documents duplicate knowledge that was already present elsewhere. This is obviously a problem when the other document is the authority and can be trusted, but it evolves all the time.

Because knowledge already exists in many places, all you need to do is to set up mechanisms to extract the knowledge from where it's located and bring it where it's needed, when it's needed. And because you don't have much time for that, such mechanisms must be lightweight, reliable, and low effort.

Identifying Authoritative Knowledge

It's important to learn to spot the authoritative sources of knowledge in your system. When knowledge is repeated in different places, you need to know where to find the knowledge that you can trust. When decisions change, where does the knowledge reflect the changes most accurately?

Therefore: Identify all the places where authoritative knowledge is located. For a given need, set up mechanisms such as automation to extract the knowledge and transform it into an adequate form. Make sure this mechanism remains simple and does not become a distraction.

Knowledge about how the software works is in the source code. In the ideal case, it's easy to read, and there is no need for any other documentation. In a not-so-ideal case, perhaps because the source code is naturally obfuscated, you just need to make this knowledge more accessible.

Where Is the Knowledge Now?

Imagine that a colleague or manager says to you, "Give me documentation on stuff X!" To handle this request, you would first need to ask yourself or the team, "Where is this knowledge now?"

The answer is often obvious: The knowledge is in the code, in the functional tests, or in the document on project goals. Sometimes it's less obvious: The knowledge is in people's brains, whether they know it or not. It may even be between people, in which case you'll need collective workshops to elucidate it. Some knowledge exists only during the evaluation of the working software, in the memory of the program at runtime.

Once you've found the location of the authoritative knowledge, how can you harness that knowledge and make it living documentation?

When the knowledge is there but in a form that is not accessible or not convenient for the target audience and for the desired purpose, it must be extracted from its *single source of truth* into a more accessible form. This process should be automated to publish a clearly versioned document, with a link to the latest version.

Sometimes the knowledge can't be extracted. For example, perhaps business behavior can't simply be extracted as English business sentences from the code, so in this case, you write these sentences by hand as functional scenarios or tests. By doing so, you introduce redundancy to the knowledge, so you need a *reconciliation mechanism* to easily detect inconsistencies, as described in the previous chapter.

When the knowledge is spread over many places, you need a way to do a *consolidation* of all the knowledge into one aggregated form. And when there is an excess of knowledge, a careful selection process—a *curation* process—is essential.

Single-Source Publishing

It's important to keep the knowledge in one single source of truth and publish from there when needed. When the authoritative source of knowledge is source code in a programming language or a configuration file of a tool in a formal syntax, it's often necessary to make this knowledge accessible to audiences that can't read it. The standard way to do this is to provide a document in a format everyone understands, like plain English in a PDF document, or as a Microsoft Office document, spreadsheet, or slide deck. However, if you directly create such a document and include all the relevant knowledge in a copy-and-paste fashion, you will have a difficult time when it changes. And on an active and healthy project, you should expect that it will change a lot.

The Pragmatic Programmer by Dave Hunt and David Thomas says that English can be considered a programming language. They suggest: "Write documents as you would write code: honor the DRY principle, use metadata, MVC, automatic generation, and so on." As an example of duplication, Hunt and Thomas mention that a database schema in a specification document is redundant with the database schema file in a formal language like SQL. One has to be produced out of the other. For example, a specification document could be produced by a tool that can convert the SQL or DDL file into plain text and diagram form.

Therefore: Keep each piece of knowledge in exactly one place, where it's authoritative. When it must be made available to audiences that can't access it directly, publish a document out of that single source of knowledge. Don't include the elements of knowledge into the document to be published by copying and pasting but use automated mechanisms to create a published document straight from the single authoritative source of knowledge.

Figure 3.1 illustrates how the authoritative knowledge that is already present can be extracted by automated mechanisms in order to publish documents.

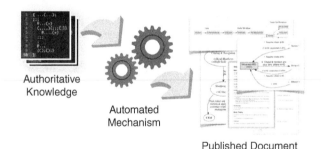

Authoritative
Knowledge

Automated
Mechanism

Published Document

Figure 3.1 *From authoritative knowledge to published documents*

Some Examples of Producing a Published Document

There are many tools available to produce documents out of source code and other technical artifacts. Here are some examples:

- **GitHub:** GitHub takes the README.md file, which is a single source of knowledge about the goals of an overall project, and turns it into a web page that is rendered to be pretty.

- **Javadoc:** Javadoc extracts the structure and all the public or private API of the code and publishes it to a website as reference documentation. You can easily create a custom tool based on the standard Javadoc Doclet in order to generate your own specific report, glossary, or diagram, as described in Chapter 6, "Automating Documentation."

- **Maven:** Maven and some other tools have a built-in way of producing consistent documentation, usually as a website, by putting together a number of tool reports and rendered artifacts. For example, Maven collects test reports, static analysis tools reports, Javadoc output folders, and any Markdown documents and organizes it all into a standard website. Every Markdown document can be rendered in the process.

- **Leanpub:** Leanpub, the publishing platform I used to write this book, is a canonical example of single sourcing with a publication mechanism: Every chapter is written as a separate Markdown file, images are kept outside, the code can be in its own source files, and even the table of contents is in its own file. In other words, the content is stored in the way it's most convenient to work with. Whenever I ask for a preview, Leanpub's publishing toolchain collates all files according to the table of contents and renders it through various tools for Markdown rendering, typesetting, and code highlighting in order to produce a good-quality book in multiple formats: PDF, MOBI, and ePUB. This is similar to how the manuscript of a novel in the publishing world can be published as a book, as a comics, and then later as a movie—all from the same initial manuscript (see Figure 3.2). You could follow this basic pattern with any templating mechanism and a bit of custom code. For example, you could produce a PDF out of the resource file that lists every currency supported by the program.

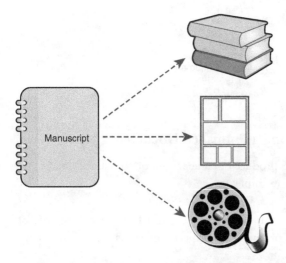

Figure 3.2 *One single source and possibly multiple documents*

A Published Snapshot with a Version Number

Any document published from a single source of truth is a snapshot: It must therefore be considered as strictly immutable and should never be edited. To avoid the risk of having someone edit a published document, you should favor document formats that prevent editing—or at least that make editing difficult. For example, prefer PDF over Microsoft Office documents, which are very easy to change. Whatever the format, consider using the locking flags to prevent edits. It's not about making it impossible for hackers to edit; rather, the idea is to make it just hard enough to make edits that it is easiest to change the authoritative source and have it published again.

Any published document must clearly identify its version and should also include a link to the location where the latest version can be found.

If you produce a lot of paper documents to be printed, you may consider putting on each of them a barcode with the link to the folder that always contains the latest version. This way, even a printed document can easily direct readers to the latest version.

Remarks

You should write by hand only what cannot be extracted from an already existing project artifact, and you should store such remarks in a file that has its own lifecycle. Ideally, this file will change much less frequently than the knowledge extracted from other places. On the other hand, if some information is missing from a document you need to publish, you should by all means try to add it to the artifact it is most related to, perhaps using annotations, tags, or naming convention, or make it a new collaborative artifact on its own.

Setting Up a Reconciliation Mechanism (aka Verification Mechanism)

Whenever knowledge is repeated in more than one place, you should set up a reconciliation mechanism to detect inconsistencies immediately. Duplication of knowledge about software is a bad thing because it necessitates recurring work to update all the places that are redundant to each other, and it also means there is a risk of getting into an inconsistent state when an update is forgotten.

However, if you must have redundancy, you can relieve the pain by using a verification mechanism, such as an automated test that checks that two copies are always in sync. This does not remove the cost of making changes in more than one place, but at least it ensures that you won't forget a change somewhere.

One reconciliation mechanism everybody is familiar with is checking the bill in a restaurant (see Figure 3.3). You know what you ate (and the evidence may be still visible in the number of dishes), and you check each line on the bill to ensure that there's no discrepancy.

Reconciliation

Figure 3.3 *Checking the restaurant bill is a reconciliation mechanism*

Therefore: When you want or have to accommodate a redundancy in the knowledge stored at various places, make sure all the redundant knowledge is kept consistent using a reconciliation mechanism. Use automation to make sure everything remains in sync and that any discrepancy is detected immediately, and you get an alert prompting to fix it.

Running Consistency Tests

As mentioned in Chapter 2, "Behavior-Driven Development as an Example of Living Specifications," with BDD, scenarios provide documentation of the behavior. Whenever a scenario and code disagree, you know it immediately because the test automation fails, much like a Roberval balance (see Figure 3.4).

This mechanism is made possible thanks to tools that parse the scenario in natural domain language to drive their implementation code. The code is driven through a little layer of glue code that you write specifically for that purpose, usually called "step definitions." These steps are adapters between the parsed scenario and the actual code being driven.

Imagine testing the following scenario:

- Given party BARNABA is marked as bankrupt

- And trade 42 is against BARNABA,

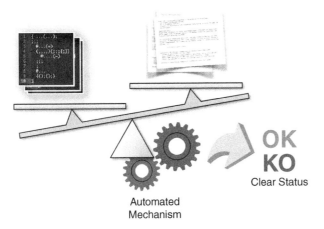

Figure 3.4 *Automated mechanism to verify that redundant knowledge is in sync*

- When the risk alerting calculation is run,

- Then an alert occurs: Trade against the bankrupt party BARNABA is triggered.

The tool parses these lines of text and recognizes the sentence "Given party BARNABA is marked as bankrupt" as one it has a step definition for:

```
1 Given("^party (.*) is marked as bankrupt$")
2 public void partyMarkedAsBankrupt(string party){
3  bankruptParties.put(party);
4 }
```

The tool does the same for each line. Typically sentences starting with *When* trigger actual computation, and sentences starting with *Then* cue the tool to check assertions:

```
1 Then("^an alert: (/*) is triggered$")
2 public void anAlertIsTriggered(string expectedMessage){
3  assertEquals(expectedMessage, actualMessage);
4 }
```

For all of this to work, the sentences need to actually drive the code with parameters (the regular expression [/*] in the middle of the sentence), and the assertions must check against the expectations from the sentences as precisely as possible.

As a counter example, it would not make sense to code the step without extracting a parameter from the sentence, or you would run the risk of inconsistency after a few changes:

```
1 Then("^an alert: Trade against the bankrupt party BARNABA is
triggered$" )
3 public void anAlertIsTriggered(){
4  assertEquals("Trade against the bankrupt party
ENRON",actualMessage);
5 }
```

The scenario would unfortunately still pass even when the hardcoded message does not fit the one in the scenario, and nobody would notice.

Reconciliation on the Test Assumptions

Usually you use the *Given* (or the equivalent *Arrange* phase in plain xUnit code) to create mock objects or to inject data into the test database.

When testing legacy systems, you often have to deal with a couple types of problems:

- It's too hard to mock the database, so you must test in an end-to-end fashion.

- You can't re-create or populate a database just for your tests, so you must work on a real shared database that can change anytime if someone else is working on it.

Despite these problems, it's still possible to use exactly the same declaration of an assumption as a *When* sentence or an *Arrange* phase in xUnit but with an implementation that checks that the assumption still holds true instead of injecting the value into a mock object:

```
1 Given("^party (.*) is marked as bankrupt$")
2 public void partyMarkedAsBankrupt(string party){
3  assertTrue(bankruptParties.isBankruptParty(party)); // calls
the DB
4 }
```

This not an assertion of the test; it's just a prerequisite for the scenario (or test) to even have a chance to pass. If this assumption already fails, then the scenario "does not even fail." I often call this kind of "tests before the tests" a *canary test*.

Such tests tell that something's wrong even outside the test focus, helping you know that you don't have to waste time investigating in the wrong place.

Published Contracts

A reconciliation mechanism that I first saw used by my Arolla colleague Arnauld Loyer is used to reconcile contracts against third parties such as external services that call your services. If your services exposes a resource with the parameter CreditDefaultType, which has the two possible values FAILURE_TO_PAY and RESTRUCTURING, you can't rename them as you wish once published. You can therefore use tests with a deliberate redundancy to enforce that these elements of the contract don't change. You can refactor and rename as you wish, but whenever you break the contract, the reconciliation tests will alert you with a test failure.

This is an example of enforced documentation. Ideally you would make the test the reference documentation for the contract, in a readable form; some tools in the API sphere enable you to do this. Here you definitely don't want to update the test through automated refactoring; rather, you want it out of reach of the refactoring so that it stays unchanged to represent the external consumer services.

The most naive implementation for this approach would be something like that the following, assuming that the internal representation of the CreditDefaultType is a Java enum named CREDIT_DEFAULT_TYPE:

```
1 @Test
2 public void enforceContract_CreditDefaultType
3  final String[] contract = {"FAILURE_TO_PAY",
"RESTRUCTURING"};
4
5  for(String type : contract){
6    assertEquals(type, CREDIT_DEFAULT_TYPE.valueOf(type).
toString());
7  }
8 }
```

Because you want to make sure that the contract for the external calling code is respected, you define this contract *again* as an array of strings, as if it's being used from the outside. And because you want to check that the contract is being honed with incoming and outcoming values, you make sure the contractual string is recognized as an input with valueOf() and that it's the one being sent as an output with toString().

Note

This example is only meant to explain the idea of this type of reconciliation mechanism. In the real world, it's bad practice to use a loop inside a test as the test reporting will not tell precisely in which loop the problem resides if there is an exception. Instead, you would use a parameterized test, making the collection of values that are part of the contract the source of parameters.

With this approach, when someone who has recently joined the team decides to rename a constant of the enum, the test immediately fails to signal that it's not possible to do that—in effect acting like defensive documentation. It's a defense against misconduct, and at the same time it provides an opportunity for the violator to learn on the spot: When the test fails, they learn that this enum constant is part of a contract that should not be changed.

Consolidating Dispersed Facts

Diverse facts put together become useful knowledge. Sometimes knowledge is spread over many places. For example, a type hierarchy with an interface and five implementing classes may actually be declared in six different files. The content of a package or module can actually be stored in many files. The full list of dependencies of the project may actually be defined partially in its Maven manifest (POM) and also in its parent manifest. Therefore, there is a need to collect and aggregate many little bits of knowledge to get a full picture.

For example, the big picture of a system is the union of the black-box view of each of its part, as pictured in Figure 3.5. The overall knowledge here is derived through a consolidation mechanism.

Figure 3.5 *From fragmented authoritative knowledge to unified knowledge*

Even if the knowledge is split into many little parts, it's still desirable to consider all those little bits as the authoritative single sources of truth. The derived consolidated knowledge is therefore a special case of published document extracted from many places.

Therefore: Design a simple mechanism to automatically consolidate all the dispersed facts. This mechanism must be run as often as necessary to ensure that the information about the whole is up-to-date with respect to the parts. Avoid any storage of the consolidated information, unless there are technical concerns like caching.

How Consolidation Works

Basically, consolidation is like a SQL GROUP BY: You take many things that have some properties in common, and you find a way to turn all those multiple things into a single thing. In practice, it's done by scanning every element within a given perimeter, while growing the result, as shown in Figure 3.6.

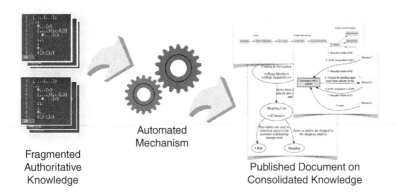

Fragmented
Authoritative
Knowledge

Automated
Mechanism

Published Document on
Consolidated Knowledge

Figure 3.6 *From dispersed facts to useful knowledge*

For example, to reconstitute the full picture of a class hierarchy within the limits of one project from its individual elements, it's necessary to scan every class and every interface of the project. The scanning process keeps a growing dictionary of every hierarchy under construction so far in the process (for example, with the mapping *top of hierarchy* > *list of subclasses*). Every time the scan encounters a class that extends another class or that extends an interface, it adds it to the dictionary.

When the scan is done, the dictionary contains a list of all type hierarchies in the project. Of course, it's possible to reduce the process to only a subset of the hierarchies of interest for a particular documentation need, such as restricting the scan to classes and interfaces that belong to a published API.

As another example, you can create a black-box living diagram of a system made of smaller components, each of which has its own set of inputs and outputs, as shown in Figure 3.7.

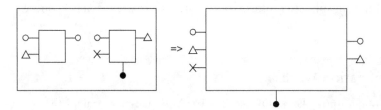

Figure 3.7 *The black-box view of the whole system can be derived through a consolidation of the black-box view of its components*

A simple consolidation can just collect the union of every input and output from each component. A more sophisticated consolidation can try to remove every input and output that match each other internally. It's up to you to decide how you want consolidation to happen for a particular need.

Consolidation Implementation Considerations

As usual, if possible, you should reuse a tool you already have that can do a desired consolidation. Some parsers for Java code can provide type hierarchies, for example. If what you want is not already in the tool, you can add it, such as by writing another visitor[1] on the programming language Abstract Syntax Tree (AST)[2]. Some more powerful tools even provide their own language to query the code base very efficiently. You might want to load the AST into a graph database if you have to do very complex queries, but if you do that, I'm afraid you're becoming a software vendor of documentation tools.

If the derived knowledge is kept in a cache for performance issues, make sure it does not become a source of truth and that it can always be properly dropped and then rebuilt from scratch from all the sources of truth.

---

1. "The Visitor Pattern" from the book *Design Patterns: Elements of Reusable Object-Oriented Software*, by Erich Gamma, John Vlissides, Ralph Johnson, and Richard Helm. Addison-Wesley.

2. A common tree structure used by parsers to represent and manipulate the structure of the source code.

For most systems, it is possible to scan all parts in sequence in a batch-processing fashion. This is typically done during a build, and it produces a consolidation that is ready for publication on the project website or as a report.

For a large system such as an information system, it is not practical to run calculations that scan all parts in sequence. In such a case, the consolidation process may be done incrementally. For example, the build of each part might contribute a partial update by pushing data to an overall consolidation state somewhere in a shared place, such as a shared database. This consolidation state is derived information; it is less trusted than the information from each build. If anything goes wrong, you should drop it and let it grow again from the contributions of each build.

Ready-Made Documentation

Most of what you do is already documented in the literature. Not all knowledge is specific to your context; a lot of knowledge is generic and shared with many other people in many other companies in the industry. Think about all the knowledge on programming languages, developer tools, and software patterns and practices; most of that is industry standard.

More and more of what we do every day gets codified by talented practitioners into patterns, techniques, and practices. And all that knowledge is properly documented in books, blog posts, and conference talks and workshops around the world. This is ready-made documentation that's readily available, for free or for the price of a book or workshop. Here are a few examples:

- *Test-Driven Development*, Kent Beck
- *Design Patterns: Elements of Reusable Object-Oriented Software*, Erich Gamma, John Vlissides, Ralph Johnson, and Richard Helm
- *Patterns of Enterprise Application Architecture*, Martin Fowler
- *Domain-Driven Design*, Eric Evans
- Everything on the C2 wiki
- Every book from Jerry Weinberg
- *Continuous Delivery*, Jez Humber and Dave Farley
- All the clean code literature
- Git workflow strategies

It is probably safe to say that if you can think about it, somebody has already written about it. Patterns, standard names, and standard practices exist, even if you don't know them yet. The literature is growing, and it's already so huge that you cannot know it all, or you would spend so much time reading you would not have any time left to create software.

> **Note**
>
> In the book *Apprenticeship Patterns*, Dave Hoover and Adewale Oshineye advocate studying the classics. For example, they suggest reading the oldest books in your reading list first.

Knowledge about mature business industry sectors is also generic knowledge. Even in very competitive areas like pricing in finance or supply chain optimization in e-commerce, most of the knowledge is public and available in industry-standard books, and only a small part of the business knowledge is specific and confidential—and only for a while at that.

For example, each business domain has its own essential reading list, and it might have a book that is often referred to as "The Bible" of that field (for example, *Options, Futures, and Other Derivatives* by John C Hull, *Logistics and Supply Chain Management* by Martin Christopher).

The good news is that generic knowledge is already documented in the industry literature. There are books, blog posts, and conference talks that describe it quite well. There are standard vocabularies to talk about it. There are trainings available to learn it faster from knowledgeable people.

Generic knowledge in itself is a solved problem. This knowledge is ready-made, ready to be reused by everyone. If you have applied this generic knowledge in your system, you just have to link to the right literature and you're done documenting.

Therefore: Consider that most knowledge is already documented somewhere in the industry literature. Do your homework and look for the standard source of knowledge on the web or by asking other knowledgeable people. Don't try to document again something that's already been well written by someone else; link to it instead. And don't try to be original; instead, adopt the standard practices and the standard vocabulary as much as possible.

In most cases, deliberately adopting industry standards is a win. What you're doing is almost certainly already covered somewhere. If you're unlucky, it will be only in a blog or two. If you're lucky, it's industry standard. Either way, you need to find where it is covered, for several reasons:

- You can refer to other sources instead of doing the writing yourself.

- Other sources might suggest improvements or alternatives that you haven't considered.

- Other sources might describe the situation in a deeper way than you did, giving you external insights.

- Such a description can validate that your approach makes sense. If you cannot find any account, beware.

- Most importantly, you will learn how the rest of the planet talks about this situation.

The Power of a Standard Vocabulary

He who controls vocabulary controls thought.

—Ludwig Wittgenstein

Talking using the same words as everybody else in the world is a fantastic advantage. It enables you to communicate using shorter sentences. Without a common vocabulary, you could spend several sentences trying to describe the design of a text editor:

> Inline editing is done thanks to an interface with several subclasses. The text editor delegates the actual processing to the interface, without having to care which subclass is actually doing the job. Depending on whether the inline editing is on or off, an instance of a different subclass is used.

However, if you're familiar with standard documented knowledge like design patterns, you can get your point across more concisely:

> "Inline editing is implemented as a State in the Controller."[3]

Each mature industry has its own rich jargon because using such understood jargon is an efficient way to communicate. Every part in a car has a specific name, depending on its role in the vehicle: A shaft is not just a *shaft*, it's a *camshaft* or a *crankshaft*. There's a *piston* in a *cylinder*, and there are *pushrods* and a *timing chain*. Domain-driven design advocates for carefully growing such ubiquitous language in the domain.

The software industry makes progress each time its standard vocabulary grows. For example, whenever Martin Fowler coins another term for a patterns that we do without thinking about it, he is helping grow our own ubiquitous language for our industry.

---

3. This example of sentence on the State Pattern is from Kent Beck, https://www.facebook.com/notes/kent-beck/entropy-as-understood-by-a-programmer-part-1-program-structure/695263730506494

Ubiquitous language is extremely helpful in documentation. If you know what you're doing and you know what it's called in the industry, you can just insert a reference to the industry standard, and you have achieved extensive documentation at low cost.

Patterns and pattern languages are particularly effective at packing ready-made knowledge into a reusable documentation. Patterns really are canned documentation. They create a standard vocabulary you can use and refer to for complete reference.

Design patterns are communication tools for experienced programmers. Not training wheels or scaffolding for beginners.

—*@nycplayer on Twitter*

100% Design Patterns?

Patterns matter. But when I started learning about design patterns, I was trying to use them whenever I could; this is so common that some even call it patternitis. Then I became reasonable and learned when not to use patterns.

Many articles have harshly criticized code that is full of patterns. However, I think they miss the point: You should learn as many patterns as you can. The idea is not to learn patterns in order to use them, though they can be useful; instead, the point is to know many patterns in order to know the standard names of what you're doing. In this view, 100% of the code could, and should, be described by the means of patterns.

Knowing the standard vocabulary also opens the door to even more knowledge: You can find books and buy training on the topic you're interested in. You can also pinpoint people with this knowledge and hire them.

Knowing the standard vocabulary is not so much about finding a solution. Even when you have a perfect solution, it's worth finding out what it's called in the industry. A standard vocabulary enables you to refer to the work of other people who describe a solution in a well-written, peer-reviewed, and time-tested fashion.

Linking to Standard Knowledge

Generic knowledge is already documented in the industry literature, in books, and online. When you use it, link to the authoritative source via an Internet link or a bibliographic reference. If something has been written well once, you should refer to it rather than redo a poorer job of documenting it again.

Of course, one big problem can be identifying the standard name for a piece of knowledge. Search engines like Google and community websites like C2 and Stack Overflow are your friends. You might have to guess how others talk about a topic. Then you can quickly scan the first search engine results to determine a more accurate vocabulary that can help you make narrower queries. Through this exploration, you'll quickly learn a lot and get to see how much of the topic is already codified and using what terminology.

Don't hesitate to ask around—in your team or on a forum—for suggestions. Other people may have experience and seniority and more time to index pointers to standard knowledge they've encountered, even superficially, over the years.

From a given term, you can also browse Wikipedia and all the various links at the ends of the articles. Keep an eye on the bottom "related" links as well, until you recognize your situation. Wikipedia is a fantastic tool for mapping a standard vocabulary to your own mental universe.

More Than Just Vocabulary

Having a shared standard vocabulary is a key advantage in communicating effectively, both verbally and in writing. That said, even a standard description may involve refinements and alternatives you haven't considered. That information is useful, too. Ready-made documentation is in fact reusable thinking, which is a great help. It's a bit like having the author, usually a seasoned practitioner, close to you so you can think together.

> YOU STILL HAVE TO THINK. BUT YOU DONT HAVE TO DO IT ALONE.
> —*@michelesliger on Twitter*

If I say that "I create an adapter on top of the legacy subsystem," this sentence implies a lot of things in a few words, because there's more than a name in the idea of the adapter pattern. For example, an important consequence in this pattern is that the adaptee—the legacy subsystem in our example—should not know about the adapter; only the adapter should know about the legacy subsystem.

When I say that a package represents the presentation layer, whereas this other package represents the domain layer, I also imply that only the former can depend on the latter—and never the other way around.

It's the norm in mathematics to reuse theorems and shared abstract structures from the literature to go further without reinventing and having to prove the same results again and again. The same goes for a standard vocabulary.

Using Ready-Made Knowledge in Conversation to Speed Up Knowledge Transfer

Here's a little conversation I had with my friend Jean-Baptiste Dusseaut ("JB" for short, @BodySplash on Twitter) to illustrate how a common culture and vocabulary can help with sharing knowledge efficiently (see Figure 3.8).

Figure 3.8 *Hello, JB. I heard you launched a new startup, Jamshake—what is it about?*

CM: Hello, JB. I heard you launched a new startup, Jamshake. What is it about?

JB: It's a social and collaborative tool for musicians. We provide both a lightweight social network to find other musicians and cool projects and an in-browser digital audio workstation, the Jamstudio, to collaborate in real time with other musicians. It's a kind of Google Doc for music (see Figure 3.9).

Figure 3.9 *It's a social and collaborative tool for musicians*

CM: Sounds really cool! On the technical side, how's your system organized in a nutshell?

JB: I know you're familiar with software craftsmanship and design, and DDD in particular, so you won't be surprised to hear that our system is made of several subsystems, one by bounded context (see Figure 3.10).

Figure 3.10 *I know you're familiar with software craftsmanship and design*

CM: Oh yes, makes perfect sense! Each one is a microservice then?

JB: Yes and no. They begin as modules very strictly decoupled in terms of dependencies—that is, ready to be extracted into their own process at runtime. But we keep them within the same process until we really need the separate processes, usually to scale with the increasing load.

CM: Yes! I call that the "microservice ready" style of code. You don't have to pay the full cost of too many physical services up front, as long as you have the option to do it at any time. But it takes discipline.

JB: Yes, and that's easy when you're just one or two developers, like we are at the moment. In practice, we regularly use these options because of the increasing load.

CB: Increasing load: that's a good problem to have when you're a startup growing and looking for financing!

JB: Yes, absolutely.

CB: I'd like to have an overview of the full system. Perhaps Bounded Context by Bounded Context?

JB: Sure. There are around five bounded contexts at the moment: Acquisition (registration of new users), Arrangement, Audio Rendering (mixing, limiter, and compression kinds of processing), Stems Management, and Reporting. They all rely on Spring Boot instances on top of separate Postgres databases, except for the Stems management built with Node.js on top of an S3 storage. Each Bounded Context is paying attention to its domain model, except Registration, which is CRUD-y based on Hibernate. It's a survivor from the early version of the system.

CB: I now have a clear picture in mind of what it's like (see Figure 3.11). Thanks a lot, JB!

Figure 3.11 *Picturing the full system while listening to JB talking*

Does Working More Deliberately Oppose Gut Feeling and Spontaneity?

When should knowing something consciously be considered less desirable than gut feeling? Consider this information from an interesting post by Steve Hawley:

> The use of patterns is like the use of literary device. There are (probably) an infinite number of ways in which the same general thought can be expressed, but I doubt you will find a single quality writer who started off a chapter thinking, "I'm introducing a character here so it's best to paint a picture of the character. That calls for simile. Yeah, simile will do it. I think I'll also use some ironic juxtaposition." This type of writing feels forced. I've read code where the application of design patterns also felt forced.[4]

Steve has a point here. I must admit that gut feeling, if trained properly on examples of good quality, may have advantages over a conscious quest for perfection, perhaps because our brains are more powerful that we often realize. And yes, very often, we pretend that what we have done was intentional and deliberate, even though we're just explaining, after the fact, a decision that was actually based on gut feeling.

Francois from Propel has raised this interesting question: Should developers know design patterns? ORM engines are rather sophisticated pieces of software, and they make big (and deliberate) use of patterns, in particular the Fowler PoEAA patterns. Francois discusses in a blog post the reasons to mention or not mention the various patterns used at the heart of the Propel ORM in the documentation of the engine:

> Propel, like other ORMs, implements a lot of common Design Patterns. Active Record, Unit Of Work, Identity Map, Lazy Load, Foreign Key Mapping, Concrete Table Inheritance, Query Object, to name a few, all appear in Propel. The very idea of an Object-Relational Mapping is indeed a Design Pattern itself.

If you know the patterns, you can understand Propel quickly; if you don't, you'll need to go through a lot more explanation to reach a higher level of expertise, and next time you encounter another ORM, you'll have to redo this discovery effort. Of course, at some point you'll recognize the patterns, and you just won't know their names. You'd just be half-conscious of the patterns.

---

4. https://www.atalasoft.com/cs/blogs/stevehawley/archive/2009/07/29/design-patterns-and-practice.aspx

Tools History

As you've seen before, a lot of knowledge is already there, and some of it is hidden in the history of the tools you use. Source control systems are an obvious example. They know about every commit—when it was done, by whom, what changes were made—and remember each commit comment. Some tools, like Jira or even your email client, also know a lot about your project.

However, this knowledge is not always readily accessible, and it is not used as much as it could be used. For example, if there's no screen to conveniently retrieve the most commonly asked question on a chat, you may never know it.

Sometimes you have to re-enter the same knowledge in another form in another tool. For example, a commit to fix a bug may have a comment that states it fixed the bug, but in many companies, you have to go to the work tracker to declare that you've fixed the bug. You also have to declare the time spent on the task, only to enter it again into the time tracking tool later in an aggregated form. This is a waste of time. Consider integrating the tools together.

Better integration between tools also helps simplify human tasks, which reduces the need for manual documentation of the tasks. However, when an integration fails, you do need documentation. Ideally, the integration component should provide this documentation. For example, an integration script should be readable and as declarative as possible.

Therefore: Exploit the knowledge stored in your tools. Decide what tool is the unique authority for each bit of knowledge. Search for plugins that can provide integration with other tools or specific reports for your documentation purposes. Learn how to use the command-line interface for each of your tools to programmatically extract knowledge or integrate various tools with other tools. Discover the APIs provided by the tools, including the email or chat integration.

As a last resort, find out how to query the internal database of a tool, but beware that a database may change at any time without prior notice, as it's usually not part of the official API.

The following are some examples of tools and their knowledge:

- **Source control:** Tools such as Git with the `blame` command can tell you who changed what and when, show you commit comments, and reveal pull request discussions.

- **Internal chat system:** Systems such as Slack can reveal questions, launch build, release information, mentions of words, activity, moods, who, and when.

- **User directory mailing lists:** These tools can list teams, team members, and team managers, which helps you know who to contact for support, who to contact for escalation, and so on.

- **Console history:** Such tools can tell you the most recently or frequently used commands or sequences of commands.

- **Services registry:** This tool can give you a list of every running service, its address, and any additional tags.

- **Configuration server:** This tool can give you environment configuration details.

- **Company service catalog:** This catalog lists services governance information, such as who to contact, time last updated, and so on.

- **Project registry:** Even a spreadsheet file on a shared drive can tell you project names, codes, leader, sponsor identification, budget codes, and so on.

- **Sonar components:** These tools can show groupings into logical units, metrics, and their trends at various levels of details and across multiple repositories and multiple technologies.

- **Project tracking tools history or release management tools history:** These tools can tell you about changes, including who, what when, and current versions.

- **Email server:** These tools are commonly used to archive the following for auditing (for example, by forwarding to the archiving address): manual reports, manual decisions such as go-live decisions, and the most knowledgeable collaborators.

Summary

Most, but not all, valuable knowledge already exists in some form in the artifacts of your system. The path to living documentation starts with acknowledging the various authoritative sources of knowledge that are already present. It also involves determining whether there is a single source of truth, which can be extracted into various kinds of documents, or whether there are redundant sources that require a reconciliation mechanism. If the knowledge is spread over many places, you may need a consolidation mechanism to put it back in one piece.

Most knowledge is already there, but not 100% of it, which suggests that you need to find ways to enrich, or *augment*, the system itself with the missing knowledge so that it becomes knowledge complete. That is the topic of the next chapter.

Chapter 4

Knowledge Augmentation

The source code might have code that is never executed, variable and procedure names that are lies, and is in general a poor way to learn the programmer's intention. To me, design is as much the decisions and the reasons as the results of the decisions. Sometimes code makes that clear, but usually it doesn't.
—Ralph Johnson, http://c2.com/cgi/wiki?WhatIsSoftwareDesign

Software is built from its source code. Does this mean that the source code tells everything there is to know over the lifecycle of the application? Sure, the source code tells a lot—and it has to. The source code describes how to build the software so that the compiler can do it. Clean code goes further, aiming to make knowledge as clear as possible for the other developers working on it.

Still, code is often not enough. When the code doesn't tell the full story, you need to add the missing knowledge to make it complete.

When Programming Languages Are Not Enough

Most programming languages have no predefined way to declare the key decisions, to record the rationale, and to explain the choice made against the considered alternatives. Programming languages can never tell everything. They focus on their key paradigm and rely on other mechanisms to express the rest: naming, comments, libraries, and so on.

A Bridge Metaphor

Consider the construction of a bridge as a metaphor here. A bridge is built based on its technical drawings. However, if at some point it is necessary to replace its wood timbers with new ones in a stronger material, such as steel, the original technical drawings wouldn't be enough. They would tell the dimensions chosen for the wooden timbers, but they wouldn't tell where the dimensions came from. They wouldn't tell about the calculations related to the resistance of materials, or fatigue of materials, or resistance against strong waters and extreme wind forces. They wouldn't tell what was considered "extreme" at the time the drawings were made. Perhaps the design needs to be reconsidered now, to accommodate more extreme conditions in light of recent events. Perhaps at the time the bridge was originally built, no one though a tsunami would be possible in this place, but now we know it could actually happen.

When it comes to documenting design decisions and their rationale, programming languages can't help much beyond simple standard decisions such as the typical visibility of members or inheritance.

When a language does not support a design practice, workarounds such as naming conventions can often do the job. Some languages with no way to express private methods prefix them with an underscore. Languages without objects adopt a convention of having a first function parameter called `this`. Yet even with the best programming language, a lot of what's in the developer's head still cannot be fully expressed by the language alone.

It's possible to add knowledge as code comments. But comments lack structure, unless you hijack structured comments like Javadoc. Also, refactoring does not apply to comments as well as it applies to code.

Therefore: Augment your programming language so that the code can tell the full story, in a structured way. Define your own way to declare the intentions and the reasoning behind each key decision. Declare the higher-level design intentions, the goals, and the rationales.

Don't rely on plain comments for this. Use strong naming conventions or use the extension mechanisms of the language, such as Java annotations and .Net attributes; the more structured, the better. Don't hesitate to write a little code solely for this documentation purpose. Create your domain-specific language (DSL) or reuse one if needed. Rely on conventions when suitable.

Keep the augmented knowledge as close as possible to the code it is related to. Ideally, they should be collocated to be totally refactoring proof. Have the compiler check for any errors. Rely on the autocompletion of the IDE. Make sure the augmented knowledge is easily searchable in your editor or IDE and ensure that it can be easily parsed by tools to extract living documents out of the whole augmented code.

Augmented code contains a lot of valuable hints for the future maintainers. One important consideration when adding knowledge related to the code is how it evolves when the code changes. Code will change because that's the way it is. As a consequence, it's essential for the additional knowledge to either remain accurate or change at the same time as the code, with no or very little manual maintenance. What happens when a class or package is renamed? What happens when a class is deleted? The extra knowledge you want to add should be refactoring proof.

Augmented code is great for making decisions explicit in the code and for adding the rationale behind the decisions.

Because it is structured, augmented code is also easy to search and to navigate in the IDE, without plugins. This means that it also works the other way: From a chosen rationale, you can find all the code that is related to it. This is quite valuable for traceability or impact analysis.

Augmented code in practice can be done with several approaches:

- Internal documentation
  - By annotation
  - By convention
- External documentation
  - With sidecar files
  - With a metadata database
  - With a DSL

Documentation Using Annotations

Extending a programming language by using annotations for documentation purposes is my favorite way to augment code in languages such as Java or C#. Annotations do not impose any constraint on naming or code structure, which means they work in most code bases. And because they are as structured as the programming language itself, it's possible to rely on the compiler to prevent errors and to rely on the IDE for autocompletion, navigation, and searching.

The main strength of annotations is that they are refactoring-friendly: They are robust when the element they are attached to is renamed, they move with it when it moves, and they get deleted when it's deleted. This means no extra effort to maintain them, even if the code changes a lot.

Therefore: Explain the design and its purpose using structured annotations. Create, grow, and maintain a catalog of predefined annotations, and then simply include these annotations to enrich the semantics of the classes, methods, and modules.

You can then create little tools that can exploit the additional information in the annotations, such as to enforce constraints or to extract knowledge into another format.

When you have annotations and you know them, you can more quickly declare a design decision: Just add the annotation. Annotations are like bookmarks for the thinking that has happened (see Figure 4.1).

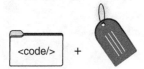

Figure 4.1 *Augmented Code = Code + Annotations*

Annotations can represent class stereotypes such as values, entities, domain services, and domain events. They can represent active pattern collaborators, such as composites or adapters. They can declare styles of coding and the default preference.

It's important that your annotations correspond to standard techniques with standard names as much as possible. If you need your own custom ones, be sure to document them in a place that everybody knows.

Placing an annotation to declare your decisions in terms of standard knowledge and standard practices encourages deliberate practice. You have to know what you're doing, and you have to know what it's called in the industry literature. Using standard design patterns and annotations can reduce the time required to complete a task.

Annotations are also searchable in the IDE, which is handy. For example, you can search for every class that is annotated by a selected annotation, which gives you a new way to navigate the design.

Structured annotations are a powerful tool, but they are probably not enough to completely replace all other forms of documentation to describe all design decisions and their intentions. You still need conversations between everyone involved. In addition, some knowledge and insights are best explained through clear writing with a sense of nuance—something that's hard to do in annotations. You may also find it desirable to keep track of more nuanced aspects like emotions involved in decision-making, such as fears, taste, distaste, political pressure. Other media, such as plain text, are better for that.

Finally, the knowledge declared using annotations is machine readable, which means tools can exploit this knowledge to help the team. Living diagrams and living glossaries, for example, rely on such possibilities. Imagine what you could do—or what you could have tools do for you—with tools that can understand your design intents!

Annotations as More Than Tags

Annotations in Java and attributes in .Net are genuine citizens of their programming language. They have a name and a module name (package or namespace). They also hold parameters and can themselves be annotated by other annotations. And because they are classes, they also benefit from the structured comments syntax used by documentation generators like Javadoc. All this means you can convey a lot of knowledge through simple annotations.

Let's look at a technical example. Annotations use meta-annotations to describe where they can be applied. For example, here the annotation Adapter can be applied to types and packages:

```
1  @Target({ ElementType.TYPE, ElementType.PACKAGE })
2  public @interface Adapter {
3  }
```

The following example involves annotations with parameters. If you were to annotate an instance of a builder pattern, you could describe the type that the builder produces as a parameter of the annotation:

```
1  public @interface Builder {
2      Class[] products() default {};
3  }
4
5  @Builder(products = {Supa.class, Dupa.class})
6  public class SupaDupaBuilder {
7  //...
8  }
```

Often the declared return types and implemented interfaces can already tell a lot of similar information, but they miss the precise semantics that additional annotations convey. In fact, more precise annotations open the door to more automation because they give tools a way to interpret the source code with higher-level semantics.

Just as the Semantic Web aims to transform unstructured data into a web of data, a code base with annotations that clarify the semantics of the source code becomes a web of data that machines can interpret.

Describing the Rationale Behind Decisions

One of the most important pieces of information worth recording for future generations is the rationale behind each decision. What may seem like a stupid choice years later was not so stupid when it was decided. Most importantly, when the rationale is referring to a context at some point in time, and now the context is different, you are in a better position to reconsider the decision now.

For example, say that an expensive database was chosen long ago because it was one of the few to be able to fully cache data in memory. Reading this rationale now, you may consider instead using NoSQL datastores for that purpose. As another example, say that an application has layers talking to each other through XML everywhere, which makes your life cumbersome and causes performances issues. The rationale for this decision explains that this architecture was meant to be distributed physically between layers in order to scale. However, after many years, it has become clear that this will never happen, so you know now that you could remove all the extra complexity. Without a clear rationale, you would always wonder if you had missed something, and you would not dare reconsidering the whole thing.

Embedded Learning

Putting more knowledge into code helps its maintainers learn while working on it. At a minimum, annotations should themselves be documented. If you have an annotation named `Adapter`, its comments should explain what `Adapter` is. My favorite way to do this is to link to a clear online definition, such as the corresponding Wikipedia page, along with a brief text description within the comment itself:

```
1   /**
2    * The adapter pattern is a software design pattern that allows the
3    * interface of an existing class to be used from another interface.
4    *
5    * The adapter contains an instance of the class it wraps, and
6    * delegates calls to the instance of the wrapped object.
7    *
8    * Reference: See <a href="http://en.wikipedia.org/wiki/\
9    * Adapter_pattern">Adapter_pattern</a>
10   */
```

```
11  public @interface Adapter {
12  }
```

This is more important than it might seem. From now on, every class with this annotation is only a tooltip away from complete documentation of its design role.

Consider the example of a random **Adapter** class in a project, in this case on top of the RabbitMQ middleware:

```
1 @Adapter
2 public class RabbitMQAdapter {
3     //...
4 }
```

When this class is opened in any IDE, when the mouse hovers over it, the tooltip displays its documentation, as shown in Figure 4.2.

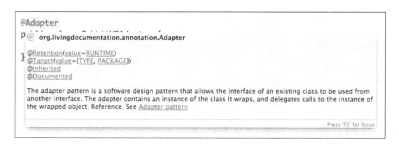

Figure 4.2 *The tooltip of the annotation displays its documentation*

The tooltip description provides a brief explanation but is especially useful for developers who already know the information but just need a refresher. Those who need more information than the tooltip provides can click the link to be redirected to more information. They will probably ask questions in the process, but at least there's an easy entry point to the learning. In this case, the annotations describe that the **Adapter** class is an instance of the adapter pattern, and they act as a gateway to learning more about the adapter pattern.

Therefore: Putting more knowledge into the code is not just for documentation; it can also help deliberately increase the skills of the teams working on it. Consider this opportunity when deciding on your augmented code strategy. When augmenting code, think about how your colleagues will react when they discover it.

An annotation could also link to the book or books that best explain the topic. Or it could link to a company e-learning program.

As an alternative to including links in comments, every annotation from the same book could have a meta-tag representing the book. In the following example, both `Adapter` and `Decorator` annotations represent design patterns from the Gang of Four book *Design Patterns*, and information about the book can be included in a meta-annotation `GoF` specifically about the book:

```
1  /**
2  * Book: <a href="http://books.google.fr/books/about/Design_
3  Patterns.html?id=6oHu\KQe3TjQC">Google Book</a>
4  */
5  @Target(ElementType.ANNOTATION_TYPE)
6  public @interface GoF {
7  }
8
9  @GoF
10 public @interface Adapter {
11 }
12
13 @GoF
14 public @interface Decorator {
15 }
```

This is only an example, and of course you are not limited to documenting design patterns! Feel free to elaborate your own scheme for organizing your knowledge based on these ideas.

Using Structured Tags Within Comments

If you are using a programming language that does not have annotations, you can use structured tags within comments:

```
1 /** @Adapter */
```

It's a good idea in this case to conform to a common style of structured documentation. The language may provide some tool support, such as autocompletion or code highlighting. The XDoclet library did that with great success in the early Java days, hijacking the Javadoc tags in order to use them as annotations.

You may also use the good old marker interface pattern, which involves implementing an interface with no method in order to mark the class. For example, to mark a class as serializable, you implement the `Serializable` interface:

```
1  public class MyDto implements Serializable {
2    ...
3  }
```

Note that this is quite an intrusive way to tag a class, and it pollutes the type hierarchy, but it provides a good illustration of what we're discussing here.

When Annotations Go Too Far

Google Annotations Gallery[1] is a retired open-source project from 2010 that proposed a collection of neat annotations to augment your code with your design decision, intentions, honest feelings, and even shame.

Discovering stupid code? You can leave a `@LOL` or `@Facepalm` or `@WTF` annotation:

```
1  @Facepalm
2  if(found == true){...}
```

Or you can leave all of them with an explanation:

```
1  @LOL @Facepalm @WTF("just use Collections.reverse()")
2  <T> void invertOrdering(List<T> list) {...
```

You can also use remark annotations to preemptively qualify your own miserable code:

```
1  @Hack public String
2  unescapePseudoEscapedCommasAndSemicolons(String url) {
```

...or to justify it:

```
1 @BossMadeMeDoIt
2 String extractSQLRequestFromFormParameter(String
params){...}
```

You can warn your team members with the `@CantTouchThis` annotation. Stumble across code that somehow works beyond all reason? Life's short. Mark it with `@Magic` and move on:

```
1 @Magic public static int negate(int n) {
2    return new Byte((byte) 0xFF).hashCode()
3    / (int) (short) '\uFFFF' * ~0
4    * Character.digit ('0', 0)
```

---

1. Google Annotations Gallery, https://code.google.com/p/gag/

```
5   * n * (Integer.MAX_VALUE * 2 + 1) / (Byte.MIN_VALUE >> 7)
6   1 * (~1 | 1);
7 }
```

And when you've done a good job of design, you can let the world know your brilliance with the literary annotations:

```
1 @Metaphor public interface Life extends Box { }
```

or:

```
1 @Oxymoron public interface DisassemblerFactory {
Disassembler
2   createDisassembler(); }
```

Documentation by Convention

Using plain conventions to document your decisions is convenient. For example, in Java, every identifier that starts with an uppercase letter is a class, and every identifier that starts with a lowercase letter is a variable name.

There are conventions for many situations, in many technologies, and you can always add your own conventions on top of any technical environment, be it code, XML, JSON, assembly, or SQL. Even old projects with old technologies rely on conventions to communicate knowledge, describe their structure, and help with navigation.

Here are some examples of documentation by convention:

- **Package names by layer:** Everything in a package named `*.domain.*` might represent domain logic, whereas everything in a package named `*.infra.*` might represent infrastructure code.

- **Package names by technical class stereotype:** It's common in many code bases to group every data access object class in a package named after the abbreviations `*.dao.*`; similarly for your Enterprise Java Beans in a package `*.ejb.*` and your plain old Java objects used by your favorite framework in a package `*.pojo.*`.

- **Commit comments:** You could use a convention such as `[FIX] issue-12345 free text`, where the square brackets categorize the type of commit as either `FIX`, `REFACTOR`, `FEATURE`, or `CLEAN`, and `issue-xxx` references the ticket ID in the bug tracker.

- **The Ruby on Rails style of convention over configuration:** In this convention, if a database table is named `orders`, the controller would be named `orders_controller`.

Living Documentation in Legacy Code with Conventions

Whenever you have an existing code base that follows conventions, you have an opportunity to go the living documentation route by exploiting all the existing conventions, without even having to touch the source code to add anything. (This is not possible with documentation by annotation.)

For example, say that an existing application follows a layered design. If you're lucky, its package names represent the layers directly through naming conventions:

```
1  /record-store-catalog/gui
2  /record-store-catalog/businesslogic
3  /record-store-catalog/dataaccesslayer
4  /record-store-catalog/db-schema
```

Your documentation is already there in the naming of the Java packages or in namespaces or subprojects in C#.

Documenting the Conventions

If everyone on a team is familiar with the conventions used, then you don't need any further documentation. Conventions published by another company are called *ready-made documentation*, and you can adopt such conventions and then just create a reference to the external documentation of the sets of conventions in the README file. In practice, though, I recommend always documenting the conventions in the README file. Here's an example of documenting conventions in a real code base:

```
1 README.txt
2
3 This application follows a Layered Architecture.
4 Each layer has its own package, with the following naming
5 conventions:
6
7 /gui/*
8 /businesslogic/*
9 /dataaccesslayer/*
10 /db-schema/*
```

```
11
12 The GUI layer contains all the code about the graphical user
13 interface.
14 All code responsible for display & data entry must be there.
15
16 The business logic layer contains all the domain-specific
17 logic and behavior. This is where the domain model is.
18 Business logic should only be there and nowhere else.
19
20 The data access layer contains all the DAO (Data Access
21 Objects) responsible to interact with the database.
22 Any change of storage technology should only impact
23 this layer and no other layer (in theory at least :)
24
25 The DB Schema contains all the SQL scripts to setup, delete
26 or update the database.
27
28 Important Rule: Each layer can only depend on the layers
29 below. No layer can depend on the layer or layers above,
30 this is forbidden!
```

Some conventions carry a cost, especially when they add noise to the naming. For example, putting prefixes or suffixes on identifiers (for example, `VATCalculation-Service`, `DispatchingManager`, `DispatchingDTO`) is a standard practice, but it's not clean code, and the names in your code do not belong to the business domain language anymore!

When every interface in a package is a service, adding the `Service` prefix adds no information, just noise. Every class in a `/dto/` package might not need the `DTO` suffix if it would be redundant information.

Consistently Adhering to Conventions

Documentation by convention works only to the extent that everyone involved has enough discipline to adhere to the conventions consistently. The compiler does not care about your conventions and won't help much in enforcing them.

One typo, and you're already not following the convention! You can, of course, tweak the compiler or your IDE parser, or you can use static analysis tools to detect some violations of conventions. Sometimes it's a lot of work, but other times it's surprisingly easy, so you may give it a try.

Relying on documentation by convention to help produce living documents such as living diagrams encourages and rewards following the conventions: If you break the convention, then your living documents will fail, which is nice.

The Limitations of Conventions

Conventions work well for categorizing sections of code, but they quickly show their limits when you try to enrich them with additional knowledge such as rationales, alternatives, and so on. In contrast, annotations may be better able to include such additional knowledge.

Conventions are often little more than free text meant for humans. However, you may still get some tool support for your conventions:

- You can configure your IDE with templates for each convention. For example, you might be able to type a few characters and have the template print the full name properly to adhere to the convention; for a commit comment with a more complicated convention, the template might print a placeholder that you can just fill in.

- You can have your living document generators interpret the conventions to perform their work.

- You can enforce rules such as dependencies between layers based on the naming conventions (for example, using JDepend, ArchUnit, or your own tool built on top of any code parser).

Compared to annotations, conventions also have the advantage of not disrupting old habits. If your team and managers are very conservative, you may prefer going the documentation by convention route rather than the documentation by annotation route. You can probably guess that I prefer documentation by annotation.

External Documentation Methods

Documentation by annotation and documentation by convention are forms of internal documentation that appear right into the code itself. In contrast, the techniques described in the following sections are forms of external documentation, as they reside at a location that is remote from the thing being documented.

Sidecar Files

When putting annotations within code is not possible, you can put them into a file next to the code. *Sidecar files*—also known as buddy files, companion files, or connected files—are files that store metadata that cannot be supported by the source file format. For each source file, there is typically one associated sidecar file with the same name but a different file extension.

For example, some web browsers save a web page as a pair of files: an HTML file and a sidecar folder of the same name but with a _folder prefix. As another example, a digital camera might have the capability to record a piece of audio while taking a picture, and the associated audio may be stored as a sidecar file with the same name as the .jpg file, but with a .wav extension.

Sidecar files are a type of external annotations. They can be used to add any kind of information, such as a classification tag or a free text comment, without having to touch the original source file on the file system.

The main problem with using sidecar files is that when the file manager is not aware of the relationship between the source file and its sidecar file, it cannot prevent the user from renaming or moving only one of the files without the other, and the relationship is broken. For this reason, I don't recommend using sidecar files unless you have no other choice.

> **Note**
>
> Old source control systems like Concurrent Versions System (CVS) used a lot of sidecar files.

Metadata Databases

When putting annotations within code is not possible, you can keep them in an outside database. A *metadata database* is a database that stores metadata referencing other source files or components. A well-known example is the iTunes database, which contains a lot of metadata associated with each song (for example, playlists, recent listening history) that doesn't fit within the song's audio file. The metadata might not fit within the file because the file format does not have a place to store the metadata or because it would not be a good idea to change the file at all.

Metadata may also reference a file but not really be intrinsic to it, and hence it should be stored somewhere else. For example, a photo should not store information about its being part of an album; it would be better to store the album somewhere else. In a similar fashion, the URL of the thumbnail of a photo is metadata that is of interest only for the photo application, and it would be intrusive to corrupt the photo file by including that kind of metadata in its own structure (assuming it were even possible).

The main problem with using metadata databases for annotations, just like the main problem with using sidecar files, is that it's easy for the metadata database and the corresponding files to get out of sync if one of these files is renamed, moved, or deleted without the database being updated.

A metadata database should be the last-resort choice when it's not possible to touch the files at all and metadata has to be stored elsewhere. However, it is also a convenient approach when the management of the metadata is done in bulk across all files at the same time, by different people than the people managing the files themselves. For example, if hundreds of photos are managed by a photographer, but the metadata database is a plain spreadsheet managed by a librarian, then it is easy for the librarian to quickly add all the metadata in a column, thanks to the copy/paste, interpolation, and calculation abilities of a modern spreadsheet application. The photographer does not have to be involved, and there is no risk of corrupting the photo file by mistake.

Common examples of metadata databases are the various key/value stores embedded in discovery registries; deployment, configuration, and provisioning tools; service catalogs; bookmarking registries; and so on. Whenever you can reference something and add tags, you have a de facto metadata database!

Designing Custom Annotations

Off-the-shelf literature is essential in quickly learning from the experience of others and sharing a common vocabulary, whatever the company, department, or continent. However, the problem with such literature is that in order to be shared with everyone, it has to give up what is specific to each particular context.

You should use this standard body of knowledge, and you can also extend it to make it even more expressive. You can evolve your vocabulary of tags and annotations from the standard literature with additions and extensions to make it more specific to your own context.

For example, we more or less all agree on a standard circle of six colors, but in your own visual charter, you certainly use custom variants of these colors, which are specific to you. Your light blue is certainly a blue, but it is up to you to define what "light" means.

Stereotypical Properties

When we design code, we think in terms of working behavior and also in terms of properties, desirable or not. Here are some examples of desirable properties:

- `NotNull`: For a parameter that cannot be null. Life is so much easier when you use it almost always!
- `Positive`: For a parameter that has to be positive.
- `Immutable`: For a class that remains unchanged.
- `Identity by value`: Where equality is defined as the equality of data.
- `Pure`: For a function or for every function of a class to avoid side effects.
- `Idempotent`: For a function that has the same effect when called more than once (which is very important in distributed systems).
- `Associative`: For a function such as (a + b) + c = a + (b + c), when doing map-reduce kinds of things.

When you use these properties, you need to make your usage clear in the code. You can do this with the type system whenever possible. For example, it is possible to express the possibility of having no result with `Option` or `Optional` if it is built in to the language or provided by a standard library. Using a Scala *case class* is in itself a shorthand for *(Immutable, Identity by value)*. When this is not possible, you can express the properties with comments or with custom annotations, along with automated tests and property-based testing.

Stereotypes and Tactical Patterns

In a language like Java or C#, everything is a class, but not every class is of the same kind or has the same purpose. Note that in functional programming languages, everything is a function, but not every function has the same purpose either. Domain-driven design proposes some fundamental categories of classes, such as *value object*, *entity*, *domain service*, and *domain event*. It also suggests borrowing from other patterns, such as using design patterns (for example, strategy and composite patterns). The point is that some (but not all) design patterns are also domain patterns.

It is interesting that these categories of classes offer compressed ways to express a lot of information. For example, when I say that the class `FueldCardTransaction` is a value object, I mean that its identity is only defined by its values, that it is immutable, that it should be without any side effects, and that it should be transferable.

It is therefore natural to declare explicitly these patterns as a simple way to do documentation.

You could introduce a set of custom annotations like the following into a project:

- `@ValueObject`
- `@Entity` or `@DomainEntity` (to prevent any ambiguity with the annotations of similar names from all the technical frameworks)
- `@DomainService`
- `@DomainEvent`

And you can declare the consequences explicitly by using the properties.

Each category of class comes with predefined properties. For example, a value object should have identity by value, should be immutable, and should be side effect free. You can easily make this explicit in a system of annotations by using annotations on annotations, as shown here:

```
1  @Immutable
2  @SideEffectFree
3  @IdentityByValue
4  public @interface ValueObject {
5  ...
```

When you mark a class as being a value object, you indirectly mark it with the meta annotations as well. This is a convenient way to group properties that go together into bundles, to declare them all with only one equivalent declaration. Of course, a bundle should have a clear name and meaning; it should not be just a random bunch of properties together.

This approach enables additional enforcement of the design and architecture. For example `@DomainEntity`, `@DomainService`, and `@DomainEvent` imply being part of a domain model and perhaps related restrictions on the allowed dependencies, which can all be enforced with static analysis.

As described later in this chapter, you can put annotations on packages in Java so that a declaration in one place collectively marks every element of the package. You can take advantage of this in an "unless specified otherwise" fashion. For example, you could define a custom annotation named `@FunctionalFirst`, meant to be put on whole packages, which would mean `@Immutable` and `@SideEffect-Free` by default for every type, unless something else were stated explicitly on a particular type.

There are many other catalogs of patterns and stereotypes of interest to express efficiently a lot of design and modeling knowledge. They provide ready-made knowledge and vocabulary related to your job as a developer, about design, and about modeling and solving infrastructure problems. But you can go further and extend the standard categories into finer-grained categories.

For example, it is possible to refine the kind of value object. Martin Fowler wrote about the quantity pattern, the null object pattern, the special case pattern, and the range pattern, which are all specialized cases of value objects. In addition, the money pattern is a special case of the quantity pattern. You can use all these patterns, choosing the most specific one possible. For example, you could chose range over just value object if it applies, as it is common knowledge that a range is a value object. If you did this, you could make it explicit that a range is a special case of a value object with an annotation on the annotation:

```
1  @ValueObject
2  public @interface Range {
3  ...
```

You can also create your own variants. In one project, I had a lot of value objects, but they were more than that. They were also instances of the policy pattern, the domain pattern equivalent of the strategy pattern. More importantly, in the business domain of finance, we would usually call them standard market *conventions*. So I created my own @Convention annotation and made it clear that it was at the same time a value object and a policy:

```
1  @ValueObject
2  @Policy
3  public @interface Convention {
4  ...
```

Using Meaningful Annotation Package Names

When you create a custom annotation, you have to choose its package name. You can choose for a package name to have a particular meaning. I like to encode a reference place for an idea in the package name. When the annotation is drawn from a book, for example, I might use the book name or an abbreviation of the book name or authors, such as com.acme.annotation.gof for a book by the Gang of Four, com.acme.annotation.poeaa for the book *Patterns of Enterprise Application Architecture*, and com.acme.annotation.ddd for the book *Domain-Driven Design*. For standard knowledge with no one golden book, I might name the package after the field (for example, com.acme.annotation.algebra).

Hijacking Standard Annotations

Many frameworks in the Java world use annotations as a form of configuration. For example, JPA (Java Persistence API) and Spring Framework offer the infamous choice between XML and annotations. Even though I advocate using annotations for documentation purposes, I am not a big fan of using annotations as an alternative to writing code. I prefer the approach found in some .Net projects, such as Fluent NHibernate, of using plain code to define the object-to-relational mappings.

However, in Java at this time, you still have to use annotations, unless you prefer XML (which I do not). When you use annotations to drive the behavior of frameworks, the annotations are code indeed, and since most of them relate to infrastructure concerns such as persistence or web service, they often have the annoying habit of polluting domain classes with non-domain noise.

Aside from my little rant, you probably wonder whether these standard annotations have any documentation value. Because they are code, at a minimum, the annotations document what they are doing—just like well-designed code. They tell the *what*.

Let's consider a few examples of particular documentation interest:

- **Stereotyping annotations (Spring):** This set of annotations includes `@Service`, `@Repository`, and `@Controller`. They are used to stereotype classes, and you can declare them for registration into the dependency injection mechanism. In fact, they alias the `@Component` annotation with more meaning, which is a nice way to hijack these noisy annotations for something more meaningful for humans rather than just for Spring.

- **Creating custom stereotypes (Spring):** This approach also supports your own custom annotations, provided that you annotate them with the `@Component` meta annotation.

- **`@Transactional` (Spring):** The `@Transactional` annotation is used to declare transactional boundaries and rules, typically on a service. If you have a hexagonal architecture, the transactional services should be your application services in their own thin layer on top of the domain model. You could thus decide that this Spring annotation in itself also means `@Application-Service` in the DDD sense. Because most Spring annotations are also meta annotations, you could actually define your own `@ApplicationService` annotation and mark it as `@Transactional` in order to express your intent in a way that Spring can recognize for doing its magic, too.

- **@Inheritance (JPA):** The `@Inheritance` annotation and its friends can be used to directly document design decisions on how to do the mapping between a class hierarchy and a corresponding database schema. This directly relates to the corresponding patterns from Martin Fowler's book *Patterns of Enterprise Application Architecture*. For example, `@Inheritance(strategy=JOINED)` corresponds to the single-table inheritance pattern[2] (but, unfortunately, under another name).

- **RESTful web service (JAX-RS annotations):** This set of annotations is clearly declarative: `@Path` identifies the URI path, `@GET` declares the `GET` request method, and `@Produces` defines the media type as a parameter. The resulting code is self-documented to a large extent. Furthermore, tools like Swagger can exploit these annotations to generate living documentation of the API.

It is possible to rely on the standard annotations for their particular documentation value, but this is almost always limited to technical concerns, where the annotation is just like particularly declarative code in that it tells the *what* but not the *why*. As mentioned earlier, it is sometimes possible to extend the standard mechanism to convey additional meaning while still playing nicely with the frameworks you depend on.

Standard Annotation: `@Aspect` and Aspect-Oriented Programming

The Spring Pet Clinic demonstrates aspect-oriented programming (AOP) by showing how to set up a simple aspect that monitors call count and call invocation time *for every repository*.[3]

It is interesting here that the requirement "to monitor every repository" is described *literally* in the aspect declaration, as shown in the following excerpt annotated with the `@Aspect` annotation from Spring AOP.

```
1  @Aspect
2  public class CallMonitoringAspect {
3      ...
4      @Around("within(@org.springframework.stereotype.Repository *)")
```

---

2. Martin Fowler, "Single Table Inheritance," ThoughtWorks, http://martinfowler.com/eaaCatalog/singleTableInheritance.html

3. https://github.com/spring-petclinic/spring-framework-petclinic/blob/master/src/main/java/org/spring-framework/samples/petclinic/util/CallMonitoringAspect.java

```
5    public Object invoke(ProceedingJoinPoint joinPoint) throws
Throwable{
6      ...
7    }
8  ...
9  }
```

This expressiveness is possible because the code has been augmented with the meaningful `@Repository` stereotype. This illustrates perfectly how augmenting the code with explicit design decisions makes it possible to talk to tools the way we humans think.

Annotation by Default or Unless Necessary

When designing custom annotations to express properties, you have a choice of creating an annotation for the case when the property is met or when it's not met:

- `@Immutable` or `@Mutable`
- `@NonNull` or `@Nullable`
- `@SideEffectFree` or `@SideEffect`

You may create both and let individuals decide which one to choose, but that might create inconsistencies, in which case the annotation means nothing at all.

You may decide on an alternative that you want to promote so that having the annotation in many places becomes a marketing campaign; for example, using `@NonNull` everywhere will encourage making everything non-null. No annotation then suggests nullability.

On the other hand, you might consider that annotations are noise and think that the fewer annotations the better. In this case, the default and preferred choice should be no annotation, and you would use an annotation only to declare a deviation from the default. If the team preference is to have every class immutable by default, you would annotate mutable classes because you want your colleagues to notice: "Oh, this class is exceptionally `@Mutable`!"

Handling Module-Wide Knowledge

In a software project, a module contains a set of artifacts (essentially packages, classes, and nested modules) that can be manipulated together. You can define properties that apply to all the elements a module contains. Design properties and quality attribute requirements (for example, being read only, serializable, stateless) often apply on a whole module, not just on distinct elements within the module.

You can also define the primary programming paradigm at the module level: object-oriented, functional, or even procedural or reporting style.

A module is also ideal for declaring architecture constraints. For example, you could have distinct areas for code written from scratch with high-quality standard and for legacy code with more tolerant standards. In each module, you could define preferences of style such as Checkstyle configuration, metrics thresholds, unit test coverage, and allowed or forbidden imports.

Therefore: When a piece of knowledge spans a number of artifacts equally within a module, you should put this knowledge at the module level directly, so that it applies to all the contained elements.

This approach can also be applied to all elements satisfying a given predicate, as long as you can find a home for this declaration, such as the pointcuts in aspect-oriented programming.

Dealing with Many Kinds of Modules

Packages are the most obvious modules in Java and in other languages. But a package x.y.z actually defines more than one module: the module of its direct members (`x.y.z.*`) and the module that also include every artifact included in its subpackages (`x.y.z.**`). Similarly, a class also represents a "module" for its member fields, methods, and nested classes—for example, `x.y.z.A#` and `x.y.z.$`.

The "working sets" in an IDE like Eclipse also define another logical grouping, similar to modules, as simple collections of classes and other resources. Tools like Ant also define filesets using lists of files and regular expressions—for example, `{x.y.z.A, x.y.z.B, x.y.*.A}`. Like modules, working sets and filesets are usually named for easy reference.

Source folders (for example, src/main/java or src/test/java) obviously define coarse-grained groupings of elements. Maven modules define bigger modules, at the scale of subprojects. Pointcuts of aspect-oriented programming also defines logical groupings elements across various "real" modules.

Inheritance and implementation implicitly define modules, too, such as "every subclass of a class or implementation of an interface" as `x.y.z.A+`, and if it includes every member of every nested member, it is `x.y.z.A++`.

A stereotype implicitly defines the set of its occurrences. For example, the value object pattern implicitly defines the logical set of every class that is a value object.

Collaboration patterns such as Model–View–Controller (MVC) and knowledge level also imply logical groupings such as the model part of MVC or each level of the knowledge level pattern (knowledge level or operational level).

Design patterns also define logical groupings by the role played within the pattern (for example, "Every abstract role in the Abstract Factory pattern" would be `@AbstractFactory.Abstract.*`).

There are many other modules or quasi-modules implied by concepts like layers, domains, bounded contexts, and aggregate roots.

The problem with large modules is that they contain huge numbers of items, which often necessitates aggressive filtering and may even require ranking to consider only the N most important elements out of many more.

Module-Wide Augmentation In Practice

All the techniques to augment code with additional knowledge apply for module-wide knowledge: annotations, naming conventions, sidecar files, metadata database, and DSL.

A common way to add documentation to a Java package is to use a special class named package-info.java as a location for the Javadoc and any annotation about the package. Note that this special pseudo-class with a magic name is actually an example of a sidecar file.

C# modules often contain projects, which can have assembly information descriptions:

```
1   AssemblyInfoDescription("package comment")
```

In most programming languages, package or namespace naming conventions can also be used to declare design decisions. For example, *something.domain* can be used to mark a package or namespace as a domain model.

Intrinsic Knowledge Augmentation

> **Caution**
>
> This section is more abstract than most others. The concepts discussed here are important but subtle. If abstract nonsense is definitely not your thing, you can safely skip this section and perhaps come back to it later.

It is important to make a distinction between what things really are for themselves and what they are for something else or for a purpose. A car may be red, may be a coupe, or may have a hybrid engine. These properties are really *intrinsic* to the car;

they are part of its identity. In contrast, the owner of the car, the car's location at a point in time, or the car's role in a company fleet are *extrinsic* to the car. This extrinsic knowledge is not really about the car in itself but about a relationship between the car and something else. As a consequence, it can change for many reasons other than the car itself. Thinking about intrinsic versus extrinsic knowledge has many benefits for design and for documentation.

If only intrinsic knowledge is attached to an element, the following would happen:

- If you were to delete the element, the attached knowledge would go away with it, without regret and without modification anywhere else. For example, when the car is recycled, its serial number is crunched at the same time, and this is okay.

- Any change that it is not intrinsically about the element would not modify the element or its artifacts at all. For example, selling the car would not modify its user manual.

Understanding the Importance of Extrinsic Properties

I first learned about the notion of intrinsic versus extrinsic in the Gang of Four book Design Patterns. The chapter that introduces the lightweight pattern considers a glyph used in a word processor. Each letter in the text is printed on the screen as a glyph, the rendered image of a character. A glyph has a size and style attributes such as italic or bold. A glyph also has an (x, y) position on the page. The core idea behind the lightweight pattern is to exploit the difference between intrinsic properties of the glyph (for example, its size, its style) and its extrinsic properties (for example, its position on the page) to enable reuse of the same instance of the glyph many times on the page.

This explanation has had a big influence on the way I design. It is a secret ingredient in improving the long-term relevance of design decisions.

Therefore: Only annotate elements with knowledge that is intrinsic to them. Conversely, consider attaching all intrinsic knowledge to the element itself. Avoid attaching knowledge that is extrinsic, as it will change often and for reasons unrelated to the element. A focus on intrinsic knowledge will reduce the maintenance efforts of the documentation over time.

> **Key Point**
>
> You may think of this attention to intrinsic knowledge as a matter of more or less judicious coupling. The key question is "How would my declared knowledge have to evolve when I change the element?" The best approach is the one that requires you to do the least work when the element changes.

The common use of annotations by popular frameworks regularly does not consider whether they're really intrinsic to the thing annotated. For example, say that you have a class that exists in itself and that can be used independently, but then you put annotations on it to declare how it is supposed to be mapped to the database or to declare that it is the default implementation for some interface. If you consider this class to really represent a domain responsibility, then this database mapping is an unrelated concern; having it attached only makes the class more likely to change for database reasons, too.

Imagine that you have a `CatalogDAO` interface with two implementations: `MongoDBCatalogDAO` and `PostgresCatalogDAO`. Marking the `MongoDBCatalogDAO` class as the default implementation of the `CatalogDAO` interface would be an example of forcing an extrinsic concern on the class. A better alternative would be to annotate each `DAO` with an intrinsic attribute like `@MongoDB` or `@Postgres` and separately make the selection *indirectly* via this intermediate attribute. For example, you could mark all `MongoDBDAO` implementations with the `@MongoDB` annotation and all `PostgresDAO` implementations with the `@Postgres` annotation. This is intrinsic knowledge with respect to the `DAO`. Separately, you could decide to inject every implementation for the technology chosen for a particular deployment. If you deploy with Postgres, we want to inject every `@Postgres` implementation. This decision to inject one selected technology is knowledge, too, but the `DAO` hierarchy shouldn't have to know.

Machine-Accessible Documentation

You code at the design level, not just the code level, but your tools cannot help you much at the design level. They cannot help because they have no idea, based on the code alone, what you are doing from a design perspective. If you make your design explicit, such as by using annotations attached to the code, then tools can begin to manipulate the code at the design level, too, and thus help you more.

Design knowledge that can make the code more explicit is worth adding. An annotation attached to the language element is often enough. For example, you can declare the layers on each top-level package in the corresponding package-info.java file:

```
1   @Layer(LayerType.INFRASTRUCTURE)
2   package com.example.infrastructure;
```

By putting the annotation @Layer on the package com.example.infrastructure, you declare a particular instance of the layer pattern, where the layer is the package itself.

As usual, there are many options for designing a custom annotation, such as declaring an ID (which may be useful for referencing it later):

```
1   @Layer(id = "repositories")
2   package com.example.domain;
```

With this design intent made explicit in the code itself, tools such as a dependency checker could automatically derive forbidden dependencies between layers to detect when they are violated.

You could do this with tools like JDpend, but you'd have to declare each package-to-package dependency restriction. This it tedious and does not directly describe the layering; it describes just the consequence of the layering.

Declaring every forbidden or acceptable package-to-package dependency is tedious, but imagine doing it between classes: It's prohibitive! However, if classes are tagged—for example, as @ValueObject, @Entity, or @DomainService—dependency checkers can enforce your favorite dependency restrictions. For example, I like to enforce the following rules:

- Value objects should never depend on anything other than other value objects.

- Entities should never have any service instance as a member field.

Once the classes are augmented with these stereotypes explicitly, you can more literally and more concisely tell the tools what you want.

Literate Programming

Let us change our traditional attitude to the construction of programs: Instead of imagining that our main task is to instruct a computer what to do, let us concentrate rather on explaining to human beings what we want a computer to do..
—*Donald Knuth*[4]

---

4. Donald Knuth, http://www.literateprogramming.com

It is hard not to mention literate programming in a book on living documentation. Literate programming is an approach to programming introduced by Donald Knuth. A literate program explains program logic in a natural language, such as English, along with snippets of macros and traditional source code. A tool processes the program, producing both a document for humans and source code that can be compiled, becoming an executable program.

Although literate programming never became widely popular, it had a profound and widespread influence on the industry, even if the idea was often distorted.

Literate programming introduced several important ideas:

- Documentation interleaved with the code, in the same artifacts, with code inserted within the prose of the documentation: This should not be confused with documentation generation, where the documentation is extracted from comments inserted into the source code.

- Documentation following the flow of thoughts of the programmer, as opposed to being constrained by the compiler-imposed order: Good documentation follows the order of the human logic.

- A programming paradigm encouraging programmers to think deliberately about each decision: Literate programming goes well beyond documentation: It is meant to force programmers to think deliberately, as they have to explicitly state their thoughts behind the program.

Keep in mind that literate programming is not a way to do documentation but a way to write programs.

Even though its use is not widespread, literate programming is still alive today, with tools available for all good programming languages, including Haskell, Clojure, and F#. The focus now is on writing prose in Markdown, with snippets of programming language inserted. In Clojure you use Marginalia,[5] in CoffeeScript you use Docco,[6] and in F# you use Tomas Petricek's FSharp. Formatting.[7]

Traditionally, documentation of a software program has involved a mix of code and prose, which can be combined in several ways:

- Code in prose: This is the method of literate programming as originally proposed by Donald Knuth. The primary document is prose that follows the human logic of the programmer. The author-programmer has full control of the narration.

---

5. Marginalia, https://github.com/gdeer81/marginalia
6. Docco, http://jashkenas.github.io/docco/
7. FSharp.Formatting, https://github.com/tpetricek/FSharp.Formatting

- **Prose in code:** This is the documentation generation approach offered by most programming languages; Javadoc is an example of a tool that creates prose in code.

- **Separate code and prose, merged into one document by a tool:** Tools are used to perform a merge in order to publish a document, such as a tutorial.

- **Code and prose as the same thing:** In this approach, the programming language is so clear that it can be read as prose itself. Unfortunately, this Holy Grail is never reached, but some programming languages get closer than others. I've seen some F# code by Scott Waschlin that is impressively close to this ideal.

Some tools, like Dexy,[8] offer a choice of how to organize the code and the prose with each other.

Recording Your Rationale

In the book *97 Things Every Software Architect Should Know*, Timothy High is quoted as saying, "As explained in the axiom 'Architectural Tradeoffs', the definition of a software architecture is all about choosing the right tradeoffs between various quality attributes, cost, time, and other factors." Replace the word *architecture* with *design*, or even with *code*, and the sentence still holds.

There are trade-offs everywhere in software, whenever a decision is being made. If you believe you're not making any trade-off, it just means the trade-off is out of sight.

Decisions belong to stories. Humans love stories and tend to remember them. It is important to preserve the context of a decision. The context of a past decision is necessary to reevaluate that decisions in a new context. Past decisions are tools that can help learn from the thinking of the predecessors. Many decisions are also more compact to describe than their consequences and hence are easier to transfer from one brain to another than all the details that result from a decision. If you tell me your intent and the context shortly, provided that I'm a skilled professional, I may come up with the same decisions that you've made. Without the intent and context, however, you are left to wonder "What were they thinking?" (see Figure 4.3).

---

8. Dexy, https://github.com/dexy/dexy

Figure 4.3 *What were they thinking?*

Therefore: Record the rationale for each important decision in some form of persistent documentation. Include the context and the main alternatives. And listen to the documentation: If you find it hard to formalize the rationale and the alternatives, then it may be that the decision was not as deliberate as it should have been. You may be programming by coincidence!

What's in a Rationale?

Any decision happens in a context and is one of the considered answers to a problem. Therefore, a rationale is not only the reason behind a chosen decision, it is also all of the following:

- **The context at the time:** The context includes the main stakes and concerns, for example the current load ("Only 1000 end users using the application once a week") or the current priority ("Priority is exploring the market-product fit as quickly as possible") or an assumption ("This is not expected to change") or a people consideration ("The development teams don't want to learn JavaScript").

- **The problem or requirement behind the choice:** Examples of problems are "The page must load in less than 800ms to not lose visitors" and "Decommission the VB6 module."

- **The decision itself instead of the chosen solution, with the main reason or reasons:** Examples of decisions and reasons are "The ubiquitous language is expressed with English words only, as it's simpler and every current stakeholder prefers it that way" and "This facade exposes the legacy system through a pretty API because there is no good reason to rewrite the legacy but we still want to consume it with the same convenience as if it were brand new."

- **The main alternatives that were considered seriously and perhaps why they were not selected or why they would be selected if the context were different:** Examples of alternative are "Buying an off-the-shelves solution would be a better choice if the needs were more standard," "A graph structure would be more powerful but is harder to map with the Excel spreadsheets of the users," and "A NoSQL datastore would be a better choice if we didn't have all this investment with our current Oracle database."

As @CarloPescio suggested in a conversation on self-documenting code, generally speaking, design rationale is very much about discarded options and so is *not typically in the code*.

Making the Rationale Explicit

You can record the rationale behind important decisions in a number of ways:

- **Ad hoc document:** You need an explicit document about the requirements, including all quality attributes. It needs to evolve slowly but still at least once a year; such a document is needed only for the main attributes that span large areas of the system, not for more local decisions. Chapter 12, "Living Architecture Documentation," describes a decision log as an example of that approach for architectural matters.

- **Annotations:** Annotations that document a decision could have fields to record the rationale: `@MyAnnotation(rationale ="We only know how to do that way")`.

- **Blog post:** A blog post takes more time to write than annotations or even an ad hoc document, and a good writing style is really helpful. However, you provides a human account of the reasoning and the human context behind a decision, even with the politics and personal agenda mentioned between the lines, and this makes it valuable. A blog post may also be searched and scanned when a question arises on a past decision.

Beyond Documentation: Motivated Design

Recording the rationale is not just for future generations or your future self; it is also useful right now, at the time you do it. You need to listen to what's difficult as a signal that something could be improved. If it is hard to come up with a rationale, or a context, perhaps the decision was not thought about seriously enough, and this should be an alert.

If it is hard to come up with two or three credible alternatives to a decision, then perhaps the first solution that fit was chosen, without any work being done to explore simpler or better solutions. Your current decision might not be optimal, and it can have consequences as lost opportunities in the future. Of course, one rationale may be "First solution that fit was chosen to go to market as quickly as possible," but at least this decision is deliberate, and those involved understand the consequence and can be ready to reconsider it next time.

In the absence of deliberate design decisions, and with a complete lack of skills, you will just have a random software structure. You just end up with a pile of details, and the only way to deal with it is to guess the intentions involved. This is typically the issues you have to deal with in legacy code, which we discuss in detail in Chapter 14, "Documenting Legacy Applications." My point is that the focus on making a rationale explicit helps make better decisions and better software.

Avoid Documenting Speculation

In the book *Building Microservices*, Sam Newman advises against documenting solutions to speculative needs. He paints a critical picture of traditional architecture documentation that explains with many pages and many diagrams how the perfect system will be but ignoring completely any unexpected future impediment when it comes to actually build it and make it work.

In contrast, rationales are decisions taken on actual needs that have been proven to be necessary. In incremental approaches, such as emerging design, we grow the solution slice by slice, and each slice is driven by the most important need at each instant. We often work in a just-in-time fashion, precisely because it is an antidote to speculation: We build it just when it becomes necessary to be built.

Overall, you should document only what has been built, in response to actual needs.

Skills as Pre-Documented Rationales

The thinking process for many small decisions has already been solved and documented in the literature. For example, the single responsibility principle says to split a class that does two things into two classes that do one thing each. There is no need to document each occurrence of a particular happening, but you may document once, in a single place, each of the principles you consistently follow; I call this the acknowledge your influences pattern and describe it a little later in this chapter.

Figure 4.4 *Without the why, they will make the same mistake again*

Recording the Rationale as an Enabler for Change

Knowing all the reasons behind past decisions can enable you to more successfully make changes because you can either respect or reject each of those decisions deliberately. The best way to know about those decisions in a reliable way is to have them recorded; otherwise, the reasoning will be forgotten (see Figure 4.4). Without the explicit rationale behind each past decision, you might wonder if a change has unexpected impacts with respect to a concern you don't have in mind. Without knowing about past decisions, you may never be sure enough to decide to change, and the status quo will dominate, even though the opportunity to improve is there in front of your eyes. Alternatively, you may actually cause harm inadvertently if you make a change that triggers a forgotten concern that you cannot see because it was not recorded.

Acknowledging Your Influences (aka Project Bibliography)

> Good books care about their bibliography. For the reader, it's a way to learn more, but it's also a way to check the influences of the author. When a word has different meanings, looking at the bibliography helps find out how to interpret it. Read the book!
>
> —*Eric Evans,* Domain-Driven Design

The mindset of the team that worked on a project is stable knowledge that's worth making explicit for future developers. It doesn't require long sentences; you can just list your bibliography and list the main points of your style.

A project bibliography provides a context for readers. It reveals the influences of the team at the time that they built the software. A project bibliography is composed of links to books, articles, and blogs either crafted by hand or extracted from annotations and comments or through a mix of both.

Declaring Your Style

As painters tend to belong to specific painting schools (for example, Surrealism, Cubism), software developers align themselves with various schools of thoughts. Some painters can switch between styles from one work to another; similarly, a developer might be able to create a module in a very functional programming style, with everything pure and immutable, and then create another module using semantic technologies and graph-oriented stores.

To provide context for documentation readers, it is useful to declare the style and the main paradigm, if any, that you have chosen for some area of code—typically for a module or for a project. This overall statement might look similar to a resume for the team or teams:

- Modeling paradigms (for example, DDD)

- Authors the team members follow

- Books the team members have read and blogs they often go read

- Languages and frameworks the team members are familiar with

- Any kind of inspiration that matters, such as "Stripe as an inspiration for developer-friendliness"

- Typical kinds of projects the team members have mostly done so far (for example, web, server, embedded)

To be refactoring proof, this information should reside within the module or project itself. It can be done with annotations such as `@Style` (Styles.FP) on packages (Java), attributes on the AssemblyInfo (.Net), or by using a style.txt file with a key/value syntax at the root of the module or project.

> **Note**
>
> An explicit style declaration is also useful for tools; for example, the declared style can be used to select a specific rulesets for static analysis tools.

Declaring your style helps enforce consistency within the code base.

> **LOL**
>
> Coined Gierke's law yesterday: from the structure of a software system you can derive the book the architect read most recently.
>
> —*From Oliver Gierke, @olivergierke on Twitter*

Commit Messages as Comprehensive Documentation

Carefully written commit messages make each line of code well documented. When committing files into source control, it is good practice to add a meaningful comment that includes the commit message. This is often neglected, and the result is time wasted opening files to discover what a change was about. When done carefully, commit messages are very valuable for several purposes, as yet another high-yield activity:

- **Thinking:** You have to think about the work done. Is it one single change or a mix of more than one that should be split? Is it clear? Is it really done? Are there new tests that should have been added or modified along with the changes?

- **Explaining:** A commit message must make the intention explicit. It is a feature, or a fix, and the reason should be written, even briefly, as in recording the rationale. This will save time for the readers.

- **Reporting:** Commit messages can later be used for various kinds of reporting, published as a changelog, or integrated into the developer toolchain.

The big idea with commit messages is that on any given line of code, asking the source control for its history gives you a detailed list of reasons and, hopefully, of rationales explaining why this line of code is what it is. As Mislav Marohnić writes in his blog post "Every Line of Code Is Always Documented," "a project's history is its most valuable documentation."[9]

---

9. Mislav Marohnić, "Every Line of Code Is Always Documented," http://mislav.uniqpath.com/2014/02/hidden-documentation/

Looking at the history of a given line of code tells you who made a change, when, and what other files were changed at the same time: for example, the related tests. This helps pinpoint to the new test cases that were added and acts as a built-in mechanism for *code to test* traceability. In the history you would also find the commit message explaining the change and the reasons for the change.

To make the most of commit messages, it might be a good idea to agree on a standard set of commit guidelines if the current quality of the messages is not satisfactory. Using a standard structure and standard keywords has several benefits. For one thing, it is more formal and, therefore, more concise. With a formal syntax, you can write:

fix(ui): change the color of the submit button to green

which is shorter to write and to read than the equivalent full English sentence:

"This is a fix on the UI area to change the color of the submit button to green."

A structure message enforces that the required information, such as the type of commit or the location of the change, will not be forgotten. And using formal syntax turns a messages into machine-accessible knowledge, for even more goodness!

Therefore: Take care with commit messages. Agree on a set of commit guidelines and use a semi-formal syntax and a standard dictionary of keywords. Work collectively or use peer pressure, code reviews, or enforcement tools to ensure that the guidelines are respected. Design the guidelines so that tools can use them to help you more.

Commit messages provide comprehensive documentation for each line of code. This information is available at the command line or on the graphical interface on top of your source control, as shown in Figure 4.5.

Commit Guidelines

A good example of commit guidelines is the Angular commit guidelines,[10] which specify strict rules for how the commit messages must be formatted. These rules, says the Angular website, lead "to more readable messages that are easy to follow when looking through the project history. But also, we use the git commit messages to generate the AngularJS change log." According to this particular set of guidelines,

---

10. AngularJS, https://github.com/angular/angular.js/blob/master/CONTRIBUTING.md#commit

the commit message must be structured as a header section, an optional body section, and an optional footer section, each separated by a blank line, as shown here:

```
1  <type>(<scope>): <subject>
2
3  <body>
4
5  <footer>
```

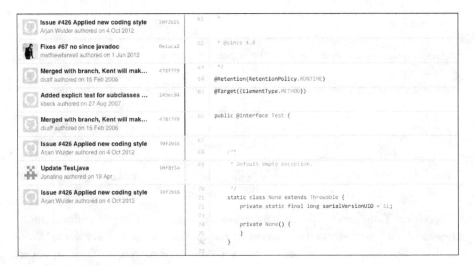

Figure 4.5 *The blame view on GitHub shows every contribution for each line, here for the famous Junit project*

Specifying the Type of a Change
type must be one of the following:

- **feat:** A new feature
- **fix:** A bug fix
- **docs:** Documentation-only changes
- **style:** Changes that do not affect the meaning of the code, such as changes to whitespace, formatting, missing semicolons, and so on
- **refactor:** A code change that neither fixes a bug nor adds a feature
- **perf:** A code change that improves performance

- **test:** Changes that add missing tests
- **chore:** Changes to the build process or auxiliary tools and libraries, such as documentation generation

All breaking changes must be declared in the footer, starting with the words *breaking change*, followed by a space and a detailed explanation of the change and of the migration aspects.

If a commit is related to issues in a tracker, the issue should be referenced in the footer as well, with the identifier of the issue in the tracker.

Here is an example of a feature related to the scope "trade feeding":

```
1 feat(tradeFeeding): Support trade feeding for negative-coupon
2 bonds
3
4 Some bonds have negative coupon rates, e.g. -0.21 percent.
5 Change the validation to not reject trades on bonds
6 with negative coupons.
7
8 Closes #8125
```

Specifying the Scope of a Change

The commit syntax shown earlier is semiformal, with a combination of keywords and free text. The first keyword, *type*, denotes the type of change (feature, fix, and so on) out of a small list. The second keyword, *scope*, denotes the scope of the change in the system or application and is specific to the context.

scope can cover various aspects of the system:

- **Environment:** Examples include `prod`, `uat`, and `dev`
- **Technology:** Examples include `RabbitMq`, `SOAP`, `JSON`, `Puppet`, `build`, and `JMS`
- **Feature:** Examples include `pricing`, `authentication`, `monitoring`, `customer`, `shoppingcart`, `shipping`, and `reporting`
- **Product:** Examples include `books`, `dvd`, `vod`, `jewel`, and `toy`
- **Integration:** Examples include `Twitter` and `Facebook`
- **Action:** Examples include `create`, `amend`, `revoke`, and `dispute`

A commit guideline could require a main scope, but you could add more, as shown here:

```
1 feat(pricing, vod): increase the rate on prime time
2 ...
```

Of course, you have to define a list of scopes, ideally as a whole team and including the three amigos, with everyone involved in the DevOps in close collaboration. Every change that could be committed to the source control should be covered in at least one of the scopes.

Keep in mind that a smart list of scopes opens the door to reasoning about impacts.

Machine-Accessible Information

A semiformal syntax for commit messages has the benefit of making it possible for machines to use these messages to automate more chores, such as generating a *change log* document.[11] Let's take a closer look at Angular.js, which provides a neat example in this area.

Under Angular.js conventions, the change log is made of three optional sections for each version, and each section is shown only when it is not empty:

- New features
- Bug fixes
- Breaking changes

The following is an excerpt from an Angular.js change log:

```
## 0.13.5 (2015-08-04)
### Bug Fixes
- file-list: Ensure autowatchDelay is working. (655599a), closes
#1520
- file-list: use lodash find() (3bd15a7), closes #1533
### Features
- web-server: Allow running on https (1696c78)
```

This change log is in the Markdown format, which enables links for convenient navigation between commits, versions, and ticketing systems. For example, each

---

11. "Keep a Changelog," http://keepachangelog.com

version in the change log links to the corresponding compare view in GitHub, show-ing the differences between this version and the previous one. Each commit message also links to their particular commits and also links to the corresponding issue(s), when applicable.

Thanks to this kind of structured commit guidelines, it is possible to extract and filter commits through command-line magic, as shown in the following example, borrowed from the Angular.js documentation:

```
1 List of all subjects (first lines in commit message) since
last release:
2 >> git log <last tag> HEAD --pretty=format:%s
3
4 New features in this release
5 >> git log <last release> HEAD --grep feature
```

The change log shown here can be generated by a script when doing a release. There are many open-source projects to do this, such as the conventional-changelog project.[12] This change log automation script relies strongly on the chosen commit guidelines, and it already supports several of them, including Atom, Angular, and jQuery.

Such automation is convenient, although if a human should review and edit the generated change log skeleton before release to the public.

Summary

It is often the case that elements of knowledge that are missing from a system are things that you want to be remembered. In particular, you should record the ration-ale behind decisions. You need to augment the code of a system to make it knowledge complete. Annotations, conventions, and other techniques are instrumental in this augmented code approach for recording the most important pieces of knowledge. And this process of augmented code is also an opportunity to spread skills to your workmates as a form of embedded learning.

---

12. https://github.com/ajoslin/conventional-changelog

Chapter 5

Living Curation: Identifying Authoritative Knowledge

The Queen's speech is like the release notes for a minor new version of the UK!
—Matt Russell (@MattRussellUK) on Twitter

Remember that most of the knowledge related to a system is already there in that system—and there is a lot of it. One crucial way to exploit all that knowledge is through curation. The idea of curation is to select the few relevant bits of knowledge out of the ocean of data in the system, in order to help people working on it in their future work assignments. Because this system is always changing, it is safest to ensure that this curation evolves naturally, without any manual maintenance.

Dynamic Curation

In art exhibitions, the curator is as important as the director in a movie. In contemporary art, the curator selects and often interprets works of art. For example, the curator searches for prior work and places that inspired the artist, and he or she proposes a narrative or a structured analysis that links the selected works together in a way that transcends each individual piece. When a work that is essential for the exhibition is not in the collection, the curator will borrow it from another museum or from a private collection or may even commission the artist to create it. In addition to selecting works, the curator is responsible for writing labels and catalog essays and overseeing the scenography of the exhibition to help convey the chosen messages.

When it comes to documentation, we need to become our own curators, working on all the knowledge that is already there to turn it into something meaningful and useful.

Curators select works of art based on many objective criteria, such as the artist name, the date and place of creation of the works, or the private collectors who first bought the works. They also rely on more subjective criteria, such as the relationships to art movements or to major events in history, such as wars or popular scandals. The curator needs metadata about each painting, sculpture, or video performance. When the metadata is missing, the curator has to create it, sometimes by doing research.

Curation is something that you already do, perhaps without being aware of it. For example, when you are asked to demo an application to a customer or to a top manager, you have to choose just a few use cases and screens to show in order to convey a message, such as "everything is under control" or "buy our product because it will help you do your job." If you have no underlying message, it's likely that your demo with be an unconvincing mess.

Unlike in art exhibitions, in software development what we need is more like a living exhibition with content that adjusts according to the latest changes. As the knowledge evolves over time, we need to automate the curation on the most important topics.

Therefore: Adopt the mindset of a curator to tell a meaningful story out of all the available knowledge in the source code and artifacts. Don't select a fixed list of elements. Instead, rely on tags and other metadata in each artifact to dynamically select the cohesive subset of knowledge that is of interest for the long term. Augment the code when the necessary metadata is missing and add any missing pieces of knowledge when they are needed for the story.

Curation is the act of selecting relevant pieces out of a large collection to create a consistent narrative that tells a story. It's like a remix or a mashup. Curation is key for knowledge work like software development. Source code is full of knowledge about many facets of the development, and different parts of it are of varying degrees of importance. On anything bigger than a toy application, extracting knowledge from the source artifacts immediately overflows our regular cognitive capabilities with too many details, and the knowledge becomes meaningless and therefore useless (see Figure 5.1).

Figure 5.1 *Too much information is as useless as no information*

The solution is to aggressively filter the signal from the noise for a particular communication intent; as the little buffoon monster in Figure 5.1 says, "Too much information is as useless as no information." What would be the noise from a particular perspective might be the signal from another perspective. For example, the method names are an unnecessary detail in an architecture diagram, but they might be important in a close-up diagram about how two classes interact, with one being an adapter to the other.

Curation as its core is the selection of pieces of knowledge to include or to ignore, according to a chosen editorial perspective. It's a matter of scope. Dynamic curation goes one step further, with the ability to do the selection continuously on an ever-changing set of artifacts.

Examples of Dynamic Curation

A Twitter search is an example of automated dynamic curation, and it is a resource in itself that you can follow just as you would follow any Twitter handle. People on Twitter also do a manual form of curation when they retweet content they have (more or less) carefully selected according to their own editorial perspective (perhaps). A Google search is another example of simple automated curation.

As another example, selecting an up-to-date subset of artifacts based on a criterion is something we do every day when using an IDE:

- Show every type with a name that ends with "DAO."

- Show every method that calls this method.

- Show every class that references this class.

- Show every class that references this annotation.

- Show every type that is a subtype of this interface.

When a tag is missing to help select the pieces, you should introduce it with annotations, naming conventions, or any other means. When a piece of knowledge is missing, in order to show a complete picture, you need to add it in a just-in-time fashion.

Editorial Curation

Curation is an editorial act. Deciding on an editorial perspective is the essential step. There should be one and only one message at a time. A good message is a statement with a verb, like "No dependency is allowed from the domain model layer to the other layers" rather than just "Dependencies between layer," where there is no message, and it's up to the reader to guess what is meant. At a minimum, dynamic curation should be given an expressive name that reflects the intended message.

Low-Maintenance Dynamic Curation

Selecting subsets of knowledge can be hazardous if done in a rigid way. For example, a direct reference to a list of classes, tests, or scenarios will rapidly become obsolete and will require maintenance. It is a form of copy and paste, and it makes change more expensive; it also is subject to the risk of someone forgetting to update it. This is not a good practice, and it should be avoided at all cost.

> **Caution**
>
> Avoid directly referencing artifacts by name or URL. Instead, find mechanisms to select pieces of knowledge based on criteria that are stable over time so that the selection will remain up-to-date without any manual action.

> **Key Concept**
>
> Select artifacts indirectly, based on stable criteria.

You can describe the artifacts of interest in a stable way by using one of the stable selection criteria described here:

- **Folder organization:** For example, "everything in the folder named 'Return Policy'"
- **Naming conventions:** For example, "every test with 'Nominal' in its name"
- **Tags or annotations:** For example, "every scenario tagged as 'WorkInProgress'"
- **Links registry over which you have control (which may need some maintenance from time to time, but at least it is in a central place):** For example, "the URL registered under this shortlink"
- **Tool output:** For example, "every file that has been processed by the compiler, as visible in its log"

When you use stable criteria, the work is done by tools that automatically extract the latest content that meets the criteria to insert it into the published output. Because it is fully automated, it can be run as often as possible—perhaps continuously on each build.

One Corpus of Knowledge for Multiple Uses

Everything can be curated—code, configuration, tests, business behavior scenarios, datasets, tools, data, and so on. All the knowledge available can be considered as a huge corpus, accessible via automated means for analysis and curated extractions.

Provided that the content of the knowledge corpus is adequately tagged, it is possible to extract by curation out of it a business view of a glossary (that is, a living glossary), a technical view of the architecture (that is, a living diagram), and any other perspective you can imagine, including the following:

- Audience-specific content, such as business-readable content only versus technical details

- Tasks-specific content, such as how to add one more currency

- Purpose-specific content, such as an overview of content versus a references section

Curation is possible only to the extent that metadata about the source knowledge is available to enable relevant selection of material of interest.

Scenario Digests

Curation is not just about code; it's also about tests and scenarios. A good example of dynamic curation is a scenario digest, in which the corpus of business scenarios is curated under various dimensions in order to publish reports tailored for particular audiences and purposes.

When a team makes use of BDD together with an automated tool such as Cucumber, a large number of scenarios are written in feature files. Not every scenario is equally interesting for everyone and for every purpose, so you need a way to do a dynamic curation of the scenarios, and for that you need to have the scenarios marked with a nicely designed system of tags. Remember from Chapter 2, "Behavior-Driven Development as an Example of Living Specifications," that tags are documentation.

Each scenario can have tags like the following:

```
1  @acceptancecriteria @specs @returnpolicy @nominalcase
@keyexample
2  Scenario: Full reimbursement for return within 30 days
3  ...
4
5  @acceptancecriteria @specs @returnpolicy @nominalcase
6  Scenario: No reimbursement for return beyond 30 days
```

```
7  ...
8
9  @specs @returnpolicy @controversial
10 Scenario: No reimbursement for return with no proof of purchase
11 ...
12
13 @specs @returnpolicy @wip @negativecase
14 Scenario: Error for unknown return
15 ...
```

Note that almost all these tags are totally stable and intrinsic to the scenario they relate to. I say *almost* because `@controversial` and `@wip` (work in progress) are actually not meant to last too long, but they are convenient for a few days or weeks for easy reporting.

Thanks to all these tags, it is easy to extract only a subset of scenarios, by title only or complete with step-by-step descriptions. The following are some examples:

- When meeting business experts who have very limited time, perhaps you could focus only on the information tagged `@keyexample` and `@controversial`:

  ```
  1 @keyexample or @controversial Scenarios:
  2 - Full reimbursement for return within 30 days
  3 - No reimbursement for return with no proof of purchase
  ```

- When reporting to the sponsor about the progress, the `@wip` and `@pending` scenarios are probably more interesting for this audience, along with the proportion of `@acceptancecriteria` passing green:

  ```
  1 @wip, @pending or @controversial Scenarios:
  2 - Error for unknown return
  ```

- When onboarding a new team member, going through the `@nominalcase` scenarios of each `@specs` section may be enough:

  ```
  1 @nominalcase Scenarios:
  2 - Full reimbursement for return within 30 days
  3 - No reimbursement for return beyond 30 days
  ```

- Compliance officers want everything that is not `@wip`. However, even in that case, they might want to have the big document show a summary of the `@acceptancecriteria` first and the rest of the scenarios in addendum.

Highlighting the Core

Some elements of a domain are more important than others. In the book *Domain-Driven Design*, Eric Evans explains that when a domain grows to a large number of elements, it becomes difficult to understand, even if only a small subset of the elements are really important. A simple way to guide developers to focus on particular subsets is to highlight them in the code repository itself. He calls that subset the *highlighted core*.

Therefore: Flag each element of the core domain within the primary repository of the model without particularly trying to elucidate its role. Make it effortless for a developer to know what is in or out of the core.

Using annotations to flag the core concepts directly in the code is a natural approach, and it evolves well over time. Code elements such as classes or interfaces get renamed, are moved from one module to another, and sometimes end up deleted. The following is a perfect simple example of curation by annotations:

```
1  /**
2   * A fuel card with its type, id, holder name
3   */
4  @ValueObject
5  @CoreConcept
6  public class FueldCard {
7     private final String id;
8     private final String name;
9     ...
```

It is an internal documentation integrated into the search capabilities of an IDE. You can see the list of all core concepts just by searching every reference of the annotation in the project, which is always up-to-date (see Figure 5.2).

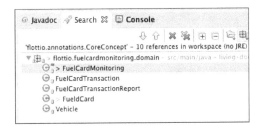

Figure 5.2 *The highlighted core is available instantly and at any time in the IDE through a search on all references to the @CoreConcept annotation*

And, of course, tools can also scan the source and use the highlighted core as a convenient and relevant way to improve curation. For example, a tool to generate a diagram may show different levels of detail in different cases, such as showing everything when there are fewer than seven elements and focusing only on the highlighted core when there are many more than seven elements. A living glossary typically uses this technique to highlight the most important elements in the glossary by showing them first or by printing them in a bold font.

Highlighting Inspiring Exemplars

The best documentation on how to write code is often the code that is already there. When I'm coaching teams on TDD, I pair-program randomly with developers on code bases I have never seen before. The developers pairing with me often behave as if they have never seen the code base before; for a new task, they might go looking for an example of something similar already there, and then they copy and paste it into a new case. A programmer might determine, for example, to find a service written by Fred, who is the team lead and is well respected by the rest of the team. However, Fred might not be great in every aspect of his code, and the flaws in his code may end up being replicated across the whole code base. In such situations, a good way to improve the code quality is to improve the examples of code that people imitate. Exemplary code should serve as a desirable model to imitate—or at least to inspire other developers. Sam Newman writes about this in his book *Building Microservices*:

> If you have a set of standards or best practices you would like to encourage, then having exemplars that you can point people to is useful. The idea is that people can't go far wrong just by imitating some of the better parts of your system.[1]

You can point your colleagues to the exemplars during conversations and during pair-programming or mob-programming: "Let's look at the class `ShoppingCartResource`, which is the most well-designed class and is exactly in the style of code we favor as a team."

Conversations are perfect for sharing exemplars, but some additional documentation can have benefits, too, when you are not present to point people in the right direction or when people are working on their own. You can use documentation to provide the equivalent of a big loud sign to signal a good examples (see Figure 5.3).

Therefore: Highlight directly in the actual production code the places that are particularly good exemplars of a style or of a best practice you would like to encourage. Point your colleagues to these exemplars and advertise how to find

---

1. Newman, Sam. *Building Microservices*. Sebastopol, CA: O'Reilly Media, Inc., 2015.

them on their own. Take care of the exemplars so that they remain exemplary, for everyone to imitate in a way that will improve the overall code base.

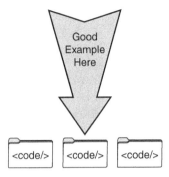

Figure 5.3 *Good example of code here!*

Annotations are, of course, a perfect fit here: You can create a custom annotation to put on the few classes or methods that are the most exemplary. Of course, exemplars are useful only if their numbers are limited to those that are very best.

Decisions on what code is exemplary or not are best made collectively by the team. Make it a team exercise to find a consensus on the few exemplars to highlight with a special annotation.

Exemplars should be actual code used in production, not tutorial code, as Sam Newman says in *Building Microservices*:

> Ideally, these should be real world services you have that get things right, rather than isolated services that are just implemented to be perfect examples. By ensuring your exemplars are actually being used, you ensure that all the principles you have actually make sense.[2]

In practice, an exemplar is hardly perfect in all aspects. It might be a very good example of design, but the code style might be a bit weak—or the other way round. My preferred solution would be to fix the weak aspect first. However, if that's not possible or desirable, you should at least clarify why the exemplar is good and what aspect of it should not be considered exemplary. Here are a few examples of exemplars:

- **On a class:** `@Exemplar("A very good example of a REST resource with content negotiation and the use of URI-templates")`

- **On a JavaScript file:** `@Exemplar("The best example of integrating Angular and Web Components")`

---

2. Newman, Sam. *Building Microservices*. Sebastopol, CA: O'Reilly Media, Inc., 2015.

- **On a package or a key class of this part of design:** `@Exemplar("A nicely designed example of CQRS")`
- **On a particular class:** `@Exemplar(pros = "Excellent naming of the code", cons = "too much mutable state, we recommend immutable state")`

Basically, marking exemplars directly in the code enables you to then ask your IDE something like "What code is a good example of writing a REST resource?" In an integrated documentation fashion, finding exemplars is only a matter of searching for all references of the `@Exemplar` annotation in your IDE. You can then just scroll the short list of results to decide which code will be the inspiration for your task.

Of course, there are caveats in the approach suggested before:

- Software development is not supposed to be as much copying and pasting as thinking and solving problems. Highlighting exemplars does not give you license to copy and paste code.

- Copying/pasting requires refactoring. As similar code accumulates, it must be refactored.

- Marking the exemplars in the code is not meant to replace asking colleagues for exemplary code. Asking questions is good because it leads to conversations, and conversations are key for improving the code and the skills. Don't reply "RTFM" ("read the flipping manual") when asked for exemplars. Instead, go through the suggested exemplars in the IDE together to determine which one would be best for the task. Always take conversations as opportunities to improve something mutually.

Guided Tours and Sightseeing Maps

It is easier to quickly discover the best of a new place with a guided tour or a sightseeing map. In a city you have never visited before, you can explore randomly, hoping to bump into something interesting. This is something I love to do during an afternoon within a longer stay, to get a feel of the place. However, if I have only one day and I want to quickly enjoy the best of the city, I take a guided tour with a theme. For example, I have excellent souvenirs from a guided tour of the old sky-scrapers in Chicago, where the guide knew how to get us into the historical lobbies to enjoy the low light that was typical of early light bulbs. One year later, I enjoyed an architecture boat tour of Chicago, from the river, which is another way to really grasp the city. In Berlin, I booked a tour dedicated to Berlin's street art, which was eye opening. For me, the same street art I see every day without really noticing gains another dimension when put in a context with one hint from a guide.

But guided tours start at a fixed hour on a few days a week only, often take a few hours, and may be expensive. If you happen to pass through a city on the wrong day, you are out of luck. But you can still get a tourist map or printed guided tours. And, of course, there is probably an app for that! Plenty of apps provide guided tours and sightseeing maps, classified by themes such as attractions, eat, drink, dance, and concerts. In Chicago, the Society of Architecture offers free architecture tours on leaflets, too. And the Internet is full of resources to help plan a visit, such as "Top 20 List of Must-See Highlights," "Itineraries to Help You Plan Your Visit," and "101 Things to Do in London."

> ### Note
>
> Sometimes these resources go a bit too far, as in the guided tour *Unusual and Original Things to Do in London*, for example, which has a stop for coffee in a public loo: As *Timeout London* says, "Don't worry, these beautifully converted old Victorian toilets were given a good scrub down before the plates of cakes were laid out. Opened in 2013, Attendant has a small bank of tables where the porcelain urinals once provided relief to gents about town."[3]

The process of becoming familiar with a code base can be similar to the process of becoming familiar with a city. The best way for someone to discover it is with another human—a colleague. But if you want to provide an alternative to a human guide, you can take inspiration from the tourism industry and provide itineraries of guided tours and sightseeing maps. This tourism metaphor comes from Simon Brown, who writes the blog "Coding the Architecture" and also wrote the book *Software Architecture for Developers, Volume 2*.

One important thing to realize is that all the tourism guidance in a city is highly curated: Only a very small subset of all the possible content of the city is presented, for various reasons ranging from the historical importance of different landmarks to more money-related reasons.

One important difference between a code base and a city is that a code base can change more frequently than most cities. As a result, the guidance must be provided in such a way that the work to keep it up-to-date is minimized; of course, automation is a good option here.

---

3. Timeout London, "Unusual and Original Things to Do in London," http://www.timeout.com/london/things-to-do/101-things-to-do-in-london-unusual-and-unique

Therefore: Provide curated guides of a code base, each with a big theme. Augment the code with extra metadata about the guided tour or a sightseeing map, and set up an automated mechanism to publish as often as desired an updated guide from these metadata. A sightseeing map or a guided tour based on tags in the code is a perfect example of the augmented code approach.

If the code base does not change much, a guided tour or a sightseeing map can be as simple as a bookmark with a list of the selected places of interest, each with a short description and a link to its location in the code. If the code is on a platform like GitHub, it is easy to link to any line of code directly. This bookmark can be created in HTML, Markdown, JSON, a dedicated bookmark format, or any other form you like.

If the code base changes frequently or may change frequently, a manually managed bookmark would require too much effort to keep up-to-date, so you might choose dynamic curation instead: Place tags on the selected locations in the code and rely on the search features of the IDE to instantly display the bookmarks. If needed, you can add metadata to the tags to enable reconstruction of the complete guided tour, simply by scanning the code base.

You might be worrying that adding tags about sightseeing maps or guided tours into the code will pollute the code—and you are right. These tags are not really about the tagged element intrinsically but about how it is used, so use this approach sparingly.

Consider your code base as a beautiful wilderness in the mountains where you go hiking. It is a protected area, and there are red-and-white hiking trail signs painted directly on the stones and on the trees. This paint does pollute the natural environment in a small way, but we all accept it because it's very useful and degrades the landscape only a limited amount.

Creating a Sightseeing Map

To create a sightseeing map, you first create a custom annotation or attribute, and then you put it on the few most important places that you want to emphasize. To be effective, you should keep the number of places of interest low—ideally 5 to 7 and certainly no more than 10.

It may well be that one of the most difficult decision here is to name each annotation or attribute. Here are some naming suggestions:

- `KeyLandmark` or `Landmark`
- `MustSee`

- SightSeeingSite
- CoreConcept or CoreProcess
- PlaceOfInterest, PointOfInterest, or POI
- TopAttraction
- VIPCode
- KeyAlgorithm or KeyCalculation

For the approach to be useful, you also need to make sure everybody knows about the tags and how to search them.

A Sightseeing Map Example in C# and Java

Say that in creating a custom attribute, you decide to put it into its own assembly to be shared by other Visual Studio projects (which also means you don't want anything to be specific to any particular project there). Here is how the attribute might look in C#:

```
1  public class KeyLandmarkAttribute: Attribute
2  {
3  }
```

You can now immediately use this attribute to tag your code:

```
1  public class Foo
2  {
3    [KeyLandmark("The main steps of enriching the Customer
4    Purchase from the initial order to a ready-to-confirm
5    purchase")]
6    public void Enrich(CustomerPurchase cp)
7    {
8      //... interesting stuff here
9    }
10 }
```

Java and C# are very similar. Here's the same example, now in Java:

```
1  package acme.documentation.annotations;
2
3  /**
```

```
4 * Marks this place in the code as a point of interest
worth listing on a sightseeing map.
5 */
6
7  @Retention(RetentionPolicy.RUNTIME)
8  @Documented
9  public @interface PointOfInterest {
10
11     String description() default "";
12  }
```

And now we can use it as follows:

```
1  @PointOfInterest("Key calculation")
2  private double pricing(ExoticDerivative ...){
3    ...
```

An alternative naming could look like this:

```
1  @SightSeeingSite("This is our secret sauce")
2  public SupplyChainAllocation optimize(Inventory ...){
3    ...
```

In C# you would use the custom attribute as follows:

```
1 public class CoreConceptAttribute : Attribute
2
3 [CoreConcept("The main steps of enriching the Customer
4 Purchase from the initial order to the ready to ship
5 Shipment Request")]
```

The wording is up to you, and you can use one generic annotation with a generic name like PointOfInterest and add the parameter Key calculation to tell precisely what it is about. Alternatively, you could decide to create one annotation for each kind of point of interest:

```
1  @KeyCalculation()
2  private double pricing(ExoticDerivative ...){
3    ...
```

Creating a Guided Tour

In the example shown in this section, the idea is to take a newcomer by the hand along the complete chain of processing of an incoming transaction, from the event listener on a message queue down to storing the outgoing report to the database. Note that even though it strictly separates the domain logic and the infrastructure logic, this guided tour spans both business logic elements with elements of the underlying infrastructure in order to give a complete picture of a complete execution path.

This guided tour currently has six steps, each of which is anchored on a code element that can be a class, a method, a field, or a package.

This example uses the custom annotation `@GuidedTour` with some parameters:

- **The name of the guided tour:** This is optional if there is only one tour, or if you prefer one annotation by guided tour, like `@QuickDevTour`.

- **A description of the step in the context of this tour:** This is in contrast to the Javadoc comment on the element, which describes the element for what it is and not necessarily for how it is used.

- **A rank:** The rank can be expressed as a number or anything comparable, and it is used to order the steps when presenting them to the visitor.

Here's an example of a guided tour:

```
1 /**
2 * Listens to incoming fuel card transactions from the
3 * external system of the Fuel Card Provider
4 */
5 @GuidedTour(name = "Quick Developer Tour",
6     description = "The MQ listener which triggers a full
7 chain of processing", rank = 1)
8 public class FuelCardTxListener {
```

It then goes through other steps, until the last one:

```
1 @GuidedTour(name = "Quick Developer Tour",
2     description = "The DAO to store the resulting
3     fuel card reports after processing", rank = 7)
4 public class ReportDAO {
5
6 public void save(FuelCardTransactionReport report){
7 ...
```

> **Note**
>
> Note that the numbering here is not consecutive; it goes from 1 to 7, but there are only 6 steps. In the good old BASIC line numbering style, you would number the lines 10, 20, 30, and so on to make it easier to add another step in between when you want to.

If you wanted to provide a simple selection of points of interest only for an audience of developers, you could stop here and rely on the user to do a search of the custom annotation to get the IDE to present the tour as a whole:

```
1  Search results for 'flottio.annotations.GuidedTour'
6 References:
2
3  flottio.fuelcardmonitoring.domain - (src/main/java/1...)
4  - FuelCardMonitoring
5    - monitor(FuelCardTransaction, Vehicle)
6  - FuelCardTransaction
7  - FuelCardTransactionReport
8
9  flottio.fuelcardmonitoring.infra - (src/main/java/1...)
10 - FuelCardTxListener
11 - ReportDAO
```

The recap is all here, but it is not pretty, and there is no ordering. This could be enough for a small list of the main landmarks that a developer can explore in any order desired, though, so do not discount the value of the integrated approach, as it is much simpler and may be more convenient than more sophisticated mechanisms.

However, this first case is not enough for a guided tour that is meant to be visited in order, from start to finish. So the next step is to create a living document out of it so that it is a living guided tour.

Creating a Living Guided Tour

Going further than in the preceding section, you can create a little mechanism to scan the code base to extract the information about each step of the guided tour and produce a synthetic report of the guided tour in the form of a ready-to-follow and ordered itinerary.

FuelCardTxListener
The MQ listener which triggers a full chain of processing.

Listens to incoming fuel card transactions from the external system of the fuel card provider.

FuelCardTransaction

The incoming fuel card transaction.

A transaction, between a card and a merchant, as reported by the fuel card provider.

FuelCardMonitoring

The service that takes care of all the fuel card monitoring.

Monitoring of fuel card use to help improve fuel efficiency and detect fuel leakages and potential driver misbehaviors.

monitor(transaction, vehicle)

The method that does all the potential fraud detection for an incoming fuel card transaction.

```
1  public FuelCardTransactionReport monitor(FuelCardTransaction
2  transaction, Vehicle vehicle) {
3    List<String> issues = new ArrayList<String>();
4
5    verifyFuelQuantity(transaction, vehicle, issues);
6    verifyVehicleLocation(transaction, vehicle, issues);
7
8  MonitoringStatus status
9    = issues.isEmpty() ? VERIFIED : ANOMALY;
9  return new FuelCardTransactionReport(
10   transaction, status, issues);
11 }
```

FuelCardTransactionReport

The report for an incoming fuel card transaction.

The fuel card monitoring report for one transaction, with a status and any potential issue found.

ReportDAO

The DAO to store the resulting fuel card reports after processing.

Note that in this guided tour, each title is a link to the corresponding line of code on GitHub. When the point of interest is a method (like the `monitor()` method), I include its block of code verbatim from GitHub, for convenience. In a similar fashion, when the point of interest is a class, I might include an outline of the non-static fields and the public methods if I find it convenient and relevant to the focus of the guided tour.

This living guided tour document is generated in Markdown, for convenience. Then a tool like Maven site (or sbt or any other similar tool) could do the rendering to a web page or in any other format. An alternative, as shown here, is to use a JavaScript library to render the Markdown in the browser, which requires no additional toolchain.

An alternative to using strings in the guided tour annotations would be to use enums, which take care of naming, descriptions, and ordering at the same time. However, this moves the descriptions of each step of the guided tour from the annotated code to the enum class, as you can see here:

```
1 public enum PaymentJourneySteps {
2   REST_ENDPOINT("The single page app call this endpoint with
the id of the shopping cart"),
3   AUTH_FILTER("The call is being authenticated"),
4   AUDIT_TRAIL("The call is audit-trailed in case of dispute
and to comply to regulation"),
5
6   PAYMENT_SERVICE("Now enter the actual service to perform
the job"),
7
8   REDIRECT("The response from the payment is sent through a
redirect");
9
10 private final String description;
11 }
```

This enum is then used as the value in the annotation:

```
1  @PaymentJourney(PaymentJourneySteps.PAYMENT_SERVICE)
2  public class PaymentService...
```

The Implementation of the Guided Tour

In Java you can use a Doclet-like library called QDox to do the implementation grunt work, which allows you to access the Javadoc comments. If you don't need Javadoc, then any parser and even pain reflection could work.

QDox scans every Java file in src/main/java, and from the collection of parsed elements, you can do the filtering by annotation. When a Java element (class, method, package, and so on) has the custom `GuidedTour` annotation, it is included in the guided tour. You can extract the parameters of the annotation and also extract the name, Javadoc comment, line of code, and other information (including the code itself, when necessary). You can then turn all that into fragments of Markdown for each step, stored in a map sorted by the step rank criteria. This way, when the scan is done, you can render the whole document by concatenating all the fragments in the rank ordering.

Of course, the devil is in the details, and this kind of code can quickly grow hairy, depending on how demanding you are with respect to the end result. Scanning code and traversing the Java or C# metamodel is not always nice. In the worst case, you could even end up with a visitor pattern. I expect that more mainstream adoption of these practices will lead to new small libraries which will take care of most of the grunt work for common use cases.

A Poor Man's Literate Programming

A guided tour is reminiscent of literate programming but in reverse: Instead of having *prose with code*, a guided tour has *code with prose*. For a sightseeing map, you only have to select the points of interest and group them by big themes. For a guided tour, you need to devise a linear ordering of the code elements. In literate programming, you also tell a linear story that progresses through the code and ends up with a document explaining the reasoning and the corresponding software at the same time.

A guided tour or sightseeing map is not just a documentation concern but also a way to encourage continuous reflection on your own work as you do it. It would therefore be a good idea to document a guided tour as soon as you are building the early walking skeleton of the application. This way, you will benefit from the thoughtful effect of doing the documentation at the same time of doing the work.

Summing Up: The Curator Preparing an Art Exhibition

As a concluding note on the topic of living curation, let's now go back to the approach of the curator in art exhibition, as illustrated in Figure 5.4.

The curator of an exhibition primarily decides on a key editorial focus, which often becomes the title of the event. Sometimes the focus is trivial, such as "Claude Monet, the Surrealist," but even in this case, there is an opiniated decision—to exclude prior art from the artist that was not yet Surrealism. Similarly, any documentation initiative must clearly deliver one key message.

Figure 5.4 *The curator in the museum*

Good exhibitions try to bring an element of surprise to create interest (for example, "You've always thought Kandinsky paintings are fully abstract, but we'll show
how the abstract shapes evolved from his prior figurative paintings."). Visitors come
not just to see the art pieces but also to expand their cultural awareness and better
understand relationships between artists, art pieces, and their era. Similarly, good
documentation adds value and new knowledge, with emphasis on relationships, by
offering a different perspective of things.

Selecting and Organizing Existing Knowledge

The curator selects art works based on the chosen editorial focus. Most of the pieces
available are left in the storage room, and only the few pieces of particular interest
for the exhibit are on display. Similarly, documentation is a curation activity that
involves deciding what's most important in a given perspective.

The curator decides which pieces to display in each room. A room may be organized around a time period, a phase in the life of the artist, or a theme. Art pieces
may be displayed side-by-side to suggest comparisons between them. They may be
displayed with an ordering that tells a story, chronologically or through a succession
of themes. Organization of knowledge is a key tool for adding meaning to a plain
collection of pieces of knowledge. We group elements by named folders, tags, or
naming conventions.

Adding What's Missing When Needed

The curator writes a few bits of text explaining the big idea of each section of the exhibition. She or he also writes a small label for each piece of art that is displayed on the wall directly next to the appropriate art piece. Similarly, documentation needs knowledge augmentation, which can occur through annotations, DSL, or naming conventions. Some limited amount of text can be useful in some places, too. This knowledge is attached to the related code elements whenever possible.

When a work considered essential for the art exhibition is not in the collection, it is borrowed or commissioned from the artist. The artist may also contribute to the organization of his or her pieces directly.

Sometimes some information is missing. The curator can have researchers conduct investigations or may request chemical analysis on the painting or by looking at written archives to find the missing piece in the puzzle. For example, the Louvre uses research results on the style of brushing colors on the canvas in order to tell visitors how much Raphael really participated in each of his paintings. And it reveals that the famous master did not touch many of them! In a similar way, documentation is a feedback mechanism that helps you notice when something is missing or wrong in the code or in the related knowledge.

Accessibility for People Who Can't Attend and for Posterity

The curator creates a catalog of the exhibition, which recaps all the content displayed: the explanative text by section, the art pieces as quality pictures, and their labels. The catalog as a book is usually organized in a way that is similar to the organization of the rooms in the exhibition venue.

Museums now sometimes offer expensive and heavyweight complete exhibition catalogs, and they also offer catalogs in a shorter form, with just a digest of the major pieces. I usually buy the shorter catalog, which is a more attractive read by far!

Documentation also involves making knowledge accessible and ensuring that the important pieces are persisted for the future. You may, for example, publish content as documents and on an interactive website, targeted for different audiences and different needs—much like the different catalogs published by the art museum.

Summary

Because the typical quantity of knowledge in any real-life code base is huge, any attempt at making use of it involves discarding most of it, through a process of curation that itself adds value to the curated knowledge by focusing on the essentials.

Living curation, inspiring exemplars, highlighting the core, and providing guided tours and sightseeing maps are some possible approaches to curation that can highlight a subset of knowledge for a particular purpose.

Chapter 6

Automating Documentation

As described earlier, living documentation does not necessarily require producing formal documents in order to deal with knowledge. However, there are a number of situations in which it is desirable to produce traditional-looking documents. In such a case, the most obvious example of documentation that is really "living" is documents that evolve at exactly the same pace as the knowledge they describe. You need automation to make living documents possible.

This chapter introduces two important, related concepts: using *automation* to help create *living documents*.

Living Documents

A living document is a document that is evolving at the same pace as the system it describes. It's prohibitively time-consuming to create a living document manually, so a living document is usually achieved through automation.

As the names suggests, *living documentation* relies a lot on living documents, which are required when other means of documentation cannot keep up with the pace of change, or are not accessible for the intended audience.

A living document works like a reporting tool that produces a new report after each change. A change is usually a code change but could also be a key decision made during a conversation.

This chapter presents a few key examples of living documents, including living glossaries and living diagrams.

Steps in Creating a Living Document

Creating a living document typically involves four main steps:

1. Select a range of data stored somewhere, such as source code in source control.

2. Filter the data according to the objective of the document.

3. For each piece of data that made it out through the filter, extract the subset of its content that is of interest for the document. It can be seen as a projection, and it's specific to the purpose of the diagram.

4. Convert the data and the relationships in the data into the target format to produce the document. For a visual document, this target can be a sequence of calls to the API of the rendering library. For a text document, it can be a list of text snippets consumed by a tool to produce a PDF.

If the rendering is very complex, the step of converting into another model may be multiple times—to create intermediate models that are then chained to drive the final rendering library.

The hard part in each step is the interplay between the editorial perspective and the presentation rules. What data should be selected or ignored? What information should be added from another source? What layout should be used?

Presentation Rules

A good document must follow particular rules, such as showing or listing no more than five to nine items at a time. There are also rules for choosing a particular layout—such as a list or a table or a chart—so that it is congruent with the structure of the problem. This is not a book on that topic, but some awareness of such presentation rules will help you make your documents more efficient.

Living Glossaries

How do you share the ubiquitous language of the domain with everyone involved in a project? The usual answer is to provide a complete glossary of every term that belongs to the ubiquitous language, together with a description that explains what you need to know about it. However, the ubiquitous language is an evolving creature, so the glossary needs to be maintained, and there is a risk that it will become outdated compared to the source code.

In a domain model, the code represents the business domain, as closely as possible to the way the domain experts think and talk about it. In a domain model, great code tells the domain business: Each class name, each method name, each enum constant name, and each interface name is part of the ubiquitous language of the domain. But not everyone can read code, and there is almost always some code that is not very related to the domain model.

Therefore: Extract the glossary of the ubiquitous language from the source code. Consider the source code as the single source of truth and take great care in the naming of each class, interface, and public method whenever they represent domain concepts. Add the description of the domain concept directly to the source code, as structured comments that can be extracted by a tool. When extracting the glossary, find a way to filter out code that is not expressing the domain.

As illustrated on Figure 6.1, the living glossary processor scans the source code and its annotations to generate a living glossary that will remain up-to-date because it can be regenerated as frequently as desired.

Living Diagram

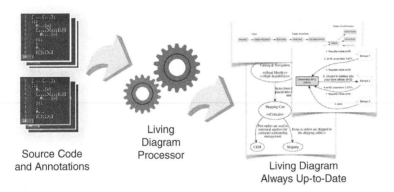

Source Code
and Annotations

Living
Diagram
Processor

Living Diagram
Always Up-to-Date

Figure 6.1 *Overview of a living glossary*

For a successful living glossary, the code must be declarative. The more the code looks like a DSL of the business domain, the better the glossary. Indeed, for developers there is no need for a living glossary because the glossary is the code itself. A living glossary is especially useful for nondevelopers who don't have access to the source core in an IDE. It brings additional convenience in being all in a single document.

A living glossary is also a feedback mechanism. If a glossary does not look good, or if you find it hard to make the glossary work, you know you have something to improve in the code.

How a Living Glossary Works

In many languages, documentation can be embedded directly within the code as structured comments, and it is good practice to write a description of what a class, an interface, or an important method is about. Tools like Javadoc can then extract the comments and create a report based on them. With Javadoc you can create your own Doclet (documentation generator) based on the provided Doclet, and it does not take a lot of effort. By using a custom Doclet, you can export custom documentation in any format.

Annotations in Java and attributes in C# are great for augmenting code. For example, you can annotate classes and interfaces with custom domain stereotypes (@DomainService, @DomainEvent, @BusinessPolicy, and so on) or domain-irrelevant stereotypes (@AbstractFactory, @Adapter, and so on). This makes it easy to filter out classes that do not contribute to expressing the domain language. Of course, you need to create a small library of annotations to augment your code.

If done well, these annotations also express the intention of the developer who wrote the code. They are part of a deliberate practice.

In the past I have used the approach just described to extract a reference business document that I could then send directly to a customer abroad. I was using a custom Doclet to export an Excel spreadsheet with one tab for each category of business domain concepts. The categories were simply based on the custom annotations added to the code.

An Example Please!

Let's look at a brief and oversimplified example of a living glossary about a kitten, because everybody loves kittens. The following code base in pseudo-code represents the main activities of a cat:

```
1  module com.acme.catstate
2
3  // The set of the main activities of a cat
4  @CoreConcept
5  interface CatActivity
6
7  // How the cat changes its activity in response to an event
8  @CoreBehavior
9  @StateMachine
10 CatState nextState(Event)
11
12 // The cat is sleeping with its two eyes closed
13 class Sleeping -|> CatActivity
```

```
14
15 // The cat is eating, or very close to the dish
16 class Eating -|> CatActivity
17
18 // The cat is actively chasing, eyes wide open
19 class Chasing -|> CatActivity
20
21 @CoreConcept
22 class Event // Anything  that can happen that matters to the cat
23 void apply(Object)
24
25 class Timestamp // technical boilerplate
```

This is just plain source code that describes the domain of the daily life of a cat. However, it is augmented with annotations that highlight what's important in the domain.

A processor that builds a living glossary out of this code will print a glossary like the following:

```
1  Glossary
2  --------
3
4  CatActivity: The set of the main activities of a cat.
5  - Sleeping: The cat is sleeping with its two eyes closed
6  - Eating: The cat is eating, or very close to the dish
7  - Chasing: The cat is actively chasing, eyes wide open
8
9  nextState: How the cat changes its activity in response to
10 an event
11
12 Event: Anything that can happen that matters to the cat
```

Notice that the `Timestamp` class and the `Event` method have been ignored here because they don't matter for the glossary. Also, each separate class that implements `CatActivity` has been presented together with the interface they implement, because that's the way we think about that particular construction.

> **Note**
>
> This is the state design pattern, and here it is genuinely part of the business domain.

Building the glossary out of the code is not an end to itself; from this first generated glossary you might notice that the entry `nextState` is not as clear as you'd expect it to be. (This is more visible in the glossary than in the code.) So you go back to the code and rename the method `nextActivity()`.

As soon as you rebuild the project, the glossary is updated because it is, after all, a living glossary:

```
1  Glossary
2  --------
3
4  CatActivity: The set of the main activities of a cat.
5  - Sleeping: The cat is sleeping with its two eyes closed
6  - Eating: The cat is eating, or very close to the dish
7  - Chasing: The cat is actively chasing, eyes wide open
8
9  nextActivity: How the cat changes its activity in response
10 to an event
11
12 Event: Anything that can happen that matters to the cat
```

Information Curation for Living Documents

The technique just described requires a parser for the programming language, and the parser must not ignore the comments. For Java, there are many options, including like Antlr, JavaCC, Java annotation-processing APIs, and several open-source tools. However, the simplest option is to go with a custom Doclet, and this is the approach described here.

> **Note**
>
> Even if you don't care about Java, you can still read on; the important information here is largely language agnostic.

In a simple project that covers only one domain, one single glossary is enough. The Doclet is given the root of the Javadoc metamodel, and from this root it scans all programming elements, including classes, interfaces, and enums.

For each class, the main question is "Does this matter to the business enough to be included in the glossary?" Java annotations can go a long way toward answering this question. If you use a "business meaningful" annotation, each class that has this annotation is a strong candidate for the glossary.

> **Caution**
>
> It is preferable to avoid strong coupling between the code that processes annotations and the annotations themselves. To avoid this coupling, annotations can be recognized just by their prefix (for example, `org.livingdocumentation.*`) or by their unqualified name (for example, `BusinessPolicy`). Another approach is to check annotations that are themselves annotated by a meta-annotation, such as `@LivingDocumentation`. Such a meta-annotation can itself be recognized by simple name only to avoid direct coupling.

For each class to be included, the Doclet then drills down the members of the class and prints everything that is of interest for the glossary, in a way that is appropriate for the glossary.

Selectively showing and hiding the relevant portions of the source code and grouping the related elements are critically important. If it weren't for this, the standard Javadoc would be enough. At the core of a living glossary are all the editorial decisions on what to show, what to hide, and how to present the information in the most appropriate way. It's hard to make such decisions outside a context. I won't tell how to do it step by step, but I do give some examples of selective curation:

- An enum and its constants
- A bean and its direct non-transient fields
- An interface, its direct methods, and its main subclasses that are not technical and not abstract
- A value object and its methods that are "closed under operation"[1] (that is, methods that only involve the type itself)

For a relevant glossary, a lot of details from the code usually must be hidden:

- You typically ignore all methods from the super-object, such as `toString()` and `equals()`.
- You typically ignore all transient fields because they are there just for optimization purposes and seldom mean anything for the business.
- You typically ignore all constant fields, except the *public static final* of the type itself, if they represent important concepts of the business.
- Marker interfaces often don't need to list their subclasses, and the same may be true for any interface that has only one method.

---

1. Evans, Eric. *Domain-Driven Design: Tackling Complexity in the Heart of Software*. Hoboken: Addison-Wesley Professional, 2003. See the section "Closure of Operations."

The selective filtering depends to a large extent on the style of the code. If constants are *usually* used to hide technical literals, then they should be mostly hidden, but if they are *usually* used in the public API, they may be of interest for the glossary.

Depending on the style of code, you can adjust the filtering so that it does most of the work by default, even if it goes too far in some cases. To supplement or deviate from this default filtering, you can use an override mechanism (for example, by using annotations).

For example, the selective filtering may ignore every method by default; in this case, you have to define an annotation to distinguish the methods that should appear in the glossary. However, I would never use an annotation named `@Glossary` because it would be noise in the context of the code. A class or method is not meant to belong to a glossary or not; it is meant to represent a concept of the domain or not. But a method can represent a core concept of the domain and be annotated as such with a `@CoreConcept` annotation that can be used to include the method in the glossary.

For more on curation, see Chapter 5, "Living Curation: Identifying Authoritative Knowledge." For more on the proper usage of annotations to add meaning to code, refer to Chapter 4, "Knowledge Augmentation."

Creating a Glossary Within a Bounded Context

In domain-driven design, a ubiquitous language can be defined with no ambiguity only within a given bounded context. If you are not comfortable with bounded contexts, don't worry; for this discussion you may replace the term *bounded context* with *module about a set of cohesive use-cases*.

If the source code spans several bounded contexts, you need to segregate the glossary by bounded context. In order to do that, the bounded contexts must be explicitly declared.

You can use annotations to declare the bounded contexts, but this time the annotations will be on modules. In Java they are package annotations, using the pseudo-class `package-info.java`:

```
1 package-info.java
2
3 // Cats have many fascinating activities, and the way they
4 // switch from one to another can be simulated by Markov
5 // chains.
6 @BoundedContext(name = "Cat Activity")
7 package com.acme.lolcat.domain
```

This is the first bounded context in the application, and you have another bounded context, again on cats but this time from a different perspective:

```
1  package-info.java
2
```

```
3 // Cats moods are always a mystery.
4 // Yet we can observe cats with a webcam and use image
5 // processing to detect moods and classify them into mood
6 // families.
7
8 @BoundedContext(name = "Cat Mood")
9 package com.acme.catmood.domain
```

With several bounded contexts, the processing is a bit more complicated because there will be one glossary for each bounded context. You need to inventory all the bounded contexts and then assign each element of the code to the corresponding glossary. If the code is well structured, the bounded contexts are clearly defined at the roots of modules, so a class obviously belongs to a bounded context if it belongs to a particular module.

The processing then proceeds as follows:

1. Scan all packages and detect each context.

2. Create a glossary for each context.

3. Scan all classes, and for each class, find out what context it belongs to. This can simply be done from the qualified class name (for example, `com.acme.catmood.domain.funny.Laughing`) that starts with the module qualified name (for example, `com.acme.catmood.domain`).

4. For each glossary, apply the selective filtering and curation process described above for building a nice and relevant glossary.

This process can be enhanced to suit your taste. A glossary may be sorted by entry name or sorted by importance of concepts.

Case Study of a Living Glossary

Let's take a close look at a sample project in the domain of music theory and MIDI. Figure 6.2 shows what you see when you open the project in an IDE.

There are two modules, each containing a single package. Each module defines a bounded context. The first one, which focuses on Western music theory, is shown in Figure 6.3.

The second bounded context, which focuses on MIDI, is shown in Figure 6.4.

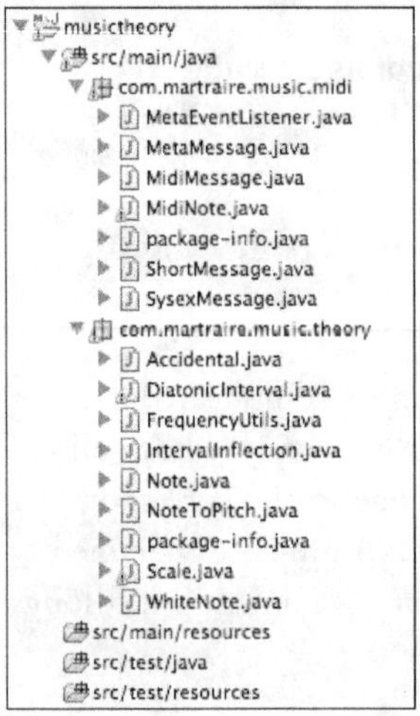

Figure 6.2 *Tree view of the code base*

```
/**
 * A representation of the theory of western music, from notes to chords, rhythm, harmony and melody.
 */
@BoundedContext(name = "Music Theory", link = "http://tobyrush.com/theorypages/index.html")
package com.martraire.music.theory;

import org.livingdocumentation.annotation.BoundedContext;
```

Figure 6.3 *Declaration of the first bounded context as a package annotation*

```
/**
 * Represents the MIDI concepts necessary for composing and recording sequences of rhythms and melodies.
 */
@BoundedContext(name = "MIDI sequencing", domain = "MIDI", link = "https://docs.oracle.com/javase/tutorial/sound
package com.martraire.music.midi;

import org.livingdocumentation.annotation.BoundedContext;
```

Figure 6.4 *Declaration of the second bounded context as a package annotation*

From the second bounded context, Figure 6.5 shows an example of a simple value object with its Javadoc comment and annotation.

From the first context, Figure 6.6 shows an example of an enum that is a value object as well, with its Javadoc comments, the Javadoc comments on its constants, and the annotation.

Note that there are other methods, but they will be ignored for the glossary.

```
package com.martraire.music.midi;

import org.livingdocumentation.annotation.ValueObject;

/**
 * Any message defined by the MIDI specification and that is sent over the wire.
 * There are several kinds of MIDI messages.
 */
@ValueObject
public interface MidiMessage {

}
```

Figure 6.5 *A value object with its annotation*

```
package com.martraire.music.theory;

import org.livingdocumentation.annotation.ValueObject;

/**
 * The accidentals alter the note by raising or lowering it by one or two half
 * steps.
 */
@ValueObject
public enum Accidental {

    /** (##) Lowered two half-steps */
    DOUBLE_SHARP("##"),
    /** (#) Lowered one half-step */
    SHARP("#"),
    /** No alteration */
    NATURAL(""),
    /** (b) Raised one half-step */
    FLAT("b"),
    /** (bb) Raised two half-steps */
    DOUBLE_FLAT("bb");

    private final String symbol;

    private Accidental(String symbol) {
        this.symbol = symbol;
    }

    public int halfSteps() {
```

Figure 6.6 *An enum with its annotation*

Starting with Something and Adjusting Manually

To create the living glossary processor, you need to create a custom Doclet that creates a text file and prints the glossary title in Markdown:

```
1  public class AnnotationDoclet extends Doclet {
2
3    //...
4
5    // doclet entry point
6    public static boolean start(RootDoc root) {
7      try {
8        writer = new PrintWriter("glossary.txt");
9        writer.println("# " + "Glossary");
10       process(root);
11       writer.close();
12     } catch (FileNotFoundException e) {
13       //...
14     }
15     return true;
16   }
```

What's left to implement is the method process(), which enumerates all classes
from the Doclet root and checks whether each class is meaningful for the business:

```
1          public void process() {
2              final ClassDoc[] classes = root.classes();
3              for (ClassDoc clss : classes) {
4                  if (isBusinessMeaningful(clss)) {
5                      process(clss);
6                  }
7              }
8          }
```

How do you check whether a class is meaningful for the business? Here you do
it only through annotation. In this case, you can consider that all annotations from
org.livingdocumentation.* mark the code as meaningful for the glossary. This
is a gross simplification, but here it's enough:

```
1  private boolean isBusinessMeaningful(ProgramElementDoc doc){
2    final AnnotationDesc[] annotations = doc.annotations();
3    for (AnnotationDesc annotation : annotations) {
4      if (isBusinessMeaningful(annotation.annotationType())) {
```

```
5       return true;
6     }
7   }
8   return false;
9 }
10
11 private boolean isBusinessMeaningful(AnnotationTypeDoc
                                       annotationType) {
12   return annotationType.qualifiedTypeName()
            .startsWith("org.livingdocumentation.annotation.");
13 }
```

If a class is meaningful, then you must print it in the glossary:

```
1  protected void process(ClassDoc clss) {
2    writer.println("");
3    writer.println("## *" + clss.simpleTypeName() + "*");
4    writer.println(clss.commentText());
5    writer.println("");
6    if (clss.isEnum()) {
7      for (FieldDoc field : clss.enumConstants()) {
8        printEnumConstant(field);
9      }
10     writer.println("");
11     for (MethodDoc method : clss.methods(false)) {
12       printMethod(method);
13     }
14   } else if (clss.isInterface()) {
15     for (ClassDoc subClass : subclasses(clss)) {
16       printSubClass(subClass);
17     }
18   } else {
19     for (FieldDoc field : clss.fields(false)) {
20       printField(field);
21     }
22     for (MethodDoc method : clss.methods(false)) {
23       printMethod(method);
24     }
25   }
26 }
```

This method is too big and should be refactored, but for the sake of this explanation I wanted to show it all on one page, as a script. As you can see, this method decides how to print the living glossary for each kind of element in the Java/Doclet metamodel (class, interface, subclass, field, method, enum, enum constant):

```
1  private void printMethod(MethodDoc m) {
2    if (!m.isPublic() || !hasComment(m)) {
3      return;
4    }
5    final String signature = m.name() + m.flatSignature()
6        + ": " + m.returnType().simpleTypeName();
7    writer.println("- " + signature + " " + m.commentText());
8  }
9
10
11
12 private boolean hasComment(ProgramElementDoc doc) {
13   return doc.commentText().trim().length() > 0;
14 }
```

You get the idea. The point is to have something working as soon as possible so you can get feedback on the glossary generator (your custom Doclet) and on the code as well. Then it's all about iterating: You change the code of the glossary generator to improve the rendering of the glossary and to improve the relevance of its selective filtering, and you change the actual code of the project so that it is more expressive by adding annotations and creating new annotations if needed so that the code tells the whole business domain knowledge. This cycle of iterations should not take a lot of time; however, it never really finishes and does not have an end state because it's a living process. There is always something to improve in the glossary generator or in the code of the project.

A living glossary is not a goal in itself. It's above all a process that helps a team reflect on its code so it can improve its quality.

Living Diagrams

Automation should make it easier to change code safely, not harder. If it's getting harder, delete some. And never automate stuff in flux.

—*Liz Keogh (@lunivore) on Twitter*

Some problems are difficult to explain with words but are much easier to explain with a picture. This is why we frequently use diagrams in software development for static structures, sequences of actions, and hierarchies of elements.

Most of the time we only need diagrams for the duration of a conversation. Quick sketches on a napkin are perfect for such a case. Once the idea has been explained or the decision made, you don't need the diagram anymore.

But you might want to keep some diagrams because they explain important parts of a design that everybody should know. Most teams create diagrams and keep them as separate documents, such as slides or Visio or CASE tools documents.

The problem, of course, is that a diagram will become outdated. The code of the system changes, and nobody has time or remembers to update the diagram. Consequently, it's very common for diagrams to be a bit incorrect. People get used to this and learn not to trust diagrams too much. The diagrams become increasingly useless until someone has the courage to delete them. From that point, it will require a lot of skills to look at the system as it is and try to recognize how it was designed and why. It becomes a matter of reverse engineering.

This is all frustrating, but the worst part is that important knowledge is lost in the process—and that knowledge was there at the beginning. Enter the living diagram: a diagram that you can generate again after a change so that it's always up-to-date.

Therefore: Whenever a diagram will be useful for the long term—for example, if it has already been used several times—you should set up a mechanism to automatically generate the diagram from the source code without any manual effort. Have your continuous integration trigger it on each build or on a special build that is run on demand at the click of a button. Don't re-create or update the diagram manually each time.

Diagrams Assist in Conversations

> Unexpected side effect of having a living diagram of the system: it makes development more tangible. You can point to things in discussions.
>
> —@abdullin on Twitter

Conversations and diagrams are not incompatible. Always being able to refer to the latest version of a diagram that reflects the current state of the software is a catalyzer of discussions.

One Diagram, One Story

When you create and maintain diagrams manually, given the time it takes, it's tempting to put as much as possible onto the same diagram to save effort, even if doing so is detrimental to its users. However, once diagrams are automated, there is no reason to make them more complicated. Creating another diagram is not so much effort, so you can create another diagram for each clearly identified purpose for an identified audience.

Diagram real estate is in limited supply, and so are the time and cognitive resources of its audience, which are the main reasons a diagram should convey only one message.

A document whose purpose is to clarify the external actors of a system for a non-technical audience should hide everything except the system as a black box and each actor with its nontechnical name and the business relationship with the system. It should not show anything about JBoss, HTTP, or JSON. It should not show components or service names. This selective perspective is what makes a document relevant or not. A document that tries to show different things at the same time requires more work from its audience and does not convey a clear message.

As illustrated with the funny poster in Figure 6.7, a living diagram should tell only a single story at a time. If you want to tell several stories, make one diagram for each of them. Remember: one diagram, one story.

Figure 6.7 *One diagram, one story*

Therefore: Remember that each diagram should have one and only one purpose. Resist the temptation to add extra information to an existing diagram. Instead, create another diagram that focuses on the extra information and remove other information that is less valuable for this new different purpose. Filter superfluous information aggressively; only the essential elements deserve to make it onto a diagram.

A related anti-pattern is showing what's convenient rather than showing what's relevant to an identified purpose. Remember the reverse-engineering/round-trip tools of the end of the 1990s? It was magical at the beginning, but eventually we all ended up with diagrams like the one in Figure 6.8 (or worse).

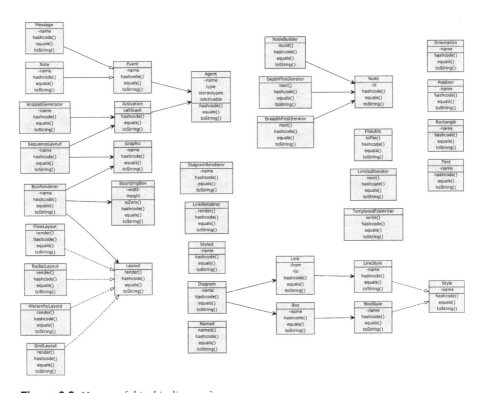

Figure 6.8 *How useful is this diagram?*

Too much information is like no information at all: It's equally useless. It takes a lot of serious filtering for diagrams to be useful! But if you clearly know the point of a diagram, you're already halfway there.

A challenge with living diagrams is filtering and extracting only the relevant data out of the mass of available data. In any real-world code base, a living diagram without filtering is close to useless; it's just a mess of boxes and wires that don't help anyone understand anything (refer to Figure 6.8).

A useful diagram tells one thing. It has a clear focus. It might show dependencies or hierarchy or workflow. Or it might show a particular decomposition of modules or a particular collaboration between classes, as in a design pattern. You name it, but you choose only one. Because a living document is automatically generated, it's easy to create one diagram for each aspect you want to explain; there's no need to try to mix them. Determining the focus of a diagram is an editorial decision.

Once the focus is chosen, the filtering step selects only the elements that really contribute to the focus and ignore the rest. Ideally there should be a maximum of seven to nine elements at this stage. Then, for each element, the extraction step extracts only the minimal subset of data that is really relevant for the focus. You should resist the temptation to show everything. If you've ever tried UML tools with magic round-trip mechanisms, you've seen what overly complex diagrams you can get.

Living Diagrams to Keep You Honest

It's important to store the code for a living diagram in the source control itself. You want to run it again and again, so that when the code changes, it's easy to generate an updated diagram. This generator could even become a plugin in the build tool that generates the latest versions of the diagrams during each build.

When a living diagram is part of a build, it provides another way to look at the current state of the code. You may have a look at it during code review, or during design meetings, or just randomly to see if everything is as expected. The biggest benefit from this kind of diagram is that it shows the code as it is, which can be a bad surprise. It keeps you honest about the quality of the design. As I discussed with Rinat Abdullin on Twitter, if you must code a new module on your own, an auto-generated diagram can be your first development feedback. And if you work with colleagues, another benefit of having a living diagram of the system is that, as Rinat said, "it makes development more tangible. You can point to things in discussions."

The Quest for the Perfect Diagram

There is a scale from traditional, manually crafted diagrams to perfect living diagrams, and each point along the way has a different level of automatic adaptations to change and requires a different level of effort. The lower in the scale, the less effort is required to produce one diagram but the more effort is required to update the diagram in reaction to changes. Here's what the scale of diagrams might look like:

- **Napkin sketch:** These throw-away diagrams are created using pen and paper. This type of diagram is perfect for the instant but disposable. There is no need for anything beyond a pen and a random piece of paper: the back of a letter, a napkin, whatever.

- **Proprietary diagram:** These diagrams look nice but take a lot of time to create and maintain. This is not the preferred option unless you want to do the layout manually, if you need more complete UML support, if you really want all the extra features the tools offer, or if you have to use these types of diagrams by law. They are time-consuming and editable only by people with the tool installed. They are hard to diff, they produce large files, and it takes time to adjust the layout and every graphical possibility.

- **Plain-text diagrams:** Plain text is easy to maintain, source control friendly and diff friendly. It supports find and replace operations, but you still have to maintain it. These diagrams are malleable, easy to change, and easy to diff. Some IDEs can propagate refactorings such as renaming to class names in text, which may help reduce maintenance, but this can constrain the text, too. ASCII diagrams are a particular flavor of plain-text diagrams.

- **Code-driven diagram:** You may author a diagram by using code rather than plain text. It could even be refactoring proof when a class is renamed (and the diagram is renamed, too) or removed (when the compiler tells you there is something wrong). These diagrams, which are more refactoring proof, are programmatic diagrams with dedicated code and/or application code (for example, driven by a DSL that includes references to code).

- **Living diagram:** The diagram is totally created from the code base or from the software system at runtime (see Chapter 7, "Runtime Documentation").

If you need a diagram only once and then you can throw it away immediately after use, choose a napkin sketch. On the other hand, if the knowledge is important enough to use over a period of time, choose another flavor of diagram from the spectrum. Choose one you feel comfortable with. For simple diagrams that won't change much except for a few additions, deletions, and renaming refactorings, I recommend plain-text diagram or code-driven diagrams.

If you need a beautiful diagram to convince or sell, then a generated diagram is probably not a good fit. Generated diagrams seldom look particularly attractive. As soon as the diagram becomes a stake in itself, it becomes worth doing it well, using the right tools to make it shiny. You may try commercial proprietary CASE tools, but you will eventually need to resort to graphical design tools or even calling a graphic designer to do the job.

LOL

"I know this diagramming tool is not friendly and you hate it, but you must use it, we have already bought an unlimited enterprise license, and there's a support team of four people to help!"

Rendering a Living Diagram

There are many possible ways to create diagrams using programming languages, and this topic could fill many other books, for various technologies and various contexts.

This chapter doesn't even try to cover them all but aims to give you a good idea of the process.

Remember that a diagram should tell a story. One story. It should hide everything that does not matter for the story. As a result, most of the work for a living diagram is in ignoring everything that is not central to the story. The story must be the sole focus of the diagram.

The generation of a living diagram depends on what kind of diagram you need to create, and it typically involves four steps:

1. Scan the source code.

2. Filter the relevant parts out of the huge number of elements.

3. Extract the relevant information from each part, including the few meaningful relationships that are relevant for the focus of the diagram.

4. Render the information using a layout that matches the focus of the diagram.

Let's look at a simple example. Say that you have a code base with many classes, some of which are related to the concept of order. You'd like to see a diagram that focuses only on the order-related classes and how they depend on each other.

The code base looks like this:

```
1  ...
2  Order
3  OrderPredicates
5  SimpleOrder
6  CompositeOrder
7  OrderFactory
8  Orders
9  OrderId
10 PlaceOrder
11 CancelOrder
12 ... // many other classes
```

First, you need a way to *scan* the code. You can use reflection or dynamically loading code for that. Starting from a package, you can then enumerate all its elements.

There are many classes in the domain model of this application, so you need a way to *filter* the elements you're interested in. Here you're interested in every class or interface related to the concept of order. For the sake of simplicity, you can do the filtering on all elements that contain "order" in their name.

Now you need to decide the focus of the diagram. In this case, say that you'd like to show dependencies between the classes, perhaps to highlight those that may be undesired. To do this, during the scan of all the classes and interfaces you will *extract* only their name and the aggregated dependencies between them. For example, you can collect all field types, enum constant, method parameters types and return types, and super types that constitute the dependencies of a class. You typically do this by using a simple parser for the Java language and with a visitor who walks through all declarations—imports, superclass, implemented interfaces, fields, methods, method parameters, method return, and exceptions—collecting all dependencies found into one set. You may decide to ignore some of them.

The last step is to *render* the diagram, using a specialized library. If you use Graphviz, you need to convert the model of classes with dependencies into the Graphviz text language. When that is finished, you run the tool and get a diagram.

Note

In this example, for each class with a name containing `Order`, you would have its name and its list of dependencies. It is already a graph that you can map to any graph rendering library, such as Graphviz.

There are many tools available for rendering, but not many of them can do a smart layout of an arbitrary graph. Graphviz is probably the best, but it's a native tool. Fortunately, it now also exists as a JavaScript library and is easy to include into a web page to render a diagram in a browser. And this JavaScript library has also become a pure Java library, graphviz-java![2] I used to use my old little Java wrapper dot-diagram[3] on top of Graphviz dot, but graphviz-java now seems like a better alternative.

A Word on Tools

Some tools and technologies that can help render a living diagram include Pandoc, D3.js, Neo4j, AsciiDoc, PlantUML, ditaa, Dexy, and many other not-so-well-known tools on GitHub and SourceForge. Creating a plain SVG file is an option, too, but you have to do the layout yourself. However, it may be a good approach if you can use it as a template, too, as you would do dynamic HTML pages with a template. Simon Brown's Structurizr is another tool.

---

2. graphviz-java, https://github.com/nidi3/graphviz-java

3. dot-diagram, https://github.com/cyriux/dot-diagram

> To scan the source code, you need parsers. Some parsers can only parse the metamodel, while others have access to the code comments. For example, in Java, the Javadoc standard Doclet or alternative tools such as QDox give you access to the structured comments. On the other hand, the excellent Google Guava ClassPath only gives access to the programming language's metamodel, which is enough in many cases.

Let's look at diagram types by layout complexity:

- Tables (which are perhaps not really diagrams, but they have a strict layout)
- Pins on a fixed background, like the markers on Google Map, which provide a way to map an (x, y) location for each element to pin on the background
- Diagram templates (for example, SVG, DOT) that are evaluated with the actual content extracts from the source code
- Simple one-dimensional flow diagrams (left-to-right or top-to-bottom), which are simple layouts you could even program yourself
- Pipelines, sequence diagrams, and in-out ecosystem black boxes
- Tree structures (left-to-right, top-to-bottom, or radial), which can be complicated but which you can do yourself if you really want to.
- Inheritance trees and layers
- Containment, which involves auto layout, for example using the cluster feature of Graphviz
- Rich layout, with vertical and horizontal layout as well as containment

Of course, if you want to be more creative, you can also try to turn a diagram into a piece of art, such as a photo collage, or even turn it into something animated or interactive.

Visualization Guidelines

Why do so many engineers think complicated system diagrams are impressive? What's truly impressive are simple solutions to hard problems.

—*@nathanmarz on Twitter*

The ultimate rule of thumb: if there is at least one line crossing another in a diagram, the system is too complicated.

—*@pavlobaron on Twitter*

There are rules for what makes a good document, such as showing or listing no more than five to nine items and choosing a layout or list style or a table or chart that is congruent with the structure of the problem.

To get the most from your diagrams, consider making everything meaningful:

- **Make the left–right and top-down axes meaningful:** Examples might include causality relations left-to-right, API on the left and SPI on the right, and dependencies top-to-bottom.

- **Make the layout meaningful:** For example, proximity between elements could mean "similarity," while containment could mean "specialization."

- **Make the size and color meaningful:** For example, the size or color of a visual element may reflect its importance, its severity, or the magnitude of some of its attributes.

Example: Hexagonal Architecture Living Diagram

The hexagonal architecture is an evolution of the layered architecture and goes further with respect to dependency constraints. The hexagonal architecture has only two layers: an inside and an outside. And there's a rule: Dependencies must go from the outside to the inside and never the other way round.

As shown in Figure 6.9, the inside is the domain model, clean and free from any technical corruption. The outside is the rest, in particular all the infrastructure required to make the software work in relation to the rest of the world. The domain is in the center, sometimes with a small application layer around it usually shown on the left. Around the domain model are adapters to integrate the domain model and ports that connect to the rest of the world: databases, middleware, servlets or REST resources, and so on.

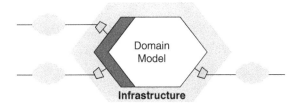

Figure 6.9 *Hexagonal architecture in a nutshell*

Say that you have to create documentation for a project that follows the hexagonal architecture, perhaps because the boss asked for it or because you'd like to be able to explain this nice architecture to a colleague. How do you do that?

The Architecture Is Already Documented

The first thing to realize is that this architecture is already documented in many places in the industry literature, starting with the website of Alistair Cockburn, who first described this pattern with the vintage diagram shown in Figure 6.10.

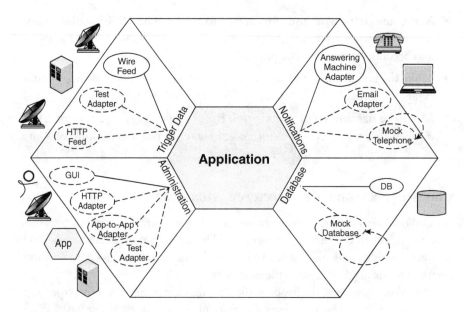

Figure 6.10 *Hexagonal architecture diagram from Alistair Cockburn's website*

This architecture pattern is also described in many books, including *Growing Object-Oriented Software, Guided by Tests* by Steve Freeman and Nat Pryce (GOOS), and *Implementing DDD* by Vaughn Vernon (IDDD). This pattern is also known in the .Net circles as the onion architecture, proposed by Jeffrey Palermo.

Because there is so much information about hexagonal architecture, there is no need for you to explain much about it yourself. You can just link to an external reference that already explains it well. Why try to rewrite what's been already written by someone else? This is ready-made architecture documentation.

The Architecture Is Already in the Code

The architecture itself is already documented in the literature, but what about its particular implementation in your custom project?

Because you're serious about your craft, the hexagonal architecture is already there in the code: The domain model is in its own package (respectively, namespace or project in .Net), and the infrastructure is in one or several other packages, clearly segregated from the domain model.

With some experience with this pattern, you can recognize it just by looking at the packages and their content. Such clean and strict segregation never happens by pure chance; it demonstrates a clear design intent. If you can recognize the hexagonal architecture just by looking at the code, you're done, right?

Well, not really. Not everyone knows about hexagonal architecture, and architecture is something everybody should be aware of. You need to make the architecture explicit in some way. It's 99% there already, but you need to add the missing 1% to make it fully visible to everyone. You need to do some knowledge augmentation, using annotations or naming conventions, both of which would work well here.

The naming convention is, in fact, already there:

- Every class, interface, and enum is in a package under the root package `*.domain.*`.

- Every infrastructure code is under `*.infra.*`.

You need this convention to be documented and, of course, stable.

You could use annotations instead of naming conventions. This would enable you or others to add more information, such as a rationale:

```
1  @HexagonalArchitecture.DomainModel(
2    rationale = "Protect the domain model",
3    alternatives = "DDD.Conformist")
4  package flottio.fuelcardmonitoring.domain;
5
6  import flottio.annotations.hexagonalarchitecture
7                          .HexagonalArchitecture;
```

Knowing What You Want for the Living Document

You can start figuring out what you expect by doodling on a napkin. What you want here is a diagram with a hexagon (or any other shape) at the center, representing the domain model with its most important elements inside. Outside and around this shape you expect to have every significant element of the infrastructure, with arrows showing their dependencies with the domain elements inside. It might look something like the diagram in Figure 6.11.

You want a layout that flows from left-to-right, from the calls to the API to the domain, and then to the service providers and their implementations in the infrastructure.

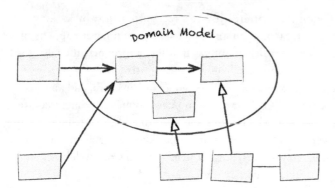

Figure 6.11 *A quick sketch of the kind of diagram you'd like to generate*

Where's the Knowledge Right Now?

As you've seen, the bulk of the knowledge about the hexagonal architecture is in the naming convention used with the packages. The rest of the knowledge is simply the list of every class, interface, and enum contained in these packages, along with their relationships.

A convenient convention when drawing hexagonal architecture is to have every element consuming the domain model on the left and every element providing services to the domain model on the right. How do you extract this information from the source code?

In the current application you have several opportunities for simplification: Every class that calls the domain model does so through its member fields, and every service provider integrates with the domain model by implementing one of its interfaces. This is a common situation, but it is not a rule; for example, a caller may be getting its response through a callback. In other cases, you may have to declare explicitly who's on the API side and who's on the SPI (service provider) side if you care about that in the diagram layout.

Filtering Out Irrelevant Details

Even in small projects, the source code contains a lot of information, so you always need to carefully decide what to keep *out* of the diagram. In this case, you want to exclude the following:

- Every primitive
- Every class that acts as a primitive (like the most basic value objects)
- Every class that is not related to other classes mentioned in the diagram

You want to include classes in the following fashion:

- Include all classes and interfaces within the domain model (apart from quasi-primitives such as units of measurement). Being in the domain model is a matter of naming convention, or of being in a package annotated as such.

- Include mutual relationships that make sense. You may want to fold type hierarchies into their supertype to save diagram real estate.

- Include infrastructure classes that have relationships with elements already included in the domain model.

- For each infrastructure class, include its relationship to the domain classes and between infrastructure elements, too. In order to have a directed diagram in the API-to-SPI direction from the left to the right, you need to help the renderer. For example you need to ensure that your *call* and *implement* relationships are in opposite directions in your generated diagram description: A *calls* B and A *implements* B must be in opposite directions. If you don't understand this now, that is no problem; you will understand it clearly as soon as you try to make it work by tweaking your rendering.

All this is just one example that works fine in one context. It is by no mean a universal solution for this kind of diagram. You should expect to try various alternatives, and you may have to filter more aggressively if your diagram gets too big. For example, you may decide to show only the core concepts, based on additional annotations.

Scanning the Source Code

For a living diagram like this one, all you need is a way to iterate through all the classes and the ability to introspect them. Any standard parser can do this, and you can even do it without any parser, just by using reflection. Because the focus is on the hexagonal architecture and nothing else, your focus is on segregating elements and highlighting the dependencies between them.

The example shown in Figure 6.12 uses standard Java reflection, with the help of the Google Guava ClassPath to scan the full class path conveniently. My own utility library DotDiagram is a convenience wrapper on top of the Graphviz DOT syntax to create the .dot files. Then it's up to Graphviz dot to do the auto-magical layout and rendering.

Working with Changes

Say that a month after you create the diagram shown in Figure 6.12, you are not happy with a name Trend for the domain interface, and you decide to rename it

`SentencesAuditing`. There is no need to update the diagram by hand; a new, up-to-date diagram showing the new name is generated on the next build.

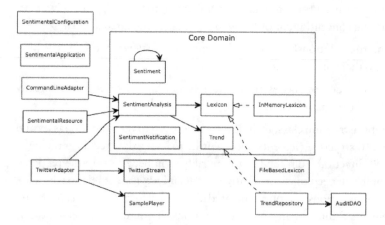

Figure 6.12 *Hexagonal architecture living diagram generated from source code*

Possible Evolutions

The hexagonal architecture constrains dependencies: They can only go from the outside to the inside and never the other way around. However, the living diagram shows all dependencies, even those that violate the rule. This is very useful for making violations visible.

It's possible to go even further and to highlight all violations in a different color, such as with big red arrows that indicate dependencies that are going the wrong direction. The line between a living diagram and static analysis to enforce guidelines is very thin.

You may have noticed that it's impossible to talk seriously about a living diagram without talking deeply about the purpose of the diagram—in other words, without talking about design. This is no coincidence. Useful diagrams must be relevant, and to be relevant when you're supposed to describe a design intent, you must really understand the design intent. This suggests that doing design documentation well converges with doing design well.

Case Study: A Business Overview as a Living Diagram

Say that you work for an online shop that was launched a few years ago. The software system for this online shop is a complete e-commerce system made of several components. This system has to deal with everything necessary for selling online, from the catalog and navigation to the shopping cart, the shipping, and some basic customer relationship management.

You're lucky because the founding technical team had good design skills. As a result, the components match the business domains in a one-to-one fashion, as illustrated in Figure 6.13. In other words, the software architecture is well aligned with the business it supports.

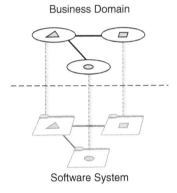

Figure 6.13 *Software components match the business domains one-to-one*

Because of its success, your online shop is growing quickly. As a result, there are an increasing number of new needs to support, which in turn means there are more features to add to the components. Because of this growth, you'll probably have to add new components, redo some components, and split or merge existing components into new components that are easier to maintain, evolve, and test.

You also need to hire new people in the development teams. As part of the necessary knowledge transmission for the new joiners, you want some documentation, starting with an overview of the main business areas, or domains, supported by the system. You could create it manually, spending a couple of hours in PowerPoint or in some dedicated diagramming tool. But you want to trust your documentation, and you know you'll likely forget to update a manually created document whenever the system changes—and you know it will change.

Fortunately, after you read a book on living documentation, you decided to automatically generate the desired diagrams from the source code. You don't want to spend time on a manual layout; a layout based on the relationships between the domains will be perfectly fine—something like what is sketched in Figure 6.14.

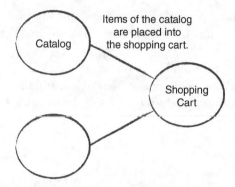

Figure 6.14 *Expected style of diagram*

Practical Implementation: The Existing Source Code

Your system is made of components that are simply Java packages, as shown in Figure 6.15.

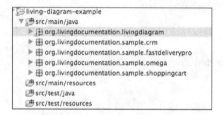

Figure 6.15 *Overview of the components as Java packages*

The naming of these packages is a bit inconsistent because historically the components were named after the development project code, as it is often the case. For example, the code that takes care of the shipping features is named Fast Delivery Pro because that's the name the marketing team gave the automated shipping initiative two years ago. This name is not used anymore, though, except as a package name. Similarly, Omega is actually the component that takes care of the catalog and the current navigation features.

You have a naming problem that is also a documentation problem: The code does not tell the business. For some reason you can't rename the packages right now, although you hope to be able to do it next year. However, even with the right names, the packages won't tell the relationships between them.

Augmenting the Code

As a result of the current naming problems in code, you need extra information in order to make a useful diagram. As you've seen before, one great way to add knowledge to code is to use annotations. At a minimum, you want to add the following knowledge to the code to fix the naming:

```
1  @BusinessDomain("Shipping")
2  org.livingdocumentation.sample.fastdeliverypro
3
4  @BusinessDomain("Catalog & Navigation")
5  org.livingdocumentation.sample.omega
```

You introduce a custom annotation with just a name to declare a business domain:

```
1  @Target({ ElementType.PACKAGE })
2  @Retention(RetentionPolicy.RUNTIME)
3  public @interface BusinessDomain {
4        String value(); // the domain name
5  }
```

Now you'd like to express the relationships between the domains:

- The catalog items are placed into the shopping cart before they are ordered.

- Then the items in orders must be shipped.

- These items are also analyzed statistically to inform the customer relationship management.

You then extend the annotation with a list of related domains. However, as soon as you refer to the same name several times, text names raise a little problem: If you change one name, then you must change it everywhere it is mentioned. To remedy this, you want to factor out each name into a single place to be referenced. One possibility is to use enumerated types instead of text. You can then make references to the constants of the enumerated type. If you rename one constant, you'll have nothing special to do to update its references everywhere. Because you also want to tell the story for each link, you add a text description for the link as well:

```
1  public @interface BusinessDomain {
2        Domain value();
3        String link() default "";
4        Domain[] related() default {};
5  }
6
7  // The enumerated type that declares each domain in one
8  // place
9  public enum Domain {
```

```
9   CATALOG("Catalog & Navigation"),
10  SHOPPING("Shopping Cart"),
11  SHIPPING("Shipping"), CRM("CRM");
12
13      private String value;
14
15      private Domain(String value) {
16              this.value = value;
17      }
18
19      public String getFullName() {
20              return value;
21      }
22 }
```

Now it's just a matter of using the annotations on each package to explicitly add all the knowledge that was missing from the code:

```
1   @BusinessDomain(value = Domain.CRM,
2           link = "Past orders are used in statistical
3           analysis for customer relationship management",
4           related = {Domain.SHOPPING}))
5   org.livingdocumentation.sample.crm
6
7   @BusinessDomain(value = Domain.SHIPPING,
8           link = "Items in orders are shipped to the
9           shipping address",
10          related = {Domain.SHOPPING})
11  org.livingdocumentation.sample.fastdeliverypro
12
13 //etc.
```

Generating the Living Diagram

Because you need a fully automatic layout that works like magic in all cases, you decide to use the tool Graphviz for the layout and rendering of the diagram. This tool expects a text file with a .dot extension that conforms to the DOT syntax. You need to create this plain-text file before running Graphviz to render it into a regular image file.

The generation process involves the following steps:

1. Scan the source code or the class files to collect the annotated packages and their annotation information.

2. For each annotated package, add an entry to the DOT file:

   • To add a node that represents the module itself

   • To add a link to each related node

3. Save the DOT file.

4. Run Graphviz dot at the command line by passing it the .dot filename and the desired options to generate an image file.

You're done! The image is ready on disk.

The code to do all this can fit inside a single class of fewer than 170 lines of code. Because you're in Java, most of this code is about dealing with files, and the hardest part of it is about scanning the Java source code.

After running Graphviz, you get the living diagram shown in Figure 6.16.

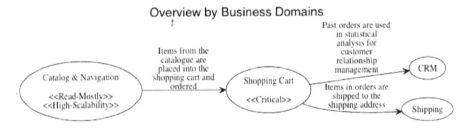

Figure 6.16 *Actual diagram generated from the source code*

After adding some additional style information, you get the diagram shown in Figure 6.17.

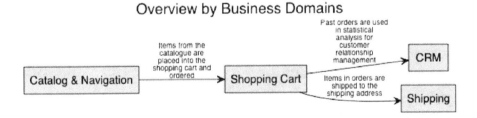

Figure 6.17 *Actual diagram generated from the source code, with style*

Accommodating Changes

After some time, the business has grown, and the supporting software system has to grow as well. Several new components have appeared—some brand new and some as a result of splitting existing components. For example, now you have dedicated components for the following business domains:

- Search & Navigation
- Billing
- Accounting

Each new component has its own package and has to declare its knowledge in its package annotation, like any well-behaved component. Then, without any additional effort, your living diagram will automatically adapt and produce the new, more complicated overview diagram shown in Figure 6.18.

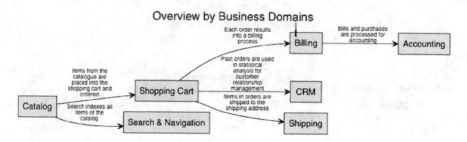

Figure 6.18 *The new diagram generated from the source code, some time later*

Adding Other Information

Now you'd like to enrich the diagram with concerns such as quality attributes. Because this knowledge is missing from the code, you need to add it by augmenting the code. You can once again use package annotations for that, as shown in Figure 6.19.

```
@Concern({ HIGH_SCALABILITY })
@BusinessDomain(value = SEARCH, link = "Search indexes all items of the catalog", upstream = { CATALOG })
package org.livingdocumentation.sample.search;

+ import static org.livingdocumentation.livingdiagram.Domain.CATALOG;
```

Figure 6.19 *Package annotations in package-info.java*

You can now enhance the living diagram processor to extract the @Concern information as well to include it in the diagram. After you do this, you get the diagram shown in Figure 6.20, which is obviously a little less clear than the previous diagrams.

Figure 6.20 *Actual diagram generated from the source code, with additional quality attributes*

This case study provides an example of what's possible with a living diagram. The main limits are your imagination and the time required to try ideas, some of which may not work. However, it's worth the time to try playing with ideas from time to time or whenever there's frustration about the documentation or about the design. Living documentation makes your code, its design, and its architecture transparent for everyone to see. If you don't like what you see, you need to fix it in the source code.

How Does the Living Diagram Fit with the Patterns of Living Documentation?

This diagram is a living document that is automatically refreshed whenever the system changes. If you were to add or delete a module, the diagram would adjust as quickly as the next build.

This case study provides an example of one diagram that tells a story from one node to the next through links that display brief descriptions.

This diagram is an example of augmented code, using annotations to augment each main module with the knowledge of its corresponding business domain. This is also a case of information consolidation spread across many packages.

Finally, the knowledge added to the source code can be used for an enforced guidelines about architecture. Writing a verifier is similar to writing a living diagram generator except that the relationships between nodes are used as a dependency whitelist to detect unexpected dependencies instead of generating a diagram.

Example: A Context Diagram

No system is an island; every system is part of a bigger ecosystem with other actors, typically people and other systems. From a developer's point of view, integration with other systems is sometimes considered obvious knowledge not worth documenting, especially in the early years of a system. But after a while the system grows and becomes deeply integrated with many other actors, and even people on the team no longer know about this ecosystem. To reconstitute the whole picture, you have to review all the code manually and interview knowledgeable people (who also happen to be very busy).

Context knowledge is essential for reasoning about impacts to or from other actors when considering changes in this system or in another external system. As such, it deserves to be made clearly visible and up-to-date at any time. Basically, a context diagram provides a recap of all actors using the system (API side) or used by the system (service providers side):

```
1  Actors using * --> System --> * Actors used
2  using the system              by the system
```

The context can be expressed as a simple list, like this:

- API (actors using the system)
  - Fuelo Card API
  - Fleet Management Teams
  - Support & Monitoring
- SPI (actors providing services to the system)
  - Google Geocoding
  - GPS Tracking from Garmin
  - Legacy Vehicle Assignment

But a visual layout has advantages too, as shown in Figure 6.21.

You can create such a diagram by hand each time you need it, tailoring it to the matter at hand. Or you could generate it.

The diagram shown in Figure 6.21 was generated from the sample Flottio fleet management system used in examples throughout this book. This diagram tells the story of the system through its links to external actors, with some brief descriptions on some of them.

System Diagram

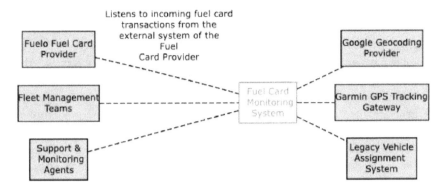

Figure 6.21 *A generated context diagram with three actors on the left and three actors on the right*

> **Note**
>
> The name *context diagram* is borrowed from Simon Brown's C4 model,[4] a lightweight approach to architecture diagrams that is becoming increasingly popular among developers.

This diagram is a living document that is automatically refreshed whenever the system changes. It is generated by scanning the augmented source code and calling a graph layout engine such as Graphviz. If you were to add or delete a module, the diagram would adjust as quickly as the next build. This diagram is also an example of a refactoring-proof diagram; if you want to rename a module in the code, the diagram will show it renamed, too, without extra effort. There is no need to fire up PowerPoint or a diagram editor each time.

Hyperlinks to the Corresponding Source Code Locations

Your living document can feature hyperlinks to the accurate locations in the code base. With these links, a user can click on any external actor on the diagram to jump to the corresponding URL in the source code repository online. (For this you can use one of the patterns for stable links from Chapter 8, "Refactorable Documentation.")

---

4. Simon Brown, Coding the Architecture blog, http://www.codingthearchitecture.com/2014/08/24/c4_model_poster.html

Note that even without a link, the wording in the diagram can be used verbatim to perform a search in the code base. Because the wording came from the code, it would be easy to find the corresponding location.

Applying Augmented Code and Knowledge Consolidation

The problem, of course, is to identify automatically the external actors and their names, descriptions, and directions of use (using or being used). Unfortunately, I haven't found a miracle solution for that.

To generate this diagram, the code has to be augmented with some annotations to declare the *external actor*. This is an example of augmented code and is also a case of consolidation of information spread across multiple packages and subpackages.

For example, the package flottio.fuelcardmonitoring.legacy takes care of the integration with the legacy system for vehicle assignments to drivers, a provider of services for the system under consideration:

```
1  /**
2  * Vehicle Management is a legacy system which manages which
3  * drivers is associated to a vehicle for a period of time.
3  */
4
5  @ExternalActor(
6    name = "Legacy Vehicle Assignment System",
7    type = SYSTEM,
8    direction = ExternalActor.Direction.SPI)
9  package flottio.fuelcardmonitoring.legacy;
10
11 import static flottio.annotations.ExternalActor
12                                    .ActorType.SYSTEM;
13 import flottio.annotations.ExternalActor;
```

Another example is the class listening to the incoming message bus, which basically uses the system to check whether fuel card transactions have anomalies:

```
1 package flottio.fuelcardmonitoring.infra;
2 // more imports...
3
4 /**
5 * Listens to incoming fuel card transactions from the
6 * external system of the Fuel Card Provider
7 */
8 @ExternalActor(
```

```
9    name = "Fuelo Fuel Card Provider",
10   type = SYSTEM,
11   direction = Direction.API)
12 public class FuelCardTxListener {
13   //...
```

You don't have to use annotations. You could also add sidecar files in the same folder as the annotation code, with the same content as the annotation inside, as a YAML, JSON, or .ini file:

```
1  ; external-port.ini
2  ; this sidecar file is in the integration code folder
3  name=Fuelo Fuel Card Provider
4  type=SYSTEM
5  direction=API
```

Say that at some point, you want to add information to the context diagram, so you add this information to the code itself, in the Javadoc of the integration code, and then the diagram gets updated as shown in Figure 6.22.

System Diagram

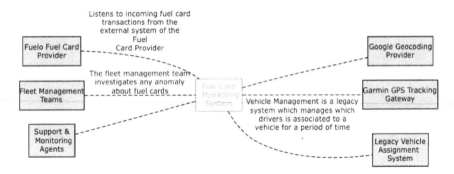

Figure 6.22 *A generated context diagram with three actors on the left and three actors on the right*

Limitations and Benefits of This Living System Diagram

Because of the need for some code augmentation with annotation files, there is a risk of not knowing about some external actors.

If in your project you can enumerate only a few ways to perform integration, you may try to detect them all and add them to the diagram unless silenced explicitly through code augmentation.

In any case, integration through the database will be hard to detect and document. You may believe the database is a private detail of your system, but if another system queries or writes into it directly, it will be hard to find out without a conversation with the culprits.

On the other hand, this diagram shows every potential integration, but it cannot tell whether the integrations are active in production. If the code base is a toolkit for a product line, it will show all the potential integrations—not just the one actually used in practice in a particular instance.

Another drawback of a generated diagram like the one shown in Figure 6.22 compared to an ad hoc manual diagram is that it is not tailored for the particular matter at hand. However, it's much faster to generate a diagram than to draw an ad hoc one.

Still, you may want to tweak the diagram generator—for example, to focus on a subset of the context.

The Challenges with Automated Generation of Design Documentation

Producing documentation of the design of a software project manually requires a lot of work and becomes obsolete very quickly after the next change or refactoring. Manually drawing meaningful UML diagrams is very time-consuming, and even choosing what to display takes a lot of time.

According to domain-driven design, the code is itself the model, but code lacks the ability to clearly express larger-than-class structures and collaborations. Therefore, some additional carefully selected design documentation is useful to show the bigger picture. And it can be generated from the code, as long as the code is augmented with the design intentions.

Using Patterns in Generating Design Documentation

The use of patterns to help with the process of generating design documentation is promising. Patterns naturally lie "on top" of the language elements. They address a particular problem within a context, discuss a solution, and have a clear intent. They involve a collaboration of several elements from the language, such as several classes and their protocols, or just relationships between fields and methods within a class. Each pattern is a chunk of design knowledge. When it comes the time to automate the description of the design, it seems natural to chunk the automation process by pattern as well.

In some projects, I've declared some of the patterns used in the code (using annotations) and created little tools to derive partial macro structures of the software design around these patterns. Each pattern come with a context, and this context helps in selecting what to show and how to show it. From the patterns declared in the code, the tool can then generate better-than-generic design documentation (for example, a diagram) informed by the knowledge chunked pattern by pattern.

So far, all the examples of living diagrams in this book have been generated from the source code at compile time, but this doesn't have to be the case; it's also possible to exploit runtime knowledge to produce them.

Summary

Living documents are great fun to produce and help bridge the gap between fast-paced projects and traditional documents that may still be desirable in some cases. The design diagrams, glossary, overview diagrams, and domain-specific diagrams described in this chapter illustrate the use of automation to produce smart documents.

But it isn't just automating diagrams that is important; deriving diagrams from known sources is also important so that when a diagram changes, the documentation does as well. As shown in this chapter, you need to augment the source code a little—for example, by declaring explicitly the patterns or design stereotype that you want to use through annotation or any other means of augmenting the code—to achieve reliable automation.

Chapter 7

Runtime Documentation

The Agile Manifesto calls for "Working Software over Comprehensive Documentation."

What if the working software were itself a kind of documentation?

It is already quite common to design the user experience so that the users can have successful interactions with an application without ever having to open the user manual. However, it's less common to design software so that its developers can understand it without even having to open the source code.

It is possible to learn the business domain just by using a related and well-designed application. The software is by itself a piece of documentation about itself and its business domain. This is why all the developers on an application should at least know how to use their application for most standard use cases, even if it is a complicated application that deals with complicated ideas (such as financial instruments).

Key Point

Anything that can answer a question can be considered documentation.
If you can answer questions by using an application, then the application
is part of the documentation.

In Chapter 6, "Automating Documentation," you saw several examples of living diagrams based on source code, but living diagrams can also be built from knowledge available at runtime. Let's look at this by using an example based on distributed tracing, which is typically used on distributed systems with multiple components.

Example: Living Services Diagram

Distributed tracing, based on Google's Dapper paper,[1] is becoming a vital ingredient of a microservices architecture. It's "the new debugger for distributed services," a key runtime tool for monitoring, typically to solve response time issues. But it's also a fantastic ready-made living diagram tool that can discover the living architecture of your overall system, with all its services, on a given day.

For example, the Zipkin and Zipkin Dependencies provide a services dependency diagram out-of- the-box, as shown in Figure 7.1. This view is nothing more than the aggregation of every distributed trace over some period (for example, for a day).

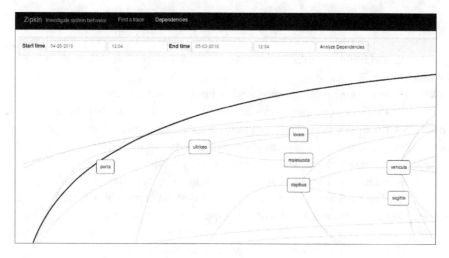

Figure 7.1 *Zipkin Dependencies diagram on screen*

A Matter of Augmented Code but at Runtime

For distributed tracing to work, you need to augment the system through *instrumentation*. Every service or component must use a tracer that conforms to the trace identifiers to declare the reception of a request, and the sending of the response, along with annotations, and additional "baggage" as a key/value store.

The trace identifiers involve a context made of three identifiers that enable you to build the call tree as an offline process:

- **Trace ID:** The correlation ID of a complete call tree
- **Span ID:** The correlation ID of this single client/server call
- **Parent ID:** The current parent call

---

1. http://research.google.com/pubs/pub36356.html

The span name can be specified, for example, with Spring Cloud Sleuth, using an annotation:

```
1  @SpanName("calculateTax")
```

Some of the core annotations used to define the start and stop of a client/server request are as follows:

- **cs:** Client start
- **sr:** Server receive
- **ss:** Server send
- **cr:** Client receive

The annotations may be extended to classify your services or to perform filtering. However, the tools may not naturally support your own annotations.

The baggage, or "binary annotation," goes further, capturing key runtime information:

```
1  responsecode = 500
2  cache.somekey = HIT
3  sql.query = "select * from users"
4  featureflag.someflag = FALSE
5  http.uri = /api/v1/login
6  readwrite = READONLY
7  mvc.controller.class = Application
8  test = FALSE
```

Here, all the tagging with metadata and other live data happens in real time. You might recognize that this approach is similar to augmented code. You need to inject some knowledge for tools to help more, and this augmentation happens at runtime.

Discovering the Architecture

The ability to inspect a distributed system in real time isn't just for front-end developers. As Mick Semb Wever writes on his blog, aggregating traces over time into a runtime service dependency graph "goes a long way to help architects and management to understand accurately how things work, negating much of the need for higher level documentation."[2]

---

2. Mick Semb Wever, The Last Pickle blog, http://thelastpickle.com/blog/2015/12/07/using-zipkin-for-full-stack-tracing-including-cassandra.html

The Magic That Makes This Work

Through sampling, some requests get instrumented as they go through each node of the system. The instrumentation generates span traces that are collected and stored in some central (logically) datastore. Individual traces can then be searched and displayed. A daily `cron` triggers then post-processes all the traces into aggregates representing the "dependencies" between services. The aggregation is something like this simplified example:

```
1  select distinct span
2  from zipkin_spans
3  where span.start_timestamp between start and end
4  and span.annotation in ('ca', 'cs', 'sr', 'sa')
5  group by span
```

The UI then displays all the dependencies using some sort of automated nodes layout.

Going Further

By getting creative on the tags and through test robots stimulating the system on predefined scenarios, a distributed infrastructure like Zipkin has a lot of potential for living architecture diagrams:

- You can create "controlled" traces from a test robot driving one or more service(s), with a specific tag to flag the corresponding traces.

- You can display different diagrams for the "Cache = HIT" and the "cache = MISS" scenarios.

- You can display distinct diagrams for the "Write part" versus the "Read part" of an overall conversation across the system.

Trying something in this area? Please let me know!

Visible Workings: Working Software as Its Own Documentation

Another idea related to *software as documentation* is to rely on the software itself to explain how it works inside, which Brian Marick calls *visible workings* and which involves making internal mechanisms visible from the outside.[3] There are many ways

---

3. Brian Marick, "Visible Workings": https://web.archive.org/web/20110202132102/http://visibleworkings.com/

to achieve this, and they all have in common relying on the software itself to output the desired form of documentation.

For example, many applications perform calculations for payroll or bank statements or other forms of data crunching. It is often necessary to describe how the processing is done for external audiences such as business people or compliance auditors.

You may think of visible workings approaches as an exporting or reporting feature that explains to end users the way it works internally. You want to be able to ask the software "How do you compute that?" or "What's the formula for this result?" and have it just tell you the answer at runtime. There should be no need to ask a developer to get the answer.

Visible workings are not often requested by customers, but they're a valid answer to a need for more documentation. Visible workings techniques are obviously very useful for development teams. Such a team should have full latitude to decide to add features to make its own life easier, since it's obviously one of the key stakeholders of its project. The key is to spend just enough time for the expected benefit.

Visible Tests

Good tests check the code against predefined assertions all the time. They are silent unless something unexpected occurs, such as a failed assertion or an error. However, I've found that tests can sometimes also be used to produce visible output such as diagrams in various domain-specific notations.

When starting in exploration mode, such as during a spike, when the problems are not clear and you're not sure how to solve them, it's hard to define accurate assertions. However, visible output provides fast feedback on whether it works as expected or not. Later, as the tests turn into non-regression tools, you can add actual assertions, but you may still decide to keep some of the visible outputs as a way to show what's happening.

Domain-Specific Notation

Many business domains have grown their own specific notations over time. Domain experts are comfortable with notation, usually doing it with pen and paper.

For example, for a supply chain, we tend to draw trees from the upstream producers to the distributors downstream, as shown in Figure 7.2.

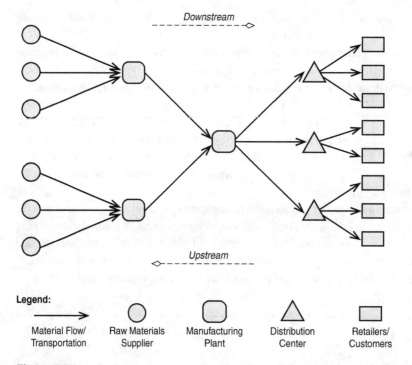

Legend:

→	◯	⬭	△	▭
Material Flow/ Transportation	Raw Materials Supplier	Manufacturing Plant	Distribution Center	Retailers/ Customers

Figure 7.2 *Supply chain tree*

For a stock exchange, we often have to draw order books when it is time to decide how the matching happens, as shown in Figure 7.3.

Bid Volume	Price	Ask Volume
	105.00	40
	104.50	30
	104.00	20
	103.50	10
10	103.00	
20	102.50	
30	102.00	50
40	101.50	
50	101.00	

Figure 7.3 *Order book for matching orders*

In finance, financial instruments pay and receive cash flows (amounts of money) over a timeline, which we draw using vertical arrows on a timeline, as shown in Figure 7.4.

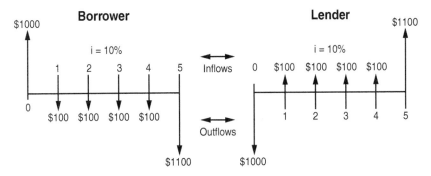

Figure 7.4 *Cash flows over a timeline*

Generating Custom Domain-Specific Diagrams to Get Visual Feedback

Long ago, at the beginning of a new project I used to create simple tests with no assertions that simply generated basic, ugly SVG files like the one shown in Figure 7.5.

Amortized Bond Coupons

EUR13469 at 20/06/2010
EUR13161 at 20/09/2010
EUR12715 at 20/12/2010
EUR12280 at 20/03/2011
EUR12247 at 20/06/2011
EUR11939 at 20/09/2011
EUR11507 at 20/12/2011
EUR11205 at 20/03/2012
EUR11021 at 20/06/2012
EUR8266 at 20/09/2012
EUR5450 at 20/12/2012
EUR2695 at 20/03/2013

Figure 7.5 *Generating an SVG file*

Compare the information shown in Figure 7.5 to the following spreadsheet table:

1	EUR13469	20/06/2010
2	EUR13161	20/09/2010
3	EUR12715	20/12/2010
4	EUR12280	20/03/2011
5	EUR12247	20/06/2011
6	EUR11939	20/09/2011
7	EUR11507	20/12/2011
8	EUR11205	20/03/2012
9	EUR11021	20/06/2012
10	EUR8266	20/09/2012
11	EUR5450	20/12/2012
12	EUR2695	20/03/2013

It's much easier to check the evolution of the amounts paid over time visually, using the diagram.

Of course, you could also dump a CSV file and graph it in your favorite spreadsheet application. Or you could even generate an XLS file with the graph inside programmatically; in Java, for example, you could use Apache POI to do this.

Figure 7.6 shows a more complicated example of a generated diagram, which shows how the cash flows are conditioned by market factors.

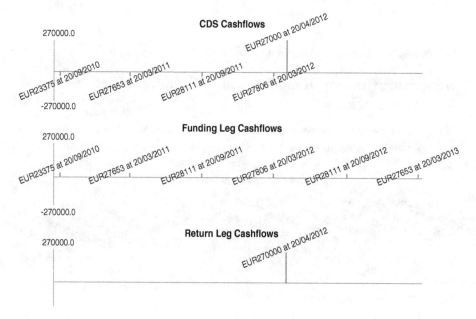

Figure 7.6 *Generating the SVG file for the cash flows of a more complicated financial instrument*

As you can see, I'm not an expert with SVG, and the figures here are just quick graphs to get visual feedback during the initial spike of a bigger project. You could use a modern JavaScript library to produce beautiful diagrams!

A Complement to Gherkin Scenarios?

I haven't tried it yet, but I'd love to have some key scenarios in Cucumber or SpecFlow produce such domain-specific diagrams in addition to the test results for their assertions. This sounds quite feasible, so if you happen to try it, please let me know!

Example: A Visible Test When Using Event Sourcing

Event sourcing is a way to capture all changes to an application state as a sequence of events. In this approach, every change to the state of an application (an *aggregate* in domain-driven design terminology) is represented by events that are persisted. The state at a current point in time can be built by applying all past events.

When a user or another part of the system wants to change the state, it sends a command to the corresponding state holder (the aggregate) through a command handler. The command can be accepted or rejected. In either case, one or more events are sent for everyone who is interested. Events are named as verbs in the past tense, using nothing but domain vocabulary. Commands are named with imperative verbs, also from the domain language.

We can represent all this in the following way:

```
1   Given past events
2   when we handle a command
3   Then new events are emitted
```

In this approach, each test is a scenario of the expected business behavior, and there is not much to do to make it a business-readable scenario in fluent English. So we are back to typical BDD goodness—without Cucumber!

Therefore: You need no "BDD framework" when you're doing event sourcing. In this approach, if the commands and events are named properly after the domain language, the tests are naturally business-readable scenarios. If you want additional reporting for nondevelopers, you can print the events and the command through simple text transformations in your event sourcing testing framework.

There are many benefits of using event sourcing, and one of them is that you get very decent automated tests and living documentation almost for free. This was initially proposed by Greg Young in various talks,[4] and Greg has made his related Simple.Testing framework available on Github.[5] This idea was later elaborated by Jeremie Chassaing.[6]

---

4. Greg Young, Skills Matter, http://skillsmatter.com/podcast/design-architecture/talk-from-greg-young

5. Simple.Testing, https://github.com/gregoryyoung/Simple.Testing

6. Jeremie Chassaing, https://twitter.com/thinkb4coding

A Concrete Example in Code

Let's consider an example of making (and eating) batches of cookies, taken from Brian Donahue on the CQRS mailing list[7] discussing Greg's approach:

Given: Batch Created with 20 Cookies

When: Eat Cookies: Amount = 10

Then: Cookies Eaten: Amount Eaten = 10, AmountRemaining: 10

For illustration purpose, I've created a similar very simple framework in Java.[8]

In this approach, and using this framework, the scenario is written literally in code, through the direct use of domain events and commands that form the event sourcing API:

```
1  @Test
2  public void eatHalfOfTheCookies() {
3    scenario("Eat 10 of the 20 cookies of the batch")
4      .Given(new BatchCreatedWithCookiesEvent(20))
5      .When(new EatCookiesCommand(10))
6      .Then(new CookiesEatenEvent(10, 10));
7  }
```

This is a test, and the "then" clause is an assertion. If no CookiesEatenEvent event is emitted, then this test fails. But it's more than just a test; it's also a part of the living documentation, since running the test also describes the corresponding business behavior in a way that is quite readable, even for nondevelopers:

```
1  Eat 10 of the 20 cookies of the batch
2          Given Batch Created With 20 Cookies
3          When Eat Cookies 10 cookies
4          Then 10 Cookies Eaten and 10 remaining cookies
```

Here the framework just invokes and prints the toString() method of each event and command involved in the test (aka scenario). It is as simple as this.

As a result, this is not as beautiful and "natural language" as text scenarios written by hand in a tool like Cucumber or SpecFlow, but it is not bad.

---

7. Brian Donahue, https://groups.google.com/forum/#!topic/dddcqrs/JArlssrEXIY

8. jSimpleTesting, https://github.com/cyriux/jSimpleTesting

Of course, there can be more than one event in the prior history of the aggregate, and more than one event can be emitted as a result of applying the command:

```
1  @Test
2  public void notEnoughCookiesLeft() {
3    scenario("Eat only 12 of the 15 cookies requested")
4      .Given(
5        new BatchCreatedWithCookiesEvent(20),
6        new CookiesEatenEvent(8, 12))
7      .When(new EatCookiesCommand(15))
8      .Then(
9        new CookiesEatenEvent(12, 0),
10       new CookiesWereMissingEvent(3));
11 }
```

This second scenario would print as the following text:

```
1  Eat only 12 of the 15 cookies requested
2          Given Batch Created With 20 Cookies
3          And 8 Cookies Eaten and 12 remaining cookies
4          When Eat Cookies 15 cookies
5          Then 12 Cookies Eaten and 0 remaining cookies
6          And 3 Cookies were missing (no more cookies)
```

This little framework is just a builder producing test cases using method chaining between the three methods Given(*Event...*), When(*Command*), and Then(*Event...*). Each method stores the events and command passed as parameters. Calling the Then() method at the end runs the full test and prints its text scenario by calling the toString() method of each event and command, prefixed with the keyword Given, When, or Then. When a keyword is repeated, it is aliased by And.

The method scenario(*title*) instantiates the SimpleTest class of the framework the way you want it to print and log. From there, you can elaborate to go further than just tests. For example, you might also use the knowledge from these tests to document the possible behaviors as living diagrams.

Living Diagrams from Event Sourcing Scenarios

In the example shown in the previous section, the test checks the behavior and prints a description of the business behavior in plain text that is readable by anyone.

There are several tests, each with different incoming events, commands, and out-coming events. The union of all these tests represents the use cases for the considered aggregate. This is often enough.

If you want to turn this test into diagrams, the event sourcing–based testing framework can collect all these inputs and outputs across the test suite in order to print a diagram of the incoming commands and the outgoing events.

Each test collects commands and events. When the test suite has completed, it's time to print the diagram in the following fashion:

```
1  add the aggregate as the central node of the diagram
2  add each command as a node
3  add each event as a node
4
5  add a link from each command to the aggregate
6  add a link from the aggregate to each command
```

When this is rendered with Graphviz in the browser, you get something like what is shown in Figure 7.7.

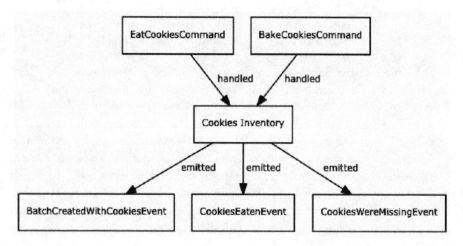

Figure 7.7 *The generated living diagram of commands, aggregate, and events for the cookies inventory aggregate*

You may or may not find this kind of diagram useful, and you can make your own based on this approach. This example illustrates that automated tests are a data source to be mined for valuable knowledge that can then be turned into a living document or a living diagram.

Note that the same content shown in Figure 7.7 could also be rendered as a table:

Cookies Inventory Commands
BakeCookiesCommand
EatCookiesCommand

Cookies Inventory Events
BatchCreatedWithCookiesEvent
CookiesEatenEvent
CookiesWereMissingEvent

You might also want to avoid mixing scenarios together, or you might decide to add more information to the same picture. You might, for example, remove the noise of the Event or Command suffixes. You can customize this idea for in your particular context.

Introspectable Workings: Code in Memory as a Source of Knowledge

At runtime, code often takes the form of an *object tree*, a tree of objects that you create by using new operators, factories, or builders or dependency injection frameworks such as Spring or Unity.

Often, the exact nature of the object tree depends on the configuration or even on a by-request basis, as illustrated in Figure 7.8.

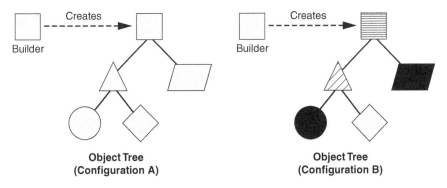

Figure 7.8 *An object tree at runtime may vary depending on the configuration or the request*

How do you know what the object tree really looks like at runtime for a given request? The regular way is to look at the source code and try to imagine how it will wire the object tree. But you would probably still like to check whether your understanding is correct.

Therefore: Introspect trees of objects at runtime in order to display the actual arrangement of objects, their object types, and their actual structure.

In languages like Java or C#, this can be done through reflection or through methods on each member of the structure to be introspected, as shown in Figure 7.9. The simplest form of this idea is to rely on the `toString()` method of each element to tell about itself and about its own members with some indentation scheme. When using a Dependency Injection (DI) container, you might as well try to ask the container to tell what it constructed.

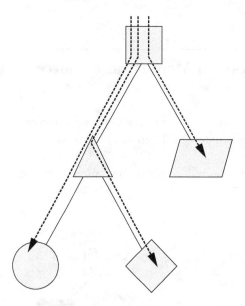

Figure 7.9 *Introspecting the object tree, from its root*

Let's look at an example of a little search engine of hip-hop beats loops. It's made up of an engine, at the root, that itself queries a reverse index for fast search queries. For indexing purposes, it also browses a repository of links contributed by users of the service, using a loop analyzer to extract the significant features of each beats loop to put into the reverse index. The analyzer makes use of a waveform processor.

The engine, reverse index, links repository, and loop analyzer are all abstract interfaces with more than one implementation each. The exact wiring of the object tree is determined at runtime and changes according to the environment's configuration.

Introspecting with Reflection

If it's an object, we can traverse it.

—*Arnold Schwarzenegger*

Introspecting a tree of objects is nothing but a trivial recursive traversal. From the given (root) instance, you get its class and enumerate each declared field because that's how classes store their injected collaborators here. For each collaborator, you carry out the traversal through a recursive call.

As you might suspect, you need to filter uninteresting elements that you don't want to include in the traversal—classes like strings and other low-level stuff. Here the filtering is just based on the qualified names of the classes. If an instance of a class that has nothing to do with the business logic is passed as a parameter, then you want to just ignore it. The following code snippet illustrates how to do that introspection while filtering uninteresting elements:

```
1  final String prefix = org.livingdocumentation.
visibleworkings.";
2
3  public void introspectByReflection(final Object instance, int
depth)\
4  throws IllegalAccessException {
5    final Class<?> clazz = instance.getClass();
6    if (!clazz.getName().startsWith(prefix)) {
7      return;
8    }
9    // System.out.println(indent(depth) + instance);
10    for (Field field : clazz.getDeclaredFields()) {
11      field.setAccessible(true);// necessary
12      final Object member = field.get(instance);
13      introspectByReflection(member, depth + 1);
14    }
15 }
```

With this code, if you just print each element with the proper indentation, the console displays the following:

```
1  SingleThreadedSearchEngine
2  ..InMemoryLinkContributions
3  ..MockLoopAnalyzer
4  ....WaveformEnergyProcessor
5  ..MockReverseIndex
```

This engine is a single-threaded one, and it uses an in-memory repository of contributed links, together with a mock of a loop analyzer and another mock of a reverse index.

With the same code, you can instead build a DOT diagram with each element and the proper relationships between them, as shown in Figure 7.10.

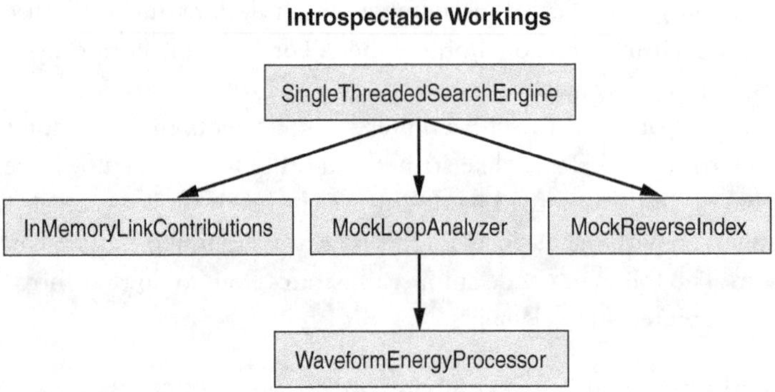

Introspectable Workings

Figure 7.10 *Introspecting the object tree, in practice*

This diagram shows the same information as the text in the console we had before, but the visible relationship could show additional information.

Introspecting Without Reflection

To introspect an object tree without using reflection, all the objects in the tree must exhibit an accessible way to enumerate their collaborators. You could accomplish this with public fields, but I do not recommend that. Instead, they can expose a public method that returns the list of their members.

In the simplest case, every element would implement some interface like `Introspectable`, becoming an instance of the composite pattern:

```
1   interface Introspectable {
2     Collection<?> members();
3   }
```

Thus the traversal of the tree would again be nothing but the recursive traversal of the composite:

```
1   private void traverseComposite(Object instance, int depth) {
2     final String name = instance.getClass().getName();
3     // Add this node to the diagram
4     digraph.addNode(name).setLabel(instance.toString());
```

```
5    if (!(instance instanceof Introspectable)) {
6        return;
7    }
8    final Introspectable introspectable = (Introspectable)
instance;
9    for (Object member : introspectable.members()) {
10       traverseComposite(member, depth + 1);
11       // Add the relationship from this node to its member to
the diagram
12       digraph.addAssociation(name, member.getClass().
getName());
13   }
14 }
```

Obviously, this approach produces exactly the same output you get by using reflection.

Which approach should you choose? If all the objects are created by the team and there aren't too many of them, I recommend the composite flavor, as long as it doesn't pollute the classes too much.

In all other cases, the approach of introspection by reflection is the best or only choice. This approach helps make the inner workings visible. In the case of a workflow, decision tree, or decision table that is built on the fly for each given business request, introspectable workings is a way to make the particular structure that was built visible for users and developers alike.

Sometimes, however, you don't need any introspection at all. When the processing is driven by a configuration, hardcoded, or from a file or from a database, displaying the workings may be simplified a lot, as this is just a way to display the configuration in a nice way. At a minimum, every workflow or processing that is driven by a configuration should be able to display the configuration that is used for a particular type of processing.

Summary

Because some knowledge is much more easily accessible when the source code is executed at runtime than from the static artifacts in the source code repository, working software can, and should, be considered a source of truth for documentation purposes. And with distributed architecture and cloud infrastructure becoming more prevalent, so will the opportunities for exploiting runtime knowledge that is also accessible by machines for better living documentation.

Chapter 8

Refactorable Documentation

Living documents are documents that are automatically generated using up-to-date knowledge from an authoritative source. In contrast, documents created using proprietary tools must be updated manually, which is tedious. Between these two extreme cases are *refactorable documents*, which must be manually updated but in a smart way, thanks to automation tools that reduce the labor-intensive burden.

For text documents, one example of a tool that enables refactorability is the Find and Replace feature of most text editors, which makes it easy to consistently change a word used in a large document. For example, this can be appealing for maintaining diagrams that change only from time to time, where each word is referenced multiple times because of the links between the words.

But the prominent example of a tool that enables refactorability is source code and the automated refactorings that apply on it. Developers spend a lot of time reading code and trying to get knowledge out of it. If you think of code specifically for its documentation value, then it becomes a key ingredient in your living documentation, an ingredient that embraces change very well.

Automated refactoring is one of the primary ways of changing a software system. In healthy projects, this process is used all the time. When renaming a class or a method somewhere, an automated refactoring tool updates the declaration and every instance of its use throughout the project—instantly. Moving a type to another module, adding a parameter to a function signature, and extracting a function out of a block of code are just a few transformations that tools do automatically. This refactoring automation, combined with tests, enables teams to make changes, including big changes, very frequently because the tools remove the pain.

Refactoring all the time is a good thing, even if it can be seen as a challenge for traditional documentation. Living documentation embraces continuous refactoring and involves documentation approaches that leverage the power of automated refactorings instead of resisting them.

Code as Documentation

Programs are meant to be read by humans and only incidentally for computers to execute.

—*Harold Abelson, Gerald Jay Sussman, and Julie Sussman, Structure and Interpretation of Computer Programs*

That, yes, but more. The source code is also the ONLY document in whatever collection you may have that is guaranteed to reflect reality exactly. As such, it is the only design document that is known to be true. The thoughts, dreams, and fantasies of the designer are only real insofar as they are in the code. The pictures in the reams of UML are only veridical insofar as they are in the code. The source code is the design in a way that no other document can claim. One other thought: maybe gloss isn't in the writing, maybe it's in the reading.[1]

—*Ron Jeffries*

Most of the time, code is its own documentation. Code is written for machines, of course, but code is also written so that human beings can understand it for its maintenance and evolution.

It takes a lot of skills and techniques to improve the ability of code to be quickly and clearly understood by people. It's a core topic in the software crafters community, and there have been many books, articles, and conference talks on the topic, which this book is not meant to replace. Instead it focuses on a few practices and techniques that are especially relevant, typical, or original with respect to the idea of code being documentation itself. As Chris Epstein once said during a talk, "Be kind to your future self." Learning how to make code easy to understand will be a big bonus for your future self.

Many books have been written on writing code that is easy to read. Of particular importance are *Clean Code* by Robert Cecil Martin (commonly referred to as Uncle Bob) and *Implementation Patterns* by Kent Beck. Kent advocates asking yourself, "What do I want to say to someone when they read this code?" and "What will the computer do with this code?" and "How can I communicate what I am thinking to people?"[2]

---

1. http://wiki.c2.com/?WhatIsSoftwareDesign
2. Beck, Kent. *Implementation Patterns*. Hoboken: Addison-Wesley Professional, 2007.

Text Layout

We usually think of code as a linear medium, but code is itself a graphical arrangement of characters in the two-dimensional space of a text editor. This 2D layout of the code can be used to express meaning.

The most common examples of text layout are the guidelines on the ordering of the members of a class:

- Class declaration
- Fields
- Constructors and methods

With this ordering, even as the class is declared as plain text, there is a visual aspect implied by the layering of the blocks of text on the page. This is not that far from how a class is visually represented in UML (see Figure 8.1). The main difference between code layout and visual notation is the absence of the border lines around the blocks of text in the code.

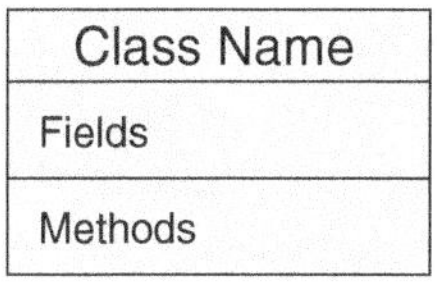

Class Name
Fields
Methods

Figure 8.1 *UML visual notation for a class*

The following sections look at other cases of code layout.

Tabular Code Layout

Take the example of a socket considered as a state machine. This state machine can be fully described through its *state transition table*, which can be expressed literally as code. In this case, the layout really matters, including the vertical alignment of the current states, the transitions, and the next states, as shown in Figure 8.2.

This type of layout is easy to do with code, except that the automatic code formatting of the IDE may often break this alignment. Putting an empty comments section (/ * * /) at the beginning of a line can prevent the formatter from reordering the lines, but it's hard to preserve the whitespace. Of course, this all depends on your IDE and its capabilities to autoformat in a smarter way.

```
public static enum State {
    CREATED, OPEN, CLOSE;
}

public static enum Action {
    CREATE, CONNECT, CLOSE;
}

public Object[][] socketStableTransitionTable() {
    final Object[][] stableTransitionTable = {
    //state,         action,        next state
    { State.CLOSE,   Action.CREATE,  State.CREATED },
    { State.CREATED, Action.CONNECT, State.OPEN },
    { State.OPEN,    Action.CLOSE,   State.CLOSE }};
    return stableTransitionTable;
}

@Test
public void testSocketStateMachine() {
```

Figure 8.2 *The transition table of a socket as a state machine with its expressive code layout*

Arrange–Act–Assert

Unit tests offer examples of how the 2D graphical layout of code can be used to express meaning. The Arrange–Act–Assert convention advocates organizing code in three different sections, each below the previous one, as shown in Figure 8.3.

```
@Test
public void aaa_distance_4km2_between_centre_pompidou_and_Eiffel_Tower() throws Exception {
    // Arrange
    final Coordinates centrePompidou = new Coordinates(48.8608333, 2.3516667);
    final Coordinates eiffelTower = new Coordinates(48.858222, 2.2945);

    // Act
    final double distance = GeoDistance.EQUIRECTANGULAR.distanceBetween(centrePompidou, eiffelTower);

    // Assert
    assertEquals(4190, distance, 10);
}
```

Figure 8.3 *The convention Arrange–Act–Assert in a unit test*

When you're familiar with this convention, the vertical layout makes it graphically obvious what each section is doing. You can tell just by looking at the composition of text versus whitespace.

Another convention in unit tests involves considering that a unit test matches a given expression on the left with another expression on the right. In this approach, the horizontal layout is meaningful: You want the full assertion on one single line, with the two expressions on both sides of the assertion, as shown in the example in Figure 8.4.

```
@Test
public void distance_4km2_between_centre_pompidou_and_Eiffel_Tower() throws Exception {
    assertEquals(4190, GeoDistance.EQUIRECTANGULAR.distanceBetween(CENTRE_POMPIDOU, EIFFEL_TOWER), 10);
}
```

Figure 8.4 *A test is about matching the expressions on the left with the expression on the right*

Much more could be said about various possible ways to organize code graphically, but this section is just meant to draw your attention to this universe of possibilities.

Coding Conventions

Programming has always relied on conventions to convey additional meaning in the code. The programming language syntax does a lot of the job. For example, in C# and Java, it's easy to recognize the method `play()` from the variable `play` because methods end in parentheses. But the parentheses are not enough to indicate the difference between class identifiers and variable identifiers. As a result, we rely on naming conventions, such as particular uses of lowercase and uppercase, to quickly distinguish between class names and variable names. Such conventions are so ubiquitous that they can be considered mandatory.

For example, in Java, class names must be in mixed case, with the first letter of each internal word capitalized (for example, `StringBuilder`). This convention is sometime called *CamelCase*. Instance variables follow the same convention except that they must start with a lowercase first letter (for example, `myStringBuilder`). Constants, on the other hand, should be all uppercase with words separated by underscores (for example, `DAYS_IN_WEEK`). When you are familiar with such conventions, you don't need to think too hard about them, and you instantly recognize classes, variables, and constants based on their case.

Note that the standard Java and C# notations are redundant with the coloring and syntax highlighting of your IDE (instance variables are blue, static variables are underlined, and so on). So, in theory, you should not even need the naming convention any longer.

The Hungarian notation is an extreme example of using a naming convention to store information. In it, the name of a variable or function indicates the type or intended use of that variable or function. The idea is to encode the type into a short prefix, as in these examples:

- **lPhoneNum:** The variable is a long integer (`l`).
- **rgSamples:** The variable is an array or a range of Sample elements (`rg`).

The visible drawback of this notation is that it makes identifiers ugly, as if they were obfuscated. I definitely do not recommend this convention.

A convention is more than just a matter of convenience; it's also a social construct, a social contract between all developers in a community. When you are familiar with a convention, you feel at home with it, and you may even feel disturbed when you encounter a different convention. Familiarity with notation makes it almost invisible, even if it's very cryptic to those who don't understand it.

The Hungarian notation originated in languages that lack a type system, and using such notation helped you remember the type of each variable. However, unless you're still coding in BCPL, it's very unlikely that you need such notation because it impedes code readability too much, for almost no benefit.

> **Caution**
>
> It's unfortunate that C# has kept the convention of prefixing every interface with I, as this is reminiscent of Hungarian notation and has no benefit. From a design perspective, we should not even know whether a type is an interface or a class; it does not matter from a caller point of view. In fact, you might start with a class and later generalize it into an interface when really needed, and this should not change the code much. However, it's part of the standard convention that should be followed, unless all developers involved in an application agree not to.

In languages with no built-in support for namespaces, it's common practice to prefix all types with a module-specific prefix, as shown here:

- **`ACMEParser_Controller`:** Module `ACMEParser`
- **`ACMEParser_Tokenizer`:** Module `ACMEParser`
- **`ACMECompiler_Optimizer`:** Module `ACMECompiler`

This is usually a bad practice, as it pollutes the class names with information that could be factored out in their package (Java) or namespace (C#):

- **`acme.parser`:** Controller
- **`acme.parser`:** Tokenizer
- **`acme.compiler`:** Optimizer

As you've seen, coding conventions try to extend the syntax of a programming language to support features and semantics that are missing. When you have no type, you must manage the type by hand with some help from the naming convention. On the other hand, types can be very helpful for documentation.

Naming as the Primary Documentation

Searching for just the right words is a valuable use of time while designing.
—@Kent Beck and Ward Cunningham, "A Laboratory for Teaching
Object-Oriented Thinking"

One of the most important documentation tools is naming. Despite its unattractiveness, naming should never be overlooked. More often than not, the names bestowed by the original authors are the only element of documentation available to retrieve those authors' knowledge. Good naming is immensely important. But good naming is difficult. Names as a social convention need agreement and shared connotations. Checking a thesaurus for alternative terms, listening actively to the words used in spontaneous conversations, and asking your workmates feedback about names can help.

Good names are not just useful when you read them; they are also useful when you're searching for something. Good naming ensures that all names are searchable. The programming language named Go provides an example of naming that fails on the searchability front, which is especially interesting considering that it originates from the "search company" known as Google.

Composed Methods: You Need to Name Them

Names don't live in isolation. In object-oriented programming languages, the set of class names form a language, and the words have various relationships to each other, gaining expressivity as a whole. In the paper "A Laboratory for Teaching Object-Oriented Thinking" (1989), Kent Beck and Ward Cunningham wrote:

> The class name of an object creates a vocabulary for discussing a design. Indeed, many people have remarked that object design has more in common with language design than with procedural program design. We urge learners (and spend considerable time ourselves while designing) to find just the right set of words to describe our objects, a set that is internally consistent and evocative in the context of the larger design environment.[3]

---

3. Kent Beck and Ward Cunningham, "A Laboratory for Teaching Object-Oriented Thinking," http://t.co/PjQfDzRZcX

For more on naming and practical advices, I suggest reading the chapter on naming written by Tim Ottinger in Robert C. Martin's book *Clean Code*.

Idiomatic Naming Is Contextual

The naming style does not have to be uniform throughout a large code base. Different areas of the system call for different idiomatic styles. For example, I always go for business domain names within a domain model or in the domain layer (for example, `Account`, `ContactBook`, `Trend`). But on the infrastructure layer or adapters (in the hexagonal architecture sense), I like to use prefixes and suffixes to qualify technologies and patterns being used in the corresponding implementing subclasses (for example, `MongoDBAccount`, `SOAPBankHolidaysRepository`, `PostgresEmailsDAOAdapter`, `RabbitMQEventPublisher`). In this example of a double standard in naming, the names must tell *what* things are within a domain model, whereas outside of a domain model, in the infrastructure code, the names must tell *how* they are implemented.

Coding Against a Framework

> But if you write an app "without a framework," you end up with an under-specified, un-documented, informal framework.
> —*Hacker News, https://news.ycombinator.com/item?id=10839081*

Coding against a popular or opiniated framework has great value for strong documentation. Code that is not written needs no documentation. When you use an off-the-shelf framework such as Spring Boot (a lightweight microservice framework) or Axon-Framework (a framework for event-sourced applications), a lot of code is already written, and your code has to conform to what the framework expects. Choosing such a framework may be a good idea for a team of limited maturity, where the framework will constrain the design to follow some structure. This might sound like a bad thing, but it's a good thing from a knowledge transfer perspective: There is less room for surprise, and when you're familiar with the framework, you can understand most of the code. In addition, such frameworks are well documented, and their use of annotations also provides documentation in the code, as shown in the following example:

```
1  @CommandHandler
2  void placePurchase(PlacePurchaseCommand c){...}
```

Type-Driven Documentation

Types are powerful vehicles for storing and conveying knowledge for both developers and tools. With a type system, you need no Hungarian notation; the type system knows which type is there. It's part of the documentation, whether it is a compile time (Java, C#) or runtime (TypeScript) system.

In a Java or C# IDE, you can see the type of everything by putting the mouse over it, and a tooltip will tell you about its type.

Primitives are types, but types really shine when you use custom types instead of primitives. For example, the following code does not tell the whole story that this quantity is supposed to represent an amount of money, and you need a comment to tell the currency:

```
1  int amount = 12000; // EUR
```

But if you create a custom type **Money**, as a class, for example, it becomes explicit. Now you know it's an amount of money, and the currency is part of the code:

```
1  Money amount = Money.inEUR(12000);
```

There are many advantages to creating types for different concepts, and documentation is a very important one. This is not a random integer anymore, it's an amount of money, the type system knows that and can tell you.

You can also check the **Money** type to learn more about it. For example, here is the class's Javadoc comment description:

```
1  /**
2  * A quantity of money in Euro (EUR),
3  * for accounting purpose,
4  * i.e. with an accuracy of exactly 1 cent.
5  *
6  * Not suited for amounts over 1 trillion EUR.
7  */
8  class Money {
9  ...
10 }
```

This is valuable information, and it's best located in the code itself rather than in random document somewhere else.

Your types are an essential part of your documentation. Type everything and name the types carefully.

Therefore: Use types whenever possible. The stronger the types are, the better. Avoid bare primitives and bare collections. Promote them into first-class types. Name your types carefully, according to the ubiquitous language, and add just enough documentation on the types themselves.

From Primitives to Types

In the following example, the code switches on a `String`; it's a type, but a weak one, which in practice is almost like a primitive:

```
1  validate(String status)
2    if (status == "ON")
3    ...
4    if (status == "OFF")
5    ...
6    else
7      // some error message
```

This kind of code is shameful. Because a `String` can be anything, you need an additional `else` clause to catch any unexpected value. All this code describes the expected behavior, but if this behavior were done by the type system—for example, by using a typed enum—there would simply be no code to write at all:

```
1  switch (Status status){
2    case: ON ...
3    case: OFF ...
4  }
```

Documented Types and Integrated Documentation

A type is a perfect place to put documentation about a concept in a Javadoc section or its C# equivalent. Such documentation will evolve throughout the life of the type: It's created when the type is created, and if the type is deleted, its documentation will go away with it. If the type is renamed or moved, its documentation remains attached to it, so there is no maintenance.

The only risk is that if you change the definition of the type without changing its documentation, you might still end up with misleading documentation. However, this risk is lower because the documentation is co-located with the type declaration.

An obvious benefit of using types with their documentation is that it gives you *integrated documentation* directly within your IDE. When you mouse over a type name anywhere in the code, the IDE shows a small popup with the related documentation. When you're using autocompletion, a brief excerpt of the documentation is shown in front of each autocompletion option.

Types and Associations

Associations in code are expressed as member fields to types. The code and its types can tell a lot, but sometimes you need something more. Let's consider a few examples. When the associations are one-to-one, and the member fields are well named, you need nothing more than this:

```
1  // nothing to say
2  private final Location from;
3  private final Location to;
```

There is no need to tell much when types can also express meaning themselves. In the following example, the annotation is redundant with the declared type, and it is common knowledge that a **Set** enforces unicity:

```
1  @Unicity
2  private final Set<Currency> currencies;
```

Similarly, the following code does not need the additional ordering declaration, as it is implied by the concrete type (but is this really the case from the caller point of view?):

```
1  @Ordered
2  Collection<Item> items = new TreeSet<Item>();
```

You could refactor into a new declared type to make the documentation redundant:

```
1  SortedSet<Item> items = new TreeSet<Item>();
```

But doing this exposes a lot of methods you may not want to expose. If you would like to expose only **Iterable<Item>**, the ordering is an internal detail.

You can see here that I prefer types over annotations.

Types over Comments

Comments can and often do lie. So does naming, though to a lesser extent. But types don't lie; if they did, the program would not even compile.

A method name may pretend to be the following:

```
1   GetCustomerByCity()
```

But regardless of its name, if the signature and its types are actually as follows, you get a much more accurate picture of what it really is:

```
1   List<Prospect> function(ZipCode)
```

And it could even be improved: `List<Prospect>` could be a type in itself, something like `Prospects` or `ProspectionPortfolio`.

With just primitives, you're on your own to decide whether you can trust the naming or not. What does the Boolean `ignoreOrFail` mean? Enums, such as `IGNORE` and `FAIL`, add accuracy.

`Optional<Customer>` expresses the possible absence of a result with total accuracy. In languages that support them, monads signal the presence of side effects with total accuracy. In these examples, the information is accurate because the compiler enforces it.

Generics such as `Map<User, Preference>` tell a lot, whatever the variable name.

In case you're still not convinced, you can read this study on the topic: "What Do We Really Know About the Differences Between Static and Dynamic Types?"[4]

A Touch of Type-Driven Development

When using types, even if you didn't name the variables, you could still determine a lot about them, thanks to their type. Consider the following variable declaration:

```
1   FuelCardTransactionReport x = ...
```

The type name tells it all. The variable name will be useful only if there's more than one instance in the scope at the same time.

The same goes for functions and methods. Even without knowing its name, you can tell that a function that takes `ShoppingCart` as an argument and returns `Money` probably has something to do with pricing or tax calculation. By just looking at the function signature, you can glean a good understanding of what the function can do.

---

4. Stefan Hanenberg, http://www.slideshare.net/mobile/devnology/what-do-we-really-know-about-the-differences-between-static-and-dynamic-types

On the other hand, if you're trying to find the code doing the pricing of a shopping cart, you have two options:

- Guess how the class or method is named and perform a search based on your guess
- Guess the signature in terms of type and perform a search by signature

Haskell has a documentation tool called Hoogle that can show every function with a given signature. In Java using Eclipse (Kepler), you can also search by method signature. In the search menu, you select the Java Search tab, select the radio buttons Search For: Method and Limit To: Declarations, and then type in the search string (see Figure 8.5):

```
1  *(int, int) int
```

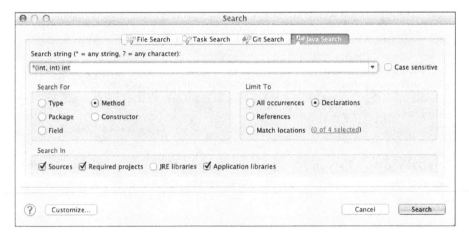

Figure 8.5 *Search by method signature in Eclipse*

You get a lot of search results of methods that take two integers as parameters and return another integer, for example:

```
1 com.sun.tools.javac.util.ArrayUtils
                        .calculateNewLength(int, int) int
2 com.google.common.math.IntMath.mean(int, int) int
3 com.google.common.primitives.Ints.compare(int, int) int
4 org.apache.commons.lang3.RandomUtils.nextInt(int, int) int
5 org.joda.time.chrono.BasicChronology
                        .getDaysInYearMonth(int, int) int
6 ...
```

This works not just for primitives such as integers but for any type. For example, if you were looking for a method to calculate the distance between two **Coordinates** objects (**Latitude**, **Longitude**), you would search for the following signature, using the fully qualified type names:

```
1  *(flottio.domain.Coordinates, flottio.domain.Coordinates)
double
```

This would find the service you are looking for, without knowing its name:

```
1  GeoDistance.distanceBetween(Coordinates, Coordinates) double
```

You might have heard about type-driven development (TDD), or type-first development (TFD). These approaches have similar ideas about types.

The Composed Method

> Clear code, like clear writing, is hard to do. Often you can only tell how to make it clear when someone else looks at it, or you come back to it at a later date.
> Ward Cunningham explained it like this. Whenever you have to figure out what code is doing, you are building some understanding in your head. Once you've built it, you should move that understanding into the code so nobody has to build it from scratch in their head again.
>
> —*Martin Fowler, "Refactoring"*

Clear code does not happen by chance. You have to make it emerge through continuous refactoring, using all your design skills. For example, it could be a good idea to follow the four rules of simple design expressed by Kent Beck.[5, 6]

Among all the design skills, the composed method pattern is particularly relevant for documentation purposes. For example, what's this block of code doing?

- It's squishing the fibbly-bar.
- So should we extract it into a **squishFibblyBar** function?

The composed method is an essential technique for writing clear code. It involves dividing code into a number of small methods, each of which performs one task. Because each method is named, method names are the primary documentation.

---

5. Martin Fowler, ThoughtWorks, http://martinfowler.com/bliki/BeckDesignRules.html

6. Corey Haines, "Understanding the Four Rules of Simple Design," https://leanpub.com/4rulesofsimpledesign

A common refactoring is to replace a block of code that requires a comment into a composed method named after the comment. Consider the following example:

```
1  public Position equivalentPosition(Trade... trades) {
2          // if trades list has no trade
3          if (trades.length == 0) {
4                  // return position of quantity zero
5                  return new Position(0);
6          }
7          // return quantity of first trade
8          return new Position(trades[0].getQuantity());
9  }
```

Here the comments suggest that you can do better, such as by simplifying the code or extracting methods into composed methods. You could extract little cohesive blocks of code into their own composed method, as shown here:

```
1  public Position equivalentPosition(Trade... trades) {
2          if (hasNo(trades)) {
3                  return positionZero();
4          }
5          return new Position(quantityOfFirst(trades));
6  }
7
8  //----
9
10 private boolean hasNo(Trade[] trades) {
11          return trades.length == 0;
12 }
13
14 private Position positionZero() {
15          return new Position(0);
16 }
17
18 private static double quantityOfFirst(Trade[] trades) {
19          return trades[0].getQuantity();
20 }
```

Notice that the first method now describes the overall processing, and the other three methods underneath describe low-level parts of the code. This is another way to make code clear by organizing the methods into different levels of abstraction.

Here the first method is one level of abstraction above the three other methods. Usually you can just read the code in the higher level of abstraction to understand what it does without having to deal with all the code in the lower levels of abstraction. This allows you to more efficiently read and navigate unknown code.

The code above also illustrates how the layout of text is meaningful: You can graphically see the two levels of abstraction one on top of the other, just through the ordering of the methods.

Fluent Style

One of the most obvious way to make code more readable is to make it mimic natural language, using a style that is called a *fluent interface*. Let's consider an example taken from a software application to calculate mobile phone billing:

```
1  Pricing.of(PHONE_CALLS).is(inEuro().withFee(12.50).
atRate(0.35));
```

You can read this pretty easily in English: "The pricing of phone calls is in euros, with a fee of 12.50, at a rate of 0.35."

The code can grow bigger while remaining readable as a quasi-English sentence:

```
1  Pricing.of(PHONE_CALLS)
2    .is(inEuro().withFee(12.50).atRate(0.35))
3    .and(TEXT_MESSAGE)
4      .are(inEuro().atRate(0.10).withIncluded(30));
```

Using an Internal DSL

Using an internal domain-specific language (DSL) usually relies heavily on method chaining, among other tricks. A fluent interface is an example of an internal DSL that is built on the programming language itself. The advantage is that you get the power of expression without giving up all the good things around your programming language: compiler checking, autocompletion, automated refactoring features, and so on.

Creating a nice fluent interface takes some time and effort, so I do not recommend making it the default programming style in all situations. It's especially interesting for your published interface, the API you expose to all your users, anything about configuration, and for testing so that the tests become living documentation that is readable by anyone.

A famous example of a fluent interface in .Net is the LINQ syntax. It's implemented through extension methods, and it manages to mimic SQL quite closely, as shown in this example:

```
1  List<string> countries = new List<string>
2   {"USA", "CANADA", "FRANCE", "ENGLAND","CHINA", "RUSSIA"};
3
4  // Find every country containing the letter 'C',
5  // ordered by length
6  IEnumerable<string> filteredOrdered = countries
7                          .Where (c => c.Contains("C"))
8                          .OrderBy(c => c.Length);
9
10
```

Here's another example of a fluent interface for data validation, from FluentValidation:[7]

```
1 using FluentValidation;
2
3 public class CustomerValidator: AbstractValidator<Customer> {
4   public CustomerValidator() {
5     RuleFor(customer => customer.Surname).NotEmpty();
6     RuleFor(customer => customer.Forename).NotEmpty()
7             .WithMessage("Please specify a first name");
8     RuleFor(customer => customer.Discount).NotEqual(0)
9             .When(customer => customer.HasDiscount);
10     RuleFor(customer => customer.Address).Length(20, 250);
11     ...
12  }
```

Implementing a Fluent Interface

As in the first step of writing tests in TDD, when implementing a fluent interface you start by dreaming. Write examples of using the ideal fluent interface by imagining that it's there and perfect, even though you haven't started to build it yet. Then take a subset of it and start to make it work. You'll encounter difficulties that will force you

---

7. https://github.com/JeremySkinner/FluentValidation

to reconsider alternative ways to express the same behavior. Martin Fowler has more to say about fluent interfaces.[8]

Fluent Tests

The fluent style is particularly popular for testing. JMock, AssertJ, JGiven, and NFluent are well-known libraries that can help you write tests in a fluent style. When tests are easy to read, they become the documentation of the behaviors of the software.

NFluent[9] is a test assertion library in C# created by Thomas Pierrain. Using NFluent, you can write test assertions in a fluent way, like this:

```
1 int? one = 1;
2 Check.That(one).HasAValue().Which.IsPositive()
3          .And.IsEqualTo(1);
```

Through method chaining and many other tricks—in particular around the C# generics—the library allows for a very readable style of tests, as shown here:

```
1  var heroes = "Batman and Robin";
2  Check.That(heroes).Not.Contains("Joker")
        .And.StartsWith("Bat")
        .And.Contains("Robin");
```

An equivalent library in Java is AssertJ.[10]

Creating a DSTL

You can create your own domain-specific test language (DSTL) to enable writing pretty scenarios in plain code. This involves test data builders.

When using builders, it is not very difficult to create an internal DSL for creating test data. Nat Pryce calls this a test data builder. You could extend the previous example with the use of a test data builder to create objects on the given section.

Test data builders can be nested. For example, you can define bundled travel as travel that groups flights, accommodations, and additional services into one basket

---

8. Martin Fowler, ThoughtWorks, http://martinfowler.com/bliki/FluentInterface.html

9. http://www.n-fluent.net

10. AssertJ, http://joel-costigliola.github.io/assertj/

so that it's more convenient to buy. You can use a test data builder to create each element independently:

```
1 aFlight().from("CDG").to("JFK")
2     .withReturn().inClass(COACH).build();
3
4 anHotelRoom("Radisson Blue")
5     .from("12/11/2014").forNights(3)
6     .withBreakfast(CONTINENTAL).build();
```

You could use another test data builder to create the bundle from each product:

```
1  aBundledTravel("Blue Week-End in NY")
2    .with(aFlight().from("CDG").to("JFK")
3    .withReturn().inClass(COACH).build())
4  .with(
5    anHotelRoom("Radisson Blue")
6    .from("12/11/2014").forNights(3)
7    .withBreakfast(CONTINENTAL).build()).build();
```

Test data builders can be so useful that you may decide to use them not just for tests. For example, I ended up moving them into the production code and made sure they were no longer "test" data builders but just regular companion builders with nothing test-specific in them.

See Martin Fowler's book *Domain-Specific Languages* for more on DSL.

When Not to Use a Fluent Style

Fluent is not an end to itself, and coding with a fluent style is not always the right thing to do:

- It makes it more complicated to create the API, and it's not always worth spending the extra effort.
- A fluent API is sometimes harder to use when writing code because of non-idiomatic use of the programming language. In particular, it can be confusing to know when to use method chaining or nested functions or object scoping.
- The methods used as part of a fluent style have names that are not meaningful on their own, like Not(), And(), That(), With(), or Is().

Case Study: An Example of Refactoring Code, Guided by Comments

This case study starts with a random class taken from a legacy C# application in the domain of finance:

```
1   public class Position : IEquatable<Position>
2   {
3       //could be just DealId
4       private IEnumerable<Position> origin;
5
6       // Position properties to be defined ...
7       private double Quantity { get; set; }
8       private double Price { get; set; }
9
10      // MAGMA properties to dispatch a job
11      public int Id { get; set; }
12      public string ContractType { get; set; }
13      public string CreationDate { get; set; }
14      public string ModificationVersionDate { get; set; }
15      public bool FlagDeleted { get; set; }
16      public string IndexPayOffTypeCode { get; set; }
17      public string IndexPayOffTypeLabel { get; set; }
18      public string ScopeKey { get; set; }
19      // end MAGMA properties to dispatch a job
20
21   #region constructors
22 ...
```

Notice that most comments delimit sections. For example, the last comment says, in plain English, "from here to there, this is a subsection that is used only by the application MAGMA." Unfortunately, plain English is code for people, and it requires developers like you to deal with it time and time again.

You can do better than these free-text comments to describe sections: You can turn them into formal sections represented by distinct classes. This way, you turn the fuzzy knowledge in plain English into strict knowledge expressed in the programming language instead. Here's how you can do this for the last section:

```
1   public class MagmaProperties
2   {
3       public int Id { get; set; }
4       public string ContractType { get; set; }
```

```
5      public string CreationDate { get; set; }
6      public string ModificationVersionDate { get; set; }
7      public bool FlagDeleted { get; set; }
8      public string IndexPayOffTypeCode { get; set; }
9      public string IndexPayOffTypeLabel { get; set; }
10     public string ScopeKey { get; set; }
11 }
```

You could apply this approach once or twice again here, on the subsets of the fields. For example, CreationDate and ModificationVersionDate probably go together as a versioning subsection that could become a generic shared class:

```
1  public class AuditTrail
2  {
3      public string CreationDate { get; set; }
4      public string ModificationVersionDate { get; set; }
5  }
```

Doing this opens opportunities to think more deeply about what you're doing. For example, when you use the name AuditTrail, it becomes obvious that this should be immutable to prevent mutation of the history.

IndexPayoffTypeCode and IndexPayoffTypeLabel also probably go together, as suggested by their similar naming:

```
1  IndexPayoffTypeCode
2  IndexPayoffTypeLabel
```

The prefix of the name acts like a module name or namespace. Again, this would be well expressed as an actual class:

```
1  public class IndexPayoffType
2  {
3      public string Code { get; set; }
4      public string Label { get; set; }
5  }
```

You could go on and on, improving the code and its design purely guided by comments and naming. When you do this, use the formal syntax of your languages instead of fragile and ambiguous text comments.

Comments, sloppy naming, and other shameful signals suggest opportunities for improving code. If you see any of this and don't know the alternative techniques, you need some external help with clean code, object-orientated design, or functional programming style.

Integrated Documentation

Your integrated development environment (IDE) already fulfills many documentation needs. This documentation is even more integrated into your coding, thanks to the autocompletion. This is sometimes called "intellisense" for its ability to guess what you need from the context. As you write code, the IDE shows what's available.

If you write the name of a class and press the period key, instantly the IDE shows a list of every method for the class. In fact, though, it's not every method but is filtered to show only what you can really access in the context of your code under the cursor. It doesn't show the private method if you're not within the class, for example.

This is a form of documentation that is task oriented and highly curated for your context.

Therefore: Acknowledge that your IDE is a key tool for documentation purposes. Learn how to use it well. Admit that the documentation use cases that your IDE handles don't have to be addressed anywhere else.

Type Hierarchy

A class hierarchy diagram is a classic element of a reference documentation. Because these diagrams usually use the UML notation, they take a lot of screen real estate. In contrast, your IDE can display a custom type hierarchy diagram on-the-fly from any selected class. The diagram is interactive: You select whether to display the hierarchy above or below the selected type, and you can expand or fold branches of the hierarchy. And because it's not using UML, it's quite compact, so you can see a lot in a fraction of the screen.

If, for example, you're looking for a concurrent list with a fixed length, but you can't remember its name, you can select the standard `List` supertype and ask the IDE for its type hierarchy. The IDE displays every type that is a list. Now you can examine each type by name, have a look at the Javadoc for each by mousing over, and select the one you want. Look, Ma, no documentation!

Indeed, this is documentation. It's just different. Again, this is a form of documentation that is task oriented and interactively curated for your context.

Code Searching

It would be unfair to talk about the IDE without mentioning the IDE's searching capabilities.

When you're looking for a class but don't remember its name, you can just type stems that belong to a class name, and the interval search engine will display a list of every type that contains each stem. The same works with just initials of a stem. For example, you can type `bis` as a shortcut for `BufferedInputStream`.

Semantics Derived from Actual Usage

A colleague at Arolla, Mathieu Pauly, once told me about the idea that meaning comes from the associations between things. Therefore, one way to learn what a class means is by looking at its relationships with all other classes that you already know.

Superficially this is something that you probably do already. Imagine that you need to find every transactional service within a code base. If the services use annotations like `@Transactional`, then it's easy: Select the annotation anywhere and ask the IDE to find all usages.

Alternatively, suppose that transactions are done through the standard Java class `Transaction` and its method `Commit()`. You can ask the IDE to retrieve the call stack for this method. Every class that is directly or indirectly calling this transaction stuff should be a transactional service. So the IDE is an assessment tool. It's far from perfect, though. You have to translate your goal into what the IDE offers. Still, all the capabilities the IDE offers replace advantageously a lot of documentation that would otherwise be necessary. The IDE is a great integrated documentation tool.

You can extend your code in an augmented code fashion by using your IDE as a user interface. Guided tours and inspiring exemplars (see Chapter 5, "Living Curation: Identifying Authoritative Knowledge") illustrate this approach.

Using Plain-Text Diagrams

Most diagrams are short-lived. A diagram may be useful for a particular discussion or to help reason on a specific design decision, but once the idea has been communicated or once the decision has been made, the diagram immediately loses most of its interest. This is why napkin sketches are the best choice for handmade diagrams. I use the word *napkin sketches* to actually refer to any low-tech visual and tangible technique. *Whiteboarding*, *CRC cards*, and *event storming* are of similar interest. They're all great tools for communicating, reasoning, and trying things in a visual fashion.

Some diagrams do remain of interest for a longer term, and in such a case, you want to persist the initial napkin sketch, set of cards or stickers, or whiteboard into something better suited for posterity. One way is to simply take a photograph of the outcome and to store it in the wiki or directly in the source control, co-located with the related artifacts. This works fine if the picture describes stable knowledge, but if it describes decisions that evolve regularly, the picture will be misleading after a while. You could try to do a Living Diagram, but this might be too hard or too much work to do, given the expected benefits. This is when you need a plain-text diagram.

Therefore: Take your initial napkin sketch or set of CRC cards and turn it into plain-text form. Use a text-to-diagram tool to render it into a visual diagram automatically. Then, on every change, maintain the plain-text description of the diagram and keep it in the source control area in the related code base.

Keep in mind that a plain-text diagram favors content over the formatting. You want to focus on the content in plain text and let the tools take care of the formatting, layout, and rendering as much as possible.

Example: Plain-Text Diagrams

Let's consider the example of a fuel card fraud detection algorithm. Say that you start with a napkin sketch (see Figure 8.6) when thinking about the problem, listing every related responsibility needed and how the responsibilities interoperate to solve the problem.

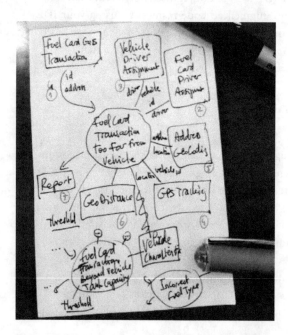

Figure 8.6 *The initial napkin sketch for a fraud detection mechanism*

After a few days, your team might agree that you need to keep the napkin sketch as part of your documentation, and you need to make it easier to read and to maintain as you expect it to change from time to time.

This diagram should tell one story. It should hide everything that does not matter for the story. To be story-oriented, you can use links as sentences:

```
1  <actor A> "does something to" <Actor B>
```

So, basically, you look at the napkin sketch and describe it by using sentences in this format:

```
1  FueldCardTransaction received into FuelCardMonitoring
2  FuelCardMonitoring queries Geocoding
3  FuelCardMonitoring queries GPSTracking
4  Geocoding converts address into AddressCoordinates
5  GPSTracking provides VehicleCoordinates
6  VehicleCoordinates between GeoDistance
7  AddressCoordinates between GeoDistance
8  GeoDistance compared to DistanceThreshold
9  DistanceThreshold delivers AnomalyReport
```

Then you can turn this set of sentences into a nice diagram by using a rendering tool.

> **Note**
>
> For the drawing shown in Figure 8.7 and 8.8, I used an online tool called Diagrammr that is not available anymore; however, Zoltán Nagy contributed a similar tool named diagrammr-lite (while attending my Living Documentation workshop at CraftConf Budapest): https://gist.github.com/abesto/a58a5e7155f38f4ac29d6c02f720a312.

The default layout of the rendered diagram is an activity-like diagram like the one shown in Figure 8.7.

But the same text sentences can also be rendered as a sequence diagram instead, as shown in Figure 8.8.

A tool like that is in fact only a thin wrapper on top of an automatic layout tool like Graphviz. Each sentence describes a relationship between two nodes. The first word of the sentence represents the start node, and the last word of the sentence represents the target node. This is a rustic approach.

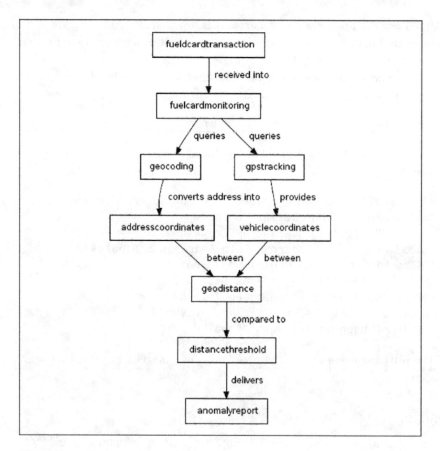

Figure 8.7 *A diagram rendered from the text*

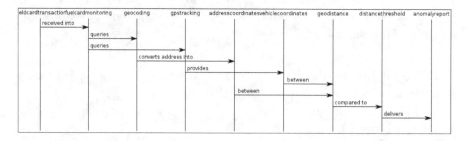

Figure 8.8 *Another layout to tell the same story in a different way*

It's not difficult to create your own flavor of this approach, using different conventions to interpret the text sentences. However, the point is to keep it really rustic. If you don't keep the syntax simple, you may end up with syntax so complicated that you have to look at its syntax sheet all the time.

When there are changes that make updates to the diagram necessary, it's easy to make them in the text. Renaming can be done through Find and Replace. Depending on your preferences, your IDE can probably have its refactoring automation reach the plain-text files, in which case you're less at risk of forgetting to update the diagram.

Diagrams as Code

An alternative flavor of a plain-text diagram is to use code in a programming language as the way to declare the nodes and their relationships. There are benefits to this method:

- You get the benefit of autocompletion.

- Checks from the compiler or interpreter can catch invalid syntax.

- You can move along with any automated refactoring to remain in sync with all changes.

- You can programmatically generate many dynamic diagrams from data sources.

There are some drawbacks, too:

- The code itself is less readable by nondevelopers than plain text would be.

- The names of identifiers cannot contain whitespace.

- It's not really a living diagram, but just a diagram created from ad hoc code.

Here is an example of a diagram generated from my little library DotDiagram,[11] which is a wrapper on top of Graphviz:

```
1 final DotGraph graph = new DotGraph("MyDiagram");
2 final Digraph = graph.getDigraph();
3
4 // Add the nodes
5 digraph.addNode("Car").setLabel("My Car")
        .setComment("This is a BMW");
6 digraph.addNode("Wheel").setLabel("Its wheels")
        .setComment("The wheels of my car");
7
8
9 // Add the associations between the nodes
```

---

11. DotDiagram, https://github.com/LivingDocumentation/dot-diagram

```
10 digraph.addAssociation("Car", "Wheel").setLabel("4*")
       .setComment("There are 4 wheels")
11       .setOptions(ASSOCIATION_EDGE_STYLE);
12
13 // Render everything
14 final String actual = graph.render().trim();
```

The diagram created from this code should render as shown in Figure 8.9.

Figure 8.9 *Rendering* `MyCar —> 4* Wheel`

Of course, the biggest benefit of diagrams as code is the ability to generate diagrams from any source of data.

Summary

Considering that many changes in a software system are done using automated refactoring, it makes a lot of sense to leverage refactorings for updating the documentation as well. In practice, this suggests a bias toward code-level techniques, from plain text to actual code, and it helps to learn many coding techniques to make the code more expressive, such as the use of types and careful naming.

Chapter 9

Stable Documentation

Stable knowledge is easy to document because it doesn't change often. A great benefit of stable knowledge is that you can use any form of documentation for it. Because there will be no need for updating the documents, even traditional forms that I would otherwise avoid, like Microsoft Word documents or wikis, are absolutely fine in this case. However, it does take some care to do it well; you need to properly design each detail to make sure everything is *really* stable.

Evergreen Content

Evergreen content is a kind of content that remains of interest for a long period of time, without change, for a particular audience. Evergreen content does not change, and yet it remains useful, relevant, and accurate. Obviously, not every kind of document contains evergreen content.

Evergreen content documents have the following characteristics:

- They tend to be short, without much detail.
- They focus on high-level knowledge—"the big picture."
- They focus on goals and intentions rather than implementation decisions.
- They focus more on business concepts than on technical ones.

These characteristics are key for the stability of a document.

Therefore: Traditional means of documentation are appropriate for knowledge that seldom changes. When this is the case and that the knowledge is useful, don't bother with living documentation techniques. Just write the knowledge in any kind of document, even in a proprietary format or a PDF document or using a content management system, slides, or a spreadsheet. But make sure to leave out of that documentation anything that is at risk of changing.

You don't have to spend a lot of time on creating evergreen content, but if you do, it will benefit the readers for a long time.

Note that just because knowledge is stable doesn't mean it's useful and worth documenting.

Requirements Are More Stable Than Design Decisions

> If you can't change a decision, it's a requirement to you. If you can, it's your design.
> —*Alistair Cockburn, https://twitter.com/TotherAlistair/status/606892091432701952*

If you can't change a decision, then from your perspective, that decision is already more stable than your design decisions. Hence, requirements tend to be more stable than design decisions. And in particular, high-level requirements may be stable enough to be expressed in evergreen documents.

Of course, it happens that some requirements change frequently, but then it's usually the details of the expected behaviors that change. For these low-level requirements that may change frequently, practices like BDD are more appropriate to deal with the changes efficiently; conversations are efficient for fast-changing knowledge, together with some automation when it fits.

High-Level Goals Tend to Be Stable

A company may have a vision to change the world. Such a high-level vision is stable and is part of the company identity. A startup at an early stage may pivot regularly, but its vision often remains the same.

In large corporations, change happens all the time everywhere, but the traditional approach to management is to consider most decisions and knowledge as certain, predictable, and stable. Within a department, team, or project, everything around can often be considered stable.

A project vision, expressed in a few sentences, like an elevator pitch, can be quite stable. And if it ever changes, the project will probably be stopped or totally reconsidered.

Why does your project exist? Who's sponsoring it? What are the business drivers? What are the expected benefits, and what are the success criteria?

You need to take extra care to keep the vision high level enough to avoid prematurely constraining the execution of the project.

For example, the project vision "Create a library to report sales to the regulator" already presumes the solution. When the vision is stated this way, the team has already lost better opportunities, such as extending two existing services so that they together can deliver the report. This example of a vision is also fragile to changes. If a new CTO decides that everything now must be services—no library allowed— the team will have to update the vision of the project. A better vision for the project would simply be "Report the sales to the regulator" or, even better, "Extend reporting to meet MIFID II regulation." With visions like these, it does not matter what you do to achieve the goal; all options remain open.

A Lot of Knowledge Is Less Stable Than It Looks

There's a limit with evergreen documents: Even if the knowledge itself does not change much, evergreen documents involve a graphical style, with a company logo and company-specific footers, and these elements of style sometimes change.

Another limit is that it's common for all documents, including evergreen documents, to reside on the same source control system as the source code. This encourages lightweight formats of documents, like text and HTML rather than Microsoft Office documents or other binary proprietary formats. Keeping knowledge in plain text is also the preferred way to go for stable knowledge.

Case Study: A README File

As an example, let's consider the following README file from a fleet management system:

```
1  # Project Phenix
2  (Fuel Card Integration)
3
4  Project Manager: Andrea Willeave
5
6  ## Syncs daily
7  Transaction data from the pump is automatically sent to
8  Fleetio.
9  No more manual entry of fuel receipts or downloading and
```

```
10 importing fuel transactions across systems.
11
12 ## Fuel Card Transaction Monitoring
13
14 Transaction data from the pump are verified automatically
15 against various rules to detect potential frauds: gas
16 leakage, transactions too far from the vehicle etc.
17
18
19 *The class responsible for that is called
20 FuelCardMonitoring.*
21
22 Anomalies are detected if the vehicle is further than 300m
23 away from the gas station, of if the transaction quantity
24 exceeds the vehicle tank size by more than 5%
25
26 When drivers enter mileage at the pump, Fleetio uses that
27 information to trigger service reminders. This time-saving
28 approach helps you stay on top of maintenance and keeps
29 your vehicles performing their best.
30
31 *This module is to be launched in February 2015. Please
32 contact us for more details.*
33
34
35 ## Smart fuel management
36 ...
```

There are many issues in this file that will require the file to be updated regularly:

- The project name Phenix will change many times for political or marketing reasons.

- The name of the project manager will also likely change, likely every two years.

- The class name will be renamed, split, or merged with another at some point if the team is doing refactoring, which is expected to be the case. This document will need to be updated each time.

- Close to the class name, there are concrete parameters that may change any time (for example, 300m may become 500m, and 5% may become 3%).

- The launch date is likely to change as it's already in the past. How do you fix that?

You can start by changing the title to be a stable name, by reference to the core business of the module. It may not be stable forever either, but at least it is more stable than a name that is driven by internal company politics. To do this, you change the following:

```
1  # Project Phenix
2  (Fuel Card Integration)
3
4  Project Manager: Andrea Willeave
```

to the following title, along with a short introduction line:

```
1  # Fuel Card Integration
2
3  Here are the main features of this module:
```

You can also get rid of the project manager name in this file, as it is not the right place for that information. Instead, it could be in a Team section of the wiki, or in the Team section of your project manifest (a Maven POM file, for example). You could also replace the project manager name with a link to the page that contains this information.

You should also remove the launch date from this file. Instead of including it here, you could link to the corporate calendar, news portal, dedicated forum or internal social network, or to the Twitter or Facebook page where the launch will be announced.

The class name has nothing to do here. If you really want to bridge from this file to the code, you might instead link to a search on the source control, something like "link to the classes tagged as @EntryPoint."

Finally, the detailed parameters values are not necessary here. If you really need them, you can either look at the code or configuration, or you can check the scenarios that describe the expected behavior and that are used by Cucumber or SpecFlow.

To sum it up, here's what the code now looks like:

```
1  # Project Phenix
2  # Fuel Card Integration
3
4  Project Manager: Andrea Willeave
5
6  Find who's in the team here // link to the wiki
7
8
9
10 Here are the main features of this module:
11
```

12 ## Syncs daily
13 Transaction data from the pump is automatically sent to Fleetio.
14 No more manual entry of fuel receipts or downloading and importing fuel transactions across systems.
15
16 ## Fuel Card Transaction Monitoring
17
18 Transaction data from the pump are verified automatically against various rules to detect potential frauds:
19 gas leakage, transactions too far from the vehicle etc.
20
21
22
23 ~~*The class responsible for that is called FuelCardMonitoring.*~~
24
25 The corresponding code is on the company Github // link to the source code repository, but not to a concrete class name
26
27
28 ~~*Anomalies are detected if the vehicle is further than 300m away from the gas station,~~
29 ~~or if the transaction quantity exceeds the vehicle tank size by more than 5%*~~
30
31
32 For more details on the business rules of the fraud detection, please check the business scenarios here // link to the living documentation
33
34
35
36 ## Odometer readings
37 When drivers enter mileage at the pump, Fleetio uses that information to trigger service reminders.
38 This time-saving approach helps you stay on top of maintenance and keeps your vehicles performing their best.
39
40
42 ~~*This module is to be launched in February 2015. Please contact us for more details.*~~
43

```
44
45 For news and announcements on this product, please check our
Facebook page link to the FB page
46
47
48 ## Smart fuel management
49 ...
```

Now you have an evergreen README.

Tips for Evergreen Documentation

The following sections present tips on how to keep your documentation current.

Avoiding Mixing Strategy Documentation with the Documentation of Its Implementation

Strategy and its implementation don't evolve at the same pace. In their book *Agile Testing: A Practical Guide for Testers and Agile Teams*, Lisa Crispin and Janet Gregory recommend not mixing the documentation of a strategy with the documentation of its implementation, using the example of the test strategy:

> If your organization wants documentation about your overall test approach to projects, consider taking this information and putting it in a static document that doesn't change much over time. There is a lot of information that is not project specific and can be extracted into a Test Strategy or Test Approach document.
>
> This document can then be used as a reference and needs to be updated only if processes change. A test strategy document can be used to give new employees a high-level understanding of how your test processes work.[1]

I have had success with this approach at several organizations. Processes that were common to all projects were captured into one document. Using this format answered most compliance requirements. These are some of the topics that have been covered:

- Testing practices
- Story testing

---

1. Crispin, Lisa, and Janet Gregory. *Agile Testing: A Practical Guide for Testers and Agile Teams*. Hoboken: Addison-Wesley, 2009.

- Solution verification testing
- User acceptance testing
- Exploratory testing
- Load and performance testing
- Test automation
- Test results
- Defect tracking process
- Test tools
- Test environments

Therefore: Don't mix documentation of a strategy and documentation of its implementation. Make the strategy documentation a pure evergreen document. Use another living documentation approach for the implementation, considering that the implementation will change more frequently.

The strategy should be documented as an evergreen document, stable and even shared between multiple projects. Omit from the strategy document every detail that could change or that would be project specific. All these details that change more frequently and that differ from project to project must be kept separate, using the techniques proposed in this book that are more suited for knowledge that changes often, such as declarative automation and BDD.

Ensuring Stability

Names describing business benefits tend to be stable, often over decades. Business is changing, but from a high-level perspective, it's still about selling, purchasing, preventing losses, and reporting. If you open an old book about doing business in your domain, you'll recognize that although the typical way of doing business has evolved since then, most words in the book are still valid and still mean the same thing. Business domain vocabulary is on the stable end of the spectrum.

On the other end of the spectrum, everything about the organization, legal stuff, and marketing is volatile: Company names, subsidiaries, brands, and trademarks change all the time. Avoid using them in more than one place. Prefer stable names instead.

Look at your company org chart now and compare it with one from two or three years ago. How are they different? New executives often change the org structure. In some companies the top management switches every three years. Departments are split and merged and renamed. A game of perpetual business and politics-driven refactoring may change the org structure without changing the underlying business operations much.

Do you want to spend time changing words everywhere in your code and in your documents to accommodate those changes? I certainly don't want that, so I choose to go for stable names whenever I can, with a preference for business domain names.

Arbitrary Versus Descriptive Names in Code

I noticed that arbitrary code names, such as `SuperOne`, that don't describe anything are more volatile than common names that describe what they do. Even if you just work with a company for two or three years, you will see some of these names changing. But arbitrary names are attractive because we change them often to match the current fashion. On the other hand, common words that describe the things they are, like `AccountingValuation`, are dull, but they are less likely to be renamed and hence are more stable. More importantly, in the latter case, the name itself is an element of documentation. Without anything else, you may know what an `AccountingValuation` component does.

Using Perennial Naming

Naming is one of the most powerful means available to transfer knowledge. Unfortunately, many kinds of names change frequently, such as marketing brands and product names, project code names, and team names. When this happens, it costs maintenance work: Somebody has to find every place where the old name is used and update each instance.

Some names last longer than others, and some names change more frequently than others. For example, it's common for marketing names, legal names, and company organization names to change every one to three years. These names are volatile.

Choosing names judiciously so that they don't change often is important for reducing the amount of maintenance work in all kinds of artifacts. This is important in the code and also in other documents.

Therefore: Use stable names over volatile names in all documentation that you maintain. Name classes, interfaces, methods, code comments, and every document using stable names. Avoid references to volatile names in all documents.

Organizing Artifacts Along Stable Axes

At the macro level, how do you organize your documentation? There are many different ways to organize documents:

- **By application name:** For example, `CarPremiumPro`, `BestSocksOnline`
- **By business process:** For example, sell car in retail, sell socks online
- **By target client:** For example, individual car buyers, urban middle-class men, B2B or B2C
- **By team name:** For example, team B2B, Team Ninja
- **By team purpose:** For example, Software Delivery Paris, R&D London
- **By project name:** For example, `MarketShareConquest`, `GoFastWeb`

For each other these organization modes, how does it evolve over time? If you think back on your past work experiences, which ones remained unchanged, and which ones were changing from time to time or even several times a year?

Projects start and end. They are canceled and sometimes resuscitated under a new name. Applications last longer than projects, but they end up being decommissioned and replaced by other projects that provide similar business benefits.

Linked Knowledge

Knowledge is more valuable when it is connected, provided that the connections are stable. Knowledge becomes more valuable when it is connected as a graph of relationships that conveys additional information and also brings structure.

On a particular topic or on a project, all knowledge is related to other knowledge in some way. On the Internet, links between resources add a lot of value: Who's the author? Where can you find more? What does this definition mean? Who's quoted here? In a book or paper, the bibliography tells you the context. Was the author aware of this publication? If it's cited in the bibliography, then you can guess that was the case. The same concept applies to your documentation.

Therefore: In your documentation, link knowledge to other related knowledge. Qualify the relationship. Define a resource identification scheme, such as a URL or a citation scheme. Decide on a mechanism to ensure that the links remain stable in the long run.

It's important to qualify a link with some metadata, such as the source, reference on the topic, review, criticism, author, and so on.

> **Caution**
>
> Be aware of the directions of the links. Just as in design, links should go from the less stable to the more stable.

A great way to link to some piece of knowledge is to make it accessible through a URL. You can expose knowledge as web resource accessible through a link. Whenever necessary, you can refer to that knowledge by using the link. Use a link registry to ensure the permanence of the links.

Many tools expose their knowledge through links: issue trackers, static analysis tools, planning tools, blogging platforms, and social code repositories like GitHub. If you want to link to a particular version of something, use permalinks. If, on the other hand, you prefer to link to the most recent version of something, link to the front page, or index, or folder, which will usually show the latest version first.

Volatile-to-Stable Dependencies

When you refer to something, make sure the direction of the reference is from the more volatile to the more stable elements. It's much more convenient to couple the volatile to the stable than it is to couple the stable to the volatile. A reference to something stable is not very expensive as there won't be many impacts from the dependency because it does not change often. On the other hand, with a reference to a volatile dependency, you'll have to make changes all the time, whenever the dependency changes. This applies to both code and documentation.

For an example in code, most programming language propose to couple the implementation to the contract or interface they implement, and not the other way around. Generic stuff is usually more stable than more specific stuff.

In the universe of representing knowledge that we call documentation, prefer references the following ways, not the other way around:

- From the artifacts (code, tests, configuration, resources) to the project goals, constraints, and requirements
- From the goals to the project vision

Broken Link Checkers

If you have a direct link to a resource, then you need a way to detect when the link is broken. Links to code at GitHub get broken when the code changes, and links to external websites get broken when the websites reorganize their content or when they disappear.

Therefore: Use a mechanism to detect broken links before your colleagues do.

You can use a broken link checker on your overall documentation for detecting broken links. (You can find many such checkers by searching online for "broken link checker.") You may also use low-tech contract tests that will fail when there is a change that breaks a link. This way, you know when you have to fix the link or the code to get them back in sync. This is another example of a reconciliation mechanism.

You can create a unit test to compare the code, which could change at any time, against hardcoded laterals that represent the external contract, such as the link. When the test fails, you know you have to update the doc or perhaps revert the change.

For example, if the qualified class name is used directly in a link, the contract test might look like this:

```
1  @Test
2  public void checkLinks() {
3    assertEquals(
4      "flottio.fuelcardmonitoring.domain.FuelCardMonitoring",
5      FuelCardMonitoring.class.getName());
6  }
```

Whenever you refactor and accidentally break the contract, this check against the hardcoded literal would fail to tell you that you need to make a fix.

Link Registry

All links need maintenance because the web is a living thing, and so is your internal company web. When a link is broken, you don't really want to have to go through every document that contains the broken link and replace it with another link.

Therefore: Don't directly include direct links in multiple places in your artifacts. Instead, use a link registry that is under your control.

A link registry is an indirection that you can change to fix broken links in one single place. A link registry gives you intermediate URLs as aliases on the actual links. When a link is broken, you just need to update the link registry in one single place to redirect to another link.

An internal URL shortener works perfectly as a link registry. Some shorteners allow to choose your own pretty short link; not only do the links become more manageable, they also get shorter and prettier.

I've seen companies install their own on-premise link registries. This is necessary for companies that care a lot about the confidentiality of their knowledge. You can find many URL shorteners that you can install on-premise, some open source and some with commercial licenses.

Bookmarked Searches

Another way to link in a way that is more robust to change is to link to a bookmarked search instead of linking to a direct resource. Imagine that you want to link to the class `ScenarioOutline` in a repository. You could link through a direct link. For example, in GitHub you would use a link like this:

```
https://github.com/Arnauld/tzatziki/blob/
4d99eeb094bc1d0900d763010b0fea495a5788d\d/tzatziki-core/src/
main/java/tzatziki/analysis/step/ScenarioOutline.java
```

The problem is that this class could move into another package, or its package might be renamed. The class itself could be renamed, too, even though that is not very likely. But any of these changes would turn a link into a broken link, and that's bad.

Therefore: Replace direct links with searches on more stable criteria. There may be more than one result, but it will help users locate the target of a link in a more robust way.

You can make a link more robust by using a bookmarked search instead of a direct link. For example, you could search for a Java class in this particular repository with `ScenarioOutline` in its name. Using the GitHub advanced search,[2] you would create the following search:

```
ScenarioOutline in:path extension:Java repo:Arnauld/tzatziki
```

where each option can help create a more relevant search:

- **`ScenarioOutline`:** Search for this term.
- **`in:path`:** The search term must appear in the path name.
- **`extension:Java`:** The file extension must be Java.
- **`repo:Arnauld/tzatziki`:** Search only in this one repo.

The result page of this search will show more than one result, but the one you're looking for is easy to grab from the list (here it is the second result in the list):

```
1  .../analysis/exec/model/ScenarioOutlineExec.java
2  .../analysis/step/ScenarioOutline.java
3  .../pdf/emitter/ScenarioOutlineEmitter.java
4  .../analysis/exec/gson/ScenarioOutlineExecSerializer.java
5  .../pdf/model/ScenarioOutlineWithResolved.java
```

---

2. GitHub, https://help.github.com/articles/searching-code/

A bookmarked advanced search is not just useful for more robust links. It is also an important tool for living documentation in general. It offers the power of an IDE for everyone who has a browser. By creating curated bookmarked searches, you create guided tours for navigating code and for quickly discovering everything related to a concept, as shown here around the concept of `ScenarioOutline`.

Categories of Stable Knowledge

As discussed in the following sections, different pieces of knowledge have different lifespans, from volatile to long term. The following typical categories of stable knowledge are good candidates for evergreen documents.

Evergreen README

> We have projects with short, badly written, or entirely missing documentation....There must be some middle ground between reams of technical specifications and no specifications at all. And in fact there is. That middle ground is the humble Readme.
> —*Tom Preston-Lerner, "Readme Driven Development"*

For a given project Blabla, the README file can be safely evergreen if it focuses on answering the following key questions:

- What is Blabla?
- How does Blabla work?
- Who uses Blabla?
- What is Blabla's goal?
- How can the organization benefit from using Blabla?
- How do you get started with Blabla? (But beware: Keep it so simple that it should not change often. In particular, don't embed the version number but instead refer to the place where you can find the most recent version number.)
- What is the licensing information for Blabla? (This could also be detailed in a LICENSE.txt sidecar file.)

This level of key information is at the same time essential and quite stable over time.

Beware of including instructions on how to develop, use, test, or help, as well as contact information, except with permanent mailing lists.

Also, when using an online source code repository like GitHub, avoid linking from the README to pages on the wiki: The README is versioned, whereas the wiki is not, so links will break, in particular when cloning or forking.

Vision Statement

A vision is a picture of the world as it will be when you're done working on it.
—*The McCarthy Show (@mccarthyshow) on Twitter*

When a manager comes to me, I don't ask him, "What's the problem?" I say, "Tell me the story." That way I find out what the problem really is.
—*Grocery store chain owner Avram Goldberg, quoted in The Clock of the Long Now*

One of the single most important pieces of knowledge everybody in a project should absolutely know is the vision of the project or of the product.

With a clear vision, the efforts of each team member can really converge to make the vision come true. A vision is a dream, but it is a dream that is also a call to action for a team that decides to make it real.

A vision often originates in a particular person, who tries to share it with other people using various means:

- A talk, lecture-style, perhaps with great visuals, like a TED talk

- Repeating the pitch of the vision often and to everyone

- Telling stories that illustrate or exemplify the vision

- Writing down a vision statement

All this is documentation. A brilliant talk recorded on video may be the best documentation of the vision.

A vision has to be simple so that it can be pitched in a few sentences. Startups love vision statements, but these statements sometimes lack depth because they just steal from existing successful startups.

The perfect companion to a vision statement is a couple of stories that illustrate it and make it more real.

A vision statement is usually on the stable end of the spectrum, at least compared to other project artifacts, such as source code and configuration data. But it is possible that a company could change its vision from time to time, such as when pivoting.

Once the vision is set, it can be split into high-level goals.

Domain Vision Statements

A particular kind of vision statement focuses on the business domain the product is about. The purpose of this statement is to describe the value of the future system to be built before it actually exists. This description may span several subdomains since at the beginning no one knows yet how the domain should be split into subparts. The point of the domain vision statement is to focus on the critical aspects of the domain.

In the words of Eric Evans:

> Write a short (1 page) description of the core domain and the value it will bring, the "value proposition." Ignore those aspects that do not distinguish this domain from others. Show how the domain model serves and balances diverse interests. Keep it narrow. Write this statement early and revise it as you gain new insights.[3]

Most technical aspects and infrastructure or UI details are not part of the domain vision statement.

Here is an example of a domain vision statement for fuel card monitoring in the fleet management business:

> Fuel card monitoring of every incoming fuel card transaction helps detect potential abnormal behavior by drivers.
>
> By looking for abuse patterns and by cross-checking facts from various sources, the system reports anomalies that are therefore investigated by the fleet management team.
>
> For example, a client using fuel card monitoring with GPS fleet-tracking features is able to catch employees who are padding hours, falsifying timesheets, stealing fuel, or buying non-fuel goods with the fuel card.
>
> Each fuel card transaction is verified against vehicle characteristics and its location history, considering which driver was assigned to the vehicle at the time and the address of the merchant of the transaction. Fuel economy can also be calculated to detect engines in need of a repair.

A domain vision statement is useful as a summary of the main concepts of the domain and how they are related to deliver value to the users. It can be seen as a proxy for the actual software that is not yet built.

Goals

The vision is the single most important piece of knowledge everybody should know and keep in mind at all times. From that vision, many decisions will be made to converge to a solution and its implementation.

---

3. Evans, Eric. *Domain-Driven Design: Tackling Complexity in the Heart of Software*. Boston: Pearson Education, Inc. 2004.

A vision alone is often not enough for people to start working, and you may have to form precise intermediate goals, such as to share work between different teams or to explore early what could be done and the alternatives.

Goals can be described as a tree of goals and subgoals, with the vision at the root. Goals are lower level than the vision, but they are high level compared to all the details that describe how a system is built. They are therefore on the stable side, and the higher the level, the more stable.

Goals are also long term must be known by most people, and they are critical because they drive many further decisions. As a consequence, they must be documented in a persistent fashion. Since they are also on the stable end of the frequency-of-change spectrum, traditional forms of documentation fit for documenting goals:

- Microsoft Word documents

- Slide decks

- Paper document

This does not mean that it's easy to make good documentation for the goals. It's still all too easy to waste a lot of time on a document that will not be read because it's too long or too boring.

Caution

Remember that there is danger in deciding goals prematurely: You may over-constrain the project too early, at a time you know very little about it. This may impede the project execution. This is why Woody Zuill advises on his blog to "keep your requirements at a very high & general level until just before use,"[4] as if they were perishable goods. You do not want to reject opportunities early because of premature subgoals.

Impact Mapping

A great technique for exploring goals and organizing high-level knowledge about a project or a business initiative is impact mapping,[5] proposed by Gojko Adzic. It advocates working on goals through interactive workshops and keeping the alternative goals together on a map to keep options open during the execution of the

---

4. Woody Zuill, "Life, Liberty, and the Pursuit of Agility" blog, http://zuill.us/WoodyZuill/2011/09/30/requirements-hunting-and-gathering/

5. Impact mapping, http://www.impactmapping.org/

project. This collaborative technique is simple and lightweight, and it involves visualizing assumptions and targets.

An impact map shows options and alternate paths to reach a goal. It therefore does not constrain the execution as much as other traditional linear roadmaps.

An impact map itself is stable, but it's recommended to reconsider it at low frequency, typically twice a year. On the other hand, tracking the project execution on the map obviously changes often if you release often, and this should not be done by modifying the map each time.

Let's take as an example the result of an impact mapping session for a company in the music industry, presented as a tree-like mind map:

```
1   Reduce processing cost of song royalties
2     IT Department
3       100x volumes
4       50% Cheaper processing
5     Sales Department
6       Hourly stats feeds
7     Billing Department
8       Online real-time reporting (2s or less)
```

Impact mapping suggests classifying the goals by main stakeholders, which would be IT department, sales department, and billing department in this example. It also requires the goals to be quantified in the impact maps, with quantitative figures of success, called "performance targets."

There are other similar techniques, such as the EVO method Gilb,[6] for exploring requirements in various ways.

With or without impact mapping, a tree of goals is ideally created with sticky notes on a wall. If you want to keep a clean representation for later, you can use any mind-mapping application, such as MindMup, MindNode, Mindjet MindManager, Zengobi Curio, or MindMeister, to record and show a cleaner layout of the map.

These applications can read and write mind maps in various forms, including as *indented text*, at least as an "import" option. As a fan of plain-text artifacts, I like indented text best!

Investing in Stable Knowledge

Stable knowledge is an investment that pays back over a long period of time. Learning a subject is a costly investment. I have a hard time learning technologies that have a half-life of a few years.

---

6. Gilb, http://gilb.com

Business domain knowledge (finance, insurance, accounting, e-commerce, manufacturing, and so on) is some of the most stable knowledge there is. But because you may not always work within the same domain, you might wonder if it's reasonable to learn the knowledge of a particular domain. But it also happens that a lot of domain-specific knowledge is reusable in some form in other business domains. As an example, the book *Analysis Patterns* by Martin Fowler describes a number of patterns taken from accounting or medical observations but that work almost directly in finance, insurance, and commerce.

In addition, the fundamentals of computing and of software architecture and design also belong to the stable knowledge category. Don't hesitate to read the old papers and the patterns that map this territory.

Therefore: Don't hesitate to invest time and effort into learning stable knowledge. In particular, business domain knowledge and fundamentals of software architecture are evergreen content that are particularly worth learning.

Domain Immersion

Domain knowledge is typically on the stable side of the spectrum, even if your understanding of it changes over time (and it should). But the core use cases, purposes, concrete examples, and conversations with business people are mostly evergreen.

Traditionally, a software project itself is the main way to learn its domain. Task after task, each work part brings new vocabulary and new concepts that are learned on the job because they are necessary to do the job. This leads to a number of weaknesses:

- There is not enough time to deliver a task and to study seriously a part of the business domain in more depth. Learning remains superficial.

- Many tasks can be done with only superficial understanding of the underlying business. Something might appear to work by coincidence while really being a time bomb for next business requirements.

- Even if you decide to dedicate two hours out of the task to learn, the domain experts may not be available at that time.

Whenever the lack of domain knowledge is a bottleneck, it's an attractive proposition to invest time early on to learn the domain. One of the best ways to do this is through immersion. Invest time early to immerse the team into the domain. Visit the place where the business takes place. Take pictures. Get copies of the documents being used. Listen carefully to the conversations of the business people. When possible, ask questions. Make sketches of what you see and take plenty of notes.

Domain immersion is also an effective practice for new joiners to quickly discover what the domain is about. It is an alternative form of knowledge transfer, directly from the field, which also means it is a genuine form of documentation.

Sometimes it is not possible to go to the field, or it is prohibitively expensive to do so, in which case you need cheaper alternatives for this precious knowledge, such as an investigation wall or simple trainings.

Investigation Wall

You might want to create a wall of findings, much like an investigation wall in a criminal investigation movie, where the detectives cover the walls with lots of pictures, notes, and maps with pins to fully immerse themselves in the crime.

Similarly, you can create a space on a wall with pictures, notes, sketches, and sample business documents to keep a feel for the actual business domain while you work on it.

Domain Training

A team or part of a team might benefit from specialized trainings about the business domain.

In one of my past projects, we decided to invest in domain knowledge early, when the pressure was not very strong, so twice a week we dedicated 30 minutes after lunch to a mini-training session. A business analyst or a product manager who was identified with an area of expertise joined the team as the domain expert to explain all we needed to know on one concept at a time (a session on bond coupons, another about standard financial options, another on a new regulation, and so on). The team considered this training useful, and the developers enjoyed it.

Live-My-Life Sessions

With "live-my-life" sessions, for a period of time from half a day to two days, one or two developers stay close to someone doing business operations to see what it's really like to work in the business, using the software tools those people have. The developers may be in the back, trying not to interfere and just watching passively. However, it's best for them to be able to ask questions at any time or during some predefined pauses.

Such an experiment may be more involved. For example, a developer might try being an assistant to a business person. Some companies go further and have employees completely switch roles for a day. As a developer, doing the job of an accountant for a day could be one of the best ways to appreciate their stakes, and therefore to improve their software. It can also do wonders for the user experience.

Shadow Users

A variant of the live-my-life idea is to watch the behavior of users as a shadow user. A developer logs in as another real user, in a read-only fashion, and sees that person's screen in real time. It can be very valuable to watch how they really use the software to achieve their business objectives.

Having shadow users is obviously not feasible in many cases—because of privacy reasons or because the installed software is not accessible.

A Long-Term Investment

All these ways of investing in stable knowledge can be seen as an *investment* because the business domain is usually quite stable. The details of doing the business change all the time, but the business still uses the same old concepts. I realized this in 2007 when I opened a book on finance written in 1992. The book was still relevant in all its content except that the examples were no longer realistic: Interest rates in 1992 were often around 12% to 15% in some currencies, whereas 15 years later they were closer to 2%. (Today they are around 0.2%!)

Even books written well before the advent of computers may remain interesting.

All the contextual knowledge gained through these ways of investing in stable knowledge will inform and improve many decisions every day. And all the domain-specific words learned will make discussions during meetings more efficient. You won't have to spend the first part of each meeting clarifying vocabulary anymore.

Summary

Even in the most fast-changing projects there is still some room for traditional documents, but only for stable knowledge, which can be documented once as evergreen content. The examples presented in this chapter are just examples, not rules.

Paying attention to how often pieces of knowledge change is a good strategy for reducing your workload over time because it means you can create documents that need to be manually updated only for knowledge that almost never changes. In other cases, you need to use the more dynamic forms of documentation described elsewhere in this book, and you must rely more on conversations, working collectively, and living documents instead.

Chapter 10

Avoiding Traditional Documentation

We embrace documentation, but not hundreds of pages of never-maintained and rarely-used tomes. #agilemanifesto

—@sgranese on Twitter

I don't know many developers who love traditional forms of documentation. I've been collecting alternatives for years, some of which look like documentation and some of which don't. As a continuation of Chapter 1, "Rethinking Documentation," this chapter rebels against the documentation establishment (see Figure 10.1) and explores a number of techniques that contribute to the preservation and sharing of knowledge but that are usually not thought of as documentation techniques.

Figure 10.1 *NODocumentation is a manifesto for exploring alternatives to traditional forms of documentation, where the "NO" actually means "Not Only." We acknowledge the purpose of documentation, but we disagree with the way it's usually done. NODocumentation is about exploring better alternatives for transferring knowledge between people and across time.*

> **Note**
> Documentation is only a means, not an end, and it is not a product.

Let's start this exploration with the recognition that healthy teams working together and having conversations already exchange knowledge efficiently.

Conversations About Formal Documentation

> Having conversations, is more important than documenting conversations, is more important than automating conversations.
> —*@lunivore (Liz Kheogh)*

> A phone call can save twenty emails. A face to face chat can save twenty phone calls.
> —*@geoffcwatts on Twitter*

Written documentation is so often the default choice when it comes to documentation that the word *documentation* has often come to be used to mean "written document." However, when we say we need documentation, we mean that there's a need for knowledge transfer from some people to some other people. The bad news is that not all media are equal when it comes to the efficiency of transferring knowledge.

Alistair Cockburn analyzed three dozen projects over the course of two decades. He reported on his findings in books and articles, and he produced a famous diagram illustrating the effectiveness of different modes of communication (see Figure 10.2).[1]

Although the diagram in Figure 10.2 is a bit dated, it recaps Alistair's observation that people working and talking together at the whiteboard is the most effective mode of communication, whereas paper is the least effective.

Most of the time, effective sharing of knowledge is best done by simply talking and asking and answering questions rather than through written documents.

Therefore: Favor conversations between everybody involved over written documents. Unlike all written artifacts, conversations are interactive and fast, they convey feelings, and they have a high bandwidth.

---

1. Alistair Cockburn. *Agile Software Development*. Boston: Addison-Wesley Longman Publishing Co., Inc., 2002.

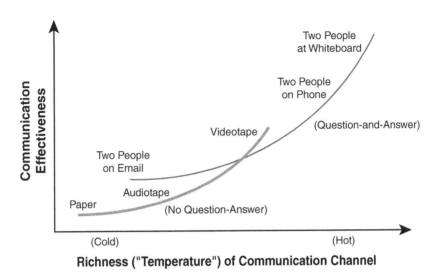

Figure 10.2 *The effectiveness of communication improves with the richness of the communication channel*

Conversations have several important characteristics:

- **High bandwidth:** Conversations offer high bandwidth compared to writing plus reading, as more knowledge can be efficiently communicated over a given period of time.

- **Interactive:** Both sides of the conversation have opportunities to ask for clarification and train the topic on what's most useful for them, whenever they want to.

- **Just in time:** Both sides of the conversation only talk about what's of interest for them.

These key properties of conversations make them the most effective form of communication for sharing knowledge.

In contrast, written documentation is wasteful because it takes time to write and also because it takes time to locate where the relevant parts are—and then it's unlikely that the content will fit the expectations. Even worse, it's likely that the content will be misunderstood.

Wiio's Laws

Professor Osmo Antero Wiio created Wiio's laws, which are serious observations formulated in a humorous way about how human communication usually fails except by accident:[2]

- Communication usually fails except by accident.

- If communication can fail, it will.

- If communication cannot fail, it still most usually fails.

- If communication seems to succeed in the intended way, there's a misunderstanding.

- If you are content with your message, communication certainly fails.

- If a message can be interpreted in several ways, it will be interpreted in a manner that maximizes the damage.

Human communication works best through interactive dialogue, with the opportunity for the receiver of information to react, disagree, rephrase, or ask for more explanation. This feedback mechanism is essential to fix the curse of one-way human communication highlighted by Professor Wiio.

Alistair Cockburn expresses similar findings in his book *Agile Software Development*:

> To make communications as effective as possible, it is essential to improve the likelihood that the receiver can jump the communication gaps that are always present. The sender needs to touch into the highest level of shared experience with the receiver. The two people should provide constant feedback to each other in this process so that they can detect the extent to which they miss their intention.[3]

A face-to-face, interactive, and spontaneous form of documentation is the best way to improve on the fate of miscommunication highlighted by Professor Wiio. If all your stakeholders are happy with talking with the team for all questions and feedback, then change nothing. You don't need written documentation.

---

2. http://jkorpela.fi/wiio.html

3. Alistair Cockburn. *Agile Software Development*. Boston: Addison-Wesley Longman Publishing Co., Inc., 2002.

> **Note**
>
> The goal of agile documentation is to "help people interact" in several ways:
>
> - Knowing who to contact
>
> - Knowing how to work on the project, guidelines, style, and inspirations
>
> - Sharing the same vocabulary
>
> - Sharing the same mental model and metaphors
>
> - Sharing the same goal

The Rule of Three Interpretations

Jerry Weinberg also wrote about the problem of making an interpretation of a received message, and he's proposing how to check your understanding thanks to what he calls the Rule of Three Interpretations:

> If I can't think of at least three different interpretations of what I received, I haven't thought enough about what it might mean.[4]

This rule doesn't prove that one of your interpretations is the one intended, but it helps avoid the illusion that the random first interpretation is the right one.

Obstacles to Conversations

There would be no need to emphasize the importance of conversations if people were easily having conversations in the workplace. Unfortunately, this is not the case often enough.

Years of working together by handing documents over the wall have trained many people not to have conversations except in meetings, where conversations are often negotiations. Corporate environments with politics and information retention have also trained colleagues not to share too much knowledge too early in order to remain in the game and to keep power, including blocking power.

People from different teams or departments or people assigned on different projects or in different locations tend to have far fewer conversations than do close neighbors in the same team and project. They tend to use colder (not interactive) and less effective modes of communication, such as email or phone calls instead of

---

4. Weinberg, Gerald M. *Quality Software Management Volume 2: First-Order Measurement*. New York: Dorset House, 1993.

face-to-face communication. It's important to note that hierarchical distance—that is, not having the same management—is at least as great an impediment to having conversations as geographic distance.

Working Collectively for Continuous Knowledge Sharing

The idea of ownership of activities is another conversation-killer:

Product "Manager"
Product "Owner"
Scrum "Master"
I have no idea why people aren't collaborating!

—@lissijean on Twitter

Defect tracking systems certainly don't promote communication between programmers and testers. They can make it easy to avoid talking directly to each other.
—Lisa Crispin and Janet Gregory, Agile Testing[5]

Separation of people by functions in separate teams, like the Dev, QA, and BA teams, is a great way to make conversations less likely. Old clichés also reduce the likelihood that people will even imagine meeting and talking together:

"I'm a tester, I must wait for the development to be finished to start testing."

"I'm a BA, so I must solve the problem by myself before handing it to the developers to implement."

"I'm a developer, my job is to execute what's been specified beforehand, and my job is not to test it once it's done."

I've heard that some business analysts have a hard time imagining not producing documents of a large enough size, for fear that their work will not be visible. They seem to believe that simply talking to help the project may not be enough to justify their role. Here we see how perverse this system has become, producing waste (large early documents) not for their value per se but to make the work visible to managers. Fear of losing a job or individual incentives feed this kind of counterproductive behavior.

---

5. Crispin, Lisa, and Janet Gregory. *Agile Testing: A Practical Guide for Testers and Agile Teams.* Hoboken: Addison-Wesley, 2009.

However, working collectively is an opportunity for continuous knowledge sharing. Make sure that everybody knows that the only goal is to deliver value. Make the work environment safe for everyone. Even with far fewer documents, there's still a role for traditional BA and QA team members, but it needs to be transformed into a continuous contribution to a collective adventure that we call a project or a product.

Therefore: Reassure everyone that it's perfectly okay to have conversations often and spend less time writing, and nobody should feel guilty about that. Promote collective work over separate job posts. Embrace the idea that close collaboration enables continuous knowledge sharing. However, ensure that the few most critical pieces of knowledge are recorded in a persistent fashion somewhere.

Have everyone, even from different teams, sit close to each other most of the time, around the same table if possible, so that spontaneous communication can happen without obstacle.

Conversations are good. When creating software, we need to have conversations, and we need to program code. It's often a great idea to do all that at once, continuously, together with one or more colleagues.

There are many good reasons for working collectively, including improving the quality of the software for its users and for its maintainers, thanks to continuous review and the continuous discussions on the design.

But working collectively, with frequent conversations, is a particularly effective form of documentation, too. Pair programming, cross programming, mob programming and the three amigos totally change the game with respect to documentation, as knowledge transfer between people is done continuously and at the same time the knowledge is created or applied on a task.

Pair Programming

OH: "Mob programming. It's like 'pair programming meets RAID6.'"

—*@pcalcado on Twitter*

Pair programming: the best way to do less email, attend fewer meetings, AND write less documentation!

—*@sarahmei on Twitter*

Pair programming is a key technique from Extreme Programming. If code reviews are good, why not do them all the time?

In pair programming, the person writing code, called the *driver*, narrates for the observer what's happening, and the observer in turn replies with acknowledgements, remarks, corrections, and any other kind of feedback. The observer, also known as the *navigator*, talks to the driver to guide the work in progress, suggesting possible next steps and expressing strategies for solving the task.

Working in pairs may not be something you are comfortable with and good at immediately, but it's something you can learn through practice, on the job or in coding dojos or on code retreats. There are various styles of pair programming, such as ping-pong pairing, where one person in the pair writes a failing test and then passes the keyboard for the other to make it pass and refactor.

For sharing knowledge as much as possible in order to have true collective ownership, in pair programming it's common to regularly change the partners in the pairs on a given task. Depending on the teams, this rotation of pairs can happen as frequently as every hour, or every day, or it may happen just once a week. Some teams don't have a fixed frequency but require that any task cannot be finished by the pair who started it.

Cross Programming

Cross programming is a variant of pair programming where the observer is not a developer but a business expert. Whenever the programming task requires a deep understanding of the business domain, it's a form of collaboration that is highly efficient but also very effective as all decisions taken by the pair in front of the computer are more relevant to the business. The name was coined by my colleague Houssam Fakih, who talked about this approach in conferences.[6]

Mob Programming

> Mob programming is a software development approach where the whole team works on the same thing, at the same time, in the same space, and at the same computer. This is similar to pair programming where two people sit at the same computer and collaborate on the same code at the same time. With Mob Programming the collaboration is extended to everyone on the team, while still using a single computer for writing the code and inputting it into the code base.
>
> —*mobprogramming.org*

> All the brilliant people working at the same time, in the same space, at the same computer, on the same thing.
>
> —*Woody Zuill*[7]

---

6. @Houssam, https://speakerdeck.com/fakih/cross-programming-forging-the-future-of-programming

7. Zuill, Woody. "Mob Programming–A Whole Team Approach," https://www.agilealliance.org/wpcontent/uploads/2015/12/ExperienceReport.2014.Zuill_.pdf

Mob programming is a recent addition to the stable of collective forms of programming and has quickly gained popularity. If Extreme Programming turned the code review knob to 10, mob programming goes even further, turning it to 11.

In mob programming, there is no question of pair rotation as everybody's always present on any task, so everybody knows about every task. That's literally collective ownership—in the same place at the same time.

In a team of five people doing mob programming full time, knowledge sharing is not an issue, as it's done continuously, every second. Whenever someone has to attend a meeting outside, the rest of the team keeps on working, almost unaffected.

The Three Amigos (or More)

A Product Owner, a Developer, and a Tester sit down to talk about something that the system under development should do. The Product Owner describes the user story. The Developer and Tester ask questions (and make suggestions) until they think they can answer the basic question, "How will I know that this story has been accomplished?"

No matter how or when it's done, these three amigos (to borrow a term from my friends at Nationwide) must agree on this basic criteria or things will go wrong.

—*George Dinwiddie, http://blog.gdinwiddie.com/2009/06/17/*
if-you-dont-automate-acceptance-tests/

The concept of the three amigos working together during specification workshops is central to the BDD approach. In contrast with pair programming, cross programming, and mob programming, the three amigos are not working on code but on concrete scenarios describing the expected business behavior of the software to build. Still, everyone involved owns the scenarios, and it does not matter who writes them down on paper or in a test automation tool (such as Cucumber). Although the common term is "three amigos," in practice there may be more than three whenever another perspective (for example, UX, Ops) is key for the success of the work.

Event Storming as an Onboarding Process

Alberto Brandolini invented Event Storming,[8] a collaborative modeling activity using sticker notes on a large wall. He says that some teams find it valuable to run a new event storming session whenever a new member joins the team, as a fast onboarding mechanism. I can testify that event storming works very well for that. As a consultant spending just a few days always in new teams with new domains, I need to learn as much as possible of the new domain in a short period of time. Recently I've used

---

8. https://www.eventstorming.com/

short event storming sessions for that, even if the team has done it several times before. It is really impressive how much you can learn in just two hours with this kind of workshop.

It happened recently that a business domain expert in an event storming session said that he had already created well-crafted diagrams on the domain. When we were mostly done with posting the events on the wall and organizing them, he drew the diagram on the whiteboard. It was interesting that his diagram was in many ways more complete than our wall of events. Still, the interactive workshop form meant that we were all much more engaged with our wall of stickers than is typically the case when just looking at a static diagram. The session became a game of comparing the diagram and the events wall to better understand both, and a lot of new insights appeared in this process.

Knowledge Transfer Sessions

Knowledge transfer (KT) sessions are common in companies that don't tend to do pair programming or mob programming. The teams plan KT as part of their scheduled work, often in addition to creating brief documents, to make sure the knowledge is actually shared and well understood. According to Wiio's laws, that is a good idea. A typical example of KT would be to exchange the knowledge on the deployment before a release, when the Ops are in another silo of the organization. One way to share knowledge in this case is to perform a dry run of the deployment, based on the deployment document and all the automated deployment manifests. This way, any issue, question, or mistake can be spotted quickly during the session—and all this happens during regular working hours.

Of course, an alternative is to directly work collectively between the developers and the Ops people to prepare, configure, and document all the deployment process. KT can be a step in this direction for traditional companies, just as code reviews are a step toward pair programming.

Continuous Documentation

Collective forms of work are optimal for continuous documentation. Face-to-face interactive conversations are the most efficient form of communication, and pair programming, cross programming, the three amigos, and mob programming organize the work precisely to maximize the opportunities for effective conversations. Documentation happens at the very time the knowledge is necessary. Everyone who must know about it is present and can immediately ask questions to clarify points.

When the task is done, those involved remember some of the key parts of knowledge and can forget the rest. If someone goes on vacation, the knowledge is safe in his or her colleagues' mind, so someone's absence does not impede the work in progress.

Truck Factor

Working collectively is very good for improving the *truck factor* of a project—that is, the number of people on a team who have to be hit with a truck before the project is in serious trouble. The truck factor measures the concentration of information in individual team members. A truck factor of one means that only one person knows critical parts of the system, and if that person is not available, it would be hard to recover the knowledge.

When several team members collaborate on every part of a project, knowledge is naturally replicated in more people. When they leave or go on vacations or just leave for a meeting, the work can carry on without them.

A small truck factor usually means someone is a hero on the project, with a lot of knowledge not shared with other teammates. This is definitely a problem for the resilience of the project, and management should be aware of it. Introducing collective forms of programming is a nice way to mitigate such risk. Moving the hero to another team nearby is another way to deal with it.

Coffee Machine Communication

Not all exchange of knowledge has to be planned and managed. Spontaneous discussions in a relaxed environment often work better and must be encouraged.

Random discussions at the coffee machine or at the water fountain are invaluable. Sometimes the best exchange of knowledge is spontaneous. You meet a colleague or two and start talking. Then you have something like a content negotiation to find topics each of you is interested in. You may land on a nonprofessional topic. In this case, you are creating a bond, which is invaluable. When you choose a professional topic, you've landed on the best type of communication: You've chosen this topic because all of you have an interest in it. You have questions about your current tasks, and the other people are happy to help with answers or stories from their own experience.

I believe that this kind of communication is the very best way to exchange knowledge. The topic is chosen freely based on shared interests. It's interactive, with questions and answers and a lot of spontaneous storytelling. It takes as long as required. I've sometimes missed meetings because the discussion at the coffee machine was way more essential to a project than the meeting I was supposed to attend.

Open space technology used for meet-ups and un-conferences replicates just this type of idea setting for larger groups. The Law of Two Feet states that everyone is free to move where the topic is most interesting. Other important principles are that "The people who are there are the right persons" and that "Whenever it starts it's the right time."

For this type of communication to work, there must be no hierarchy pressure around the coffee machine. Everybody must be free to chat with the CEO without being formal or shy.

Therefore: Don't discount the value of random discussions at the coffee machine or water fountain or in the relaxation area. Create opportunities for everyone to meet and talk at random in a relaxed setting. Decree that the rank in the hierarchy must be ignored within all relaxed conversations.

Google and other web startups propose fantastic facilities to encourage people to meet and talk. Just ask Jeff Dean, the famed Googler who often is referred to as the Chuck Norris of the Internet. As the 20th Googler, Dean has a laundry list of impressive achievements, including spearheading the design and implementation of the advertising serving system. Dean pushed limits by achieving great heights in the unfamiliar domain of deep learning, but he couldn't have done it without proactively getting a collective total of 20,000 cappuccinos with his colleagues. "I didn't know much about neural networks, but I did know a lot about distributed systems, and I just went up to people in the kitchen or wherever and talked to them," Dean told Slate. "You find you can learn really quickly and solve a lot of big problems just by talking to other experts and working together."[9]

La Gaité Lyrique, a cultural venue in Paris devoted to digital arts, has offices and meeting rooms, but the staff working there often prefer to host meetings in the foyers that are open to the public (see Figure 10.3). They even serve beer there, but I haven't seen people from the staff drink beer during the day.

I've spent countless hours in their foyers writing this book. I've experienced benefits that would be missed in a traditional work environments with closed meeting rooms:

- **The atmosphere:** Because there is a mix of people from the outside, many working and other having fun around tea or beer, the atmosphere is quite relaxed. This is pleasant, and it encourages thinking more creatively. You have the choice of low sofas and lounge chairs or dining tables with kitchen chairs. On a tense topic, I'd go for the lounge setting each time! To work on a diagram, I'd choose the dining table.

---

9. Tech Crunch, http://techcrunch.com/2015/09/11/legendary-productivity-and-the-fear-of-modern-programming/

Figure 10.3 *One of the informal foyers where most meetings take place*

- **Impromptu discussions:** For example, the general director of La Gaité Lyrique had a meeting with two people from the staff. They didn't book a space. When that conversation was done, the general director looked around to see who was there and went on to have very brief side discussions with colleagues who were attending another meeting in the foyer.

Thinking back on all the frustrations of planning meetings with busy clients in the corporate world, in boring meeting rooms, I was jealous that the staff working at La Gaite Lyrique had such a better collaboration experience.

Being there with the staff also means I had the opportunity to ask questions to the director of the venue himself in an impromptu fashion—no appointment, no secretary to filter access. Wow.

The director told me he definitely encourages informal meetings. Spending leisure time in the foyer instead of working is not a problem because everyone owns their responsibilities, regardless of how, when, where, or how long they work. Impromptu meetings can be totally improvised or planned in an informal space, like in the coffee machine area.

Coffee machine communication is not suited for every case, of course. There is no guarantee that you'll find the people you want to talk to around the coffee machine unless you plan the meeting. There's also no flip chart, no whiteboard, and unfortunately no teleconferencing system. And there is no privacy.

> **Note**
>
> Conversations, working collectively and places for spontaneous knowledge sharing represent the ideal form of documentation for most knowledge. However, this approach doesn't scale to large groups of people and is not enough for knowledge that is essential in the long term, when all team members are gone or have forgotten knowledge from the remote past. It's not enough for knowledge that is of interest to a large number of people, and it's not enough for knowledge that's too critical to be left as spoken words. Sometimes you need something more, and a way to gradually evolve from the informal to the more formal.

Idea Sedimentation

"Memory is the residue of thought." - simple but profound realization that is so important to my work. I intend to honor it more fully.

—*@tottinge on Twitter*

It can take time to find out whether a piece of knowledge was important or not. A lot of knowledge is important only at the moment it's created. You might debate design options, try one, find out it's not right, and try another. After some time, it may be obvious that it was the right choice, and the choice is visible in the code. It's already there. There is no need to do anything more.

You discuss options around the coffee machine. You mentally simulate how they will perform. Everybody agrees on the best option. Then a pair goes back to their computer to implement it. The knowledge exchanged and created during the discussion was important *at that particular time*. But the next day, it's already nothing more than a mere detail.

Once in a while, some of this knowledge remains important even after a while. It gets reinforced until it's worth recording to be shared with a larger audience and for the future.

Therefore: Within small groups of people, favor quick, fast, cheap interactive means of knowledge exchange such as conversations, sketching, and sticky notes. Only promote to more heavyweight forms of documentation the fraction of knowledge that has repeatedly proven to be useful, that is critical, or that everybody should know, especially at a larger scale.

Start with impromptu conversations and later turn the key bits into something permanent, whether it be augmented code, evergreen content, or anything durable.

The knowledge exchanged live can be captured as traces, through a photograph taken with your smartphone, handwritten notes, and so on (see Figure 10.4). But these forms of documentation will often be ignored later on.

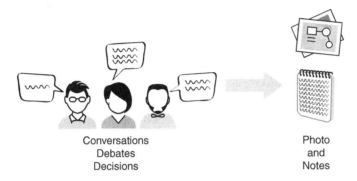

Conversations
Debates
Decisions

Photo
and
Notes

Figure 10.4 *Conversations to traces*

The sedimentation metaphor relates ideas that are flowing to sand flowing in a stream. The sand particles move along quickly, but some of them become sediment at the bottom of the stream, where they accumulate slowly. A similar process is at work in a wine decanter (see Figure 10.5).

Figure 10.5 *Particles settling to the bottom of a wine decanter*

Make a napkin sketch to document a design aspect, and later if it proves essential, turn it into something maintainable, like a plain-text diagram or a living diagram or a visible test.

Use bullet points to document the quality attributes, and later if it hasn't changed much, turn the bullets into executable scenarios.

Throw-Away Documentation

Some documentation is useful for only a limited period of time and can then be deleted. For example, you need a specific diagram while you're designing around a problem. When you're done with the problem, the diagram immediately loses most of its value because nobody cares anymore about the focus of that diagram. And for the next problem, you need another completely different diagram with another focus.

Therefore: Don't hesitate to throw away documentation that is specific to a particular problem.

When it's worthwhile to archive a diagram, turn it into a blog post, telling the story with the diagram as an illustration.

One important set of transient documentation is everything about planning, like the user stories and everything about estimation, tracking, and so on. A user story is useful only just before development. A burndown chart is useful only during an iteration. (You may want to keep the stats to check later how hard it is to plan and estimate, but that is something different.) You can throw away user story sticky notes after the iteration.

On-Demand Documentation

The best documentation is documentation that you really need and that suits actual purposes. The best way to achieve it is to create the documentation on demand, in response to actual needs.

A need you have right now is a proven need from a real person. It's not a speculation of *something* that *someone* could find useful in *some future*. The need you have right now is precise and has a purpose, and it can be expressed as a question. The documentation to be created will just have to answer the question. This is a simple algorithm to decide *when* to create documentation about *what* topic.

Therefore: Avoid speculating on what should be documented. Instead, pay attention to all questions asked or questions that were not asked but that should have been asked, as signals that some knowledge needs to be documented.

Just-in-Time Documentation

Documentation is best introduced just in time. The need for documentation is a precious feedback, a "knowledge gap" signal that should trigger some documentation action in response. The most important bit of documentation may be the documentation that is missing. Listen to knowledge frustrations to decide when to fill the gap.

> **Note**
>
> The idea of just-in-time documentation is inspired by the pull system Lean. A *pull system* is a production or service process that is designed to deliver goods or services as they are required by the customer or, in the production process, when required by the next step.

You might not invest time in some documentation action on each question. There's a need for some threshold:

- Some follow the "Rule of Two": When you must answer the same question twice, start documentation about it.
- Open-source projects sometimes rely on community votes to decide what to spend time on, including for the documentation.
- Commercial products sometimes rely on website analytics to decide what to spend time on, including for the documentation.
- Peter Hilton on Documentation Avoidance has his own take on this process, which is similar to the Rule of Two:

  1. Don't write the docs.

  2. Bluff, "it's on the wiki."

  3. Still don't write the docs.

  4. If they come back, feign ignorance.

  5. Then write it.

  6. Later, casually mention that you "found it."[10]

---

10. Peter Hilton, https://www.slideshare.net/pirhilton/documentation-avoidance

In practice, you can keep it low tech: Every time you're asked for information for which you don't have any documentation already available, log the request as a sticky note on a wall.

Whenever you have repeated requests for a similar kind of information, you can decide as a team to invest some minimal work to create it, using a rustic voting mechanism on the wall.

Start manual and informal. Observe and discuss the sticky notes during team ceremonies; throw them away or promote them to clean automated documentation tasks if that is what the team decides.

Then start by explaining interactively, using any existing and improvised support: browsing the source code, searching and visualizing in the IDE, sketching on paper or a whiteboard, or even using PowerPoint or Keynote as a quick drawing pad. (It's sometimes easier to use a tool when you need a lot of "copy-paste-change a little" kinds of sketches.) Then immediately refactor the key parts of the explanation into a little section of documentation. You know what parts of the explanations are essential from the interactions with your colleagues. If something was difficult to understand or surprising or came as an "Aha!" moment, then it's probably worth keeping for other people later.

Peter Hilton has another fantastic trick for write documentation, which he calls "reverse just-in-time doc":

> Instead of writing documentation in advance, you can trick other people into writing JIT documentation by asking questions in a chat room (and then pasting their answers into the docs).[11]

Provoking Just-in-Time Learning Early

Fixing bugs or making small evolutions, from the code to production, is a great way to quickly learn about an application and its complete development process. That's why many companies include bug fixing and minor evolution tasks as part of the immediate onboarding process for newcomers. This creates needs for knowledge, which in itself triggers the need to find sources of knowledge: people, artifacts, whatever.

Some startups have a policy that you must deliver something into production by yourself, with some guidance, within your first two days on the job. This forces you to quickly discover the full process and all colleagues involved, if any. It's also a mark of trust: You are trusted enough to be allowed to deliver something immediately, for real. It's also a mark of confidence in the process, the tests, and the deployment

---

11. Peter Hilton, https://www.slideshare.net/pirhilton/documentation-avoidance

automation strategy. You not only learn the code, you also learn that you can trust the delivery approach and that the typical timeframe of a change is very short. It's also a great way to get fresh feedback on the process. If the installation and the prerequisite workstation setup takes two days or more, there's no way you can deliver something in two days. If someone has to help often during the local developer setup, then you need better documentation at a minimum or, preferably, better automation of the process. The same goes for the full delivery pipeline and any other matter.

If you have a weird in-house or proprietary stuff that new joiners have to learn, newcomers will tell you that there is a standard alternative that you could switch to.

Astonishment Report

Newcomers' superpower is to be bring a fresh perspective. An astonishment report is a simple yet effective tool for learning both about what should be documented and what could be improved.

Ask all newcomers to report all their surprises during their very first days on the job. Even if they come from the same company or from a similar background, they might bring fresh perspectives. Suggest that each newcomer keep a notebook and take notes immediately after noticing an astonishment before they forget it. It's paramount to preserve the candor, so keep the observation period short, such as two days or a week. Even two days might be long enough to get so acclimated that weird stuff is no longer so weird. Improve based on the remarks.

Including Some Upfront Documentation

> Be the adult you wish you had around when you were a child. Write the documentation you wish you had when you started on this project.
>
> —*@willowbl00 on Twitter*

Sometimes an on-demand documentation approach can be supplemented by some upfront documentation. The danger is that you might create speculative documentation that may never be useful. The benefit is that obviously essential knowledge becomes available to help people without waiting for the Rule of Two to trigger.

Imagine yourself as a beginner on the project, knowing nothing. If you remember what it was like when you joined, it's simpler. Then create the ideal documentation that you would have loved to find.

However, the curse of knowledge can make this approach mostly ineffective. You simply might not be able to imagine anymore what it's like not knowing something that you know now.

It's extremely hard to guess in advance what information will be useful for other people you don't know yet, trying to do tasks you can't predict. Still, there some heuristics can help you decide when a piece of knowledge should be documented right now:

- Everybody agrees it should be documented.

- It's a hot topic (controversial).

- It's been discussed for a long time, such as during the sprint planning ceremony.

- There has been a profound or shocking misunderstanding by some people involved.

- It's important, and there's no way it can be guessed or inferred from the code.

- It should be refactored to avoid the need for documentation, but it's not practical to do that now. Andy Schneider[12] has really nice words on improving the documentation every day, with a focus on empathy: "Make the value you've added permanent."

The maxim "Comment code that you are working on so the next person doesn't have to go through the same pain" does not tell you precisely when or when not to do something documentation related. It's still up to your judgment. But it brings home the point that it's all about protecting value for other people.

Techniques to stimulate on-demand documentation are to define the content of the documentation with the help of a skills matrix or through a knowledge backlog.

Knowledge Backlog

For a knowledge backlog, let each team member write on sticky notes the pieces of knowledge they'd like to have. Then have everyone put their notes on a wall and have them decide by consensus or by voting with dots what should be documented first. This could become your knowledge backlog. Every few weeks or every iteration, you can take one or two items and decide how to address them, whether through pair programming, augmenting the code to make the structure visible in the code itself, or documenting specific knowledge of the area as an evergreen document on the wiki.

The knowledge backlog creation session can be done within your retrospective.

However, beware of backlogs growing and avoid using an electronic tracker; stickers at the bottom of your whiteboard are enough, and the lack of room will remind you to keep the backlog small.

---

12. Andy Schneider was an attendee of the OOPSLA 2001 Workshop on Software Archeology who wrote the position paper "Software Archaeology: Understanding Large Systems," https://web.archive.org/web/20081121110405/http://www.visibleworkings.com/archeology/schneider.html

Skills Matrix

An alternative to creating a knowledge backlog is to create a skills matrix with pre-defined areas and ask each team member to declare his or her level of proficiency for each area. One limitation here is that the matrix will reflect the views of the person creating it and will ignore the skills areas ignored or neglected by this person.

You could use a skills matrix as a chart with many quadrants, as described by Jim Heidema in a blog post.[13] This is a chart that can be posted in the room to identify the skills needed and the people on the team. In the left column you list all the team members. Along the top you list all the various skills you need on the team. Then each person reviews his or her row, looking at each skill, and then identifies how many quadrants of each circle he or she can fill in, based on the range below the chart. The range is from no skills through teaching all skills in each column:

0: no skill

1: basic knowledge

2: perform basic tasks

3: perform all tasks (expert)

4: teach all tasks

Whenever the skills matrix reveals a lack of skills, you need to plan a training or improve the documentation in some way.

Interactive Documentation

Written documents don't have the opportunity for interaction. As Jukka Korpela comments on Wiio's laws, whenever a written document "such as a book or a Web page or a newspaper article, miraculously works, it's because the author participated in dialogues elsewhere."[14]

It takes more work than just typing text for a written document to be useful. George Dinwiddie advises in his blog to "document questions the reader may have" and to "get it reviewed by multiple people."[15] Written documentation should be like a record of an interactive conversation that worked, which makes it more likely to work again.

13. Jim Heidema, Agile Advice blog, http://www.agileadvice.com/2013/06/18/agilemanagement/leaving-your-title-at-the-scrum-team-room-door-and-pick-up-new-skills/

14. Jukka Korpela, http://jkorpela.fi/wiio.html

15. George Dinwiddie, http://blog.gdinwiddie.com/2010/08/06/the-use-of-documentation/

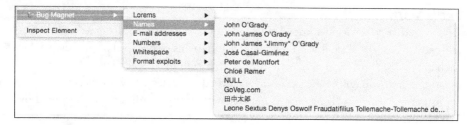

Figure 10.6 *BugMagnet*

But you can also push the limits of written words on paper, thanks to the available technologies all around us. You can create documentation that is interactive to some extent.

For example, Gojko Adzic turned a checklist of test heuristics into an additional menu in the browser, as a small assistant called BugMagnet (see Figure 10.6).[16]

Clicking on Names and then NULL in the menu directly fills the edit field in the browser with the string `"NULL"`. This could have remained a plain checklist to input manually into forms, but Gojko took the extra step of making it a little more interactive. Note the suggestive effect of navigating the menu: It calls for being used, at least more than a printed checklist.

Therefore: Whenever possible, prefer documentation that is interactive over static written words. Use hypermedia to navigate to the content through links. Turn the documentation into tools like checkers, tasks assistants, or search engines.

You already know several examples of interactive documentation as it is all around:

- Hypermedia documentation with navigable links, as generated by Javadoc and equivalent systems in other languages.

- Tools like Pickles that turn Cucumber or SpecFlow reports into interactive websites, or Fitnesse, which has been interactive from the start.

- Tools like Swagger that document a web API into an interactive website, with built-in capability to directly send requests and show the responses.

- Your IDE, which offers a lot of documentation features with a keystroke or a mouse click: call stack, search for type or reference, type hierarchy, find occurrences, find in the programming language abstract syntax tree, and so on.

---

16. BugMagnet, https://github.com/gojko/bugmagnet

As described in the next section, putting documentation into an automated form that is also readable allows for interactive discovery: You can execute and tinker with the automation code (scripts and tests) to understand the topic in more depth as you change it and see the effects.

Declarative Automation

Every time you automate a software task, you should take the opportunity to make it a form of documentation as well. Software development is increasingly making use of automation in all its aspects. Over the past decades, popular tools have changed the way we work, replacing repetitive manual tasks with automated processes. Continuous integration tools automate the building of software from its source, and they automate tests executions, even on remote target machines.

Tools like Maven, NuGet, and Gradle automate the burden of retrieving all the required dependencies. Tools like Ansible, Chef, and Puppet declare and automate the configuration of all IT infrastructures.

There's something interesting in this trend: You must describe what you want in order to automate it. You declare the process, and then the tool interprets it to do it so that you don't have to. The good news is that when you declare the process, you are documenting it—not just for the machine but also for humans as you have to maintain it, too.

Therefore: Whenever you automate a process, take the opportunity to make it the primary form of documentation for this process. Favor tools with a declarative style of configuration over tools that rely on a prescriptive style of scripts. Make sure the declarative configuration is meant primarily for a human audience, not only for the tool.

The goal is for the declarative configuration to be the single source of truth for the process. This is a great example of documentation that is both documentation for humans and documentation for machines.

What did we do before all the new automation tools? In the worst case, the process was done manually by someone with tacit knowledge of how to do it. When he or she was away, there was no way to do it at all. When we were a little luckier, there was a Microsoft Word document describing the process in a mix of text and command lines. However, the few times you tried to use it, you could hardly succeed without asking questions of the author: Some parts were missing and other were obsolete, with wrong indications. It was a manual process with deceiving documentation. When we were really lucky, there was a script to automate the process.

However, when it was throwing errors, we again had to ask the author for help to fix it, as the script code was quite obscure. And there was a separate Microsoft Word document, incomplete and obsolete, pretending to describe the process to please the management. It was an automated process, but still with no useful documentation.

Now we know better, and the key words to fix all the earlier problems are *declarative* and *automation*.

Declarative Style

For an artifact to be considered documentation, it must be expressive and easy to understand by people. It should also explain the intentions and the high-level decisions, not just the details of how to make it happen.

Imperative scripts that prescribe, step by step, what to do fail for any nontrivial automation. They only focus on the *how*, whereas all the interesting decisions and reflections that led to the *how* can only be expressed through comments, if at all.

On the other hand, declarative tools are more successful at supporting nice documentation, thanks to two factors:

- They already know how to do a lot of typical low-level things, which have been codified well by dedicated developers into reusable ready-made modules. This is an abstraction layer.

- They offer a declarative domain-specific language on top, which is at the same time more concise and expressive. This DSL is standard and is itself well documented, which makes it more accessible than your in-house scripting language. This DSL usually describes the desired state in a stateless and idempotent fashion; by moving the current state out of the picture, the explanations become much simpler.

Automation

Automation is essential to force declared knowledge to be honest. With modern approaches to automation, you tend to run the process very often, even continuously or dozens of times per hour. There is good pressure to keep it reliable and always up-to-date. You have to be smart to reduce the maintenance. Automation you rely on therefore acts as a *reconciliation mechanism* that makes it obvious when the declared process becomes wrong.

There has been a revolution, or perhaps an evolution. At last you can have knowledge that is up-to-date and that really explains what you want, the way you would talk about it. Tools are getting closer to serving the way we think, and that's changing the game in many aspects, in particular with respect to documentation.

Declarative Dependency Management

In the build automation landscape, *dependency managers*, also known as *package managers*, are tools that play a key role in the build process. They reliably download libraries, including their transitive dependencies, resolve many of the conflicts, and support your dependency management strategy, even across many modules.

Before that automation, dependency management was a chore done manually. You would manually download the libraries in some version into a /lib folder, later stored in the source control system. If the dependency had dependencies, you had to look at a website and download all of those, too. And you had to redo all of this whenever you had to switch to a new version of a dependency. It was not fun.

Popular dependency managers are available for most programming languages: Apache Maven and Apache Ivy (Java), Gradle (Groovy and JVM), NuGet (.Net), RubyGems (Ruby), sbt (Scala), npm (Node.js), Leiningen (Clojure), Bower (web), and many others.

To do their job of automating, these tools need you to declare all the direct dependencies you expect. You usually do this in a simple text file, often called a *manifest*. This manifest is the bill of materials that dictates what to retrieve in order to build your application.

When using Maven, the declaration is done in an XML manifest called pom.xml:

```
1  <dependency>
2  <groupId>com.google.guava</groupId>
3  <artifactId>guava</artifactId>
4  <version>18.0</version>
5  </dependency>
```

In Leiningen, the declaration is done in Clojure:

```
1  [com.google.guava/guava "19.0-rc1"]
```

Whatever the syntax, the declaration of the expected dependencies always happens in a tuple of the three values: group ID, artifact ID, and requested version.

In some of the tools, the requested version can be not only a version number, like 18.0, but a range such as [15.0,18.0) (meaning from version 15.0 to version 18.0 exclusive), or a special keyword such as LATEST, RELEASE, SNAPHOT, ALPHA, or BETA. You can see from these concepts of range and keywords that the tools have learned to work at the same level of abstraction we think at as developers. The syntax to express the necessary dependencies is declarative, and this is a good thing.

With declarative automation, the declaration of the requested dependencies is also the single source of truth for the documentation of the dependencies. The knowledge is already there, in the dependency manifest. As a consequence, there is no need to list these dependencies again in another document or in a wiki. If you made such a list, you would just risk forgetting to update it.

But, as usual, there's one thing missing so far in the declaration of the dependencies: You'd like to declare not just what you request from the tool but also the corresponding rationale. You need to record the rationale so that future newcomers can quickly grasp the reason behind each dependency included. Adding one more dependency should never be done too easily, so it's good to always be able to justify a dependency with a convincing reason. One way to do this is with comments next to the dependency entries in the file:

```
1  <dependencies>
2    <!-- Rationale: A very lightweight alternative to JDBC,
with no magic -->
3    <dependency>
4        <groupId>org.jdbi</groupId>
5        <artifactId>jdbi</artifactId>
6        <version>2.63</version>
7    </dependency>
8  <dependencies/>
```

You might be tempted to add a description, but you don't have to because it's already included in the POM of the dependency itself. In an IDE such as Eclipse, it's very easy to navigate to the POM of the dependency by pressing Ctrl (or Cmd on a Mac). As your mouse hovers over the dependency element in your POM, it turns into a link that allows you to directly jump to the POM of the dependency, as shown in Figure 10.7. That's integrated documentation mixed with declarative automation. Pure awesomeness!

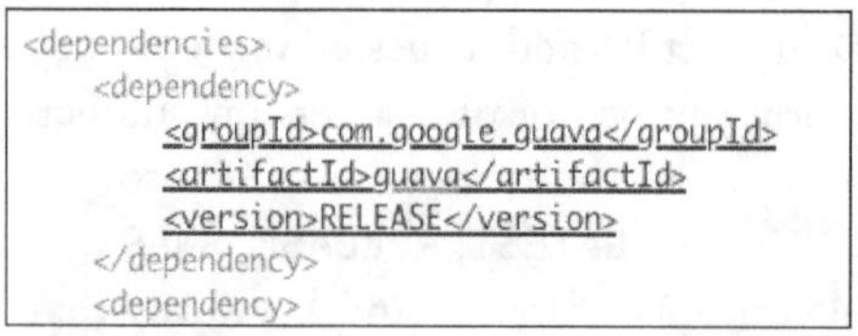

Figure 10.7 *Navigating the Maven dependencies in the Eclipse POM Editor*

Is that knowledge on the dependencies and their version accessible? It depends on the audience. For developers, the most accessible way is to look at the manifest and use the IDE, so there's no need to do anything more. One issue may be that when using ranges or keywords for the versions, you don't know the exact version being retrieved at a given point in time just by looking at the manifest. However, developers know how to query the dependency manager to get this information on demand. For example, in Maven they would run the following:

```
mvn dependency:tree -Dverbose
```

For nondevelopers, you would want to extract and publish the interesting content into an Excel document or to the wiki. But are nondevelopers really very interested in that kind of knowledge?

Declarative Configuration Management

> Sorry this is taking so long, I lost my bash history and therefore have no idea how we fixed this last time.
>
> *—@honest status page on Twitter*

Configuration management is much more complex than dependency management. It involves resources such as applications, daemons, and files, each with many attributes and with all their dependencies. However, some tools have taken a declarative approach similar to that of the dependency managers and their manifests. When using these tools, you are not supposed to use the command line much, as opposed to the situation in Figure 10.7.

The most popular tools for managing configuration are Ansible, Puppet, CfEngine, Chef, and Salt. However, some of them are imperative (Chef), while others are declarative (Puppet and Ansible).

For example, Ansible states that it "uses a very simple language [...] that allow you to describe your automation jobs in a way that approaches plain English,"[17] which is typical of a declarative approach, as explained on the Big Panda blog:

> Ansible's philosophy is that playbooks (whether for server provisioning, server orchestration or application deployment) should be declarative. This means that writing a playbook does not require any knowledge of the current state of the server, only its desirable state.[18]

---

17. https://www.ansible.com/overview/how-ansible-works
18. https://www.bigpanda.io/blog/5-reasons-we-love-using-ansible-for-continuous-delivery/

Puppet has a similar philosophy. Here's an excerpt of a Puppet manifest for managing NTP:

```
1  # Some comment if necessary...
2  service { 'ntp':
3    name      => $service_name,
4    ensure    => running,
5    enable    => true,
6    subscribe => File['ntp.conf'],
7  }
8
9  file { 'ntp.conf':
10   path    => '/etc/ntp.conf',
11   ensure  => file,
12   require => Package['ntp'],
13   source  =>  "puppet:///modules/ntp/ntp.conf",
14 }
```

Puppet emphasizes that its manifests are self-documented and provide proof of compliance even for many regulatory bodies:

Self-documentation

Puppet manifests are so simple, anyone can read and understand them, including people outside your IT and engineering departments.

Auditability

Whether it's an external or internal audit, it's great to have proof that you pass. And you can easily validate to your own executives that compliance requirements have been met.[19]

A declarative language like the ones used in these tools allows you to communicate the expected desired state not only to the too, but to the other humans on your team or to external auditors.

Again, what's often missing to make these manifests complete and useful documentation for humans is the rationale for each decision. If you consider that a Puppet manifest as-is is accessible to all the interested audience, then it would make sense to document the rationales and other high-level information into the manifest—for example, with comments.

Because the knowledge about the configuration is declared in a formal way for the tools, it also becomes possible to generate living diagrams when it can help reasoning. For example, Puppet includes a graph option that generates a .dot file of a diagram showing all the dependencies. This is useful when you experience an issue in the dependencies or when you want to have a more visual view of what's in the manifests.

Figure 10.8 shows an example of a diagram generated from Puppet.[20]

Relationships

Figure 10.8 *A diagram of resources dependencies, generated by Puppet*

---

20. John Arundel, http://bitfieldconsulting.com/puppet-dependency-graphs

This kind of diagram can be handy for refactoring the manifests to make them cleaner, simpler, and more modular. As John Arundel writes in his blog describing this feature of Puppet:

> As you develop Puppet manifests, from time to time you need to refactor them to make them cleaner, simpler, smaller and more modular, and looking at a diagram can be very helpful with this process. For one thing, it can help make it clear that some refactoring is needed.[21]

Declarative Automated Deployment

Much as with configuration management, a number of tools can automate your deployment, including the necessary company workflows and rollback procedures, and that can deploy only what needs to be changed. Some of these tools include Jenkins with custom or standard plugins and Octopus Deploy (.Net).

Here's an example of a deployment workflow from the Octopus website:[22]

- Redirect load balancer to a "down for maintenance" site

- Remove web servers from load balancer

- Stop application servers

- Back up and upgrade the database

- Start application servers

- Add web servers back to load balancer

In a tool like this, the deployment and release workflow is typically set up by clicking on the UI, and it is persisted in a database. Still, the workflow is described in a declarative manner that everyone can understand when looking at the tool screens. Whenever you want to know how it's done, you just have to look it up in the tool.

Because it's declarative and because the tool knows about the basics of deployment, it is possible to describe complex workflows in a concise way, closer to the way we think about it. For example, it is possible to apply standard continuous delivery patterns such as canary releases and blue-green deployment. Octopus Deploy manages that with a concept call *Lifecycle*, an abstraction that is useful for easily taking care of this kind of strategy.

---

21. John Arundel, http://bitfieldconsulting.com/puppet-dependency-graphs
22. https://octopus.com/blog/octopus-vs-puppet-chef

Tools can not only automate the work itself and reduce the likelihood of errors but also provide ready-made documentation for the standard patterns you could, or should, be using. This is therefore more documentation you don't have to write by yourself!

Say that you decide to adopt a blue-green deployment for your application. You can configure the tool to take care of it, and this is all you have to do now:

- Declare in a stable document such as a README file that you have decided to do blue-green deployments.

- Link to authoritative literature on the topic, such as the pattern on Martin Fowler's website.[23]

- Configure the tool and the lifecycle to support the pattern.

- Link to the page on the tool website that describes how the pattern is taken care of specifically in the tool.

The following is a description of the pattern in the context of the tool:

> Staging: when blue is active, green becomes the staging environment for the next deployment.
> Rollback: we deploy to blue and make it active. Then a problem is discovered. Since green still runs the old code, we can roll back easily.
> Disaster recovery: after deploying to blue and we're satisfied that it is stable, we can deploy the new release to green too. This gives us a standby environment ready in case of disaster.[24]

For an automation to be a case of declarative automation that provides documentation, the configuration of the tool has to be genuinely declarative, whether in text or on a screen and in a database. It also has to be at an abstraction level close to what matters for everyone involved. It cannot be obscure imperative steps with a lot of conditionals based on low-level details such as the absence of a file or the state of an operating system process.

Scaffolding a Step-by-Step Guide

Whenever you join a new team or a new project, you need to set up your work environment, and you need some documentation for that—at least this is how it still goes in many companies. There may be a Newcomers page on the wiki with a long list of

---

23. Martin Fowler, ThoughtWorks, http://martinfowler.com/bliki/BlueGreenDeployment.html

24. Octopus Deploy, http://docs.octopusdeploy.com/display/OD/Blue-green+deployments

steps to go through in order to start working on an application. Such a list is often not totally up-to-date. Links may be broken. Essential information may be missing because it was obvious in the mind of the author. Such issues exist even when newcomers join regularly.

Some teams have taken a further step, providing an installer for newcomers. You run the installer, it prompts for some specific questions, and you're done! These installers don't always work very well when they're custom in-house scripts, but the idea is there: Why document in text what could be automated, and documented, as a tool?

This approach, often called *scaffolding*, is not just for newcomers, but also allows users to start an application quickly. Ruby on Rails is probably the most popular tool for this approach.

Many tools can be used to do scaffolding. You can do scaffolding with custom scripts, Maven archetypes, Spring Roo, JHipster, and many others. Configuration management tools can sometimes also be used to create a working setup for new team members or to set up templates of applications that can be modified later.

If the resulting automation is rock solid, documentation of what it does is less of an issue, but in general I favor standard tools over in-house scripts, and I definitely would choose tools that are themselves well documented and maintained and that have a declarative configuration that can be considered itself as the documentation.

The scaffolding has to be really easy to use without a user guide. It should ask simple questions, guide the user step by step, provide sensible default values, and have very good examples of answers.

There is an open-source tool for scaffolding called JHipster.[25] It works with a command-line wizard, and here are some of the questions prompted when creating a new application from scratch:

- What is the base name of your application?
- Do you want to use Java 8?
- Which type of authentication would you like to use?
- Which type of database would you like to use?
- Which production database would you like to use?
- Do you want to use Hibernate second-level cache?
- Do you want to use clustered HTTP sessions?
- Do you want to use WebSockets?

---

25. JHipster, http://drissamri.be/blog/technology/starting-modern-java-project-with-jhipster/

- Would you like to use Maven or Gradle?
- Would you like to use Grunt or Gulp.js for building the front end?
- Would you like to use the Compass CSS Authoring Framework?
- Would you like to enable translation support with Angular Translate?

For each question, there is a clear narrative explaining the possible answers and the consequences to help make the decision. This is also inline, tailored help. The resulting code is the result of all the decisions. If you've chosen MySQL as the database, then you have a MySQL database setup.

It would be interesting to record the responses to all the questions of the wizard into a file (they're only kept as logs or in the console) to provide a high-level technical overview of the application. It might be included in the README file, for example.

A wizard should design helpful exceptions that precisely tell you what, how, and where to fix a problem that is thrown.

Machine Documentation

Before the cloud, we had to know our machines one by one, and there was often an Excel spreadsheet somewhere with a list of machines and their main attributes. This list was often obsolete.

Now that machines are moving somewhere in the cloud, we can no longer afford to keep a spreadsheet, as the information changes much too frequently, sometimes many times a day. But because the cloud itself is automated, very accurate documentation now comes for free, through the cloud API.

The cloud API is similar to declarative automation. You declare what you want, such as "I want a Linux server with Apache," and then you can query your current inventory of machines available and all their attributes. Many of these attributes are tags and metadata that add a higher level of information to the picture: Perhaps it's not a "2.6GHz Intel Xeon E5," but it's a "High-CPU machine," for example.

Remarks on Automation in General

> Don't do the same thing twice. If it's déjà -vu, then it's time to automate.
> —*Woody Zuill, in a conversation*

People are good for novel stuff. Machines are good for repeated stuff. Automation provides benefits—but at a cost. It is not an end in itself but a mean to save time and to improve reliability on repeated tasks. But there is always a point where the cost exceeds the benefits. You should invest in automation as long as the cost is low compared to the recurring benefits.

On the other hand, if a task is new or different each time, you should wait until you see enough repetition somewhere in the task before thinking about automation. Decide what to keep manual.

Enforced Guidelines

The best documentation does not even have to be read, if it can alert you at the right time with the right piece of knowledge.

Making information available is not enough. Nobody can read and remember all the possible knowledge ahead of time. And there is a lot of knowledge that you'd need without having any way to figure out that you need it.

> **Note**
>
> You don't even know that you don't know something that you should know.

Consider code guidelines. Many companies and teams spend time writing guidelines, but the resulting documents are seldom read and often ignored.

How do you document all the decisions that have been made and that everybody should conform to when doing their work? Examples of these decisions include the main architectural decisions, coding guidelines, and other decisions about style and team preferences.

A common approach is to spend time writing these decisions into a guideline or style book. The problem is that these decisions quickly add up to more pages than you expected, and a 12-page-long document full of "you shall do this" and "you shall not do that" is far from an exciting read. As a consequence, most of these documents are like legal documents: They are so boring that most team members never read them—even once. They pretend to have read them on arrival, but in fact they hardly went further than the second or third page.

Even when they've actually read them, the format as a list of rules is not memorable, and unless you like all the rules, you won't remember most of them. In practice, these guides are useful as a reference in case of doubt, and not much more.

However, without guidelines, code is at the mercy of everybody's own style, preferences or lack of skills. A consistent set of shared guidelines is essential to really work in a collective ownership fashion.

So how do people learn about all the decisions and style they have to conform to for real? They learn all that by reading other people's code, through code reviews, and through feedback from static analysis tools that catch rule violations.

Reading code works well when the code is exemplary, which is not always the case. Of course, code review and static analysis help improve that. Code review works well as long as the reviewers have all the decisions and style preferences in mind and all agree with them. Static analysis works well for every rule or decision that doesn't need nuance or contextual interpretation. And because static analysis tools must be configured to be useful, once configured, they are themselves naturally the reference documentation about all the guidelines.

Therefore: Use a mechanism to enforce the decisions that have been made into guidelines. Use tools to detect violations and provide instant feedback on violations as visible alerts. Don't waste time writing guideline documents that nobody reads. Instead, make the enforcement mechanism self-descriptive enough so that it can be used as the reference documentation of the guidelines.

Code analysis tools help maintain a high level of quality anywhere in the code, which in turn helps the code to be exemplary. And it also helps as a reference when the programmers are hesitant about a rule during a code review or while pair programming.

The point of enforced guidelines is to accept that documentation does not even have to be read to be useful. The best documentation brings you the right piece of knowledge at the right time—when you need it. Enforcing rules, properties, and decisions through tools (or code reviews) is a way to teach the team members the knowledge they need precisely at the moment they ignore it.

> **Note**
> Enforced guidelines provide persistent knowledge made interactive again.

Some Examples of Rules

Cosmetic rules help with code consistency and when merging code. The following are examples:

- Curly brackets must not be omitted.

- Field names must not use Hungarian notation.

Rules on metrics help discourage overly complicated code. The following are some examples:

- Avoid deep inheritance trees (max = 5).

- Avoid complex methods (max = 13).

- Avoid overly long lines (max = 120 chars).

Rules provide a way to encourage or enforce better code. The following are some examples:

- Do not destroy the stack trace.
- Exceptions should be public.

Some rules can directly avoid bugs:

- `ImplementEqualsAndGetHashCodeInPairRule`
- Test for NaN correctly.

Even some architectural decisions can be made as rules. Consider these examples:

- `DomainModelElementsMustNotDependOnInfrastructure`
- `ValueObjectMustNotDependOnServices`

Then you can add some gamification on top of the rules, as illustrated in Figure 10.9.

Figure 10.9 *The guidelines enforcement force*

Evolving the Guidelines

Guidelines have a purpose, such as helping a team work together, reducing issues like bugs or errors when merging code, and preserving quality attributes such as performance and maintainability. There's no such a thing as an ideal and definitive set of guidelines. Instead, you should start with some guidelines, use them, and evolve them to make them as relevant as possible.

The best guidelines don't come from above. The best guidelines grow from the team or teams doing work and talking to each other to agree on shared guidelines that are useful. Don't hesitate to change the guidelines when necessary. Of course, you may not want to change the length of lines of code every day.

The following is a list of sample guidelines for a greenfield project:

- Unit test coverage >80%

- Complexity by method <5

- LOC by method < 25

- Inheritance depth < 5

- Number of args < 5

- Number of member data fields < 5

- All base Checkstyle rules

Enforcement or Encouragement

On a greenfield project, you typically start with a lot of enforced guidelines in a strict fashion, and every new line of code that violates them has its commit rejected. Other the other hand, on a legacy project, you usually can't do this because the existing code likely already contains thousands of violations, even for a small module. Instead, you might choose to enforce only the few most important guidelines and make every other guideline a *warning*. Another approach is to have stricter rules only for new lines of code.

Some teams start with some guidelines, and when they are comfortable with them, they add more rules and make the existing guidelines stricter in order to progress.

When your company requires every application to follow a minimum set of guidelines, each team or application can decide to make it stricter but not weaker. Tools like Sonar provide inheritance between sets of guidelines, called *quality profiles*, to help do that. You can define a profile that extends the company profile and add more rules or make the existing rules stricter to suit your own taste.

Declarative Guidelines

Because sets of guidelines, or quality profiles, can be named, their names are also part of the documentation on guidelines. You can simply refer new joiners to the build configuration, where they will find the name of the set of guidelines. From there, they can look it up on the tool and find out that it extends the company sets of guidelines. They can browse the rules by category or severity and check parameters as they wish, in an interactive fashion. There's even a search engine.

Each given rule has a key, a title, and a brief description of what it is and why. With the key or the title, you can look up more complete documentation on the tool or directly on the web.

For example, if you look up `ImplementEqualsAndGetHashCodeInPairRule` on the web, you immediately find its reference documentation, from the Gendarme plugin for .Net:

> This rule checks for types that either override the `Equals(object)` method without overriding `GetHashCode()` or override `GetHashCode` without overriding `Equals`. In order to work correctly types should always override these together.[26]

Such reference documentation usually includes several code samples, a bad example, and a good example to illustrate the point of the rule. This is great, because the documentation is already there. Why write it again when it has been already done well by someone else?

A Matter of Tools

Compilers, code coverage, static code analysis tools, bug detectors, duplication detectors, and dependency checkers are common examples of tools for setting up enforced guidelines in practice.

Sonar is a popular tool that itself relies on many plugins to actually do its job. When the configuration of tools is not meant to be documentation with verbose XML and rules identifiers, tools like Sonar can make the configurations of coding rules more accessible in a convenient UI, to the point of becoming the reference about guidelines.

Even when plugins are actually configured via an XML file, Sonar displays the list of coding rules nicely onscreen, and you can modify them there, along with the reference description in prose. This information can also be exported in a spreadsheet format. If you really want to spend time documenting coding guidelines manually, just give the overall intentions, priorities, and preferences and let the tools provide the details!

Other guidelines may be enforced by access control. Say that you have decided that a legacy component is frozen from now on, and nobody has the right to commit on it. You can simply revoke the write grants to everyone. But this in itself does not

---

26. https://www.mono-project.com/docs/tools+libraries/tools/gendarme/rules/design/#implementequal
sandgethashcodeinpairrule

explain why you're making the decision. You should therefore expect questions, and the knowledge transfer will happen as a conversation.

Most automated means are not 100% relevant at any time, so sometimes enforcement will be violated. This is not necessarily a disaster, as long as the enforcement maintains enough continuous awareness about the guidelines.

If an element of the guideline is not enforceable, then perhaps it is not really an element of a guideline. You might want to add it to a short checklist for manual code review or review during pair programming. But it is not an enforced guideline any longer.

However, if you have new rules, you may consider extending the existing tools with a new rule or new plugin. Compilers often have extension points where you can hook your own additional rules. Tools like Sonar are extensible with custom plugins, and checkers are extensible with new rules, sometimes with XML and sometime only with code.

Guidelines or Design Documentation?

Imagine that your set of guidelines for the domain model is as follows:

- Functional first (immutable and side effect free by default)
- Null free
- No framework pollution
- No SQL
- No direct use of a logging framework
- No import of any infrastructure technology

At the time of this writing, existing static analysis tools and plugins don't support all this out of the box, so you can't do enforced guidelines unless you create your own tool. However, these guidelines are design decisions that can be documented in the code itself, perhaps by using annotations, as discussed in Chapter 4, "Knowledge Augmentation."

In fact, such design declarations expressed as annotations make it possible to enforce your coding standards and other guidelines with analysis tools. Once you declare that your code should be all immutable in a given package, it becomes possible to check the main violations using a parser.

Immutability and null-free expectations can be enforced programmatically. This is far from perfect, but it is enough for any new joiner to learn the style after a few commits.

Warranty Sticker Void if Tampered With

Hamcrest[27] is a popular open-source project that provides matchers to write beautiful unit tests. It provides a lot of matchers out of the box, and you can also extend it with your own custom matchers. Usually when you do that you should read the developer's guide, but not everyone does that. Therefore, Hamcrest uses naming in a creative way to make it very unlikely to break a design decision by ignorance:

```
1   /**
2    * This method simply acts a friendly reminder not to implement\
3    * Matcher directly and instead extend BaseMatcher. It's easy
4    * to ignore JavaDoc, but a bit harder to ignore compile errors
5    *
6    *
7    *
8    * @see Matcher for reasons why.
9    * @see BaseMatcher
10   * @deprecated to make
11   */
12     @Deprecated
13 _  void _dont_implement_Matcher___instead_extend BaseMatcher_();
```

The Hamcrest `Matcher` method doesn't implement a matcher but extends `Base Matcher`, which is an impossible-to-miss and otherwise useless documentation method. You can still break it deliberately, but the point is that you're aware of doing that. It's a kind of "warranty void if tampered" sticker. This is an original way to do unavoidable documentation.

The funny things is that in this example of enforced guidelines, the enforcement is done by the potential violator himself or herself.

The following are some more similar examples:

- **Documentation by exception:** Say that you decide to turn a legacy component from read-write to read-only. You can document this with text or annotations, but how can you make sure nobody will add write behavior? One way is to keep the write methods on all the data access objects but have them throw exceptions is to use `IllegalAccessException("The component is now READ-ONLY")`.

---

27. Hamcrest, http://hamcrest.org

- **License mechanism:** You can create a module that nobody should import except into one particular project, and you have no way to do that within the package manager itself. You can implement a very simple license mechanism: When you import the module, it throws exceptions, complaining that it's missing a license text file or license ENV variable. The license can be text such as "I should not import this module" acting as a disclaimer. You can hack it, but if you do, you accept the disclaimer!

Trust-First Culture

Enforcing guidelines as automated rules or through access restrictions may express a lack of trust to the teams, but it depends a lot on your company culture. If your culture really is a culture of trust, autonomy, and responsibility between everyone, then introducing enforced guidelines should be decided by consensus after discussions between everyone involved. In the worst case, introducing enforced guidelines could send the wrong signal and undermine trust, which would be a greater loss than the benefits you're after.

Constrained Behavior

Rather than document, you can influence or constrain the behavior instead. Enforcing guidelines is not the only approach to bring the right piece of knowledge at the right time to the developers; an interesting alternative is to influence or constrain them to do the right thing in the first place, without them being necessarily aware of it.

Making It Easy to Do the Right Thing

For example, you could decide that "from now on, developers MUST create more modular code, as new small services that MUST be deployed individually." You could even print this on the guidelines document and hope everyone will read it and follow this decision.

Or you could invest in changing the environment:

- **Provide good self-service CI/CD tools:** By making it easy to set up a new build and deployment pipeline, you make it more likely that developers will create new separate modules rather than put all new code into the same big ball of mud that they know how to build and deploy.

- **Provide a good microservices chassis** (see Chris Richardson's website, https://microservices.io): You can encourage modularity by making it easy to bootstrap a new microservice without spending time wiring together all the necessary libraries and frameworks.

In his book *Building Microservices*, Sam Newman writes on making it easy to do the right thing, with what he calls *tailored service templates*:

> Wouldn't it be great if you could make it easy for all developers to follow most of the guidelines you have with very little work? What if, out of the box, the developers had most of the code in place to implement the core attributes that each service needs?
>
> …
>
> For example, you might want to mandate the use of circuit breakers. In that case, you might integrate a circuit breaker library like Hystrix. Or you might have a practice that all your metrics need to be sent to a central an open source library like Dropwizard's Metrics and configure it so that, out of the box, response times and error rates are pushed automatically to a known location.[28]

The most famous tech companies embrace this approach with open-source libraries that you, too, can use. In the words of Sam Newman:

> Netflix, for example, is especially concerned with aspects like fault tolerance, to ensure that the outage of one part of its system cannot take everything down. To handle this, a large amount of work has been done to ensure that there are client libraries on the JVM to provide teams with the tools they need to keep their services well behaved.

The environment is also passing information. It's implicit and passive, and we don't often pay attention to that. You can make it deliberate and decide what message to pass by designing the path of least resistance in the environment to be the one that you favor.

More generally, you want to make behavior not just *easier* but also more *rewarding*. By showing the commit history as a nice pixel art diagram, GitHub makes it a rewarding thing to commit often. Developers' pride is powerful!

A major point of living documentation in general as advocated in this book is to offer simple ways to document to encourage doing it more.

Making Mistakes Impossible: Error-Proof API

Design your API in a way that makes it impossible to misuse. This reduces the need for documentation, since there's nothing to warn the user about.

---

28. Newman, Sam. *Building Microservices*. Sebastopol, CA: O'Reilly Media, Inc., 2015.

Michael L. Perry lists many common API traps in a blog post:

- You must set a property before calling this method.
- You must check a condition before calling this method.
- You must call this method after setting properties.
- You cannot change this property after calling a method.
- This step must occur before that step.[29]

These traps should not be documented; instead, they should be refactored to be removed! *Otherwise, the documentation will be a great case of shameful comment.*

There are endless ways to make an API impossible to misuse, including the following:

- Use types only to expose methods you can actually call, in any order.
- Use enums to enumerate every valid choice.
- Detect invalid properties as early as possible (for example, catch invalid inputs directly in the constructor), well before they are actually used, and then repair whenever possible, such as replacing nulls with null objects in the constructors or setters.
- It's not just about errors but also about any harmful naive usage. For example, if a class is likely to be used as the key in a hashmap, it should not make the hashmap slow or inconsistent. You could use internal caches to memorize the results of any slow computations of `hashcode()` and `toString()`.

A common objection is that experienced developers don't make these easy mistakes, so there is no need to be so defensive. However, even good developers have more important things to focus on than avoiding the traps of your API.

Don Norman calls advice on how to guide the use of something *affordances*.[30]

Design Principles for Documentation Avoidance

During QCon 2015, Dan North talked about a model in which code is either so old and well established that everybody knows how to deal with it, or it's so young that

---

29. Michael L. Perry, QED Code blog, http://qedcode.com/practice/provable-apis.html
30. Norman, Donald A. *The Design of Everyday Things*. New York: Basic Books, Inc., 2002.

the people doing it are still there, so they know all about it. Problems happen when you're in a gray zone between these two extremes.

Dan emphasizes the central role of knowledge sharing and knowledge preservation as a key ingredient of successful teams. He goes further, suggesting alternative ways to deal with this issue.

Replaceability First

Designing for replaceability reduces the need to know how things work. You don't need much documentation for components you can replace easily. Sure, you need to know *what* the components were doing, but you don't have to know *how* they were doing it.

In this mindset, you could give up maintenance. If you must change something, you could just rebuild it all. For this approach to work, every part has to be reasonably small and as independent as possible from every other component. This shifts the attention to the contracts that are between components.

Therefore: Favor a design that makes it easy to replace a part within the whole. Make sure that everybody knows exactly what the part does. Otherwise, you need documentation for the behavior—for example, the working software you can easily play with, self-documented contracts of the inputs and outputs, or automated and readable tests.

When the team does not care enough about design, the components grow and get hairy. They quickly get coupled to everything. As a result, you can never really replace them totally. Making the code easy to replace is still an act of design; it does not happen out of pure luck or without skills and care. It takes discipline. One obvious way is to limit the size of the component—for example, up to one page on the screen. Another way is to create strict restrictions on what components can call each other and preventing them from sharing data storage.

Even with an approach that favors replaceability, design skills remain necessary. For example, the open/closed principle is indeed a case of making the implementation replaceable easily; another is its good friend the Liskov substitution principle. Other solid principles also help. They are usually discussed at the class and interface levels. But they also apply at the level of components or services. But to be really replaceable at low cost, they have to be small—hence the idea of microservices.

Consistency First

Consistency in the code base is when code that you've never seen looks familiar so that you can deal with it easily.

—*Dan North at QCon London 2015*[31]

---

31. https://qconlondon.com/london-2015/speakers/dan-north.html

Being consistent reduces the need for documentation. In practice, consistency is hard to maintain beyond bounded areas; consistency is more natural within one component, within one programming language, and even within one layer. You often don't follow the same programming style for GUI logic as for server-side domain logic.

For a given area of the code base with a consistent style of code, once you know the style, there's nothing more to say for all elements in the area. Consistency makes everything standard. Once you know the standard, there is nothing else to tell.

The level of consistency depends on the surrounding culture. For example, in a JEE-heavy company, there would be no need to tell why you decided to use EJB, but you'd need to explain when you decide not to use it. In another company with better taste, it would be the opposite.

If you decide as a team that no method is allowed to return null within your domain model, then this decision only has to be documented in one place, such as in the root folder of the domain model source control system. Then there's no need to talk about it anymore on each method.

Therefore: Agree as a team on concrete guidelines to apply within chosen bounded areas. Document them briefly in one place.

There have to be exceptions to the rule. Not every class will be consistent. However, as long as the number of exceptions is low, it's still cheaper to document the exceptions explicitly than to document everything on every class.

Here's an example of the guidelines that a team created for a domain model:

- No abbreviations in naming of public signatures
- Business-readable names in all public interfaces and their methods
- Null-free: no null allowed as a return type or as a method parameter
- All classes immutable by default
- All methods side effect free by default
- No SQL
- No import of frameworks at all, including javax
- No import of infrastructure (such as middleware)

Enforced guidelines provide a way to document the guidelines in a way that is effective even if nobody reads them.

Example: The Zero Documentation Game

I've heard of a team that decided to forbid documentation. They're proudly doing zero documentation. It's not as insane as it might at first seem: Zero documentation is an approach that forces better naming and better practices in general to share knowledge without additional prose.

When you understand that most of the time written documentation in the form of prose or diagrams is a poor substitute for expressing the knowledge better within the work product itself in the first place, it makes sense to minimize it. And because striving for zero documentation sounds radical and a bit insane, it's stimulating and becomes a game. This makes it more likely to stick in team members' minds, driving their behavior for the better, hopefully.

I haven't tried it myself, but my colleague told me that zero documentation usually drives virtuous behavior in practice.

Because we don't all share the same definition of the word *documentation*, a game of zero documentation must clarify its rules. The previously mentioned team refuses comments in the code and on methods, all forms of written prose, external documents, and traditional Office documents. It happily embraces tests and Gherkin scenarios (Cucumber/SpecFlow), favors simple code, and enjoys working collectively as a primary means of sharing knowledge. The team is happy with all this.

I think augmenting the code with annotations, keeping a simple README file, and generating living documents would still fit within the rules of the game, but you decide where to put the cursor!

Continuous Training

As general knowledge becomes more widespread, the less you need to document. Investing in continuous training is therefore a way to reduce the need for documentation.

Learning standard skills also makes it easier to use more ready-made knowledge instead of original solutions. This is good for the quality of the solution, and it alleviates the need for specific documentation.

More consistency of skills and shared culture also helps speed up decision making. It's not about removing all diversity in the team, since diversity is an essential ingredient. Still, we don't need all diversity in every detail, and there's a lot that we can make more consistent without losing much.

Investing in continuous training may involve the following:

- Coding dojos on CodeKata (for example, at lunchtime every Friday)
- Short training sessions during the day

- Interactive mini-trainings (for example, half an hour twice a week right after lunch)

- Time for deliberate practice (for example, a 20%-time policy devoted to side projects)[32]

Summary

The best documentation is doesn't look like documentation. Interactive conversations and working collectively rank very high when it comes to sharing knowledge. In addition, the serendipity and spontaneity of meeting at the coffee machine is an essential complement.

On a different note, making process automation more declarative, by discipline or through better tools, also makes it the proper authority of knowledge for a process. Having tools that scream when you do something wrong is yet another form of documentation, and it is one of the most efficient, since it brings the right knowledge at the right time even to people who weren't aware of it.

In all the cases listed in this chapter, the key point is that we need to turn up the documentation value of all the activities already carried out by the development teams in order to reduce the work that is specifically done on documentation tasks. Just because something doesn't look like typical documentation doesn't mean it's not a valid form of knowledge sharing and preservation. The more developers and their managers understand this, the more efficient they will collectively be.

---

32. https://www.inc.com/adam-robinson/google-employees-dedicate-20-percent-of-their-time-to-side-projects-heres-how-it-works.html

Chapter 11

Beyond Documentation: Living Design

This book has so far focused on how to record and transfer knowledge about what has been done in a software project. However, when you start paying attention to this knowledge explicitly, an additional benefit kicks in: You start to see improvements in your design. As you're working to create living documentation, you often also see design improvement, a benefit that can quickly be far more important than just the documentation aspect. Your initial goal of living documentation that can follow design changes morphs into living documentation that begins to suggest even more changes to the design! This chapter explores a number of patterns that can help you exploit this bonus effect to the max.

As one more bonus effect, making the inside of the software system more visible to all stakeholders will make it increasingly likely that it will be well designed.

Listening to the Documentation

So you've learned a bit about living documentation, and you want to try it. If you try to create a living diagram but find it hard to generate one from the current source code, this is a signal. If you try generate a living glossary but find this almost impossible to achieve, this is also a signal. As illustrated in Figure 11.1, you should listen to the signals.

Figure 11.1 *Listen to your documentation!*

Nat Pryce and Steve Freeman wrote, "when code is difficult to test, the most likely cause is that our design needs improving."[1] Similarly, if you find it hard to generate living documents from your code, it's a signal that your code has design issues.

What Happened to the Language of the Domain?

If you're into DDD and you find it hard to generate a living glossary of the business domain language, then it's probably because this language is not expressed clearly enough in the code. Any of the following might be happening:

- The language might be expressed in other words, such as technical words, synonyms, or (worst) legacy database names.

- The language might be mixed with technical concerns in a way that is impossible to recover; for example, business logic may be mixed with data persistence logic or presentation concerns.

- The language might be completely lost, and code may be doing business stuff without any reference to the corresponding business language.

Whatever the issue, if you're finding it difficult to do living documentation, you should take it as a signal that you're doing DDD—and domain modeling in general—incorrectly. The design should be aligned as much as possible with the business domain and its language, word by word.

---

1. Freeman, Steve, and Nat Pryce. *Growing Object-Oriented Software, Guided by Tests.* Boston: Pearson Education, Inc. 2010.

So instead of trying to make a complicated tool to generate a living glossary, you should take the opportunity to redesign the code so that it better expresses the domain language. Of course, it's up to you to decide whether it's reasonable to do this and when and how to do it.

Programming by Coincidence Design

We don't know what we're doing, and we don't know what we've done.

—*Fred Brooks*[2]

If there is no choice to be made, you're not doing design.

—*Carlo Pescio*[3]

To generate a design diagram, first you have to know what particular design decision you expect the diagram to explain. But can you tell what your design is like? The most common difficulty when trying to generate living diagrams is simply that you often don't know clearly enough what your design is like or why it's that way. This suggests that you may be programming by coincidence.[4] You might know how to make your design work, but you don't really know why, and you haven't really considered alternatives. Such a design is arbitrary rather than deliberate.

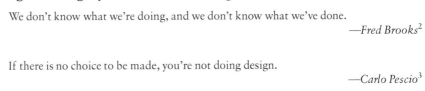

Note

I love Carlo Pescio's essays. I don't actually like his writing style much, but do I like the way he writes about his mind musing on hard and deep matters of software development. He's got some crazy ideas and some stretched metaphors but a lot of insights to spark my imagination about future breakthroughs in our field. To see what I mean, visit http://www.carlopescio.com.

Building software involves continuous decision making. Big decisions usually get a lot of attention, including dedicated meetings and written documents, and decisions deemed less important tend to be neglected. The problem is that many of the neglected decisions end up being arbitrary rather than well-thought-out, and the

---

2. This quote from Fred Brooks (1999 Turing Award) was the summary of his working group on the role of science in design, as reported on page 15 in "Software Language Engineering: 6th International Conference," SLE 2013, Indianapolis, IN, USA, October 26-28, 2013.

3. Carlo Pescio, "Design, Structure, and Decisions," http://www.carlopescio.com/2010/11/design-structure-and-decisions.html

4. Hunt, Andrew and David Thomas. *The Pragmatic Programmer: From Journeyman to Master.* Boston: Addison-Wesley, 2000.

accumulated effect (even a compounding effect) may be to make the source code hostile to work with.

"Why does this function return null instead of an empty list?" "Why do some functions return null and others return an empty list inconsistently?" "Why are most of the DAO, but not all, in this package?" "Why do we have the same method signature in five different classes but without a common interface to unify them?" Such neglected decisions sometimes get close to better solutions but miss them due to failure to properly thinking about the matters at hand. All these examples represent lost opportunities for better design.

> **Tip**
>
> Whenever you find out something unexpected in code or in code design, consider thinking about the question, "What would it take to come back to the standard situations in the literature?"

I encourage deliberate thinking. Documenting decisions as they are made is one way to encourage deeper thinking because trying to explain a decision often reveals its weaknesses.

> **Note**
>
> If you can't explain something simply, you don't understand it well enough.

Sometimes it's frustrating when working with a team at a customer site to observe decisions being made without anyone being clear on the reasoning. "Just make it work right now" seems to be the motto. In one instance I took notes about one such situation:

> We've been discussing for one hour the semantics of the messages between a legacy app and a new event-sourcing-based app. Is it event or command? As usual, the discussion doesn't lead to a clear conclusion, and yet the unclear choice works. Had we decided to document the semantics of all integration interactions clearly, we would have had to decide, and to turn it into a tag or something written and visible. Then we would have to conform to it, or to question it explicitly when it's no longer relevant.
>
> Instead, we're going to live with the continuous confusion. Each contributor will interpret as he or she wishes. And it will bite us.

A year later, I can see that the team has matured, and now such a discussion would converge to sound reasoning.

Deliberate Decision Making

The path to better design and better documentation starts by making more decisions deliberately. It is very difficult to document random decisions. It is like attempting to describe noise: There are at the same time too many low-level details and almost nothing to tell at a higher level. In contrast, when decisions are deliberate, they are clearly and consciously made, and documentation is a simple matter of putting them into words.

If a decision is pretty standard, it's ready-made knowledge that has been already discussed in a book under a standard name, such as a pattern. Documenting in such a case involves just making a mark in the code that refers to the standard name, along with some brief reasons, motivation, context, and main forces that led to the decision.

> **Tip**
>
> If a decision is deliberate, it's already half documented.

Being deliberate in the way we do our work is a big recurring theme in agile circles. Software craftsmanship encourages deliberate practice to improve the craft. We dedicate time to practice katas and coding dojos to achieve that goal of getting better at our craft. In the BDD community, Dan North explains that projects should be seen as learning initiatives, a mindset he calls *deliberate discovery*.[5] He claims that we should do whatever it takes to learn as quickly as possible as early as possible. Being deliberate is about expending extra effort to do better work in a conscious way.

Deliberate design involves thinking clearly about each design decision. What is the goal? What are the options? What do we know for sure, and what do we suspect? What does the literature say on this kind of situation?

In addition, the better the design, the less there is to document. Better design is simpler, and "simpler" actually means fewer but more powerful decisions that solve more of the problem:

- **Symmetries:** The same code or interface takes care of all symmetric cases.

- **Higher-level concepts:** The same code deals with many special cases at once.

- **Consistency:** Some decision is repeated everywhere without exception.

---

5. https://dannorth.net/2010/08/30/introducing-deliberate-discovery/

- **Replaceability and encapsulation:** Local decisions within a boundary do not matter, as they can be reconsidered or redone later, even if knowledge about them is lost.

The quantity of specific knowledge needed to document a piece of software is an indicator of the maturity of the design. Software that can be described in 10 sentences has a better design than software that needs 100 sentences of description.

Engineering Is a Deliberate Practice

In French engineering schools and other *grandes ecoles*, from mechanical engineering to electronic engineering or even industrial design, it's primarily important for students to demonstrate that all decisions they have made are substantiated. Arbitrary decisions are just not acceptable.

During final exams, the most important aspects of the evaluation involve framing the work precisely, and then at each step of designing the solution, each decision has to be justified against enough alternatives and chosen according to explicit criteria: budget, weight, feasibility, or other constraints.

In software development, we are seldom so deliberate in every detail, but we should be. Whether every decision is recorded in writing or not, making more conscious decisions often improves the decisions.

If you know what you're doing, what it's called in the literature, and why you've made a particular decision, all it takes for complete documentation is to add that information in the code in one line: a link to the literature and some text to explain the rationale. Once you've got the thinking right, the writing takes care of itself.

You have to realize, of course, that thinking takes time. It looks slow and may be confused with slack, and in many companies people often think, "We don't have time for that!" However, alternatives to thinking only give the illusion of speed, at the expense of accuracy. As Wyatt Earp said, "Fast is fine, but accuracy is everything." Accuracy requires rigorous thinking. Thinking with more than one brain, as in pair programming or mob programming, also improves accuracy and helps you create more deliberate designs. With more brains, it's more likely that someone knows the standard solutions from the literature for any situation.

You have probably heard this saying: "You don't really understand something until you can explain it to someone else." Having to clarify your thoughts for documentation purposes is virtuous because, well, you have to clarify your thoughts. Having to justify decisions in a persistent form is another incentive to think with more rigor.

Note

Deliberate design works particularly well when doing TDD. TDD is a very deliberate practice with rules. Starting with naive code that just works, the design emerges from successive refactorings, but it's the developers who are driving the refactorings, and they have to think before applying each refactoring. "Do we really need to make that more complex?" "Is it worth adding an interface now?" "Shall we introduce a pattern to replace these two IF statements?" It's all about trade-offs, which requires clear thinking.

Living documentation encourages attention to virtuous practices—design in particular. Living documentation makes bad design clearly visible. One of the great rewards is that you can improve the design, and your design documentation comes almost for free as a result.

A Confession from the Author

Deliberate design is my ulterior motive in writing this book. People don't pay enough attention to design, and I'm very sorry about that. Living documentation is a Trojan horse, or a gateway to get more people addicted to better design.

"Deliberate Decision" Does Not Mean "Upfront Decision"

With emerging design, the natural decision emerges by listening to the working code and its flaws. For example, noticing duplication may trigger a refactoring to something better. When you reach such a point, you have to make a conscious, deliberate decision: What is the "better" you want to refactor to? *Deliberate* means that you understand the troubles, can imagine the benefits you are looking for, and have found more than one way to improve. *Deciding* means choosing one way out of all the possible others. This is a deliberate decision.

Documentation Is a Form of Code Review

Documentation makes a product and the development process more transparent. As such, documentation is also a useful feedback tool that helps you adjust and correct over the complete lifecycle of an application. Decisions with no rationale have nowhere to hide. With living diagrams and the other ideas of living documentation, the neglected design areas become quite visible, making it harder to ignore them. This increases the pressure to put more care into every aspect of code quality.

Living documentation generated from source code, especially diagrams, also works great as a debugging tool to detect mistakes such as unexpected cycles in the dependencies or excessive coupling, shown as too many arrows on the diagram. You might have been expecting some design structure, but when trying to render it as a diagram, you may have to admit that the code does not exhibit much structure. You might have been expecting the code to tell the business domain, but when trying to make it into a glossary, it may appear that the business is mangled in the middle of the processing, and there is no easy way to get it out.

It is interesting to compare the top-down documentation you might have done before building the code with the actual bottom-up documentation generated from the sources. The differences can help you spot inconsistencies or, even better, to realize once again that it is difficult to speculate about what the code will be like before it is actually developed.

Indeed, even before making living diagrams, just trying to document by hand on paper can reveal design issues. Maxime Sanglan, a lead developer from one of my clients, reacted when reading an early version of this book: "That's totally what happened when I started to have the team do sketching workshops around Simon Brown's C4 model on the legacy system."

Shameful Documentation

Just because it is documented, it doesn't make it less stupid.

—@dalijap on Twitter

When documentation is up-to-date and accurate, it is often considered a good thing. However, there are a number of cases where quite the opposite occurs: The existence of the documentation itself demonstrates the presence of a problem. The infamous troubleshooting guide is the best example in this category. Someone decided to take the time to document the known troubles, usage traps, and other anomalies of behavior, and this effort demonstrates that the issues are important enough to be worth documenting. However, it also means that these issues are not fixed, and it is possible that no one even plans to fix them.

Such documentation is what I call *shameful documentation*; it's documentation you should be ashamed of. This documentation, by its sole existence, should be seen as a confession of something to be fixed. The time spent creating this documentation should have been allocated to fixing the troubles instead.

Therefore: Recognize the situations when documentation is a poor substitute for actually fixing a problem. Whenever possible, decide against adding more documentation and instead allocate time to fixing the problem.

Of course, there are many reasons teams might add documentation instead of fixing the issues:

- **Budget:** There might be money allocated for documentation but no more money for working on the code.

- **Laziness:** It may seem easier to add some quick documentation on troubleshooting rather than actually tackle the root issue.

- **Lack of time:** Documenting the issue might be faster than fixing it.

- **Cost:** It may be genuinely difficult to address some issues. For example, some issues would require releasing a new version of the application to dozens of clients, which would be prohibitively expensive.

- **Missing knowledge:** Sometimes the team knows about issues but is missing knowledge and skills required to fix the issues.

If there is no time available to fix an issue now, then the right place to document the issue is the defect tracker. However, in the mindset of shameful documentation, a defect tracker is also in itself a demonstration of a deeper issue: Defects should not accumulate but should be prevented earlier or fixed immediately as much as possible. And are defects that can remain for a long time without being fixed really defects?

If a feature is implemented so badly that it requires a manual with many pages of warnings and workaround instructions or a lot of assistance from the support team, you might consider removing it until it is implemented correctly; chances are that almost nobody manages to use it anyway or that using it is so expensive that it's not worth it.

Example: Shameful Documentation

In a past mission at a customer site, I discovered a 16-page document on how to run and test an application. This guide was for the all users, including end users. I'll call this application Icare to protect the innocents. This was not a new project; it was used several times every day by dozens of people in the company. The document was full of screenshots highlighted in red color bubbles to show how to proceed because the steps were not unintuitive. However, most of the 16 pages described where to "pay attention": "Pay attention...[this may not work properly]. Please note that... [there is a bug here]." "Pay attention, Icare is launched from another directory!" "Take really good care to not launch these tasks any time because it will kill everything on the corresponding environment!" It might as well have said "Pay attention; we're not professional."

Half of everything written was about traps waiting to bite users. "Pay attention to the name of the trigger; sometimes, it's not correctly named, so check in the trigger." Remember that this was a document for end users. And it got even better: "After an export in XML, you should do a test of re-import to be sure that it works well." You can see that a developer had the time to write this document instead of fixing the code.

The document also said, "Pay attention: Partitions Icare_env1 and Icare_env2 are inversed between UAT and PROD!!!" Ah, so everyone knew about this, and it had been like that for years, but it wasn't anyone's plan to fix it? Or was the process so heavyweight that you'd first have had to find a sponsor to pay for the fix?

The Troubleshooting Guide

Finally, at the end of the documentation was the infamous "known problems" section, shown here:

```
1  1 Known problems
2
3  1.1 Icare Job does not start
4
5  It often happens. First, try to launch it directly from Icare (so
6  launch the application manually from the correct directory
7  [c:/icare/uat1/bin for UAT, c:/icare/prod/bin for PROD]).
8
9
10 If you are not able to launch it manually, it's because
configuration of the job is not correct
11  (missing or incorrect parameter date or calculation date,
etc.).
12 If it runs well, there is a problem when launching Icare in
command line, so you need to check the log (to find where
13 it logs, check the icarius_mngt.exe.log4net).
14
15
16 In the past, there was also a problem for the first
execution.
```

```
17 It requires to have made a manual connection to the
environment with the good login (IcariusId).
18
19 When a first connection was established, the batch mode was
correctly working.
20
```

Notice the inconsistent naming of the application as Icarius and Icare.

Shameful documentation does not always mean bugs; it may instead suggest opportunities for more Ops-friendliness, as shown in this example:

```
1 "you have to check the caches are up otherwise they will hit
2 the DB and degrade performance results"
3
4 [...]
5
6 "Very important :
7 As we are not able to guarantee the synchronization of the
8 two environments for the duration of jobs, we cannot launch
9 different type of jobs".
```

When you listen carefully to the documentation, you see that it is a source of suggestions. What about having a way to automatically monitor the caches or, even better, a mechanism to ensure that they are always preloaded before operations? What about adding a safety mechanism so that if you make the error, you're warned, and you can avoid the issue?

Shameful Code Documentation

You don't have to tolerate documented pain. Say no. Writing such documentation is wasting time, and reading it is wasting time, too, and it will not even prevent anyone from falling into the trap completely, which will waste yet more time—again and again.

The Icare troubleshooting guide is just one example of shameful documentation. Any document that is getting too big becomes a case of a shameful documentation. A developer guide with 100 pages reveals issues of code quality, and a thick user manual is not user-friendly. You might need a big user guide for an application that is not intuitive to use, but addressing the real issue instead would be a better investment if you care about the users.

Similarly, with software design, if it takes a lot of pages and many diagrams to explain the architecture of an application, then it is most likely poor. (See Chapter 12, "Living Architecture Documentation," for more on documenting the architecture.)

Finally, shameful documentation also applies to code. Every time a developer feels the urge to add a comment like this, it should trigger a reaction to remove the comment and immediately fix the questionable code instead:

```
1  // beware this tricky case
2  ...
3  // should never happen
4  ...
5  // FIXME: remove this hack!
```

Documenting Errors or Avoiding Errors?

Comments in code are not the only signals which suggest that someone needs to improve the code. Code that specifically deals with handling errors and that traditionally deserves its specific documentation can become redundant if you learn to avoid the error cases altogether by using better design and coding practices.

Consider the example of a function that calculates an inverse. If the divisor is zero, then there is no result. This is often a case of error management, but an alternative is to make the function a *total function*, a function that works for the values of all parameters. In this case, to make a function total, you need to extend the number type with the special value NotANumber. Then the function can just return NotANumber when there's a division by zero instead of taking the error management road.

Documentation-Driven Development

> Here's a secret about documentation. It's not just useful to read. It's the act of writing that pushes for quality in the same way as tests.
>
> —*@giorgiosironi on Twitter*

In any project, it is typically a good idea to start with a focus on the end result you are aiming for. By focusing on the end, you first focus on where the value is, to make sure it's really there. Then you can derive what's really necessary to achieve the goal—no less and no more—and avoid unnecessary work. Start by explaining your goal or end result, such as how your system will be used, in order to drive the construction and to help notice early potential inconsistencies.

Chris Matts, in his talk "Driving Requirements from Business Value" at the BDD eXchange conference 2011 in London, gave a great example on the most typical British goal of *having a cup of tea*. Starting with this goal, you can derive the need for hot water, a clean cup, a tea bag, and so on.

Some developers find that starting with a piece of documentation helps start from the goal. Dave Balmer said this in a blog post:

> I can start by documenting only that which is important. That satisfies the "write this down before I forget" part of documentation and frees me up to improve it in later drafts.[6]

Test-driven development and its close cousin BDD exploit this effect by focusing on the desired behavior first, as a test or a scenario or an example written before starting the coding. If you're practicing TDD or BDD, you're already doing a form of documentation-driven development, too.

When uncertainty is very high, at the very inception of an idea, writing the README file *as if the project were already done* helps clarify the purpose and flesh out expectations. Once materialized in writing, ideas become objects of deeper scrutiny; they can be criticized, reviewed, and shared with other people early.

If you are alone, just let a few days pass before going back to these notes: When you see them again with a fresh set of eyes, you can review your own work in a more objective fashion, thanks to the documentation from your past self to your future self.

Documentation to Keep You Honest

Continuous improvement starts with honest retrospectives on how well we have performed. At the end of a project, it is easy to forget about our past assumptions and either blame the environment in the case of failure or congratulate ourselves for the success. Opportunities for improvement occur in looking back at our assumptions to learn from them. You might think, "Next time I will not assume that" or "I will first check the assumption before investing more time."

Therefore: Document early what you assume and the experiments you try in order to have reliable and honest data when it is time for retrospection.

This is a way to be a little more data driven. And there are tools for it! For example, growth.founders.as offers their Founders Growth Toolbox with a template to declare your assumptions and to describe your experiments.

---

6. Dave Balmer, Webkit Developments blog, https://davebalmer.wordpress.com/2011/03/29/source-code-documentation-javadoc-vs-markdown/

The Apparent Contradiction Between Documentation Driven and "Avoiding Documentation"

At this stage, you might be confused at the apparent contradiction between being *documentation driven* and trying to avoid documentation, as advocated in Chapter 10. The contradiction is a matter of ambiguity of words indeed. When talking about documentation-driven development, even though we use the word *documentation*, we don't mean it as a way to share knowledge among people. Instead, it's just a cheap way to explore the requirements at the very inception of a project, before we move on to more expensive material like tests and source code.

The fundamental idea is that it can be desirable to use different material at different levels of uncertainty: At the very start of a project, conversations are usually the best material. During the early stages, conversations, notes and sketches on paper, low-fi mockups, a README file with intentions and scenarios, code exploration in a REPL, writing code in a spike without tests, and using a scripting or dynamic language might be the idea materials to learn and explore. A bit later, when things start to stabilize, another programming language with tests and even with TDD might become the material of choice. In this light, documentation early is basically a material to get started.

Apart from this case, however, documentation must not drive the development but must capture and help present ideas and what has been developed that the system and its code cannot explain themselves (see Figure 11.2). Making the code as self-documenting as possible is the goal. Whenever we fail at making the code self-documenting, we have to resort to some documentation effort, but we keep it to the minimum.

There's no contradiction between *documentation driven* and *avoiding documentation*. They just involve different meanings of the word *documentation*.

Explore   Capture   Present

Figure 11.2 *Explore versus capture and present*

Abusing Living Documentation (Anti-pattern)

So you're now a fan of living documentation, and you're generating diagrams during each build. You like the idea so much that you spend your time figuring out what new kind of diagram could be generated. You want to generate everything!

You pretend to apply DDD, but you actually spend your time on exciting tools that generate diagrams, if not code or bytecode. We all know that DDD is primarily about tools, right? Oh, yes, you remember some folks used to do that seriously, and they called it MDA. Ouch!

You prefer working on the diagram generator rather than fixing bugs in the production code. Of course, it's way more fun than boring production issues! Is all that really a good thing?

It's easy to abuse living documentation, and doing so can backfire. If you spend too much time using tools to generate glossaries, reports, and diagrams instead of doing the work to be done, it's not professional, and management may decide to stop and forbid any documentation-improving initiative. You don't want that.

Therefore: Keep your efforts in automating living documentation reasonable compared to the actual delivery work. Remember that living documentation is just a mean to an end and not an end in itself. The goal of living documentation is to help deliver more and with better quality, not just produce documentation or have fun. Ideally, every effort in improving your living documentation should yield short-term demonstrable benefits in delivery, quality, or user satisfaction.

As the author of this book on living documentation, I don't want this topic to get bad press because people abuse it. Please don't say that this book is asking you to put in place every example described into your own project, because that's not true. All the examples are, well, examples, not requirements.

It is true that the point of this book is to excite your inner geek to try the ideas of living documentation. But I would never advise you to do it all without a good reason for each of the ideas in the book.

Living documentation is not a free license to rehash old ideas from the 1990s. In particular, beware of the following failure modes, which are *not* living documentation:

- **Doing living documentation for end-user documentation:** Keep in mind that this book is not about end-user documentation at all. Some patterns may apply, but you still need skilled technical writing in order to produce high-quality documentation for end users.

- **MDA and everything code generation:** No, code is not a dirty detail to replace or generate; it is the reference and the preferred media whenever possible. You should extend your language or choose a better programming language rather than generate code from diagrams.

- **Documenting everything, even automatically:** Documenting has a cost, which must be weighed against the benefits. The ideal case is code being so self-descriptive that it needs nothing else, but even that is not an absolute. Perfection and the quest for purity often amount to procrastination—and should be avoided.

- **UML obsession:** Some basic UML is fine, but it is not an end in itself. Chose the simplest notation that the intended audience will really understand with as few explanations as possible. Don't obsess over generic notations; problem-specific or domain-specific notations are often more expressive.

- **Design patterns everywhere:** Knowing patterns can be helpful, and you can use them to help document a design thanks to the vocabulary they bring. But don't abuse patterns. Simplicity should be your first priority. Two IF statements might be better than a strategy pattern at times.

- **Analysis paralysis:** Having a whole team spend 15 minutes together on the whiteboard before each important design decision is time well spent. Spending many hours or even days is a waste. I encourage you to start new features as a whole team, on the whiteboard for a short while but then moving on quickly to the IDE. And you can just invite the whole team again next time you face a prominent decision, unless you're into mob programming, which makes the whole team together the permanent state.

- **Living documentation masterpiece:** Aiming for perfection is really a form of procrastination. Keep in mind that living documentation is a means to help deliver production code, not the other way around.

- **Documentation before building:** Documentation should reflect what's actually built rather than prescribe what will be built. If a project is interesting, then nothing can beat starting the code. Detailed design specs are a waste. Beyond a short statement or a documentation-driven README as described earlier in this chapter, your team should code and reflect along the way, collectively, in a just-enough, just-in-time fashion.

Procrastination by Living Documentation

As developers, we are often tempted to make things more complicated than they need to be. This is true for production code, and it also true with living documentation tools.

When the everyday work looks boring, making it technically more complicated is a great way to have fun. However, it's not professional. If you consider yourself a software craftsperson, you know you should not be doing that. However, we all fall for it from time to time, usually without being aware of it.

Therefore: If you really need a space where you can have fun and make things needlessly overcomplicated, then by all means do it in the code of your living documentation tools, not in your production code. Your life and the life of your colleagues will be better as a result.

I'm not saying that you should gold-plate your living documentation tools. I'm just saying that if you're lucky enough to have some slack time and want to play, do it with your documentation, not with your code!

Biodegradable Documentation

You should understand by now that living documentation is not an end in itself but a means to an end. Trying to set up living documentation can reveal issues about the design or other aspects of your code. This provides an opportunity to improve the root cause, which is above all good for the project and the product; it also helps improve your living documentation. Making such improvements repeatedly leads to a stream of simplifications and standardizations. Eventually, everything becomes so simple and so standard that you don't need documentation any longer—and that would be perfect.

Therefore: Consider what it would take for documentation to become unnecessary. This is the direction you should move.

It does not matter whether you actually reach this point or not, but it has to be the goal: The goal of a living documentation initiative is to achieve the level of quality where documentation is mostly unnecessary. The process starts with setting up a documentation effort (see Figure 11.3), which will reveal some issues, which you fix, reducing the need for more documentation—and you repeat as needed. The goal of living documentation is not to end up with a lot of beautiful generated diagrams and documents. Instead, those documents and diagrams should be considered workaround solutions or intermediate steps toward better solutions that need less documentation.

One former Arolla colleague once told me of an experience at a bank:

> In that bank, I joined a team that took pride in conforming to every standard. I mean market standards, not in-house standards. The result was that I was able to be productive as soon as the first day! Since I knew the technologies and their standard usage, I was immediately familiar on all the project perimeter. No need for documentation, no surprise, no need for any specific customization.

Make no mistake, this was taking a real and continuous effort indeed. Find out the standards, find out the way to solve specific issues while still conforming to standards. This was a deliberate approach, and the benefits were real, for everyone but especially for new joiners!

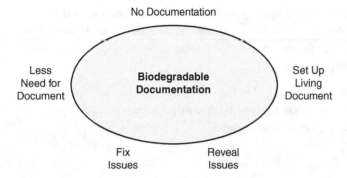

Figure 11.3 *The long-term goal of living documentation is for documentation to become unnecessary*

In the book *Apprenticeship Patterns: Guidance for the Aspiring Software Craftsman*, Dave Hoover and Adewale Oshineye advocate creating feedback loops.[7] Living documentation with generated diagrams, a glossary, a word cloud, or any other media is a feedback loop that can help you evaluate what you're doing and check against your own mental model. This feedback loop becomes particularly useful when your mental model and the content of the generated documents don't match.

Hygienic Transparency

Internal quality refers to the quality of code, the design, and, more generally, the whole process from the nebulous needs to working software that delights people. Internal quality is not meant to satisfy ego or to be a source of pride; by definition, it is meant to be economical beyond the short term. It is desirable for saving money and time sustainably, week after week, year after year.

The problem with internal quality is that it's internal, which means you can't see it from the outside. That's why, to a developer's eyes, so many software systems are awful in the inside. Nondevelopers like managers and customers can hardly

---

7. Hoover, Dave, and Adewale Oshineye. *Apprenticeship Patterns: Guidance for the Aspiring Software Craftsman*. Sebastopol, CA: O'Reilly Media, Inc. 2009.

appreciate how bad the code is inside. The only hints for them are the frequency of defects and the feeling that new features are delivered more and more slowly.

Everything that improves the transparency of how software is made helps improve its internal quality. When people can see the ugliness inside, there's pressure to fix it.

Therefore: Make the internal quality of software as visible as possible to developers and nondevelopers alike. Use living documents, living diagrams, code metrics, and other means to expose the internal quality in a way that everyone can appreciate, even without any particular skills.

Use all this material to trigger conversations and as a support to explain how things are and why they are this way and to suggest improvements. Make sure the living documents and other techniques look better when the code gets better.

Keep in mind that the techniques that help make software more transparent can't prove that the internal quality is good, but they can highlight when it is bad, and that's useful.

Le Corbusier and The Law of Ripolin

Le Corbusier, in his book *The Decorative Art of Today*, explains in 1925 his fascination for Ripolin, a brand famous for its white paint. In the chapter "A Coat of Whitewash: The Law of Ripolin," he imagines every citizen being required to replace everything with a plain coat of Ripolin white paint (see Figure 11.4): "*His home* is made clean. There are no more dirty, dark corners. Everything is shown as it is. Then comes *inner* cleanness…once you have put Ripolin on your walls you will be the master of *your own house*."[8]

Good documentation should have a similar effect on the inner cleanness of the code—its design and any other aspect that becomes visible so that people can see its dirty facets.

Diagnostic Tools

The line is very thin between typical documentation media like diagrams and glossaries and diagnostic tools like metrics and word clouds.

---

8. Le Corbusier. The Decorative Art of Today. MIT Press, 1987.

Figure 11.4 *In a house with everything painted white, dirt is immediately visible*

Word Clouds of the Language in the Code

A word cloud is a very simple diagram in which words that occur frequently appear in a bigger font than less frequent words. One way to quickly assert what an application is really talking about is to generate a word cloud out of the source code.

What does a word cloud really tell you about your code? If technical words dominate, then you know the code does not really talk about the business domain (see Figure 11.5). On the other hand, if the domain language is dominant (see Figure 11.6), you must be doing a better job.

Figure 11.5 *With this word cloud, either your business domain is on string manipulation, or it's not visible in the source code*

Figure 11.6 *In this word cloud, you can clearly see the language of Flottio fuel cards and fleet management*

Creating a word cloud out of source code is not difficult; you don't even have to parse the source code but can simply consider it as plain text and filter the programming language keywords and punctuation, like this:

```
1 // From the root folder of the source code, walk recursively
2 through all *.java files (respectively *.cs files in C#)
3
4 // For each file read as a string, split by the language
5 separators (you may consider to split by CamelCase too):
6
7
8 SEPARATORS = ";:.,?!<>><=+-^&|*/\" \r\n {}[]()"
9
10 // Ignore numbers and tokens starting with '@', or that are
11 keywords and stopwords for the programming language:
12 KEYWORDS = { "abstract", "continue", "for", "new",
13 "switch", "assert", "default", "if", "package", "boolean",
14 "do", "goto", "private", "this", " break", "double",
15 "implements", "protected", "throw", "byte", "else",
16 "import", "public", "throws", "case", "enum",
17 "instanceof", "return", "transient", "catch", "extends",
18 "int", "",  "short", "try", "char", "final", "interface",
19 "static", "void", "class", "finally", "long", "strictfp",
20 "volatile", "const", "float", "native", "super", "while" }
21
22
```

```
23 STOPWORDS = { "the", "it","is", "to", "with", "what's",
24 "by", "or", "and", "both", "be", "of", "in", "obj",
25 "string", "hashcode", "equals", "other", "tostring",
26 "false", "true", "object", "annotations" }
24
```

At this point, you could just print every token that was not filtered, and copy/paste the console into an online word cloud generator such as Wordle.com.

You can also count the occurrences of tokens yourself by using a bag (that is, a multiset from Guava):

```
1  bag.add(token)
```

You could render the word cloud within an HTML page with the d3.layout.cloud.js library by dumping the word data into the page.

Signature Survey of the Shape of Code

Another low-tech idea for visualizing the design of code out of the source code is the signature survey proposed by Ward Cunningham.[9] The idea is to filter out everything except the language punctuation (commas, quotation marks, and brackets) as pure string manipulation on the source code files.

For example, consider this signature survey, which has three big classes:

```
BillMain.java ;;;;;;;;;;;;{;;{"";;"";;{"";""; }
{;;{;;}};;;;{{;;;{;;}{;;};;;}}{;}"";}{;}{;;"";"
";;;"",;"",;;;"",;"",;;;;;;"",;"",;;;;"",;"";;;};;;{;{
"";{;}""{;}""{;}""{;}""{;;;;;}""{;}""{;}""{;};"
"{;;;;;}""{;;;;;}};}{;;;;;""{"";"";;}""{"";"";;
"";{;}}""{"";"";;""{;}};{;}""{;}{;};;;;;}{;;;;;;
}{;;;;;;}{;""{;{;}{;};;}{;{;}{;};;};}{{"";}{"""
";}{"";};;{;}{"";};}{{;};";";;;{""{{"";};}}{{;;
;}}{;};}{;{;}";";;;{""{{"";};}}{;;{""{{"";}""{;
}{;}}}};{;;;}{""";;;;;;;;}}{;{;}{;};}{;""{;}{;};
}{;{{"";};}{{"";};};}{;;;;;;;;;;{{"";};;}{{"";};
;;};}{;;;;;;;;;;{;;;{"";}{{"";};}{{"";};;};}\;}{
;;""{;}{;};}{;;{""{"";}{"";};;}{;}{{{;}{;}}};}}
```

---

9. Ward Cunningham, "Signature Survey: A Method for Browsing Unfamiliar Code," http://c2.com/doc/SignatureSurvey/

```
CallsImporter.java ;;;;;;;{;;{{"";};{;;"";;;{;}
{;;{;};};{;"";{;;};;{;;{;};};}{;}{;};;}}{;}{{{;}{;
}}}}{""{;}""{;}""{;}""{;}""{;}""{;}""{;}""{;}""
{;}""{;}""{;}""{;}""{;}""{;}""{;}""{;}""{;
}""{;}""{;}""{;}""{;}""{;}""{;}""{;}""{;}"
"{;}""{;}""{;}""{;}""{;};}}
UserContract.java ;;{;;;;;{;}{;}{;}{;}{;}{;}{;}
{;}{;}{;}}}{{""
```

Now compare the signature survey above with this one, which does exactly the same thing but with more smaller classes:

```
AllContracts.java ;;;;;{;{;}}{{;}}{""";}}
BillingService.java ;;;;;;;{;{"";}{;;;;;}{""
;;}{;;"";}{;}{;}{""";;;;}{""";;}{;;{{;;}};}{;}}
BillPlusMain.java ;;;;;;{{;"";"";"";"";"";"";}}
Config.java ;;;;;;;{;{;{"";;}{;}{{{;}{;}}}}{;}{
;;}{""";}{""";}{""";}{""";}{""";;}{;";";{;};}}
Contract.java ;;;;{;;;;{;;;;}{;}{;}{;}{;}{;}{;}{"""""""";}}
ContractCode.java ;{"""""""""""""""""""";;;{;}{;}}
ImportUserConsumption.java ;;;;;{;;{;;}{{;}{;}}{;{;;}}
{;"";;;;{;};}{{;}{;}}{""";;;{;{;}};}}
OptionCode.java ;{"""""""";;{;}{;}}
Payment.java ;;;{;;;{;;;{"";}}{;}{;}{;}{;}{{;}"";}{;}{;;;;;}{;}
{"""""";}}
PaymentScheduling.java ;;;;{{{;;;}}{{;;;}}{{;;;}};{;;;;}
{;;{;};;}{;;;;;;;;}{;}}
PaymentSequence.java ;;;;;;{;;{;}{;;}{;}{;}{;;;}{"";}}
UserConsumption.java ;{;;{;;}{;}{;}}
UserConsumptionTracking.java ;{{;}{;}}
```

Which one do you prefer to work on?

It's possible to imagine similarly low-tech yet useful plain-text visualization approaches. Let me know if you have any ideas.

Positive Pressure to Clean the Inside

One huge issue in the field of software development is that internal quality is not visible at all for the people who manage budgets and make the biggest decisions, such as saying yes or no to developers, contracting to another company, or offshoring. This lack of insight impedes these people from making good, informed decisions. Instead, it promotes decisions from people who are more convincing and seductive in their arguments.

Developers can become more convincing when they can show the internal quality of code in a way that nontechnical people can apprehend emotionally. A word cloud or a dependency diagram that is a total mess is easy to interpret even by nondevelopers. Once they understand by themselves the problem shown visually, it becomes easier to talk about remediation.

Developers' opinions are often suspect to managers. In contrast, managers appreciate the output of tools because tools are neutral and objective (or at least they believe this is the case). Tools are definitely not objective, but they do present actual facts, even if the presentation always carries some bias.

The ideas behind living documentation are not just to document for the team but to be part of the toolbox used to convince others. When everyone can see the disturbing reality—the mess, the cyclical dependencies, the unbearable coupling, the obscurity of the code—it becomes harder to tolerate it all.

LOL

To respect the acyclic dependencies principle: Have only one package!

Living documentation involves making the internal problems of code visible to everyone, creating positive pressure that encourages cleanup of the internal quality.

Design Skills Everywhere

Even if you start a living documentation journey with the goal of solving the documentation problem, you'll quickly discover that your actual problem is that the design is poor or arbitrary, perhaps a result of "design by coincidence." To solve the documentation problems, you have to solve the design problems. This is all good news indeed!

Through the focus on documentation, you end up with concrete visible criteria for everyone to see the big mess that is the current state of the design. There is then positive pressure to improve the design, which has benefits that well exceed the obvious benefits of documentation. But as mentioned before, there's even more good news: *Good design skills also make good living documentation skills.* Focus on living documentation and focus on software design skills. Practice both together, and everything will get better!

Software design involves deciding carefully among all the possible ways to code the same behavior. Or, in Jeremie Chassaing's words, "It's picking one in gazillions of possibilities with good reasons."[10] "But it's the same thing at the end!" is a frequent objection during design discussions. Yes, it is. If you just care about making the code work, design is irrelevant. Design means caring about concerns beyond just making it work.

Design skills include thinking about coupling and cohesion, hiding implementation details, considering contracts and the governance of data, keeping options open for later, minimizing dependencies, and dealing with their relative stability, among other things.

Reporter Porter Interviewing Mr. Living Doc Doc

The following is an interview Reporter Porter (on the right in Figure 11.7) conducted with Living Doc Doc, an expert on living documentation (on the left in Figure 11.7).

Figure 11.7 *Living Doc Doc interviewed by Reporter Porter*

What is good documentation?

The best documentation is code that makes everything so obvious that you understand it immediately, with naming that is so good it's instantly clear. Good documentation is so integrated in the workflow and into the daily tools that you don't even think about it as being documentation. One striking example is when a tool reminds you of something you forgot or didn't know right when you need it. We

---

10. On Twitter @thinkb4coding https://twitter.com/thinkb4coding/status/837250039688933376

usually don't call that documentation, but the end purpose of bringing the right piece of knowledge at the right time really is a form of documentation.

Why is living documentation not popular?

I think many of the practices are popular, but nobody noticed. Remember all the focus on UML in the early 2000s? Now projects are bigger today, and we don't use UML much. Instead, every IDE offers instant, integrated, and highly contextual type hierarchy trees, outlines, smooth hypermedia navigation between classes,… and all this is more useful than hundreds of static UML diagrams. Still, we take it for granted and still feel bad about the "lack of proper documentation." And there are new technologies as well.

How have new technologies changed the picture?

Most people still haven't realized all the potential of newer tools and practices when it comes to transferring knowledge.

Consul and Zipkin offer live recaps of what's actually there, even as living diagrams. They offer a tag mechanism to customize and convey intents.

Monitoring of key SLA metrics with thresholds gets us close to documenting the SLA.

Puppet, Ansible, and Docker files allow for a declarative style for describing what you expect. Imagine all the Word documents they advantageously replace!

So you need not do anything special now?

Almost. But not totally. All the new technologies and practices are fantastic for documenting the *what* and the *how*, but the weak point mostly everywhere remains the rationale, the *why*, which is often forgotten. That's why you still need to find a way to record the rationale for each of the main decisions. An immutable append-only log, code augmentation with tags, and a few evergreen content in traditional documents for the overall vision can be invaluable to complete the picture.

And what about the code?

Code should be self-documenting as much as possible. Tests and business-readable scenarios are an important part of this recorded knowledge. But sometimes you have to add extra code just to record your design decision and intention right inside the corresponding code; custom annotations for documentation and naming conventions are your tools of choice here.

Okay, but these days systems are made of dozens of services. How do I work with such fragmented systems?

You just apply the same techniques but at a different level. For example, annotations become tags in your service registry and in your distributed tracing system. Naming conventions of packages and modules become naming conventions of services and their endpoints. It involves similar thinking and similar design skills but different implementation.

Do we really need documentation? We've been living with little or no documentation for years, and we're still alive!

Of course, we can live without express documentation. Anyone can take an unknown system and make it work—at least under some definition of *work*. But just "making it work" is a very low bar, and "making it work" may take a lot of time. Documentation accelerates delivery because it shortens the time to rebuild your mental model of the system to work on. But the other effect of documentation is that trying to record the knowledge about the system is a great way to learn what's not right about the system. Paying attention to documentation is an investment for later, obviously, but less obviously there's also a return for right now!

Thank you very much!

No, thank *you* very much!

Summary

The main thesis of this book as a whole is that if you start with documentation, you end up with better design.

Most teams initially embrace BDD for non-regression testing purposes and end up realizing that the bigger benefits are somewhere else—in the early conversations using concrete examples and in the resulting living documentation. Similarly, by reconsidering documentation; adopting practices that encourage speed, deliberateness, hygienic transparency, and interactions between people; and by listening to the signals throughout this process, good things happen.

Chapter 12

Living Architecture Documentation

Architecture can be defined in many ways: "Architecture is what everybody in the project should know" or "Architecture is what is important, whatever that is" or "Architecture is about the decisions that are hard to change later." What is implied in all these definitions is that architecture involves exchanging knowledge about some decisions between multiple people over time. These decisions are not isolated events but are decisions in the context at the time.

So documentation is a significant part of architecture. A number of documentation approaches have been proposed, and there are many books on this topic. This chapter focuses on how living documentation can help with architecture, especially in the context of teams practicing evolutionary architecture, where the architecture can change all the time.

In this view, architecture is not a phase but a continuous activity. Moreover, it is not necessarily performed only by architects; rather, it is the domain of any software developer who has the skills to do it. This creates a need for even more people to share architectural decisions.

A software architecture usually ends up being materialized as code in multiple places. This code is the consequence of the past architectural decisions. You can recognize many of these past decisions just by looking at the code base. With the right skills, you can recognize, or even *reverse engineer*, many of the past decisions just by noticing the happy coincidences in the code base: You might realize, "It cannot be that well-structured by chance, so it must have been designed for that." The decisions are there, even if they are implicit.

With the right skills, usually grown from experience, you can read from the design what it is and how it is expected to be extended. This is similar to the power strip in Figure 12.1 that is visibly ready for extension if you just plug additional cords into it.

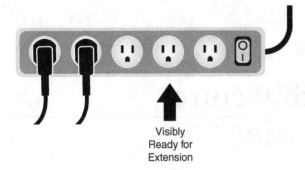

Visibly
Ready for
Extension

Figure 12.1 *Visibly ready for extension*

However, because the decisions in code are implicit, by just looking at the code, you may miss much of the architectural intent, depending on how familiar you are with the styles being used. Helping you and others discover more of the architectural intent is one major goal of architectural documentation: You want to make the implicit explicit!

Living documentation for architecture is precisely about finding practices that help explain more decisions accurately and explicitly, without slowing down the continuous flow of changes that are expected and encouraged.

The chapters so far in this book have mentioned a number of examples of architectural aspects, such as living diagrams and hexagonal architecture, context diagrams, guided tours, code as documentation, and some enforced guideline examples. This chapter expands on all that and is dedicated to applying living documentation to software architecture.

Documenting the Problem

Architecture always starts with really understanding all the objectives and constraints of the problem that needs to be solved. You won't build the same point-of-sale system for a brand with 50 hot dog stands in the street as you would for 1,500 high-end sandwich and salad shops around the world, even if they have the same high-level basic features.

The high-level goals and the main constraints are "things that everybody should know" (see Figure 12.2), and as such they are always part of the architecture.

Therefore: **Whatever your definition of *architecture*, make sure it is considered as much a documentation challenge as a technical one. Focus discussions and written records on the problems to solve, not just on the solutions. Make sure the essential knowledge about the problem is well described in a persistent form, and ensure that it is in everybody's mind.**

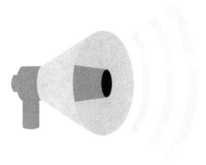

Figure 12.2 *Architecture is about things that everybody should know*

You might ask random questions from time to time to check whether everyone involved knows about the essential business knowledge. I regularly like to do this to make sure we don't waste a lot of time in every discussion.

Keep in mind that a written form of documentation is never enough; not everyone will read it. You need to complement written documentation with random discussions and roadshows to present it to every team during official work time.

An Example of a Problem Brief

Here is an example inspired by a real-world project on a legacy system for one of my customers. The brief is not in the wiki but in a single Markdown text file at the root of the source code repository of the new component. It may even be in the README file.

Vision Statement

Date: 01/06/2015
Delight the users with great UIs and new features delivered frequently

Description

The INSURANCE 2020 program aims at revamping the legacy software supporting the insurance claim management processes, with two main goals in target:

1. User experience (UX) and user-friendliness UIs

2. Continuous delivery: reduced time to market and reduced cost of change

Stakeholders

The primary stakeholders are the insurance adjusters. Other stakeholders are:

- Actuaries
- Management

IT-related stakeholders are:

- Development team
- Central architecture group
- Support and Ops teams

Business Domain

The business domain focuses on the claim management part, and in particular the Claim Adjustment phase. This starts at the early mention of a claim to start every investigation necessary to plan, witness the damages, contact the police officers, lawyer in order to propose a monetary amount to give to the policy holder.

The main business capabilities include, for example, the following:

- Take note of a claim without much information about it
- Enrich the claim whenever more information is available: parties involved, checks, evidences, photographs…
- Prepare the claim with one or more settlement offer(s) (each made of one or more monetary amount(s))
- Manage the claim team and the related workflows
- Report the current state of one or all pending claims
- Help users see their tasks to do at any time

Explicit Quality Attributes

In software, quality attributes shape the solution. The technical solution to a given business problem would be radically different for millions of concurrent users than it would be for 100 concurrent users, and the solution for real time would be quite different from the solution for daily use or if each minute of downtime cost the company $500,000.

Because of the challenges involved, everybody on a team should be aware of the most challenging quality attributes. They should also understand that other quality attributes that are not as challenging present opportunities to keep the architecture simple. Pretending that your design should support millions of concurrent users when you really have only thousands is a dangerous misuse of the sponsor's money and time.

Therefore: At the start of a project and after each change of context, clarify the main quality attributes in writing. This can be as simple as a list of bullet points. Make it clear how to interpret the quality attributes, such as by using maxims as guidance.

The following is an example of describing the main quality attributes: "The system shall respond to user requests with a response time within 1 second for 98% of the transactions. The system shall support 3,000 concurrent users."

The book *Site Reliability Engineering*, and especially the "Service-Level Objectives" chapter, offers an in-depth discussion of quality attributes, introducing the concepts of service-level indicators, service-level objectives, and service-level agreements.[1]

Quality attributes could come with some internal guidance on how to interpret the them, as in this example:

Over-quality is NOT quality

Design for ~10X growth, but plan to rewrite before ~100X[2]

These quality attributes can then be turned into executable scenarios against the system, and you can express the quality attributes in plain English sentences (see the section "Test-Driven Architecture," later in this chapter).

Stake-Driven Architecture Documentation

There are many perspectives on architecture. Some developers consider architecture as being all about the large-scale system, with its infrastructure, expensive middleware, distributed components, and database replication. It is normal for different

1. Beyer, Betsy, Chris Jones, Jennifer Petoff, and Niall Murphy. *Site Reliability Engineering*. Boston: O'Reilly, 2016.
2. Jeff Dean, "Challenges in Building Large-Scale Information Retrieval Systems," Google, http://static.googleusercontent.com/media/research.google.com/en//people/jeff/WSDM09-keynote.pdf

people working on different systems to focus on different aspects of software and call it *architecture*: They may use the term *architecture* for the aspects of the software that are most at stake in their context.

This diversity of perspectives is made obvious when doing an architectural kata. In this workshop format, proposed by Ted Neward[3], groups of people are tasked with creating an architecture for a given business problem. Each group has 30 minutes and a big piece of paper with markers to prepare and present a proposal. The rules clearly emphasize that the group members should be able to justify any decision made. The workshop ends with each group presenting its architecture to everyone else, as if defending the proposal in front of a client. Other attendees are invited to ask questions to challenge the proposal, as a skeptical client would do.

Such a workshop provides a very interesting way to think about architecture. It is in itself a communication exercise. It is not just about the decisions made but also about expressing them in a convincing way. Invariably, a kata reveals how very differently people think about the same problem.

> ## Caution
>
> You might be tempted to use the kata method on real business cases, as a form of competitive engineering, with different groups proposing different views that are later compared. However, the risk is that on a real case, you would have "winner" and "loser" groups at the end. You should practice the kata idea several times as pure katas first, without real stakes. You will get a lot of value and thinking out of it, and you will also learn how to avoid the "winner versus loser" effect.

What I have learned from katas is that different business problems call for focusing on different areas. The main aspects of a point-of-sale system for a hot dog vendor in the street are to be lightweight, low cost (in case it is stolen), and easy to use while making hot dogs in a hurry in the middle of a little crowd. In contrast, a mobile app meant to sell itself on an app store has to be primarily visually attractive. As yet another example, an enterprise system meant to serve millions of transactions per second should above all focus on performance as its main stake. In addition, with some systems the main stake is deeper understanding of the business domain.

The key stakes of the system are the primary information to record for everyone to know. You wouldn't, for example, want to spend too much of your time documenting the server technology stack when the main stake of the whole project is on the UX.

---

3. https://archkatas.herokuapp.com

Therefore: Identify early the main stake of the project, such as business domain challenge, technical concern, quality of the user experience, or integration with other systems. You may answer the question, "What would most easily make the project a failure?" Make sure your documentation efforts primarily cover the main stake.

Explicit Assumptions

When knowledge is incomplete, as it usually is at the beginning of any interesting project, we make assumptions. Assumptions make it possible to move on, but at the expense of potentially being shown to be incorrect later on. Documentation makes it cheaper to rewind the tape when you reconsider an assumption. A simple way to create such documentation is to explicitly mark decisions with the assumptions they depend upon. This way, when an assumption is reconsidered, it is possible to find all its consequences so you can reconsider them in turn. For this to work efficiently, it should all be done as internal documentation, in place within the decisions (usually in the source code itself).

Brevity Suggests Quality

A good architecture is simple and looks obvious. It is also easy to describe in just a few sentences. A good architecture is a few key decisions, sharp and opinionated, that guide every other decision.

If architecture is "what everyone should know," then this puts an upper bound on its complexity. Anything that is complex to explain will not be understood by most.

> **Tip**
>
> I saw a good example of a good architecture in Fred George's talk at Øredev 2013 on microservices architecture. Fred manages to explain the key ideas of this architecture in minutes. It sounds as if it was simplified, and it probably is—deliberately. There is a lot of value in a simplified architecture that can be quickly understood by everyone. Optimizing every detail is harmful if it makes the whole impossible to explain quickly.

Therefore: Try to express an architecture out loud in less than two minutes as a test of its quality. If you succeed, write it down immediately. If it takes much longer and too many sentences to explain the architecture, then it can be improved a lot. Of course, an architecture may be too complicated to be explained in detail in two minutes. But this test challenges the presence of a high-level structure. An architecture should be more than just an inventory of details.

Evolving Continuously: Change-Friendly Documentation

The best architecture is an evolving creature, since it is hard to get it right on the first try, and then it has to adapt to the changing context.

A good architecture is easy to explain succinctly and minimizes the number of decisions that are hard to change. Anything that is hard to change or that everybody should know has to be documented. It has to be persistent over time and made accessible to everyone, by definition.

This means that anything that makes an architecture or its documentation hard or expensive to change must be avoided. Your team should learn how to make reversible decisions or to defer irreversible decisions. And if you fear changing the architecture because you have a lot of static documentation about it that would have to be redone, your documentation is harming you, and you should reconsider how you do it.

Pay attention to how many words and diagrams are needed to explain the architecture; the fewer being the better. Keep it all evolving, and remove any process or artifact that would impede continuous change.

Decision Logs

Why does the project use this particular heavyweight technology? Hopefully it was chosen because of some requirements, following some evaluation. Who remembers that? Now that the work has changed, could you switch to something simpler?

What do you talk about during meetings with the stakeholders? From inception meetings to sprint planning meetings and other impromptu meetings, a lot of concepts, thinking, and decisions are covered. What happens to all this knowledge? Sometimes it only survives in the minds of the attendees. Sometimes it is quickly written as minutes of the meeting and sent by email. Sometimes a snapshot of the whiteboard is taken and shared. Some put everything into the tracker tool or in their wiki. One common problem is that this knowledge often lacks structure in the way it is organized.

Therefore: Maintain a decision log of the most important architectural decisions. It can be as simple as structured text files in a folder at the root of the code repository. Keep the decision log versioned with the code base. For each important decision, record the decision, its rationale (why it was made), the main alternatives considered, and the main consequences, if any. Never update the entries in the decision log; instead, add a new entry that supersedes the previous one and provide a reference to it.

Michael Nygard calls such a decision log an *architectural decision record*, or ADR for short.[4] Nat Pryce created adr-tools to support ADRs from the command line.[5]

The structuring assumptions that shape a solution are part of the decision log, as part of the rationale for an important decision. For example, if you assume that articles published in the past 24 hours represent over 80% of the visits on your website, then it will show in the rationale for the decision to partition *recent news* and *archived news* as two distinct subsystems, each with a different local architecture.

In practice, it's not always easy to record the rationale for major architecture decisions, especially when the decisions are made for the wrong reasons (see Figure 12.3). For example, management might have insisted on including this technology or the developers might have insisted on trying this new library for resume-driven development reasons. It's hard to make such rationales explicit in writing for everyone to see!

Figure 12.3 *Decision log recording a not-so-solid rationale*

You can find good examples of ADRs online in the Arachne-framework repository of ADRs.[6]

An Example of a Structured Decision Log

In the example shown here, the decision log is maintained as a single Markdown file at the root of the new Claim Management repository, after the vision statement and the descriptions of the business domain and the main stakeholders.

---

4. Michael Nygard, Think Relevance blog, http://thinkrelevance.com/blog/2011/11/15/documenting-architecture-decisions

5. Nat Pryce, https://github.com/npryce/adr-tools

6. Arachne-Framework/architecture, https://github.com/arachne-framework/architecture

The Main Decisions

To improve the overall user experience, it has been decided:

A UX approach, with a focus on beautiful and user-friendly screens, responsive across mobile devices, consistent between them regardless of the actual application behind, and with fast perceived response times. The focus is also on making sure that common tasks can be fulfilled efficiently, with few clicks and few pages navigation.

The context of the existing legacy software makes it hard to achieve the vision stated above. This is why a large part of the program is to revamp the legacy, by decommissioning it as much as possible. To mitigate the risks of this decommissioning, the following decisions have been made:

- A progressive approach, with frequent delivery: no Big Bang. New modules and legacy modules will co-exist, with a progressive migration to new code.

- A domain-driven design approach to help partition the legacy in a way which makes sense at the business domain level, to better understand the domain mechanisms, and to be easier to evolve when the business rules change.

Another challenge is that many business rules are tacit in the mind of senior adjusters and need to be formalized. On top of that, with claims taking months to complete, these rules may change during the life of a pending claim. As a consequence, the following decision has been made:

- A business process modeling approach to formalize tacit domain business rules in one place which can be easily audited and changed.

Consequences

Risks

One risk is the lack of expertise in the selected approaches. To mitigate this risk, external experts have been involved:

- UX experts (from the internal UX center)
- DDD expert (from Arolla)

Another risk comes from the legacy context, in particular:

- **Cost of testing:** The lack of automated tests of all kinds makes each release expensive (manual testing) and/or dangerous (not enough testing)

- **User-perceived performance:** The legacy system is slow, which makes it not suited for the expected response time perceived by end users.

To reduce the cost of testing, and to not impede the users during all the changes in the legacy, test automation will be key (unit tests, integration tests, non-regression tests) in order to protect the system against regressions or defects.

On the issue of user-perceived performance, the design will have to find workarounds to improve the perceived performance even though the legacy code behind may remain slow.

Technical Decisions

New Claim Management as Single Source of Truth Until the Claim Is Accepted by the Customer

Accepted on 01/12/2015

Context
We want avoid confusion arising from unclear authority of data, which consumes developer time to fix failing reconciliations. This requires that only source of truth (aka Golden Source) can exist at any point in time for a given piece of domain data.

Decision
We decide that Claim Management is the only source of truth (aka golden source) for claim on claim inception and until the claim is accepted by the customer, at which time it is **pushed** to the legacy claim mainframe. From the moment it is pushed, the only source of truth is the legacy claim mainframe (LCM).

Consequences
Given the legacy background, it is unfortunately necessary for some time to have a different golden source across the life of a claim. Still, at any point in the life of the claim, the authoritative data are clearly in one single source. This should be re- considered to move to one constant single source whenever possible.

Because of that discrepancy, before the push: commands to create or update a claim are sent to Claim Management, with events sent around and in particular to LCM to sync the LCM data (*Legacy claim mainframe as a Read Model*). After the push: remote calls to LCM are used to update the claim in LCM, with events sent back to Claim Management to sync it (*Claim Management as a Read Model*).

See "CQRS, Read Models and Persistence" on InfoQ (https://www.infoq.com/news/2015/10/cqrs-read-models-persistence).

CQRS and Event Sourcing

Accepted on 01/06/2015

Context

In the claim adjustment domain, audit is paramount: We need to be able to tell what happened in an accurate fashion.

We want to exploit the asymmetry between write and read actions to the Claim Management models, in particular to speed up read accesses.

We also want to keep track of the user intents by being more task oriented.

Decision

We follow the CQRS approach combined with EVENT SOURCING.

Consequences

We chose AxonFramework to structure the developments with its ready-made interfaces, annotations, and boilerplate code already written.

Value-First

Accepted on 01/06/2015

Context

We want to avoid bugs that arise from mutability.

We also want to reduce the amount of boilerplate code necessary in Java to create value objects.

Decision

We favor value objects whenever possible. They are immutable, with a valued constructor. They may come with a builder when needed.

Consequences

We chose Lombok framework to help generate the boilerplate code for value objects and their builders in Java.

Journals or Blogs as Brain Dumps

An alternative to using a formal decision log is to dump your brain by telling the full story of what happened, what you learned, and how the team came up with a decision, a trade-off, or a particular implementation detail.

In the book *Apprenticeship Patterns: Guidance for the Aspiring Software Craftsman*, Dave Hoover and Adewale Oshineye advocate recording what you learn and sharing what you learn.[7] A blog written by team members is a nice complement to any other kind of documentation. It is more personal, and it tells stories that are more compelling than most documentation. It tells important bits of the adventure, and the feelings of the people who were part of it.

Dan North (@tastapod) seems to agree. He said the following on Twitter, when talking to Liz Kheogh (@lunivore) and Jeff Sussna (@jeffsussna):

> I like having a product and/or team blog. Journaling decisions and conversations as you have them documents history. It also shows how decisions got made, and lets you see changing tastes or learnings over time.

Fractal Architecture Documentation

When dealing with a large system, you should give up on the idea of having one single uniform architecture everywhere. A system is made of several subsystems, and each should have its own architecture, plus the overall architecture of how they're interrelated.

Therefore: Consider your system as several smaller subsystems, or "modules." They may be physical units, such as components or services, or just logical modules at compile time. Document the architecture independently for each module and describe the overarching architecture between the modules as one system-level architecture.

Typically, you document the architecture of each module with internal documentation, using a combination of package naming conventions, annotations in the source code, and a little plain text. You would document the overall architecture with more evergreen documents in plain text and perhaps some specific DSL if you have one that fits. However, the documentation of the overall architecture could also use some generated documents built by consolidation of the knowledge extracted from each module.

---

7. Hoover, David H., and Adewale Oshineye. *Apprenticeship Patterns: Guidance for the Aspiring Software Craftsman*. Sebastopol, CA: O'Reilly Media, Inc. 2009.

The Architecture Landscape

Your architecture deserves more than just a random bunch of diagrams and other documentation mechanisms; all these efforts can be organized into a whole that we can call an *architecture landscape*, drawing inspiration from what Andreas Rüping calls a *document landscape* in his book *Agile Documentation: A Pattern Guide to Producing Lightweight Documents for Software Projects*. In this book, Andreas suggests organizing the documents into a "landscape that team members use as a mental map when they retrieve or add information."[8] The idea is that the structure of the documents helps users navigate them and may also add knowledge in itself. In the case of living documentation, the problem is to imagine an overarching structure linking documents and diagrams, generated or not.

Therefore: As your documentation grows to include a number of documentation mechanisms, organize it into a consistent whole that people can learn to navigate efficiently. Document your documentation or conform to standards for that.

Ready-made architecture document templates may provide inspiration, if you happen to like them:

- Arc42

- IBM/Rational RUP

- Company-specific templates

Some templates try to plan for every possible bit of architectural documentation need. I loathe having to laboriously fill in large templates.

LOL

I've spent one week working on a Software Architecture Document, friendly called SAD. No acronym would be more appropriate.
—*@weppos on Twitter*

---

8. Rüping, Andreas. *Agile Documentation: A Pattern Guide to Producing Lightweight Documents for Software Projects*. Chichester, England: John Wiley & Sons, Ltd. 2003.

Templates are most useful as checklists. For example, the ARC 42 "Concepts"[9] section is a nice checklist that can help you find out what you may have forgotten to consider. The following is an abbreviated list from the original template:

- Ergonomics
- Transaction Processing
- Session Handling
- Security
- Safety
- Communication and Integration
- Plausibility and Validity Checks
- Exception/Error Handling
- System Management and Administration
- Logging, Tracing
- Configurability
- Parallelization and Threading
- Internationalization
- Migration
- Scaling, Clustering
- High Availability

How many of these aspects do you neglect in your current project? How many of them do you neglect to document?

You can draw inspiration from all these established formalisms to derive your own documentation landscape, on a *module-by-module* basis. As seen previously in the section, "Stake-Driven Architecture Documentation," focus each documentation landscape on what matters most for the stakes of this subsystem.

On a module with a rich business domain, you would focus primarily on the domain model and its behaviors as key scenarios. On a more CRUD-ish module, there might be very little to say, as everything is standard and obvious. On a legacy system, the testability and migration may be the most challenging aspects and would deserve the documentation.

---

9. arc42, http://www.arc42.org

Your documentation landscape might be a plain-text file with predefined bullets and tables, or it can take the form of a small library of annotations, directly marking the source code elements with their architectural contributions and rationales. It could be a specific DSL. In practice, you would mix all these ideas according to what works best. You might even use a wiki or proprietary tools that might instantly solve all your problems.

A typical documentation landscape for a system would have to at least describe the following points:

- The overall purpose of the system, its context, users, and stakeholders
- The overall required quality attributes
- The key business behaviors and business rules and business vocabulary
- The overall principles, architecture, technical style, and any opinionated decision

This does not mean at all that you need to create documents with all this information. Living documentation is all about reducing the need for manually written documents and using alternatives that are cheaper and remain up-to-date.

For example, you could use plain-text evergreen documents for the first point, system-level acceptance tests for the second point, a BDD approach with automation for the third point, and a mix of a README, a codex, and custom annotations in the source code for the final point.

Architecture Diagrams and Notations

Many authors have for a long time proposed formalisms to describe software architecture. A number of standards are available, such as IEEE 1471, "Recommended Practice for Architecture Description of Software-Intensive Systems," and ISO/IEC/IEEE 42010, "Systems and Software Engineering Architecture Description." Kruchten's "4+1 model" has gained recognition in the enterprise world. However, all these approaches are not precisely lightweight, and they require some learning curve to be understood. Each provides a set of views to describe different aspects of the software system, with a logical view, a physical view, and so on. Overall, these approaches are not particularly popular among developers.

Simon Brown acknowledged the need for a lightweight alternative and consequently proposed the C4 Model,[10] a lightweight approach to architecture diagrams that is becoming increasingly popular among developers. This approach draws in

---

10. Simon Brown, Coding the Architecture blog, http://www.codingthearchitecture.com/2014/08/24/c4_model_poster.html

particular from the work of Nick Rozanski and Eoin Woods, in their book *Software Systems Architecture*,[11] and has the benefit of being usable without prior training. It suggests four simple types of diagrams to describe a software architecture:

- **System context diagram:** A starting point for diagramming and documenting a software system, which allows you to step back and look at the big picture

- **Container diagram:** To illustrate the high-level technology choices, showing web applications, desktop applications, mobile apps, databases, and file systems

- **Components diagram:** A way to zoom into a container, by decomposing in a way that makes sense to you (services, subsystems, layers, workflows, and so on)

- **Classes diagrams:** (Optional) To illustrate any specific implementation detail with one or more UML class diagrams

My favorite is the system context diagram, which is both simple and obvious but is often neglected.

I think that these generic notations will never be enough. Strong architectural styles should be expressed with their own specific visual notation. So while it's obviously a good thing to learn the standard notations, you shouldn't limit yourself to them but should feel free to explore your own or more specific alternatives if they are more expressive.

An Architecture Codex

When describing a solution to people, the most critical part is to share the thinking and reasoning that led to the solution.

Rebecca Wirfs-Brock was at the ITAKE un-conference in Bucharest in 2012, and during her talk and the later conversations we had about it, she gave the example of EcmaScript, where the thinking process is clearly documented. She mentioned the following as some of the rationales for decisions in ECMAScript:

- Invoke similarities with other existing folklore

- Usually we want to learn and understand as little as possible to do the job

- Recipe for making change: Figure out how similar change has been done before

---

11. Rozanski, Nick, and Eoin Woods, *Software Systems Architecture*. Boston: Pearson Education, Inc., 2012.

Later I was working on a departmentwide architecture in a bank, and I introduced this idea of a codex of principles guiding all the architecture-sensitive decisions (see Figure 12.4). The codex was built from the accumulation of concrete cases of decision making by trying to elucidate formally the reasoning behind the decision. Often, the principle was already in the heads of other senior architects, but it was tacit, and nobody else knew about it.

Figure 12.4 *The all-mighty codex*

Some of these principles were as follows:

- Know your golden source (that is, single source of truth).
- Don't feed the monster; improving the legacy only helps it last longer.
- Increase the straight-through processing automation ratio.
- Customer convenience should come first.
- The API should come first!
- A manual process is just a special case of an electronic process.

This codex proved useful for everybody involved in the architecture. The goal was to publish the codex for everyone, even if it was incomplete and not always easy to understand. At least it was useful for provoking questions and reactions. It was never formally published, but the content of the codex leaked on many occasions and has been used several times for more consistent decision making.

On a recent consulting gig I found it helpful to express the value referential of the team as a list of preferences, including the following:

- Code over XML.
- The templating engine is okay, but keep the logic out.

Of course, it is a good idea to adopt standard principles already that are documented in the literature, too, as they provide ready-made documentation. For example:

- "Keep your middleware dumb and keep the smarts in the endpoints."[12]

This codex addresses the need to spread the knowledge about architectural reasoning across more people than just the architecture team, which is a concern you should have.

Therefore: Start paying attention to how decisions are made and make the tacit principles, rules, and heuristics underneath explicit into a codex. It can be as simple as a bulleted list of single sentences. Keep it short and easy to grasp for most people, such as by using a short concrete example next to each item. Share this codex with people whenever the opportunity arises. You don't have to get it formally approved to be useful. Change it continuously to keep it short and relevant.

It is very important to keep a codex a working document that is never finished. Whenever you hit a contradiction in its principles, it's time to fix it or evolve it. This should not be seen as a failure but as an opportunity for collective decision making to be even more relevant. Architecture involves consensus, doesn't it?

An architecture codex can be a text file in the source control, a set of slides, or even expressed in code. The following is an example of using a simple enum to materialize the principles of a codex:

```
1  /**
2   * The list of all principles the team agrees on.
3   */
4  public enum Codex {
5
6      /** We have no clue to explain this decision */
7      NO_CLUE("Nobody"),
8
9      /** There must be only one authoritative place
         * for each piece of data. */
10     SINGLE_GOLDEN_SOURCE("Team"),
11
12     /** Keep your middleware dumb and keep the smarts
         * in the endpoints. */
13     DUMP_MIDDLEWARE("Sam Newman");
```

---

12. Newman, Sam. 2015. *Building Microservices*. Sebastopol, CA: O'Reilly Media, Inc., 2015.

```
14
15    private  final  String author;
16
17    private Codex(String author) {
18        this.author  = author;
19    }
20 }
```

In his book *Building Microservices*, Sam Newman says that his colleague Evan Bottcher created a big poster on the wall, displaying the key principles visibly, organized into three columns from left to right:

- Strategic Goals (for example, enable scalable business, support entry into new markets)

- Architectural Principles (for example, consistent interfaces and data flow, no silver bullet)

- Design and Delivery Practices (for example, standard REST/HTTP, encapsulate legacy, minimal customization of COTS/SAAS)

This is a nice way to sum up the system vision, principles, and practices in one place!

Transparent Architecture

When architecture documentation becomes embedded within software artifacts in each source code repository, with living diagrams and living documents generated out of them automatically, every individual has access to all the architecture knowledge. In contrast, in some companies the architecture knowledge remains in tools and slide decks only known by the official architects and not kept up-to-date.

One consequence of embedding architecture documentation within software artifacts is that it enables decentralization of the architecture and the decision-making dependent on architecture knowledge. I call this *transparent architecture*: If everyone can see the quality of the architecture by himself or herself, then everyone can make decisions accordingly, by themselves, without necessarily asking the people in an architect role (see Figure 12.5).

For example, in a microservices architecture, a transparent architecture can make use of living system diagrams generated out of the working system at runtime.

This knowledge is already there in the distributed tracing infrastructure (for example, Zipkin). You may have to augment it a bit with custom annotations and binary annotations added in your instrumentation.

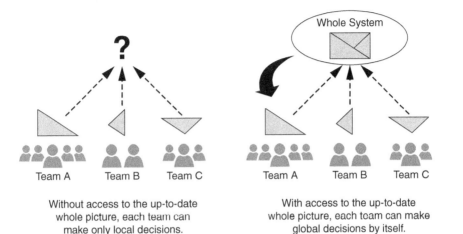

Figure caption:

Without access to the up-to-date whole picture, each team can make only local decisions.

With access to the up-to-date whole picture, each team can make global decisions by itself.

Figure 12.5 *With access to the whole picture, each team can directly make decisions that are consistent with respect to the whole system*

You might as well rely on your service registry (for example, Consul, Eureka) and its tags to produce living documents. Dependencies between services can also be derived from consumer-driven contracts if you apply this practice. And if you care about the physical infrastructure, it can be made visible through custom living diagrams generated with Graphviz from data you get from your cloud through its programmatic API.[13] Note that more "virtuous" practices also make living documentation easier!

You can achieve transparent architecture through augmented code, annotation in architectural documentation, decision logs and architectural enforced guidelines, which together can unlock the benefits of an architectural reality check, as described later in this chapter.

Architectural Annotations

Any design information that can make the code more explicit is worth adding. If you follow the layers pattern, you can document code by using the custom annotation `@Layer` on the package `com.example.infrastructure/package-info.java` at the root of each layer:

---

13. James Lewis has been showing in some of his talks an example of a living diagram of a cloud infrastructure generated from cron, Python, Boto, pydot, and Graphviz.

```
1  @Layer(LayerType.INFRASTRUCTURE)
2  package com.example.infrastructure;
```

Stereotype-like patterns represent intrinsic roles or properties that qualify a language element like a method. Consider this example:

```
1  @Idempotent
2  void  store(Customer customer);
```

Also consider this example:

```
1  @SideEffect(SideEffect.WRITE,  "Database")
2  void  save(Event e){...}
```

Specific risks or concerns can also be denoted directly on the corresponding class, method, or field, as shown here:

```
1  @Sensitive("Risk of Fraud")
2  public final class CreditCard {...
```

Design patterns in general are good candidates for design annotations. You place an annotation on an element that participates actively in the pattern. You can check it by considering whether you should keep the element if you removed the pattern. If not, you can safely declare the pattern on it; the class or method is only there to realize the pattern. It is often the element in the role that has the name of the pattern itself, such as adapter or command.

Sometimes you need values in your annotations. For example, if you wanted to declare an occurrence of the DDD repository pattern that is manipulating a particular aggregate, you could do it like this:

```
1  @Repository(aggregateRoot  =  Customer.class)
2  public interface AllCustomers {...
```

You can create your own patterns catalog with the patterns you use most commonly. It might include patterns from the Gang of Four, DDD, Martin Fowler (analysis patterns and PoEAA), EIP, some PLoP and POSA patterns, and several well-known and/or trivial basic patterns and idioms, plus all your custom in-house patterns.

In addition, you might create custom annotations to classify some important sources of knowledge, such as business rules, policies, and so on, as shown here:

```
1  @BusinessRule
2  Public Date shiftDate(Date date, BusinessCalendar calendar)
{...}
```

Here are some more examples:

- `@Policy` to highlight the major company policy expressed in the software
- `@BusinessConvention` to denote the lower-level policies that are just conventions in the business domain
- `@KeyConcept` or `@Core` to emphasize what's important
- `@Adapter` or `@Composite` to denote the use of a pattern
- `@Command` or `@Query` to clarify the semantics of write or read on a module or
- `@CorrelationID` or `AggregateID` on a field

Enforced Design Decisions

Thanks to the augmentation of code with design knowledge (using annotations, naming conventions, tags in your service registry, or any other mechanism), you can delegate conformity checks to tools. You can check dependencies according to the declared patterns and stereotypes knowledge. I like to raise an anomaly if a class annotated as a value object has field-level dependencies to classes annotated as entity or service. That's my taste, and I often ask tools to check these things for me:

```
1  if (type.isInvolvedIn(VALUE_OBJECT)) {
2    if (dependency.isInvolvedIn(ENTITY) ||
3      dependency.isInvolvedIn(SERVICE)) {
4        ... raise an anomaly
5  }
```

You can also create custom rules in your static analysis tool. For example, using the SonarQube built-in architectural constraint template or a specialized architectural assertion library such as ArchUnit,[14] you could create these rules:

- **"Persistence layer cannot depend on web code":** Forbid access to `.web.` from classes in `**.dao`.
- **"Hexagonal architecture":** Forbid access from `.domain.` to `.infra`.
- **"Value objects should not have services injected as member fields":** Classes annotated by `ValueObjects` should not have fields of a type annotated by `DomainService`.

---

14. ArchUnit, https://github.com/TNG/ArchUnit

For example, the following enforces a naming guideline mentioned in Chapter 8, "Refactorable Documentation":

```
1 @Test
2 public void domain_classes_must_not_be_named_with_prefix() {
3   noClasses().that().resideInAPackage("..domain..")
4     .should().haveSimpleNameEndingWith("Service")
5     .check(importedClasses);
6   noClasses().that().resideInAPackage("..domain..")
7     .should(new DomainClassNamingCondition())
8     .check(importedClasses);}
```

In this case, `DomainClassNamingCondition` is custom code to check that the name doesn't end with a prefix from this list: `Service`, `Repository`, `Value-Object`, `VO`, `Entity`, `Interface`, `Manager`, `Helper`, `DAO`, `DTO`, `Intf`, `Controler`, or `Controller`.

The following rule enforces the hexagonal architecture constraint "forbid access from domain code to infrastructure code":

```
1 @Test
2 public void domain_must_not_depend_on_anything() {
3   noClasses().that().resideInAPackage("..domain..")
4     .should().accessClassesThat()
5       .resideOutsideOfPackage("..domain..")
6     .check(importedClasses);
7 }
```

The name of the rules and its declarative description clearly document and protect the design decisions—as plain source code.

Architectural Reality Check

> Architecture should not be defined but discovered, refined, evolved, and explained. #theFirstMisconceptionAboutArchitecture
>
> —@mittie on Twitter

The old-fashioned idea of architecture as something to perform *before* doing the implementation doesn't fit well with modern projects. Change is expected everywhere and at any time, in the code and in the architecture—whatever you call architecture.

You want to ensure that the major quality attributes of the overall system are met (for example, conceptual integrity, performance, maintainability, security, fault tolerance) and that the most important decisions are being communicated to everyone involved. But you don't want old-fashioned architecture practices to slow down the project. You want fast documentation that can help communicate knowledge to everyone and that can also help reason and make sure the quality attributes are satisfied.

But there is another problem: The concrete implementation of the architecture may not match its intent. Coding decisions may drift day after day, one small mistake at a time, until the system bears no resemblance to the architecture it was meant to implement. This problem is called *architecture erosion*.[15]

Note that the quality attributes requirements usually don't change very frequently, but the decisions in the code do.

Therefore: Regularly visualize the architecture as the software changes. Compare the architecture as implemented to your architecture as intended. If they differ, you may want to adjust one or the other. With automated support of living diagrams or other living documents, this comparison can be done as often as during each build.

All this assumes that you have some vision of what your intended architecture should be. But if you don't have one, you can gradually reverse engineer it from your architecture as implemented.

There are tools available that can help with architecture visualization and checking, and you can also create your own living diagram generator totally dedicated to your own specific context.

Test-Driven Architecture

Test-driven development has a mindset that is not just for writing code "in the small." It's a discipline that involves first describing what you want, before you implement it, and then you make it clean to enhance your work in the longer term.

You can try to follow this same process at the architecture scale. The challenges you face are the larger scale of *everything* and the longer feedback loops, which means you may forget what you were after when you eventually get the feedback.

Ideally, you would start by defining the desired quality attributes as tests. They will not pass for weeks or months; when they eventually pass, they become the only

---

15. Ricardo Terra, Marco Tulio Valente, Krzysztof Czarnecki, and Roberto S. Bigonha, "Recommending Refactorings to Reverse Software Architecture Erosion," 16th European Conference on Software Maintenance and Reengineering, 2012: gsd.uwaterloo.ca/sites/default/files/Full%20Text.pdf

really sincere documentation of the current quality attributes. For example, consider this performance quality attribute:

> 10k requests over 5mn with less than 0.1% error and response time within 100ms at 99.5 percentile

First write it down in a bulleted list of quality attributes, such as in a Markdown file. Then implement this criterion as literally as possible as a Gatlin or JMeter test on a realistic environment (even on production). It's not very likely that it will pass right away. Now the team can work on it, along with other things, depending on the priorities. It may take a few sprints to make it pass.

You might already do something similar if you create test scripts for proofs of concepts. Instead of throwing away these scripts afterward, it doesn't take much more effort to turn experiments you're already doing on a one-off basis into maintainable assets that can assert that you still meet the requirements and that can document them at the same time.

Quality Attributes as Scenarios

A test should describe the quality attribute as declaratively as possible. One way to do this is to dress the criterion as a special Cucumber scenario:

`@QualityAttribute @SlowTest @ProductionLikeEnv @Pending`

Scenario: Number of requests at peak time

Given the system is deployed on a production-like environment

When it receives a load of 10k requests over 5mn, the error rate is less than 0.1%, and the response time is below 100ms at 99.5 percentile

Note the custom tags here:

- `@QualityAttribute:` To classify something as a quality attribute requirement
- `@SlowTest:` To launch something only as part of the nightly slow tests run
- `@ProductionLikeEnv:` To flag that this test is relevant only in a production-like environment for the metrics to be meaningful
- `@Pending:` To signal that this scenario is not passing yet

With this approach, as soon as the scenario is written, it can become the single source of truth for the corresponding quality attribute. Moreover, the scenario tests reports becomes the table of contents for these "non-functional requirements," too.

Note that the quality attributes scenarios are useful even if they are never actually implemented as true tests.

You might describe the quality attributes this way:

- **Persistence:** "Given that a purchase has been written, when we shut down and then restart the service and then the purchase, we can read all the purchase data." Is it going too far to document the obvious like this?
- **Security:** "When we run *standard* penetration testing suites, zero flaw is detected." Note that here the trick is the word *standard*, which refers to a more complete description somewhere outside the scenario. This external link is part of your documentation, too, even if you didn't write it yourself.

When the quality attribute can be checked at compile time, it will be part of your quality dashboard (for example, in Sonar). In this case, you can turn this tool into your table of contents for these quality attributes. And you might use something like the Build Breaker plugin to fail the build in case of too many violations. This is another way of implementing enforced guidelines.

Quality Attributes at Runtime in Production

Some quality attributes are too difficult to test outside their natural habitat. Such situations call for a more monitoring-oriented approach. Netflix introduced the Chaos Monkey to assert fault tolerance at the service level. Later it introduced the Chaos Gorilla at the data center level:

> Chaos Gorilla is similar to Chaos Monkey but simulates an outage of an entire Amazon availability zone. We want to verify that our services automatically re-balance to the functional availability zones without user-visible impact or manual intervention.[16]

The mere description of these two Chaos engines, along with their configuration parameters in terms of outage frequencies, is in itself a documentation of the fault-tolerance requirements.

Some cloud providers or container orchestration tools support automatic roll-back if some metrics are degraded following a deployment. This configuration de facto documents what's considered "normal" metrics (for example, CPU/memory usage, conversion rate).

---

16. The Netflix tech blog, http://techblog.netflix.com/2011/07/netflix-simian-army.html

Other Quality Attributes

> To keep track of your expectations before doing experiments on the product, its successes and failures: http://growth.founders.as #startup #hypotheses
>
> —*@fchabanois on Twitter*

Some quality attributes cannot be tested automatically (for example, financials expectations, user satisfaction). These attributes often reside within spreadsheets on shared drives. Alternatives exist online to encourage sincere declarations of the objectives before comparing them against actual achievements. These kinds of tools encourage working in a TDD-ish fashion for startup objectives.

From Fragmented Knowledge to Usable Documentation

The approach described in this section can end up producing many fragmented and heterogenous sources of truths about all the quality attributes. They need to be curated and consolidated into one or two living tables of content.

Therefore: Dress your quality attribute tests as Cucumber scenarios and put them in a separate "Quality Attributes" folder (and hence into a separate chapter in the corresponding living documentation). Use tags to classify them more precisely. Decide on one existing tool to host the main table of content as the single point of entry for all the quality attributes documentation, with references to any other tool.

For example, you might decide that Cucumber is the main table of contents. You can then add pseudo-scenarios to link to the Sonar configuration and to the permalinks to the configuration of each static analysis tools. You might also mention the Chaos Monkey as a scenario and a link to its configuration on some Git repository.

Alternatively, you might decide on your build tool as the main table of contents. By adding custom steps in the build pipeline (for example, Jenkins, Visual Studio), you can pinpoint to Cucumber reports, Sonar reports, and the Chaos Monkey configuration.

These tools can at the same time be a table of contents and fail the build in case one of the quality attribute is not met anymore. This helps keep the documentation sincere. If you just use a wiki as the main table of contents, you no longer have that enforcement.

Small-Scale Simulation as Living Architecture Documentation

Large and complex software applications or systems of applications are challenging in terms of documentation. Judging by the size of the source code and configuration they're made of, the amount of knowledge that is necessary to describe them is so huge it is useless as is. And at the same time, the critical higher-level design decisions and all the thinking that went into building the systems are often implicit.

If a system were smaller, it would be easier to understand. Just by reading the handful of classes, running the few tests, exploring what happens when playing with the code in a REPL, and watching the dynamic behavior at runtime, you could quickly get a sound understanding of its purpose and of how it works. Even if the thinking that led the design were lost, you would be able to recover it from observing the small-scale system in action. This would be tacit knowledge, but it would still be much better than nothing.

Therefore: Create a small-scale replica of your software system, such as a stripped-down reimplementation of just the key bits of code with some tests, for the sole purpose of documentation. Through aggressive curation, select a small subset of features and code that focus only on the one or two aspects that matter and that fits on your brain as a whole. Simplify every other distracting aspect, even if doing so makes it slower and gives it a limited set of features. Make sure this small-scale replica works realistically, producing accurate, if not perfect, results, though it does not necessarily need to do so in all cases.

The advantage of small-scale simulation is that it becomes human-scale; it fits in your head. Note that here when I say small-scale, I'm primarily talking about reduced complexity, not just reduced size.

I've tried small-scale simulation several times:

- When developing an exchange system for financial products, the core of the matching engine was growing larger and more complex because of various optimizations, and other concerns, such as timing, scheduling, and permissions management, were blurring the overall picture. We created a smaller version of the core of the matching engine, with just a minimal set of basic and naive classes that could make matching work in its most interesting aspects. In this case, the smaller system was not a replica but was built mostly from the same elements as the actual system because the design was flexible enough to accommodate that.

- In a very large legacy system with a few applications and many batches running in the background several times a day, the overall behavior of the system was quite nebulous. We created a small-scale, simplified Java emulation of the most important batch so that we could better understand it and explore its interactions with our new code.

- In two startups with a rich domain, we pair-programmed for a few days to create a small-scale model that worked for just one very simplified case.

This gave us an opportunity to quickly explore and map the domain, discover the main issues and stakes, grow a vocabulary, and agree on a shared vision of the whole system. From that small-scale system, later discussions had a concrete reference code to ground the discussions. We found that this was really a communication tool we could point at during conversations.

At a big company where everything takes ages, creating a small-scale model under the name "proof of concept" is a great alternative to doing never-ending studies delivering nothing but slides and illusions. The focus on working code helps converge and makes it harder to elude the tough questions. You probably already build proofs of concepts at the beginning. But do you keep them for their explanatory power later?

The Desirable Properties of a Small-Scale Simulation

A small-scale simulation must have the following characteristics:

- **It must be small enough to fit in the brain of a normal person or of a developer:** This is the most important property, and it implies that the simulation will not account for everything of the original system.

- **You must be able to tinker with it, and it must be inviting for interactive exploration:** The code should be easy to run partially, by just being able to do something with a class or function without having to rebuild the full simulation.

- **It must be executable to exhibit the dynamic behavior at runtime:** The simulation must predict results through its execution, and you must be able to observe it easily, even during the computation, if possible, in debug mode, with traces or just by running its phases independently.

A small-scale software project that is executable and works in a realistic fashion is valuable for reasoning on the system. You can reason on its static structure just by observing it in the code. You can also tinker with it by creating one more test cases or by interacting with it in a REPL.

This approach is also useful as an inexpensive proxy to impractical legacy or external systems; instead of running a complex batch that depends on the state of the database and that has numerous side effects all over the place, you can run its emulation to get a grasp of its effect in relationship to what you're doing.

Techniques to Simplify a System

To achieve a small-scale simulation, you want to simplify aggressively the full system, with an exclusive focus on the one or two aspects that matter. Just like any other documentation, documentation of a system should explain 1 thing well rather than explain 10 things badly. (There's already the real system for that.) Note that you can still decide to build more than one small-scale simulation, such as one for each important point to explain.

A simplified small-scale system will lose a lot of details and will *not* show a lot of otherwise valuable knowledge. This simplification is harder to do than it seems because when you're attached to a system you've built, you'd like to tell about all its interesting facets, but you have to refrain from doing so and learn to focus.

Interestingly, the techniques used to build a small-scale simulation are the techniques you already use to create convenient tests.

Concretely, you can simplify a system in many ways, always by deciding to ignore one or many distracting concerns:

- **Curation:** Give up the idea that it has to be feature complete. Get rid of all the member data that is not central to the current focus. Ignore side stories and secondary stuff like special cases that don't intersect the current focus.

- **Mocks, stubs, and spies:** Give up performing all the computations. Instead, use the usual test companions to totally get rid of all the non-centrally relevant subparts. Use in-memory collections instead of middleware and simulate third parties.

- **Approximation:** Give up on strict accuracy and settle only on realistic accuracy that looks good enough, such as the right value without the digits or 1% correct.

- **More convenient units:** Give up the ability to really put in production the simulation with the actual data. For example, if the dates are only used to decide if something happens before or after a given data, you might replace the dates that are cumbersome to manipulate by hand with plain integers.

- **Brute-force calculation:** Give up the optimizations that are not central to your current focus. Instead, make the simulation work using the algorithm that's the simplest to grasp or the one with the most explanatory power.

- **Batch versus event driven:** Turn the original event-driven approach into a batch mode, or the other way around, if it's simpler to code and understand, assuming that this approach is not central to the current focus.

Building a Small-Scale Simulation Is Half the Fun

You learn a lot by creating a small-scale simulation. You have to clarify your thoughts, and nothing's more demanding than simple, working code to force that.

From a design perspective, cutting through the details to focus on the essentials gives you a lot of insights that can help you improve the design of the original system. For example, if you can replace dates with integers in the simulation, the original functions don't really need to operate on dates but can operate on anything comparable.

If the simulation can work without all these distracting aspects, this also means the original design should follow the single responsibility principle and, therefore, separate all the concerns. You know when you've reached that state when you can create your small-scale simulation by reusing the same code from the original system just by assembling a naive subset of its elements.

This idea used in the context of starting a project is known under various names in the literature: Alistair Cockburn talks about a *walking skeleton*.[17]

This idea is also similar in many aspects to the pattern *breakable toys* described in the book *Apprenticeship Patterns: Guidance for the Aspiring Software Craftsman* by Dave Hoover and Adewale Oshineye.[18] A small-scale simulation can be used to try things much faster than the actual system. This comes in handy for trying two or three competing approaches quickly to decide on the best one, based on actual facts rather than on opinions.

Such a tinkerable system is very valuable because new joiners can build their own mental models about it. If, as Peter Naur[19] claims, it's very hard to express a theory using codified rules such as text, having the ability to form your own theories about a system by just playing with it without risk can help. This is how kids learn about all the laws of physics.

System Metaphor

If you run trainings, you know how hard it is to explain something to an audience you don't know. You need to determine what they know already so you can build on that.

---

17. Cockburn, Alistair. *Crystal Clear: A Human-Powered Methodology for Small Teams*. Boston: Pearson Education, Inc., 2004.

18. Hoover, David H., and Adewale Oshineye. *Apprenticeship Patterns: Guidance for the Aspiring Software Craftsman*. Sebastopol, CA: O'Reilly Media, Inc. 2009.

19. Naur, Peter. "Programming as theory building." *Microprocessing and Microprogramming* 15, no. 5 (1985): 253-261.

Metaphors get their power by leveraging on things most people are already familiar with, so it's possible to explain new stuff more efficiently.

Explaining a System by Talking About Another System

> A simple shared story of how the system works, a metaphor.
> —*C2 Wiki, http://c2.com/cgi/wiki?SystemMetaphor*

When I explain monoids and how they compose, I usually use the metaphor to the tangible world, such as real glasses of beers that I can stack or chairs that can be stacked or anything else that is stackable. This helps elucidate the idea of monoid-esque composability, and it's fun, which is also very good for learning.

Suggestive metaphors we're all familiar with include an assembly line, a water pipeline, Lego building blocks, a train on its rails, and a bill of materials.

The system metaphor was used in Extreme Programming (XP) to unify an architecture and provide naming conventions.

The famous Extreme Programming project C3 "was built as a production line," and the other famous XP project VCAPS "was structured like a bill of materials." Each chosen metaphor acts as a system of names, relations, and roles working together toward a shared purpose. When using a metaphor, you invoke all the prior knowledge of the audience to be reused in the context of the system being considered. You know that an assembly line is typically linear, with multiple machines in line alongside a conveyor belt that is moving parts from one machine to the next. You also know that any defect upstream will result in defects downstream.

Useful Even Without Prior Knowledge

The last time I was on a team that built a rich cash flow calculation engine that was able to re-create cash from any complicated financial instrument, the team used the metaphor of a modular synthesizer. Now I have to admit that not everyone is familiar with modular synths, but in that team, several people knew about them. The interesting thing is that the metaphor helped even the people who didn't know about them.

It's intriguing that a metaphor remains somehow useful even for people who don't know it, just as a redundancy mechanism. Imagine that you're trying to mentally picture the cash flow engine as an interpreter pattern, and you're not fully sure you got it right. Now, if I explain what a modular synth is ("a set of electronic modules full of buttons and knobs, wired together in an arbitrary fashion via patch cords plugged into them"), it should help. The patching combinations between every connector are nearly infinite for a large variety of sounds to be produced, just as is the case with the financial engine.

A Metaphor in Another Metaphor

A good metaphor is a model with some generative power: If I know that stopping a production line is very expensive, I can wonder if and how that would translate into a software system. It does, and just as on a production line, we should perform strict validation of the raw materials in inputs to protect the line. But the metaphor may not stand on this aspect, and that's it.

The more common culture that exists, the more ideas available to use as metaphors. When you know what a sales funnel is (see Figure 12.6), you can talk about it to explain key aspects of an e-commerce system, with its successive business stages from visitor to inquiries, to proposals, to new customer. It's called a funnel because the volume at each stage decreases significantly.

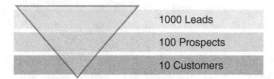

Figure 12.6 *A sales funnel*

This knowledge comes in handy when you're doing architecture, as it informs scalability reasoning: The upstream stage, like the catalog, needs more scalability than the downstream stage, like the payment.

Summary

Documentation of software architecture doesn't have to be slideware or models in proprietary modeling tools. It is best done in a living documentation fashion, in situ in the system itself, and organized into an architecture landscape that people become familiar with.

The ultimate form of this approach is a transparent and living architecture that is also test driven. In this setting, the important architectural knowledge is accessible, enabling anyone to make informed changes quickly and any time, and it's machine accessible for continuous reality checks and feedbacks, thanks to automated assertions.

Chapter 13

Introducing Living Documentation to a New Environment

Living documentation starts with someone willing to improve the current state of affairs in either the documentation or the way software is done. Since you are reading this book, you are that person. You may want to start living documentation because you're afraid to lose knowledge, or because you'd like to go faster with the relevant knowledge more readily available. You may also want to start it as a pretext to show flaws in the way the team is making software, such as in the lack of deliberate design, and you expect the documentation to make it visible and obvious to everyone.

A difficult step is to find a compelling case of missing knowledge. Once you have a demonstrated case and provided that you can solve it with one of the living documentation approaches, you're on the right track.

Undercover Experiments

If you feel alone in your interest in living documentation, you may want to start gently and slowly, without making a lot of noise about it and, most importantly, without asking for authorization. The idea is that documenting, whatever way it is done, is part of the natural work of a professional developer.

Therefore: Introduce nuggets of living documentation naturally as part of the daily work. Start annotating your design decisions, intents, and rationales at the time you make them. When there is some slack time or a genuine need for documentation, use the allotted time to create simple documentation automation such as a simple living diagram or a basic glossary. Keep it simple enough to have it work in a few hours or less. Don't talk about it as a revolution but just as

a natural way to do things efficiently. Emphasize the benefits, not the theory from this book.

Of course, when people become more interested in the approach, you can talk about living documentation as a topic and direct them to this book.

Official Ambition

Another way to introduce living documentation is through an official ambition, though I don't recommend this one as a starting point.

Going the official route usually begins with management, or at least requires management sponsorship. Documentation is often a source of frustration and anxiety for managers, and therefore this topic is often promoted even more by managers than by the development team.

Having a sponsor is good news: You have dedicated time and perhaps even a team to implement. The counterpart is that as an official ambition, it will be highly visible and closely monitored, and there will be pressure to deliver something visible quickly. This pressure may endanger the initiative by forcing success. But living documentation is a discovery journey, there's an experimental side to it, and there is no clear path to success in your own context. You'll have to try things, decide that some are not applicable, and adjust some things to your own cases. This is best done without excessive scrutiny by higher-ups.

I therefore recommend starting with undercover experiments and promoting the topic as an official ambition only after you've found the sweet spots of living documentation in your environment.

New Things Have to Work and Have to Be Accepted

A typical path I advise is to start with creating appetite, then try for quick opportunities to show benefits, and then to grow from there:

1. Start by creating awareness in the larger audience. A great way to do this is through an all-audience talk that is informative and entertaining. The point is not to explain how to do things but to show how life could be better compared to the current state of affairs. Nancy Duarte's book *Resonate*[1] is full of advice on how to do this well. Listen to the feedback at the end of the session and a few days later to decide whether there is appetite to go further. Otherwise, you may want to try again some weeks or months later, or you might decide to go undercover first.

---

1. Duarte, Nancy. *Resonate*. Hoboken: John Wiley and Sons, Inc. 2010.

2. Spend some time with the team or an influencer team member to identify what knowledge most deserves to be documented. From there, propose quick wins to try as short items in the backlog or as part of time dedicated to making improvements. Retrospectives are also a good time to consider living documentation issues and propose actions. It is important to focus on real needs that many people find important.

3. Build something useful in a short period of time and demo it as you would any other task. Collect feedback, improve, and collectively decide on whether to expand now or later, if needed.

Starting Gently

As a consultant, I regularly sit with teams in companies of all sizes. When they ask to create more documentation, I tend to suggest several steps.

First of all, I remind them that interactive and face-to-face knowledge transfer must be the primary means of documentation, before anything else.

Next, I tell them, we can then consider techniques to record the key bits of knowledge that have to be known by everyone, that every newcomer has to learn, and that matter in the long run.

At this point someone might say, "Let's write that stuff in our wiki." That is fine, as long as we understand that a wiki is a nice place for evergreen content, for knowledge that does not change often. For everything else, we can do better.

Where to start? I like to mention various ideas very quickly to scan the interest of the team members. For example, I would mention briefly each of the following:

- We could add a simple README describing what the project is about.

- We could add a simple decision log as a Markdown file in the base directory of the project, with a recap of the three to five main architectural and design decisions since its inception.

- We could tag the code with a custom annotation or attribute to highlight the key landmarks or the core concepts. Combined with the search by reference in the IDE, this becomes a simple yet effective way to provide a sightseeing map of the code base.

- On a similar note, we could tag the code with guided tour annotation or attributes to provide a simple way to follow a request or processing end-to-end across the various fragments of code, across the various layers or modules, in a linear fashion. Again, this relies on search by reference in the IDE.

- We could turn the most important napkin sketch into an ASCII diagram in the decision log file.

This list deliberately contains only stuff that can be done and committed within a short period of time. For example, a team I've worked with has been able to add and commit a decision log with five past key decisions, marking three key landmarks plus a guided tour with five steps within two hours. This included the creation of the two custom attributes for the key landmarks and the guided tour, respectively, ensuring that the search in the IDE worked well, and ensuring that the Markdown rendering was fine in TFS.

The goal at this stage is to create awareness and interest by reaching attractive results quickly. The goal is to hear, "Wow, I really like that approach. I'm hooked now!"

Another goal is for the team members to already experience the "beyond documentation effect" after just going through these simple steps: "Ouch, I now realize how sloppy and half-finished our structure is." That's a lot of goodness for two hours!

Given genuine interest from the team and some available time, you can go further and try word clouds, a living glossary, or living diagrams.

Going Big and Visible

After a gentle start, you might want have bigger ambitions. I'm not saying that is always a bad idea, but it can be dangerous for several reasons:

- Visible ambitions usually need to exhibit symbolic progress shown by a quantity of outcomes or even KPIs. But does it mean anything "to be 40% living documentation"? Doing living documentation just to do it will eventually discredit the approach.

- The benefits can be deferred by months, and it can be difficult to show the return on investment if measured over three months.

- As mentioned earlier, it may take various adjustments when applying the techniques from this book in your particular context; these adjustments may be perceived as failures in the meantime.

- What's useful for the team may not be what management expected. If this is the case, put yourself in management's shoes: What would make you happy with respect to documentation? If you can make previously hidden knowledge accessible to nondevelopers, it might be a good thing for everyone. Managers will be able to judge something by themselves, based on objective facts extracted from the code base. And when you set up the living diagram or some other mechanism, you have an opportunity to do the curation and the presentation in a way that promotes your agenda (for example, to encourage good things or to warn against bad ones).

In any case, remember that documentation, living or not, is not an end in itself but a means to accelerating delivery. This acceleration of delivery can be direct, when decisions are made faster thanks to the knowledge readily available through the living documentation. It can also be indirect, when creating the documentation raises awareness on everything sloppy in the system, in the thinking or in the communication between the stakeholders. By fixing the root cause, you improve the whole system, which in turn accelerates delivery.

Case Study: A Tale of Introducing Living Documentation to a Team Member

I met with a team member who was interested in learning more about living documentation. He was just curious, not convinced, but his curiosity was a good start.

Conversations First

I tend to start explaining living documentation with questions in a conversational style. Instead of explaining what living documentation is, I start by putting myself in the shoes of another team member willing to learn about the project. I ask the team member to tell me about the current project, and I tell her I'm going to take notes and sketch what we say on a flipchart. Then I begin to ask questions like these:

What's the name of the project? What is its purpose, and who is it for?

What is the ecosystem, including the external systems and external actors? What are the overall input and outputs?

What's the execution style? Is it interactive, a nightly batch, a GitHub hook? What's the main language: Ruby, Java, Tomcat, or something else?

These are all standard questions so far. Answers come naturally. But then I ask:

What is the core domain, in your opinion?

This comes as a surprise. The team member needs some time to think about it. She is surprised that the answer was not obvious, after several months on the project. "Oh, now that you mention that," she says, "I realize that our core domain is probably the way we insert deep links that point to our system in the feed we provide to the external partners, so that they bring us qualified inbound web traffic. I didn't think about it this way before, and I'm not sure everyone on the team is aware of it."

"Is this deep link thing the raison d'être for the whole project?" I ask.

"Yes," she says, "absolutely."

I press further: "Do you think everyone should know about that?

"Obviously, yes," she said.

"So we should document that somewhere?" I ask.

"Of course!" she replies.

The First Debriefing

After I learn what I am interested in through having conversations, I can hold a debriefing to introduce the basic concepts of living documentation.

Living documentation is primarily about *having conversations to share knowledge*. My goal in the conversations so far was to learn a lot of what matters to me, quickly and without wasting time on any other stuff. Interactive conversations and the high bandwidth of talking are hard to beat, especially with the support of a flipchart, which helps me ensure that I understand the other person's message.

The second point I can introduce now is that some of the knowledge we talked about so far needs to be recorded in a persistent form. And the good thing to recognize is that most of this knowledge so far is *stable over time*. This is lucky, so in this case we can use *evergreen documents* in any form: wiki, text and so on. But we must make sure not to mix any volatile and short-lived knowledge, or we immediately loose the benefits of evergreen documents, which are documents that don't need any maintenance yet remain true forever (or for a very long period of time).

There is a third point here already: The concept of "deep linking" we uncovered is a standard concept already documented in the online literature. As such, it's *ready-made knowledge*. We can link to it on the web, so there is no need to explain what it is again. We're lazy.

One last point we begin to see in this example is that by paying attention to the documentation, even the person with the knowledge also learns and gains additional awareness in the process. That illustrates the benefits "beyond documentation," and it's probably the biggest value of living documentation.

Time to Talk About the Code

After all my questions on the context and on the problem side, I'd like to know more about the solution side—in other words, the code. So I ask how the code is organized.

Then we draw the folder hierarchy on the flipchart, and the structure is very close to the hexagonal architecture. At this point I provoke the team member a bit: "Imagine that you're all gone after the project is delivered, and there is no budget left to keep you. Then a year later, the project has to resume, and additional features need to be delivered, so a new team is formed. What risks do you see that the new team will degrade the current system?"

In this fictitious situation, it's easier for the team member to answer: "I'd say junior developers new to the project might put business logic in the REST endpoints, and that would bad."

"Sure," I say. "It would be bad. Still, I think there should be no need to say this today, as it's supposed to be known by professional developers these days."

The team member says that they were doing everything pretty much standard, with no surprises. To me this means there's no need for documentation on all the standard stuff. Also, the code is rather clean, and it shows *how* it's done. However, it doesn't tell *why* it's done this way.

I ask whether there is a risk that any other new team members could degrade the design of the system by accident.

"In fact," says the team member, "we designed an includelist and an excludelist mechanism to filter content that we export, depending on the external partner. But we did it in such a way that the code is totally agnostic with respect to the external partner. Only their configuration is specific."

"You mean that effort to be totally agnostic does not necessarily show from the code without giving any hint?" I ask.

She replies, "Yes, it's likely that a newcomer would quickly add an IF statement around the next partner-specific behavior he or she needed to support and would break the design as a result."

Decision Logs and Guided Tours

I tell the team member that we should record the design decision she just described. We can do that in a *decision log* as a plain Markdown file at the root of the project, in the source control system. It's quite concise: date, decision, rationale, consequence. Three sentences would be enough.

What else? The code of the project is not bad, but it is still not obvious enough to follow a user request through all its stages in the system.

"For that we could do a guided tour," I say. And I explain and show how to create the custom annotation @GuidedTour to mark each step in the guided tour. The team member quickly devises the best seven steps of the guided tour and adds the annotation on each of them. It takes 20 minutes to introduce the first tour.

Furthermore, through the tour, I find out that a significant part of the overall behavior is a cache on calculations on web services, in a *read-through* fashion: That's ready-made knowledge again, that is described online!

We then create another custom annotation, `@ReadThroughCache`, to mark that knowledge, with a brief definition and a link to a standard explanation on the web.

After 2.5 hours talking and creating annotations to support our very first living documentation, it's time to get feedback from the team member, and what I hear sounds encouraging: "I like the idea of using annotations for documentation: It's lightweight and easy to add without asking the right to do it. I can start solo and locally. In contrast, other techniques like a living diagram are more like team decisions, I think. And linking to ready-made knowledge saves time and is more accurate than if I tried to explain it myself in writing."

I concur, mentioning that it's part of an embedded learning approach: "Simple annotations in the core also hint to your team members about interesting ideas in the literature they may not know otherwise."

But she's not totally convinced that this embedded learning works for everyone: "Yes, some of my colleagues will realize that they don't know and will be curious to learn more. Some will read the links and learn by themselves, but some will probably not and will ask me instead."

"But I see that as a feature," I say. "It invites discussion, and that's another opportunity for learning, probably for both of you."

Common Objections to Living Documentation

Your desire to start doing living documentation doesn't mean everyone around agrees. Perhaps they don't have the need or they don't see the benefits.

Annotations Are Not Meant for Documentation

One of the most common objections to living documentation is that annotations are not meant for documentation. This is how a conversation about this objection might go:

> Team member: "I don't like to use annotations for documentation because I don't like adding code that does not execute"
>
> Me: "You know, you do it already when you mark code as `[Obsolete]` or `@Deprecated`."
>
> Team member: "Oh, yes. Fair point."

I suggest framing the "comments versus annotation" choice as "good versus bad": "Comments are bad and should be avoided; but if the information to record is really important, then it's worth its own custom annotation."

"We Do It Already"

If you're having lots of technical meetings, it MAY indicate that your internal documentation could be better.

—@ploeh on Twitter

"We do it already" is a standard objection to almost anything. To some extent, everything looks like everything.

Yes, you probably do apply a number of the practices in this book, but are you really taking a living documentation approach? The key word here is *deliberate*. If you happen to do some of the things discussed in this book by chance, it's fine, but it would be even better to do those things deliberately. It's up to your team to decide where to put the cursor and to decide on a documentation strategy. Such a strategy has to be emergent and deliberate. It must fit your particular context and be accepted by everyone involved.

Your documentation strategy will mix practices you already do, push some of them further, and introduce new practices that sound promising. And you will adjust all this over time to get the most benefits with minimal effort.

Someone might say, "We have all the knowledge that we need."

Perhaps this team does have all the knowledge because he or she was there before the rest of the team. But does everyone else feel so comfortable?

Perhaps you just hate documentation, and I can totally understand that. But it's important to acknowledge what you don't know.

Migrating Legacy Documentation into Living Documentation

If you have legacy documentation, you may leverage on it. Doing so avoids the blank page syndrome and offers an opportunity to review past knowledge in a new light. You have old PowerPoint documentation? Turn it into living documentation! Put the knowledge from the PPT back into the source code, wherever it fits best:

- Vision and goals could go into the README file, as Markdown.

- Pseudo-code or a sequence diagram could be made into a plain-text diagram or ASCII diagram, or you could just replace it with a reference to a test doing the same scenario.

- Description of main modules and methods could be done within the source code itself, through some class- and module-level comments, annotations, and naming conventions.

- Comments can be put in config items.

Notice that all this knowledge can be pulled from shared drives and wikis to find a new home in the source control.

It's also striking that the old content that was all concentrated within a few slide decks or Word documents becomes spread all over the code base when you move to living documentation. This might sound like a bad thing. Sometimes you might prefer to have some overview slides kept together as one document. But for most of the practical knowledge, the best location to keep it is as close as possible to the place where you need it.

You could perform documentation mining on all existing written documents: emails, Word documents, reports, meeting minutes, forum posts, entries into various company tools such as application catalogs, and so on. Every time a piece of knowledge "still sounds relevant after all this time," it's probably worth preserving.

In practice, you would deprecate or remove the old content, possibly with a redirection to the new location for the similar knowledge or an explanation on how to find it from now on. A former colleague, Gilles Philippart, calls such migration "strangling your documentation," which is similar to Martin Fowler's strangler application pattern for rewriting parts of legacy applications.

Marginal Documentation

Your documentation endeavor does not have to be complete on the first attempt. It should evolve over time. One approach that's often a good idea when you're willing to improve something is to focus on the marginal work. You might say, for example, "From now on, every new piece of work will follow a much higher standard."

Improve your documentation marginally. By paying close attention to what you do from now on, even the parts of the legacy code that still matter will be taken care of over time. And don't worry too much about the rest.

Sometimes you can segregate new additions to live in their own clean bubble context; this makes it easier to clearly meet a higher standard of living documentation, which is nothing but a higher standard of everything: naming, code organization, top-level comments, clear and bold design decisions made visible in the code, and the more "typical" living documentation stuff like a living glossary and diagrams, enforced guidelines, and so on.

Case Study: Introducing Living Documentation in a Batch System

This real-world example is about batches to export credit authorizations from one application to external systems. Members of the team stay less than three years, on average, and therefore the need for some documentation is not controversial here. The team and the managers heard about living documentation and are interested, so we eventually spent an hour discussing what could be done.

When considering what to do, we tried to focus on everything that should be documented in order to improve the life of the development team. Then, by looking at the current state of the available documentation, we could propose actions to better manage the knowledge.

Currently, team members say, "there are some documents, but they are out of date and not reliable. We usually have to ask the most knowledgeable team member all the time to get the knowledge needed to perform any task."

There's a lot of potential for improvement here, including some quick wins. We could introduce all the items discussed in the following sections to start a living documentation journey.

README and Ready-Made Documentation

The source code repository does not have a README file at its root. Therefore, the team could first add a README file at the root of the module.

In this README file, the team should mention clearly that this module follows the data pump pattern, with a brief explanation of the pattern and a link to a reference on the web. From a living documentation perspective, the team would be referencing ready-made documentation.

To be more useful, the team can elaborate a little bit on the data pump with a description of its main parameters in the README file:

- **Target system and format:** A company-standard XML dialect is used.
- **Governance:** This data pump belongs to the *Spartacus Credit Approval* component and is managed as part of it.
- **Rationale:** The data pump pattern is chosen over more standard integration through services endpoints because the target system imposes a bulk integration style, with lots of data to transfer between the two systems daily.

All this remains a bit abstract, so it's desirable to include in the README file a link to a folder containing some sample files describing the inputs and outputs of the component:

```
1 Sample input and output files can be found in
2 '/samples/' (with a link to 'target/doc/samples')
```

Business Behavior

The core complexity of the module is the determination of the domain concept of *eligibility*. It is best described by business scenarios that are already partially automated in Cucumber JVM, in a feature file named eligibility.feature.

The team can reuse some of these scenarios to generate the sample files mentioned before. This way, the sample files will remain up-to-date.

Having business-readable scenarios is nice, but this team needs to make these scenarios accessible to nondevelopers. The basic Cucumber report can show the scenarios as a web page online. The team could consider the alternative tool Pickles for the living documentation to be available online to anyone in a better form and with a search engine.

Visible Workings and a Single Source of Truth

The transcoding used to generate the XML report is defined in code and in an Excel file as well:

```
1  | input field name | output field name | formatter           |
2  | trade date       | TrdDate           | ukToUsDateFormatter |
```

The team realizes that there is duplication of knowledge for no particular benefit here. Who's the authority in case of disagreement? Usually it should be the spreadsheet file, but after a while, it will be the code.

The team could improve that situation by deciding that the spreadsheet file is the single source of truth (aka the golden source) of the transcoding. The code then parses this file and interprets it to drive its behavior. In this approach, the file is directly its own documentation. For example, the parser code could look like this, in pseudo-code:

```
1  For each input field declared in a data dictionary (e.g. the
   XLS file)
2      Fetch the value from the input field
3      Apply the formatter to obtain the value
4      Lookup the corresponding output field
5      Assign the formatted value to the output field
```

The team might go the other way around and decide that the code is the single source of truth and so generate a file directly out of the code. This won't work if the code is mostly made of a lot of IF statements. Being able to generate a readable file from the code imposes a generic structure to the design of the code. Basically, the code would embed the equivalent of the former spreadsheet file, but hardcoded as a dictionary (for example, in a map in Java).

This data structure can then be exported as a file in various formats (.xls, .csv, .xml, .json, and so on) for nondeveloper audiences.

Integrated Documentation for Developers and a Living Glossary for Other Stakeholders

Does the team really need to produce Javadoc reports? It's so easy to browse the code in the IDE that the team probably won't use the Javadoc reports much. The Javadoc reports are now available directly at their fingertips in your IDE. The same is true for UML class diagrams of classes and their type hierarchies. All this is already integrated documentation that is built in to the team's editors.

If the team really needs a reference to give access to the concepts to nondevelopers, it might introduce a living glossary, which scans the code in the /domain package to generate a Markdown and HTML glossary of all the business domain concepts in the code, extracted from classes, interfaces, enum constants, and perhaps some method names and Javadoc comments. Of course, for the glossary to be good, the team will probably have to review and fix many of these Javadoc comments.

A Living Diagram to Show the Design Intent

If the internal design follows a known structure, such as the Hexagonal Architecture, the team can make it visible with the naming conventions of the corresponding modules. This naming convention and the name of the structure must be documented in the README file:

```
1 The design of this module follow the Hexagonal Architecture
pattern (link to a reference on the web).
2
3
4 By convention, the domain model code is in the
6 src/*/domain*/ package, and the rest is all infrastructure
7 code
```

This is more ready-made documentation.

The team might include a link to the domain model package, but it has to survive refactoring changes such as moving the domain folder into another folder. To make the link more stable, the team can make it a bookmarked search directly based on the naming convention as a regular expression: src/*/domain*/.

Contact Information and Guided Tours

Who should someone contact for questions? The service registry, Consul in this case, should have this information, as required by the company architects.

A guided tour just for the batch is not very difficult to create with a custom annotation, but it may not be very useful for developers. The batch is built with the very standard and well-documented Spring Batch framework. This framework completely controls the way the processing takes place. It is safe to assume that all the developers know about this framework and the way it works or that they can learn about it from the standard documentation and tutorials. There is no need to create an additional custom guided tour for that.

Microservices Big Picture

How does the data pump module fit within the bigger system made of many microservices? Answering this question takes some effort. One approach would be to regularly run a *journey test* (an end-to-end scenario that goes through a large number of components of the system) on some environment with distributed tracing enabled. Tools like Selenium for running the test and Zipkin for distributed tracing may come to mind. The team could then visualize the distributed traces to produce a guided tour that reveals what happens between services during each journey test, to provide a big picture of the system. As is usual for living documents, the curation is key to filtering what matters (for example, what services are talking to what other services in this scenario) out of a huge number of details (all the calls between services and all the events on the messaging bus between them).

Selling Living Documentation to Management

A common question about any new approach is "How do I convince my management to try it?" There are different answers to this question, depending on the context.

The first, and my preferred, answer is that it is up to the team to select the way to meet the expectations of other stakeholders. It is everyone's business to require that knowledge be shared, but does the team really need approval to decide how to perform its work efficiently? Keep in mind that everyone on the team—developers, testers, and business analysts—are also stakeholders of the project. To better deliver to other stakeholders, they have to take care of themselves first. They also need enough autonomy to try practices, and then, as Woody Zuill says, "to amplify the good[2]" and perhaps stop what does not.

---

2. https://www.infoq.com/news/2016/06/mob-programming-zuill

If your company and managers are proud to be "really agile" and to "empower their teams," then they should trust the team, and you should not need any formal approval to try living documentation or any of the related recommended practices, even the most radical ones, like pair programming and mob programming. Of course, this autonomy comes with the full responsibility for the actual results.

That said, it may be the case that putting in place a living glossary or a living diagram for the first time requires somewhere between half a day and two days of work. This might be too long to do the effort without having it in a formal backlog, in which case you need to convince someone.

If there is a documentation budget or if documentation tasks are planned already, you might also want to reuse that time to invest in living documentation instead. Again, this might require approval.

Starting with an Actual Problem

When introducing new approaches, you shouldn't preach. Instead, you should show the benefits, and the best way to do this is on a real problem that is ready to be tackled.

To find out a real knowledge problem, you might ask those around you, "Is there anything you would not feel comfortable working on alone?" or "Is there anything that is not clear to you?" Or you might not ask anything but just pay attention to the questions asked during the day, during the week, or during the iteration. Some of them will hint at candidates for documentation.

One efficient way to know what's important is to carefully take notes on everything you mention or explain to each newcomer during the onboarding period. If you ask new joiners for an astonishment report, it will contain candidates for stuff that should be either fixed or documented.

If you have identified a knowledge-sharing issue, make sure everyone acknowledges that it is a genuine documentation problem worth tackling. Then propose a solution, inspired from this book. You don't have to use the term *living documentation* but can just mention that you know of an approach that has already been done in other companies, in large-ish corporations, and in small early startups, too.

You may also start with something small, done on your own time, that you can show to the managers you want to convince. It could be a report, or a diagram, or a mix of a documentation plus some indicators that managers are particularly interested in. Emphasize how you can save time and improve satisfaction by using to the approach.

Once your project is done, the benefits should be enough to convince people to keep the approach. And if the benefits are not there, please tell me, so that I can improve this book. Still, even in the worst case, you will learn something valuable in the process, and you will probably have one example of traditional documentation that was just a bit more expensive than typical.

A Living Documentation Initiative

If there are a lot of pressing documentation issues, you might want to start with a somewhat ambitious initiative on living documentation. This book can help you push the idea forward and make it a standard package that can be a reference. Show the book to the people you want to convince. Show a video of talks on the same topic (see, for example, https://vimeo.com/131660202). I've done many such videos that have been well received.

Showing the benefits on a "pilot" case within a company is usually the best option to start with. Nobody will pay much attention at first, but with early successes, more people will try to replicate or even formalize the initiative for the benefit of their careers.

As soon as we're talking about an identified initiative, we have to convince upper management that it is worth investing time in the teams, as well as possibly some additional coaching and consulting. One way to sell living documentation is to consider that it is a prerequisite to achieve sustainable continuous delivery, and a bit like testing is a prerequisite, too: Just as you need an automated testing strategy to go fast, you also need a living documentation strategy.

Many of the key reasons to adopt a living documentation approach are already in front of your eyes and show up in your weekly time-tracking and in the current state of your knowledge management.

Overall, my feeling is that documentation is a concern close to managers' hearts. The matter of skills and knowledge transmission between team members is already a common source of anxiety for management; it represents a cost in time and also, more importantly, in defects and mistakes:

- Skills matrix creation and updates
- Turnover rate
- Time spent onboarding newcomers
- Anxiety related to the truck factor (the risk of losing key knowledge if a team is hit by a truck when coming back from lunch)
- The ratio of defects and incidents caused by "I didn't know that"

Lack of documentation is a hidden cost, just like the lack of tests. Every change needs a complete investigation and an assessment, sometimes even a pre-study.

The hidden knowledge has to be mined again each time. Alternatively, changes will be made in a way that is not in line with the previous vision of the system, which makes the application increasingly bloated and makes matters worse over time. This may show up in the following as

- Increased time to deliver a change.
- Negative trends of any code quality metrics, the most telling of which being the mere size of the code base. (If it grows regularly, it is probably a sign that the design is too weak. There is not enough refactoring to start with, and each change is an addition.)

And there are also arguments on the documentation, or lack thereof, in itself:

- Documentation tasks that are not done, or documentation that is visibly not updated frequently enough
- Compliance requirements with respect to documentation
- Time spent writing documentation or updating existing documentation
- Time lost searching the right documentation
- Time lost reading documentation that is incorrect

You might want to perform a review of the quality of the existing documents that pretend to be the documentation, with a focus on various indicators, such as the following:

- The number of different places where documentation can be found (including the source code, the wiki, each shared drive, and team members' machines)
- The time of last update
- The proportion of authors of the last updates who left the team
- The amount of rationale (explaining *why* rather than just *what*) in the documentation
- The number of pages or paragraphs or diagram that can still be trusted
- The among of knowledge that is redundant between the source and another kind of documentation
- A short survey such as "Do you know where I can find knowledge on that?" on a random set of concerns

You can come up with many other ideas to help realize the actual state of documentation. If everything is fine and under control, then the only thing that living documentation might improve is the long-term cost, thanks to team members working together more, automation, and reduction of various types of waste.

If everything is *not* fine and under control, living documentation can make documentation feasible again, at a reasonable cost and with identified value added.

On the value side, it is worth putting the emphasis on the biggest benefits, which are not just the sharing of knowledge but especially the side benefits of improving the software in the process (see Chapter 11, "Beyond Documentation: Living Design").

Contrasting the Current Situation with the Promise of a Better World to Match People's Aspirations

In her book *Resonate*, Nancy Duarte offers suggestions on how to stimulate excitement and enthusiasm through presentations. It starts with knowing why you want to change things. If you've decided to introduce living documentation to your team or company, you could start by answering these questions: "Why do I want to share and promote that?" and "Why am I excited?"

Then you can contrast the current situation with the new practice you'd like to promote. Here are examples of common frustrations that could be contrasted with the benefits of a living documentation approach:

- You don't write documentation, and you feel guilty about that.

- Explaining things to team members, new joiners, and stakeholders outside the team takes a lot of time on an ongoing basis.

- You write documentation, but you'd prefer to write code.

- You're looking for documentation, and when you find some, you cannot trust it because it's out of date.

- When you create diagrams, you're frustrated that it takes so much time.

- Looking for the right document takes so much time for such a small benefit that you often give up and try to do the work without it.

- When you collaborate the agile, way with lots of conversations, you feel uncomfortable because your organization expects to deliver more traceable and archived documents.

- You do a lot of tedious work manually, including deployment, explaining stuff to external people, and paperwork, and you have a feeling it could be avoided.

Of course, it's up to you to customize and decide which items have the most impact in your context and to decide what part of living documentation remedies that frustration most.

The following generalizations tend to be true of developers:

- They don't like writing documentation.
- They like to write code.
- They love code and find that doing more with code is appealing.
- They hate manual, repetitive tasks.
- They love automation.
- They are proud of beautiful code.
- They love plain text and their favorite tools.
- They love logical things (for example, text-first, DRY).
- They love to exhibit mastery and geek culture.
- They want recognition of skills.
- They empathize with real-life messy situations.

On the other hand, the following generalizations tend to be true of managers:

- They love more transparency on the work of their teams.
- They love to see things presented in ways they can feel so that they can understand whether it's getting better or worse.
- They like documentation they can themselves show someone else and be proud of.
- They want documentation to be more turnover-proof.

It's important to see both sides. It's critical for a documentation strategy to exhibit a vision that everybody would genuinely like to happen.

Compliance in Spirit

A living documentation approach can work with even the most demanding compliance requirements by aiming for the spirit instead of aiming for the letter.

If your domain is regulated or if your company requires a lot of documentation for compliance reasons (for example, ITIL), you probably spend a lot of time on documentation tasks. The ideas from living documentation can meet the compliance goals, reducing the burden for the teams and saving time, while improving the quality of the produced documentation and of the product at the same time.

Regulators often focus on requirements tracking and change management as a way to improve quality. For example, the U.S. Food and Drug Administration writes in its "General Principles of Software Validation; Final Guidance for Industry and FDA Staff":

> Seemingly insignificant changes in software code can create unexpected and very significant problems elsewhere in the software program. The software development process should be sufficiently well planned, controlled, and documented to detect and correct unexpected results from software changes.
>
> Given the high demand for software professionals and the highly mobile workforce, the software personnel who make maintenance changes to software may not have been involved in the original software development. Therefore, accurate and thorough documentation is essential.[3]

The same FDA document also describes the importance of testing and of design and code reviews.

It might look at first glance as though agile practices are less documentation oriented and therefore are not well suited for demanding compliance requirements. But quite the opposite is true. When agile practices, which are part of the living documentation spectrum, are applied, what you actually have is a documentation process that is more rigorous than all the traditional documentation-heavy processes.

Specification by example (BDD)—with scenarios with automation, living diagrams, and a living glossary—provides extensive documentation on each build. If you commit five times in an hour, you get your documentation updated five times per hour, and it is always accurate. Paper-heavy processes cannot dream of this level of performance!

Working collectively with colleagues to ensure that at least three or four people know of each change is also an important contribution to various compliance requirements, even though the knowledge is not necessarily written outside the source code.

You see the idea here: A development teams with a good command of agile development practices and principles, including living documentation and other continuous delivery ideas, is already quite close to matching most compliance requirements, even the notoriously heavy ones like ITIL.

Keep in mind that agile practices in general do not necessarily meet the *implementation details* of your company compliance guidelines, which are often full of

---

3. U.S. Food and Drug Administration, "General Principles of Software Validation; Final Guidance for Industry and FDA Staff," http://www.fda.gov/RegulatoryInformation/Guidances/ucm085281.htm

burdensome procedures and paperwork. Still, agile practices often meet or even exceed the higher-level goals aimed for by the compliance bodies, which revolve around risk mitigation and traceability. Agile or not, in the development team or in the compliance office, we all want risk mitigation, some reasonable amount of traceability, quality under control, and improvement in everything. You don't have to follow 2,000 pages of boring ITIL guidelines. You can substitute alternative practices that are more efficient and still be able to check most checkboxes in the checklist of the high-level objectives.

Therefore: Review the compliance documentation requirements, and for each item, identify how it could be satisfied with a living documentation approach, typically by using lightweight declarations, knowledge augmentation, and automation. Mandatory formal documents based on company templates can easily be generated from knowledge managed in a totally different fashion (for example, from the source control system, the code, and the tests). When the compliance expectations are too burdensome, go back to their higher-level goal and identify how this goal could be directly satisfied with your practices instead. Whenever there is a real gap, it's an opportunity to improve your development process. Finally, make sure your lightweight process is reviewed from time to time by the compliance team, so that it can grant your team a permanent preapproval stamp.

You'll be surprised how your living documentation can meet or exceed compliance expectations.

Case Study: Compliance with ITIL

Paul Reeves says in his great blog post "Agile vs. ITIL":

> Often people believe that rapid deployment / continuous deployment / daily builds etc. can't work in an environment that is highly process oriented, where rules and process have to be followed. (Usually they just don't like someone else's rules.)
> Well, the process is there to ensure consistency, responsibility, accountability, communication, traceability, etc. and of course it CAN be designed to be a hinderance. It, alternatively, CAN be designed to allow quick passage of releases. People blaming process or ITIL are just being immature. They may as well blame the weather.[4]

My experience from applying the ideas of continuous delivery has shown indeed that it is possible to map from a lightweight, agile, low-cycle-time process inside the development team to a more traditional, usually slower and paper-intensive process

---

4. Paul Reeves, Reeves's Results blog, http://reevesresults.blogspot.fr/2011/03/agile-vs-itil.html

outside. In contrast to common beliefs, your agile process is probably more disciplined than the other project managed in an ITIL-by-the-book fashion: It's hard to beat a process where automation can produce extensive functional documentation, extensive test results and coverage, security and accessibility checks, design diagrams, and release notes with links to the requested features in a tool and archived emails for the release decision, on each build, several times a day!

When strict procedures are important, using automation and enforced guidelines is the best way to make sure they are respected while reducing the burden of manually applying them. Procedures are great for machines, not for people. The right tools protect a development team and remove the manual chores at the same time. However, and it may seem like a paradox, good tools still draw attention to the quality expectations by making very visible whenever they are not met. With this protective harness, every team member is learning the quality expectations on the job, while having the satisfaction of always doing productive work.

The ITIL Example

Let's focus on an example of managing requests for change under the ITIL conceptual framework by looking at Table 13.1 and Table 13.2.

Note that agile practices promote slicing the work as thinly as possible. It is inconvenient to track every slice in a tracking tool when an iteration contains dozens of slices, each only a few hours long. But this level of granularity does not matter much

Table 13.1 *Request for Change Management*

Change Activity	Example of Agile Forgotten Practice	Example of Documentation Media
Collection of change requests	User stories or bugs and enhancements with description, origin, requestor, date, business priority, and expected benefits	Stickers on the wall and a tracking tool (such as Jira)
Study and impacts	BDD, TDD, tests	All living documentation artifacts
Decisions	Decision, names of decision makers, target version, date	CAB report (email as PDF)
Follow up	Not started, in progress, done), assignee	Tracking tool (such as Jira)

Table 13.2 *Release Management*

Release Activity	Example of Agile Practice	Example of Documentation Media
Content	Release notes with a link to related change(s), dates, downtime, test strategy, impacts (business, IT, infrastructure, security)	Ticketing tool (may be automated as a mix of prewritten documents and generated release notes)
Impacts	Based on the change study plus the feedbacks from the iteration demo	Living documentation, archived as PDF
Release checks	Automated test, including tests on SLA, deployments tests in pre-production environments, smoke tests	CI tool, deploy tool results, tests reports
Approval	Decision, names of the decision makers, actual delivery date, target version, rollout date, decision date, go/no-go conditions	Email saved as PDF
Deployment successful	Deployment and post-deployment tests	Deployment tool and post-deployment test reports
Continuous improvement	Retrospectives notes, with names, action plan, issues	Wiki, email, picture of the whiteboard

for the management of requests for change; as a consequence, you may only track cohesive aggregates of slices in the tool.

The point here is really to realize that your living documentation can meet or exceed the toughest compliance expectations while keeping the extra compliance-specific work to a minimum. This could be an incentive in itself to introduce living documentation if you're in a compliance-intensive environment.

Summary

Introducing living documentation is best done undercover first, to build the confidence to expand to bigger and more visible initiatives. As a start, you can decide to migrate painful traditional documentation into its more living equivalent, using some of the patterns discussed in this book.

If you need budget or time to expand your efforts, remember that managers are often concerned about retaining knowledge. And when facing the objection that your situation is special because you're regulated or you have to follow some strict compliance framework, remember that you can meet and even exceed requirements by sticking to the spirit instead of the letter.

Chapter 14

Documenting Legacy Applications

*The universe is made of information, but it doesn't have meaning - meaning is
our creation. Searches for meaning are searches in a mirror.*

—@KevlinHenney

This quote illustrates the case with legacy systems: They are full of knowledge, but it
is usually encrypted, and we have lost the keys. Without tests, we have no clear definition of the expected behavior of a legacy system. Without consistent structure, we
have to guess how it was designed and for what reasons and how it is supposed to be
evolved. Without careful naming, we have to guess and infer the meaning of variables, methods, and classes, as well as what code is responsible for what.

In short, we call systems "legacy" when their knowledge is not readily accessible.
They exemplify what we could call "documentation bankruptcy."

Documentation Bankruptcy

Legacy applications are quite valuable, and they cannot be simply unplugged. Most
attempts to completely rewrite large legacy systems eventually fail. Legacy systems
are a problem of rich organizations, which lived and became profitable long enough
to grow a legacy.

Still, legacy applications raise issues when they have to evolve due to changing
context because changing them is usually expensive. The prohibitive cost of change
is related to many issues, including duplication and lack of automated testing, and
also to the lost knowledge. Any change requires a long and painful reverse engineering of the knowledge from the code base, including a lot of guesswork, before one
line of code is eventually touched at the end.

All is not lost, though. In the following pages, you'll see a few living documentation techniques that particularly apply when working in or from legacy systems.

Legacy Application as Fossilized Knowledge

You've seen before that anything that can answer a question can be considered documentation. If you can answer questions by using an application, then the application is part of the documentation. This is of great relevance in the case of a legacy system with lost specifications. You have to use it to know how it behaves.

In the context of rewriting part of a legacy system, considering the legacy system as a source of knowledge can be handy since the new system will probably inherit a significant part of the behaviors of its predecessor. For each feature that will make it into the new system, the specifications can draw on the former system. In practice, while doing the specifications workshops, you can check how the legacy application behaved to get inspiration for the new one.

The "Rewriting with the Same Specs" Fallacy

One common failure mode of rewriting legacy systems is to rewrite them with exactly the same specifications. It makes little sense to rewrite a system without changing anything; doing so is just a lot of risk and a lot of waste. Changing only the technology stack hardly does any good idea either, unless your hardware is no longer available commercially and there is no emulator.

Rewriting a piece of software is an expensive endeavor, even from a purely technical perspective, and the best way to improve the return is by taking the opportunity to reconsider the specifications at the same time. Many features are no longer useful. Many features should be adapted to new usages and contexts. The UI and its UX have to change drastically, and the changes will have impacts on the underlying services. You'll also want the new application to be cheaper to deliver more frequently, so you'll want automated testing, too, which comes cheaper when you start from clear specifications as concrete examples, as advised by BDD.

I strongly suggest not rewriting with the same specs. Rewrite a limited portion of the system and consider it as a project from scratch, with the legacy system, the working application, and its source code as a bonus to draw inspiration from.

Therefore: In the context a rewriting a part of a legacy system, consider the legacy system as documentation to complement the discussions on the

specifications, not as the given specifications. Make sure a business person such as a domain expert, business analyst, or product owner works closely with the team. Don't fall for the fallacy that the legacy system is in itself a sufficient description of the new system to be rebuilt. Take the opportunity of the rewriting to challenge every aspect from the legacy system: the functional scope, the business behaviors, the way it is structured into modules, and so on. Regain control of the knowledge from the start, with clear specifications expressed as concrete scenarios and a clear design.

The ideal configuration is a whole team, with all skills and roles inside the team, using the idea of the three amigos: business perspective, development perspective, and quality perspective.

Having access to both a working legacy application and its source code is a nice bonus compared to projects starting purely from scratch. It's like having another expert on the team, even if it is an old, sometimes irrelevant, expert. After all, the legacy system is the result of a patchwork of the decisions of many different people over a long period of time. It's a fossil.

A perfect example of when a legacy system can be instrumented is when it can provide the answer to the question "How often is this feature used?"

Archeology

> Software source code is one of the most densely packed forms of communication we have. But, it is still a form of human communication. Refactoring gives us a very powerful tool for improving our understanding of what someone else has written.
> —*Chet Hendrickson, Software Archeology: Understanding Large Systems*

When you ask questions of a legacy code base, you need a piece of paper and a pen close to your keyboard at all times to take notes and draw. You need to create an on-demand map of the terrain for the task at hand. While exploring the code and playing with it at runtime or with the debugger, you need to write down the inputs, outputs, and all the affects you discover. You need to take note of what's read or written because the side effects are ultimately what matter. Knowing this information is also essential for mocking up or estimating the impacts of a change. You should sketch how each responsibility depends on its neighbors, a technique Michael Feathers calls an *effect map* in his book *Working Effectively with Legacy Code*.[1]

It's important to keep the process low tech so that it does not distract from the task at hand. This documentation work needs to be dedicated to a specific task, and there is therefore no need to make it clean and formal right now. However, when you're done with the task, you may review the notes and sketches and select the one

---

1. Feathers, Michael. *Working Effectively with Legacy Code*. Boston: Pearson Education, Inc., 2004.

or two key bits of information that are general enough that they would help for many tasks. They can be promoted into a clean diagram, an additional section, or an addition within an existing document. You grow your documentation by a sedimentation mechanism (see Chapter 10, "Avoiding Traditional Documentation").

Of course, you might have questions that the code does not answer. Perhaps the code is obscure or surprising. In such a case, you need help, ideally from colleagues nearby, and human communication comes back into the picture. The legacy system is not just code; there are documents of all ages, slides, old blog posts, and pages on the wiki, and of course they are all wrong to some extent now.

A legacy environment also includes people who were there at the beginning. The old developers may have moved to other positions now, but they might be able to answer questions, especially about the context that led to the decisions years ago.

Bubble Context

Even in a legacy system, you want to work as much as possible in the ideal land where everything is nice and clean. If you have some number of features to build, then you might decide to build the new features in their own new clean bubble context. In practice, it can be a new specific module, namespace, or project, which means it is then easy to document by using annotations, naming conventions, and enforced guidelines. A bubble context brings the comfort and the efficiency of writing software from scratch in a brand-new project but integrated within a bigger legacy surrounding (see Figure 14.1).

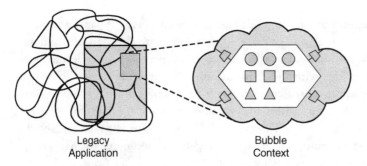

Legacy   Bubble
Application   Context

Figure 14.1 *A clean bubble context integrated within a legacy mess*

As a bubble context is a project from scratch inside a legacy project, it is also a perfect place to practice TDD, BDD, and DDD on a limited functional area to deliver a bulk of related business value.

Therefore: If you need to make a lot of changes on a legacy system, consider creating a bubble context. A bubble context defines boundaries within the rest of the system. Within these boundaries, you can rewrite in a different way, such as driven by tests. In the bubble context, you can invest in knowledge by following a living documentation approach. Conversely, if you really need full documentation of a part of a legacy application, consider rewriting that part as a bubble context, using the state-of-the-art practices for the tests, the code, and the documentation.

It is a good idea to start with high expectations for the code inside the bubble context. Its architecture and guidelines should be enforced using automated tools, as a set of enforced guidelines. For example, you might want to forbid any new commit from having direct references (Java `import` or C# `using`) on a deprecated component. You might require and enforce test coverage higher than 90%, no major violation, a maximum code complexity of 2, and a maximum of five parameters by method.

Going further in the coding style, if you use the bubble context approach, you can declare demanding requirements for the full bubble as a whole, such as by using package-level annotations, as shown here:

```
1  @BubbleContext(ProjectName = "Invest3.0")
2  @Immutable
3  @Null-Free
4  @Side-Effect-Free
5  package acme.bigsystem.investmentallocation
6
7  package acme.bigsystem.investmentallocation.domain
8  package acme.bigsystem.investmentallocation.infra
```

The first annotation here just declares that this module (package in Java or namespace in C#) is the root of a bubble context corresponding to a project named Invest3.0. The other annotations document that the expected coding style in this module favors immutability and avoids nulls and side effects. These coding styles can then be enforced by pair-programming or code review.

The bubble context was introduced by Eric Evans in 2013.[2] A bubble context is a perfect technique for rewriting part of a legacy system, as in the strangler application

---

2. Eric Evans, *Getting Started with DDD when Surrounded by Legacy Systems*, 2013, http://domain language.com/wp-content/uploads/2016/04/GettingStartedWithDDDWhenSurroundedByLegacy SystemsV1.pdf

pattern by Martin Fowler.[3] The idea is to rebuild a consistent functional area that will progressively take over the old system.

Superimposed Structure

Especially when creating a bubble context integrated within a bigger legacy application, it is hard to define the boundaries between the old and new systems. It is even difficult to just discuss it very clearly because it is hard to talk about a legacy system. You would expect to see a simple and clear structure, but what you actually discover is a big unstructured mess (see Figure 14.2).

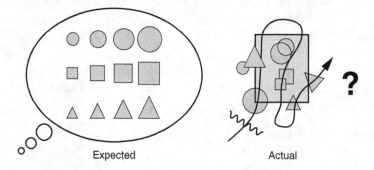

Figure 14.2 *Mental expectations versus actual situation*

Even when there is a structure, it is often arbitrary and can mislead more than it helps (see Figure 14.3).

```
⌐ com.acme

  + ⌐ com.acme.dao

  + ⌐ com.acme.dto

  + ⌐ com.acme.service

  + ⌐ com.acme.controller

  ...
```

Figure 14.3 *Typical project structure*

---

3. https://www.martinfowler.com/bliki/StranglerApplication.html

With legacy code, you usually start with lots of effort to make it testable. Tests enable you to make changes but are not enough. To make changes, you also need to reconstruct a mental model of the legacy application in your head. This can be local within a function, or it can be as big as the full business behavior plus the complete technical architecture.

You need to read code, interview older developers, and fix bugs to better understand the behavior. At the same time, you need to use your brain to make sense of what you see. The result is a structure in your head that you *project* over the existing application. Since the existing application does not show this structure, it is up to you to superimpose a new clear structure onto the existing application.

Therefore: In the context of creating a bubble context and adding a feature or fixing a difficult bug in a legacy system, create your own mental model of the legacy system. This model does not have to be visible at all when reading the legacy code. Instead, this new structure of the old system is a projected vision, an invention. Document this vision using any form of documentation, so that it becomes part of your language for future discussions and decisions.

This new structure is a hallucination, a vision, that is not directly extracted from the system as it is currently built. You might see it as a description of the system *as it should have been built* as opposed to *how it is built*, in retrospect, now that everyone knows better.

You can show the new model as a superimposed structure on top of the legacy system, as a plain sketch that you show to everyone involved. It is desirable to show how the new structure relates to the current state, but it can be too hard to achieve as soon as you want some details, given that the current system may have a totally different structure. You can invest time in making it a proper slide deck to present to every stakeholder during a roadshow. You might instead decide to make it visible within the code itself to make it more obvious and to pave the way for further transformations.

The following are some examples of mental models superimposed on top of legacy systems:

- **Business pipeline:** This perspective of the business is similar to the standard sales funnel of salespeople. It focuses on the system as a pipeline of stages in the order in which they happen in a typical user journey: A visitor navigates the catalog (catalog stage), adds items to the shopping cart (shopping cart stage), reviews the order (order preparation stage), pays (payment stage), receives a confirmation and the product, and gets after-sale service if things go wrong. This model assumes that the volume decreases by a large factor at each stage, which is a nice insight for designing each stage technically and from an operational point of view.

- **Main business assets, as in asset capture (Martin Fowler):** This perspective focuses on the two or three main assets of the business domain, such as the customer and the product in the case of an e-commerce system. Each asset can be seen as a dimension that can itself be split into segments, such as customer segments and product segments.

- **Domains and subdomains, or bounded contexts (Eric Evans):** This perspective requires some maturity in terms of both DDD and the overall business domain, but it also has the most benefits.

- **Levels of responsibility:** There are operational, tactical, and strategic levels, from a business perspective. Eric Evans mentions this in his book *Domain-Driven Design*.

- **A mix of these views:** For example, you might consider three dimensions—customer, product, and processing—each segmented into stages, customer segments, and product segments. You can also mix a business pipeline from left to right and the operational, tactical, and strategic levels from the bottom up.

Whatever the superimposed structure, once you have it, it becomes simpler to talk about the system. You might, for example, propose to "rewrite everything about the payment stage, starting with products that can be downloaded as a first phase." Or you might decide to "rewrite the catalog part only for B2B customers." Communication becomes more efficient when you have a superimposed structure.

However, it is up to every member of the team to interpret these sentences the way they see them. It is therefore useful to make the superimposed structure more visible.

Highlighted Structure

The superimposed structure can be linked to the existing code. If you're lucky, the mapping between the superimposed structure and the existing structure of the code is just a large number of messy one-to-one relationships. If you're not lucky, this can just be an impossible task.

You can add the intrinsic information of the superimposed structure on each element. For example, one DTO shown in Figure 14.4 is part of the billing domain, another is part of the catalog domain, and so on.

To make the new structure visible, you can use annotation on classes, interfaces, methods, and even modules or project-level files. Some IDEs also offer ways to tag files in order to group them, but it depends on the IDE, and the tags are not usually stored within the files themselves. In the following example, you would tag the classes in each module with annotations to denote the subdomain they are about:

```
1   module DTO
2     OrderDTO @ShoppingCart
3     BAddressDTO @Billing
4     ProductDTO @Catalog
5     ShippingCostDTO @Billing
```

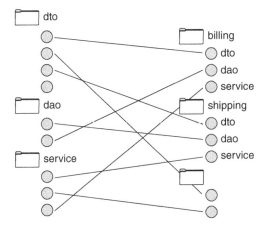

Figure 14.4 *Example of mapping between a technical structure and a business-driven structure*

This will help prepare for the next step: Move the classes that deal with billing into the same billing module. But even before you do that, your code now has an explicit structure showing the business domain if you search by the @Billing annotation:

```
1   module Billing
2     BillingAddressDTO //renamed to fix the abbreviation
3     ShippingCostDTO
4     ShippingCostConfiguration
5     ShippingCost @Service
```

The end purpose of a superimposed structure should be to become the primary structure of the system so that it is no longer superimposed. Unfortunately, in many cases, this never happens because the effort will not reach the "end state." However, this approach is still valuable because it can help deliver precious business value in the meantime. Even if the legacy code is badly structured, as long as you reason about it using a better structure, you are getting the benefits of better decisions.

External Annotations

Sometimes we don't want to touch a fragile system just to add some knowledge to it. It is sometimes hard to touch and commit in large code bases just to add extra annotations. You don't want to risk introducing random regressions. You don't want to touch commit history. It may be so hard to build that you don't want to build it unless absolutely necessary. Or your boss may not allow you to change the code at all "just for documentation."

In such a situation, it is still possible to apply most techniques of living documentation, except that the internal means of documentation (for example, annotations, naming conventions) have to be replaced with an external document. For example, you might need a text file that maps package names to tags:

```
1   acme.phenix.core = DomainModel FleetManagement
2   acme.phenix.allocation = DomainModel Dispatching
3   acme.phenix.spring = Infrastructure Dispatching
4   ...
```

With such a document, it is possible to build tools that parse the source code and exploit these external annotations just as they would exploit the regular internal ones (see Figure 14.5).

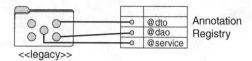

Figure 14.5 *Using a registry so that the code is not touched*

The issue with this approach is that it is an external kind of documentation, and hence it is fragile to changes in the legacy system. If you ever rename a package in the legacy system, for example, you have to update the related external annotations.

Biodegradable Transformation

Documentation of a temporary process should disappear with it when it is done. Many legacy ambitions involve transformations from one state to another. Such a transformation might take years and may never really reach the end state. However, you need to explain this transformation to all teams, and you should show it as part of your living documentation.

Example: Strangler Application

Say that you're building a strangler application that is expected to replace an older application over time. This strangler application will probably live in its own bubble context. You could just annotate this bubble context as being a strangler application. However, that it is playing the role of a strangler is a temporary fact and is not necessarily intrinsic to the new application; when it has successfully strangled the old one, it will just become the nominal application, and its annotation will be meaningless. The strangler application strategy is therefore a *biodegradable transformation*.

In the meantime, every developer needs to know to use the new strangler application instead of the one being strangled. Therefore you'd need to add a `StrangledBy("new bubble context application")` annotation to the strangled application to explain that a strangling is pending (see Figure 14.6). When it can be safely deleted, the annotation will go away with it.

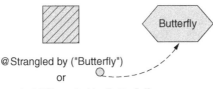

Figure 14.6 *An application annotated as being strangled by another*

Of course, you could still tag the new application `StranglerApplication`, but you will have to clean up this tag eventually, when you are done. And if the strangling never completes, this will by a hint pointing to the unfinished initiative.

Example: Bankruptcy

Some legacy applications are so fragile that they break any time you try to change them, and it takes weeks of work to stabilize them again. When you recognize this, you might decide to declare such applications officially "bankrupt," which means nobody should ever change them.

In large legacy systems with new applications strangling older ones, you don't want to perform maintenance on two applications at the same time, so you can mark the older one as "frozen" or "bankrupt," too. You can mark the application as bankrupt by using a number of means:

- Use annotation on the package or an attribute in the `AssemblyConfig` file
- Use a BANKRUPTCY.txt file to explain what you need to know and to do (or avoid doing)

- Remove the commit privilege from everyone, and if anyone tries to commit and asks why it is not possible, take the opportunity to explain that it is bankrupt

- As a weaker alternative, monitor the commits and raise an alert when changes are met in a bankrupt application

Agree on Maxims

Big changes to legacy systems are made by a number of people who share common objectives; you can use maxims to share the vision, as advised in the book *Object-Oriented Reengineering Patterns*.[4]

When you have a legacy transformation strategy, you need to make sure everyone knows about it. You may have created a superimposed structure. You may have annotated your bubble context in the code of the project. However, of all the things you need to share with everyone, there are a few key decisions you really want everyone to keep in mind at all times. Maxims are a powerful answer for such situations, and they have been around for ages.

Therefore: Invent maxims to spread the most critical pieces of knowledge to everyone. Repeat these maxims often to advertise them. Make them rhyme to boost their effect.

When your project is to rewrite only a portion of a large legacy system, and you don't want to rewrite more than what's absolutely useful now (that is, the billing engine) and nothing else, you can use a maxim like this: "One work site at a time (the billing engine)." This has been one of my favorite maxims in a big legacy project. It was meant to remind everyone not to get distracted when working on the project; they needed to focus on the main worksite only.

"When in Rome, do as the Romans do." This was the counterpart to the single-work-site maxim. In other words, when you happen to walk outside the main work site, don't innovate or change much; just do the minimum in the local style, even if you don't like it. Be conservative when working in the legacy code that will not be rewritten.

---

4. Demeyer, Serge, Stéphane Ducasse, and Oscar Nierstrasz, *Object-Oriented Reengineering Patterns*. San Francisco: Morgan Kaufmann Publishers, 2003.

Another legacy maxim that was proposed by Gilles Philippart is an extremely powerful one: "Don't feed the monster! (Don't improve the legacy Big Ball of Mud; it would only make it live longer)."

I've found maxims to be a valuable form of documentation. The point is to repeat them often, whenever it makes sense to do so, ideally at least once a day. The maxim format is made to stick, and that is why you might want to give it a try. Maxims can also help share the conclusions of your team retrospectives, as agreed upon by the team.

Enforced Legacy Rules

Legacy transformations can last longer than the people doing them; automate the enforcement of the big decisions to protect them.

Say that in a legacy application, you've decided that some method should not be called anymore, except from one specific place. For example, you might have decided to turn a read-write legacy application into a *legacy read model*, which should not accept any request to update it except from the listener responsible for syncing this read model from the other authoritative model. The design decision can be stated in a decision log:

> This model is a read model. It is therefore read-only. Don't call this Save method, unless you are the listener that syncs this read model from the events sent from the authoritative write model.

You might include with it the following rationale:

> The legacy system has proven to be unmaintainable, so we don't want to develop in it anymore. This is why we're building another system as a replacement. But because so many external systems are integrated with it, we can simply remove it in one go. This is why we have decided to keep this old system just as a legacy read model for integration purposes.

You could also document this directly in the code:

- Mark the design decision with the custom annotation `@LegacyReadModel` and include the message and the rationale
- Mark the method as `@Deprecated`

However, being in a legacy system also means there are probably legacy teams around, some of them remote or in other departments, and you can never be sure they will read your documentation or emails or that they will pay attention when you mention the design decision in the daily standup. And you know that if some developers don't respect the design decision, bad things will happen. You'll get bugs and pay the cost of extra accidental complexity due to the inconsistent data management strategies.

My colleague Igor Lovich came up with a simple way to document such a decision as an enforced guideline. Say that you express a design decision as follows:

> Never call this deprecated method unless you're in the white-list of the one or two classes responsible for the sync.

This is a custom design rule that can then be enforced at runtime with some additional code:

- Capture the stack trace in the method to find out who's calling it and ensure that it's the allowed piece of code (for example, throw an exception within a `try-catch` and extract its stack trace in Java).

- Check that at least one caller in the stack trace belongs to the white-list of allowed callers' methods.

- Make the check into a Java `assert`, if you want to fail-fast in some environments but not all of them.

- Log when the check fails in a way that will trigger specific follow-up. (If it gets fired, then it's actually a defect.)

In addition, you could turn the maxim "Don't feed the monster! (Don't improve the legacy)" into an enforced legacy rule, too, by forbidding commits into a particular area of the code base. Or you might raise a warning when a commit is done there. Such enforcement is simple and more effective than long explanations that people tend to miss or ignore.

In practice, legacy systems make everything more complicated than expected. It takes courage and some creativity to come up with relatively "not too bad" solutions!

Summary

Legacy systems raise extensive challenges with respect to living documentation. They come with a pessimistic perspective of the code and its knowledge, which is mostly there but is obfuscated as a fossilized knowledge, so you need ad hoc techniques to make it accessible again, like superimposed structure and highlighted structure. When the code is too fragile or can't reasonably be changed, you must resort to external annotations.

Because a focus on legacy is often in the context of a legacy migration, it implies major changes, adding and removing entire sections—all these changes performed by many people over large time spans: this calls for biodegradable documentation means that go away with the deleted code. Then beyond the knowledge materialized in the artifact, you also need a way for people to act with some consistency, for example through shared maxims. And obviously, you also need a lot of courage!

Chapter 15

Extra: Conspicuous Documentation

The most common myth of communication is that it happened.

—@ixhd from Twitter

Just because you have a documentation mechanism in place does not guarantee that people will notice it, remember the knowledge, or contribute to it. There are many techniques to get the message through with fewer words, more quickly, more accurately, without wasting people's time, and in a fun way. Using such techniques can boost the efficiency of your living documentation by helping to infuse the living documentation into your culture. This extra chapter enumerates some of these techniques.

Focusing on Differences

When describing a specific thing, such as a dog, we focus on its differences from the generic thing, such as a mammal. If the generic thing is well known or well described before the specific thing is mentioned, we can describe the specific thing with just a few points—one for each significant difference.

The important concept here is *salience*, defined as "a striking point or feature."[1] We primarily want to describe the salient points out of the mass of information.

---

1. By Permission. From Merriam-Webster.com © 2019 by Merriam-Webster, Inc. https://www.merriam-webster.com/dictionary/salience.

How Is Your Lemon?

During a training session I've attended during Øredev 2013, Joe Rainsberger told a story about lemons while discussing BDD. I don't remember the exact story, but I do remember the key insight, so here's my own totally distorted account of the story:

> The trainer asked everyone to describe what a lemon's like. The group described the typical lemon shape, yellow color, acid taste, and grained texture of a lemon. The trainer then gave each attendee a real lemon and asked them to carefully study their lemons for a few minutes.
>
> The trainer also analyzed his own lemon. One end of the lemon was bent in a weird way. There was a variation of color somewhere in the middle. The lemon was kind of small compared to the average lemon.
>
> He then asked everyone to put their lemons back together into the basket, and then asked each person to recognize his or her lemon among all the other lemons. This was surprisingly easy! Each attendee realized that he or she had learned a particular lemon very intimately. "It's my lemon!" they all said! They even felt a bit of attachment to their individual lemons.

By looking carefully at a specific lemon *in contrast to the generic concept* of a lemon that everybody knows, you can describe it very effectively. Your description is at the same time precise with lots of details and efficient because you don't have to describe the generic thing.

I've seen colleagues use this technique to describe concepts from a business domain. For example, during a presentation to new joiners on financial asset classes, the trainer was mentioning only the five to seven bullet points that were distinctive to a particular asset class, such as commodities, in contrast to a generic well-known asset class such as equities.

In the electricity market, a specificity is that the prices are very seasonal during the day and during the year, in contrast to company stocks. In the oil market, geography matters, as oil is not shipped just anywhere.

Tell Only What's Unknown

There is no point in explaining something to people who already know it. The key is to identify what the audience knows. During conversations, it is possible to assert what the people you're talking to already know or don't know, based on their questions, by watching their body language, and by asking them directly. In written form, this is more difficult, but it is not impossible. There are several ways to do it.

Segmenting by Known Audience

For each audience, you can get feedback on the most frequently asked questions, and if there's a support team, you can talk to them to better learn what's well known and what needs to be explained more. Then you can focus on what's unknown for each audience.

Flexible Content

You should organize written content so that it can be skimmed, skipped, and read partially. You should also clearly mark optional sections and make titles informative enough so that readers can decide whether a section is what they are after.

For example, Martin Fowler suggests writing duplex books.[2] The idea is to split the content into two big parts, where the first part is a narrative designed to be read cover to cover, and the second part is reference material that is not meant to be read cover to cover. You read the first part to get an overall understanding of the topic, and you keep the rest for when you actually to need it.

Low-Fidelity Content

> Use low fidelity representation for output as long as you want people feel invited to add their input.
>
> —*@kearnsey on Twitter*

Too often a diagram that was meant for brainstorming, exploring, or proposing ideas is misunderstood as a piece of specification. This results in premature feedback on details such as "I'd prefer another color," even though the whole thing will change a lot in the next hours or days. This situation is especially true for everything done on a computer, since it is quick and easy to create nice-looking documents, pictures, and diagrams using the proper piece of software.

Therefore: When the knowledge is still being shaped, make it clear in the documents by using low-fidelity content such as wireframes and sketchy rendering.

Visual Facilitation

"I'm talking about *that*" when pointing a finger at a box on a diagram on the whiteboard or on a screen (see Figure 15.1) is much more concise and precise than "I'm talking about this thing that takes care of filtering the duplicate entries upstream of

---

2. Martin Fowler, ThoughtWorks blog, http://www.martinfowler.com/bliki/DuplexBook.html

the real-time secondary calculation engine." As Rinat Abdulin said on Twitter during a conversation we had about living diagrams, "Stuff 'you can point on to' during discussions helps communicate faster and with better accuracy." Having conversations supported by visual media is a powerful technique.

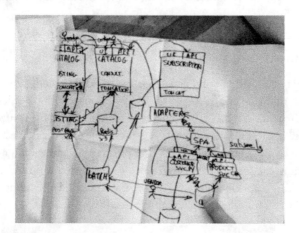

Figure 15.1 *Communication is improved when you can point your finger at what you're talking about on a shared visual support*

During meetings or an open-space session, the visual notes on the flipchart not only report on what has been said: they also *influence* further discussions just by being in front of everyone's eyes. This influence is even stronger if the scribe who has the marker on the whiteboard is skilled in visual facilitation. He or she rearranges the way the information is organized, sorting concepts, using a meaningful layout, noting links, making side remarks, and drawing little decorations about the connotations involved in the discussions.

Therefore: Don't discount the importance of visual supports during discussions. Invest in some visual facilitation skills and learn how visual supports can help shape the dynamics of the work.

Visual notes are redundant with has been said and therefore help if you did not catch a word or an idea immediately. They help as a way to catch up and help everyone remain involved in the session. When done well, visual facilitation is also an opportunity to make people smile, thanks to some visual humor.

Search-Friendly Documentation

Making information available is not enough. You have to know where to find what you need when you need it, and it needs to be easily searchable.

Being easily searchable is first of all a matter of using distinctive words.

Distinctive Words

"Go" as a name of a programming language, from a company like Google that is into search, is not search friendly. A more search-friendly name is golang.

The piece of knowledge should mention clearly the user needs it addresses, since this is the question that will be searched for. To help with this, keywords should be added, including words that don't really occur in the actual content but that are likely to be used when someone is searching for it. It is helpful to use words from actual users, found from the analytics of failed searches, for example.

Remember to mention synonyms, antonyms, mistranslations, and common confusions for improved discoverability by search.

All this is usually considered only for written text in a traditional document, but it applies just as well in the code, which is considered text, too. And you may even use annotations to add keywords.

Concrete Examples, Together, Now

Make sure to have every attendee agree on concrete examples when discussing specifications.

This probably sounds familiar:

Now that we're in agreement on this change, we can stop this meeting. You will work on test cases and the detailed design and screen mockup, and we'll discuss them next week. In the meantime, feel free to ask if you have any questions.

The lost opportunity here is that everyone involved will most likely waste time after the meeting. The collective agreement during the meeting is often an illusion. As the saying goes: "The devil is in the details." It's only when starting to create the mockup for the new screen that the issues will really start to jump out. It's only when trying to code the *abstract* requirement that the misinterpretation will happen, and it may only be detected days or weeks later.

A better approach is to reply on this type of unorthodox proposition:

Why about creating a concrete example together, right now, during this meeting?

I often use a similar strategy:

I believe we're all in agreement on what needs to be done. But to be 100% sure, just in case, we should take a few minutes to draft a concrete example all together right now.

It might sound like a waste of time to do this sort of thing right away. "We don't have time for the low-level details here" is an objection I sometimes hear. And it's true that it can be painful to observe your colleague slowly working the collage of buttons and panels on a screenshot in Microsoft PowerPoint on the big video screen. However, at the same time, you're saving much more time in decision making, because everybody is there to confirm, adjust, or raise an alarm—instantly.

Therefore: Whenever there's a workshop on specifications, make sure to have every attendee agree on concrete examples during the meetings—right away during sessions. Resist the temptation to save time by doing it offline. Acknowledge that decision making is often the main bottleneck, not drafting concrete examples. Some of the resulting examples will be important parts of your documentation.

It does not matter if the examples are scenarios expressed in text, data tables, flipchart sketches, visual screen mockups in a tool projected on a big screen, or something else. What matters is that everyone involved understands the examples so that they can immediately notice whether something is wrong in them. For this purpose, it is essential that examples be concrete. Don't settle on abstract agreement. Everybody may agree that "the discount is 50%" but how do you handle it when the price is $1.55? How do you take care of the rounding? You need concrete examples to notice issues such as this.

In Practice

You are likely to hear many common objections the first time you suggest creating concrete examples during the meeting. *Concrete* seems verbose and slow, whereas *abstract* seems concise and fast. This is true in the very short term, but in the longer term, in the context of specifications, it's rather the opposite: Concrete is faster.

In fact, you may be painfully aware of this and might suggest doing the examples offline: "I don't want to waste your time, so tell me how to do it, and I'll do it later on my own." Instead, however, consider using the following sentence: "Sorry you'll have to wait for three minutes while I fire the tool, but then we know for sure we're in agreement on the solution. This way we can avoid a ping-pong of emails and further meetings in the coming days and weeks."

When it comes to specifications, where communication is particularly fallible, keep in mind the following:

- **DON'T:** "We can stop there to save time. I'll go on alone, and then we'll have another meeting to discuss the results."
- **DO:** "Let's go as far and as quickly as we can together so that we know quickly what the troubles are and where we may disagree."

Fast Media and Prior Preparation

It helps to choose fast media, such as the following, to create consensus on concrete examples:

- Flipchart or whiteboard and markers, written on carefully so that everybody can read
- Big pages of paper on the table, with pens
- People talking and a spokesperson taking verbatim notes, regularly restating the notes to other attendees
- A simple text editor shown on a big screen
- A screen mockup tool that you know well so that you're quick with it
- Microsoft PowerPoint to do a collage of preselected screenshots if you're comfortable with the solution

It helps to do some prior preparation and have some ready-made materials. I once had a colleague bring a file folder full of screenshots from all the important screens and printed diagrams of the main workflows of the application to every meeting to improve communication during discussions. I've used a similar approach but electronically, keeping a default PowerPoint full of screenshots and other stuff, just in case it is needed during specification workshops to answer questions or to be reused as part of a screen collage.

The same ideas can be generalized to other aspects of specifications, such as quality attributes. When discussing performance, latency, and fault tolerance requirements, it would be a good idea to not only define the expectations but to go the extra mile and collectively agree on the acceptance criteria. The acceptance criteria should then become a test that will not only document but also ensure that the quality attributes are actually met.

Together, Now

The power of "together, now" suggests going the extra mile after an agreement is made until all attendees together consider and agree to a solution proven by concrete examples (for example, UI mockup, interaction workflow, impact map, scenarios of expected business behavior as text or sketches with accurate numbers on it).

Productive specification meetings that really produce concrete examples are valuable. They rely on face-to-face conversations for effective communication, and they produce quality documentation as an outcome.

The canonical example is, of course, specification workshops where the three amigos define the key scenarios. There are many similar examples of interactive collaborative creation of concrete results in the literature on agile software development:

- **Mob programming:** All the brilliant minds together, on the same task, on the same machine
- **CRC Cards:** A technique for instant, interactive, and collaborative modeling with CRC cards on a table (from Ward Cunningham and Kent Beck)
- **Modeling with stickers on the wall:** Examples are model storming (from Scott Ambler)[3] and event storming (from Alberto Brandolini)[4]
- **Code analysis:** Modeling directly in code in a programming language during a meeting with the domain expert (from Greg Young)

Stack Overflow Documentation

Several times I have heard colleagues or even candidates say that Stack Overflow (SO) is by far the best place to go for documentation, and my experience tends to corroborate this. Official documentation pages are often boring and seldom task oriented. The funny thing is that people answering on SO have often had to use the official documentation pages to build their own knowledge, together with trial and errors or even having to read the source code sometimes.

People answer questions very quickly on SO. It's another form of *living* documentation: Contribute a question, and people all over the world quickly contribute answers, making the documentation a really living thing.

Therefore: When the topic is popular enough, let SO provide good task-oriented documentation on top of the reference documentation you provided. Let your teams post questions on SO and let them answer other people's questions as well.

---

3. http://www.drdobbs.com/the-best-kept-secret/184415204
4. https://www.eventstorming.com/

Posting on SO requires your project to be published online, usually with its source code. It especially requires the project to be successful, with enough demand to attract contributors.

Or you can keep your project internal and closed source and use equivalent on-premises Stack Overflow clones.[5] However, a domestic Stack Overflow clone will probably not have the scale to work as efficiently as the true worldwide site.

One downside with Stack Overflow is that a product that is awful will be seen as awful. However, you can't prevent that from happening on the web unless you make the product better, of course. You may also dedicate many employees to answer questions in a positive way to improve the user experience.

Affordable and Attractive

> We can make information available, but we cannot make people care for it. Journalism as a solution?
>
> —*Romeu Moura*

To paraphrase my Arolla colleague Romeu Moura, documentation should be attractive for the same reason flowers are attractive: for self-preservation.

Specs Digest

I once saw a project where the team decided to curate all the accumulation of design and specifications documents into a much shorter (about 10 pages long) "specs digest" document. This was mostly done by copying and pasting the best parts out of various existing documents, and it was updated, fixed, and supplemented with the obviously missing bits in the process. This digest was a highly valued document for the team.

A specs digest is strongly organized into sections, each typically a half page long, with clear titles recapped in a table of contents. The structure allows for skipping any section safely to jump directly to the part of interest.

The content mostly focuses on everything that is not obvious: business calculations (dates, eligibility, financial and risk calculations), principles, and rules. But it may also describe key semi-technical aspects such as the versioning scheme between multiple related concepts.

Note that if you already have living documentation based on scenarios in a tool such as Cucumber, you should move all this content into the feature files themselves or into sidecar "preamble" Markdown files in the same folders.

---

5. StackExchange, http://meta.stackexchange.com/questions/2267/stack-exchange-clones

Easter Eggs and Fun Anecdotes

Having fun is the best way to learn. You can make any kind of documentation more engaging by hiding anecdotes from the project, its sponsors, and team members in the document as a way to encourage reading. Add simple illustrations.

As Peter Hilton mentions in his talk on documentation avoidance:

> Use humor. There's no rule that says that jokes aren't allowed. Insufficiently serious documentation is probably not your biggest problem. Staying awake might be.[6]

Promoting News

Adding knowledge somewhere is not enough for its audience to notice and use it. Provide ways to promote the documentation, especially when it changes:

- A "Recent Changes" page should provide the bare minimum.

- A changes feed (using Swagger, for example) can be pushed to Slack.

- Slackbot custom replies can remind you where a document is in response to keywords.

- Release notes might not be necessary. Determine whether you really read them.

- When you're really serious about knowledge sharing, hire a real professional journalist to work on-site.

Unorthodox Media

The corporate world tends to be unoriginal. When it comes to documentation, the traditional media remain mighty email, Microsoft Office with the boring mandatory templates, SharePoint, and all the various enterprise tools that are notorious for their outstanding user experience. But life does not have to be so dull. Shake up your team or department by using unexpected, unorthodox media for communication and documentation.

The following sections provide various ideas to use as inspiration to spice up your communication in general and to share knowledge and objectives.

---

6. Peter Hilton, "Documentation Avoidance for Developers," https://www.slideshare.net/pirhilton/documentation-avoidance

Maxims

When your current initiative is to improve the code quality come up with a catchy maxim, such as "Fix a bug? Add a test." or "Fight legacy code. Write unit tests."

Don't necessarily copy and paste maxims that others have used. Create your own that will stick in your culture. The only way to know if a maxim will stick is to say it out loud on different occasions to see if it resonates and if anyone mentions it later.

Note

You might want to read the book *Made to Stick: Why Some Ideas Survive and Others Die* by Chip Heath and Dan Heath to learn more on this topic.

Good maxims are useful and amusing at the same time. This one is from @BeRewt on Twitter: "If in doubt, do it the way Erlang does it."

Once you have a maxim, your job is to repeat it as often as possible (without becoming a spammer, of course).

Tip

Repetition also works inside a maxim. For example, "Mutable state kills. Kill mutable state!" has internal repetition that can help make it more memorable.

A maxim has to remain trivially simple because complicated stuff does not scale over larger audiences. You need to broadcast your maxims, so be ready to trade nuance for stickiness. You can only give one or two key messages. Make sure they are the most important messages. Take care of the other less important messages in a different way.

Note

Statements that rhyme are more believable than those that don't. This is referred to as the *rhyme-as-reason effect* or the *Eaton-Rosen phenomenon*.

Posters and Domestic Ads

Think of your communication as a marketing campaign. You can use the same tools but internally.

When you have maxims, you can turn them into illustrated posters. The first thing you can do is start with an image search. For example, consider the maxim "The only way to go fast is to go well!" This maxim exhibits internal repetition and symmetry around the word *go*, which makes it sticky.

A Google image search turns up a ready-made meme with this exact maxim text over a picture of Uncle Bob, which is not surprising considering that he likes to repeat this maxim (Figure 15.2 gives a taste of this meme reinterpreted as cute monsters).

Figure 15.2 *Robert C. Martin: The only way to go fast is to go well!*

Meme-Based Posters

Now consider that you don't have a maxim yet, but you'd like everyone to remember to close the door of the bathroom after use. You can easily create a motivational poster for that, thanks to all the available free online meme generators. From a given idea, you can browse the most common memes until you find one that fits your message best. Here we found a "Mr. T" meme (see Figure 15.3, again re-interpreted as a cute monster, because hey, it's really cute). (This example is a real one I've seen at a customer site. The poster was awesome on the bathroom door.)

ARE YOU AWESOME?

CLOSE THE DOOR ONCE YOU'RE DONE.

Figure 15.3 *Are you awesome? Close the door once you're done.*

One drawback of memes is that they tend to become annoying when used too frequently.

Pro Tip

Display a cute kitten along with or between your messages. Everybody loves cute kittens.

Information Radiators

Posters don't necessarily have to be printed and pinned on walls or windows to be visible. Some companies have TV sets on the walls or in elevators and show on them a variety of slides for internal communication. This is a nice place for your posters.

The downside is that you have to go through an acceptance process, and you might be rejected.

Still, you can insert your posters as banners into your build walls, screen savers, or pair-programming blocker screens.

Humor and Cheap Media

You might have seen already the very cheap, yet quite efficient, poster shown in Figure 15.4.

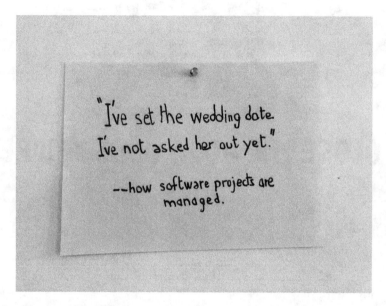

Figure 15.4 *An effective story*

Storytelling is very powerful, even when the story is this short. It takes training or pure luck to author this kind of gem. Fortunately, you can reuse (steal or hijack) many existing such gems for your own purposes. Twitter is a great source of very short, and often funny, stories to plagiarize. But keep in mind that having everyone doing it does not mean it's legal.

Maxims can be short enough to fit within a hashtag. Our software industry also loves using hashtags as a way to name new practices; consider #NoEstimates, #BeyondBudgeting, and #NoProject.

Note that hashtags are not just for Twitter and Facebook. You can use them IRL (in real life), and even verbally, which sounds deliciously awkward.

Tip

Name your Wi-Fi network after a maxim. For example, if you'd like to encourage environmentally friendly behavior, you could rename your Wi-Fi network ReduceReuseRecycle.

Goodies/Swag

Goodies (for example, t-shirts, card decks, cheat sheets, large takeaway posters, mugs, pens, postcards, stickers, sweets, relaxation widgets) are not always green, but sometimes they are useful. Goodies have traditionally been used to repeat a message. You might consider printing a maxim, rather than your brand, on goodies.

The conference DDD Europe recently did a great job of this with different t-shirt designs with different maxims such as

- *MAKE THE IMPLICIT EXPLICIT* (see Figure 15.5)

- *THROW AWAY THE MODEL*

Figure 15.5 *MAKE THE IMPLICIT EXPLICIT t-shirt*

Comics

You can use comics as a compelling way to tell a story, such as a story of frustrated users who dream of better software. You might use comics to document and explain the rationale for a new project.

Stories of users doing their job and sharing their most important stakes are also great for explaining—and documenting—in an accessible way the fundamental business stakes of a business activity.

I once used childish comics in corporate environments to explain a process for the development team. Another time I used less childish comics to help explain a governance process to senior management in a big, serious bank. In both cases, it worked and was appreciated.

Several online comics generators can help you create basic comics from libraries of characters, settings, and effects. They make it possible to anyone to create a comic, even without any drawing skill.

Infodecks

Infodecks are slides used as documents to be read onscreen rather than projected in front of an audience. Infodecks offer many advantages:

- You can use spatial layout to help with your explanation.
- They are approachable and do not use long prose that people won't read.
- It's easy to include diagrams as primary elements in the communication.

The important thing is not to confuse infodecks with slide decks that are meant to be projected to a large audience. An infodeck should contain very little text. The text it does include should be in a very big font size, and there should be many illustrations.

Martin Fowler says, "Infodecks are an interesting form to me, if only because it seems nobody takes them seriously....A colorful, diagram-heavy approach that uses lots of virtual pages is an effective form of document, especially as tablets become more prevalent."[7]

Visualizations and Animations

Animations and animated visualizations, which are a bit more difficult to produce than some of the other options listed here, are perfect for explaining temporal behaviors.

---

7. Martin Fowler, ThoughtWorks blog, http://martinfowler.com/bliki/Infodeck.html

A great example is the beautiful visualization of distributed consensus in Raft, which shows how nodes elect their leader in the face of various events.[8] Another personal favorite is the apparently crazy idea of showing how sort algorithms work by using sound along with a crude display.[9]

LEGO Bricks

LEGO bricks have become popular in agile circles over the past years, and now we often use LEGO bricks during meetings, as a planning tool, or even to represent a software architecture physically in 3D. Other system of avatars or construction blocks can be used as mediation tools during conversations. The problem with these constructions, however, is that people tend to forget what they meant after a few days.

Furniture

Even your furniture can tell stories. Fred Georges explained in one of his talks that tables express the internal organization of a startup: Each table represents one project team. No more room on the table means the team has reached its maximum size. If a table isn't full, you're welcome to join the team if you feel like it: It's a direct proposition!

Furthermore, you can tell from the huge iMac screens where the designers are, whereas Linux machines more likely suggest developers' workspaces.

3D Printed Stuff

3D printed models are now easy to produce. You can, if you like, project a particular view of your application and print it in a solid material. This helps everyone use their visual and world-sensing strength to grasp visually and by touching the elements. 3D and removable layers are useful for representing several dimensions of a problem stacked on each other and well aligned.

Summary

Having documentation doesn't mean it's useful. Keeping in mind some principles and ideas to make documentation more compelling—such as a focus on the audience, discoverability, and the fun factor—can help you optimize the effectiveness of your living documentation initiatives.

8. The Secret Lives of Data, http://thesecretlivesofdata.com/raft
9. "15 Sorting Algorithms in 6 Minutes," http://m.youtube.com/watch?v=kPRA0W1kECg

Index